A Field Guide to White Supremacy

A Field Guide to White Supremacy

Edited by Kathleen Belew and
Ramón A. Gutiérrez

UNIVERSITY OF CALIFORNIA PRESS

University of California Press
Oakland, California

Chapter 1 was previously published in *NAIS: Journal of the Native American and Indigenous Studies Association* 6, no. 2 (Fall 2019). Chapter 2 was previously published in Keeanga-Yamahtta Taylor, *From #BlackLivesMatter to Black Liberation* (Haymarket, 2016). Chapter 5 is reprinted from "A Rape a Minute, a Thousand Corpses a Year," *Guernica,* January 25, 2013. Chapter 6 originally appeared in *Slate,* May 1, 2018. Chapter 10 was previously published as the foreword to *On Antisemitism: Solidarity and the Struggle for Justice* by Judith Butler and Jewish Voices for Peace (Haymarket, 2017). Chapter 15 is excerpted and updated from Adam Goodman, *The Deportation Machine: America's Long History of Expelling Immigrants* (Princeton, NJ: Princeton University Press, 2020)

Library of Congress Cataloging-in-Publication Data

Names: Belew, Kathleen, 1981- author. | Gutiérrez, Ramón A.,
   1951- author.
Title: A field guide to white supremacy / Kathleen Belew and Ramón
   A. Gutiérrez.
Description: Oakland, California : University of California Press, [2021] |
   Includes bibliographical references and index.
Identifiers: LCCN 2020058505 (print) | LCCN 2020058506 (ebook) |
   ISBN 9780520382503 (cloth) | ISBN 9780520382527 (paperback) |
   ISBN 9780520382534 (ebook)
Subjects: LCSH: White supremacy movements—United States. |
   Anti-racism—United States.
Classification: LCC E184.A1 B348 2021 (print) | LCC E184.A1 (ebook) |
   DDC 320.56/909—dc23
LC record available at https://lccn.loc.gov/2020058505
LC ebook record available at https://lccn.loc.gov/2020058506

Manufactured in the United States of America

30 29 28 27 26 25 24 23 22 21
10 9 8 7 6 5 4 3 2 1

Contents

              TO MAINSTREAM

15.   A Recent History of White Supremacy   251
      Ramón A. Gutiérrez

16.   From Pat Buchanan to Donald Trump: The Nativist
      Turn in Right-Wing Populism   265
      Joseph E. Lowndes

17.   The Alt-Right in Charlottesville: How an Online
      Movement Became a Real-World Presence   287
      Nicole Hemmer

18.   The Whiteness of Blue Lives: Race in American Policing 304
      Joseph Darda

19.   There Are No Lone Wolves: The White Power
      Movement at War   312
      Kathleen Belew

      Conclusion   325
      Ramón A. Gutiérrez and Kathleen Belew

      Notes   335
      Acknowledgments   385
      Contributors   387
      Index   393

Thoughts on the *Associated Press Stylebook*

Kathleen Belew with *Khaled Beydoun, Adam Goodman,*
Carly Goodman, Emily Gorcenski, Nicole Hemmer,
Cassie Miller, Cynthia Miller-Idriss, Jessica Ordaz, Croix Saffin

As the field standard for journalists, the *Associated Press Stylebook* plays a major role in fixing the parameters of political debate and imagination. Consider that the most recent edition included contextual entries as long as a paragraph for the Islamist terror groups Al Qaeda, Islamic State, and the Muslim Brotherhood, but no entries for the white power terror groups Ku Klux Klan or neo-Nazis. White power activists have carried out an overwhelming majority of domestic terror fatalities and attacks in recent years, and the Department of Homeland Security now considers these the largest terrorist threat to the United States—outstripping radical Islamist terrorism.

Yet journalists using the *AP Stylebook* are ill-equipped to describe white power and militia groups. Our aim in this section is to briefly provide journalists with an overview of the terms and understandings agreed upon by most scholarly specialists and to encourage the editors of the *Stylebook* to reconsider some of the book's guidance.

On close reading of the *AP Stylebook*, we noticed that scholars and journalists often use completely different language to discuss the same social problems. The recommendations here, focused on the terminology and reporting around race, gender, immigration, and political extremism, are meant as a starting point in what we hope will be a longer conversation about how we name and acknowledge white supremacy. In some contexts, we have no recommendations, only questions. In all cases, we welcome feedback from journalists and other scholars in how best to use our shared understanding to achieve clarity and accuracy.

. . . . .

antisemitism

The AP Stylebook currently recommends hyphenating. We disagree, because we understand Semite and Semitism to be invented terms with a long history in pseudoscience.

. . . . .

immigration

We urge consideration and modification of the existing entry. Immigrants are people who move. People who move do so for many reasons: to seek better work opportunities, to reunite with family members, to flee danger or persecution. But the context for immigration involves more than individual choices: inequality, persecution, conflict, war, and exploitation by more powerful countries may frame immigration. Likewise, the United States has policies that draw people; immigration is not something that happens to the United States but is part of a process that has been facilitated by U.S. actors. Often when Americans think about immigration, they are thinking about U.S. policies that manage migration, including both admissions and restrictions. Lawful immigrants outnumber unauthorized immigrants. The United States admits people through a few categories (family, labor, humanitarian). Enforcement and restriction produce the category of *undocumented*.

We urge the *AP Stylebook* to discourage the use of immigration metaphors that might inspire fear or disgust or might dehumanize immigrants (flood, stream, wave, tide, swarm, horde, etc).

anti-immigrant *(no current entry)*

The *Stylebook* does not currently cover one of the most potent political forces of the moment. *Anti-immigrant* refers to a group, person, or policy that opposes immigration.

deportation, removal, inadmissibility, and voluntary departure

We urge reporters to use specific terminology around these procedures. For instance, documented immigrants can still be deported.

. . . . .

race

In addition to the current category, "Race-related Coverage," we urge the *Stylebook* to consider defining race itself as a socially constructed category of political identity that has changed over time.

caucasian
This is an outmoded term based on pseudoscience. We urge journalists not to use this term.

Black *(capitalized)*
Following several prominent media outlets, we agree that Black should be capitalized when it refers to a cultural and racial identity.

Indigenous *(capitalized)*

Latinx *(capitalized)*
As the most inclusive and encompassing term, we recommend use of this term, but journalists should defer, when possible, to how people self-identify. Many individuals prefer other terms. Latinx should not be used to refer to people in the past, when the term was not used in self-identification.

"reverse discrimination"
This term should be used sparingly and in quotation marks. Because racism is a system of power, we see it as incorrect to refer to "racism" against white people in a white supremacist society. Such arguments often disguise racist policies.

tribe/tribal
These words refer to an Indigenous nation. Do not use *tribal* to discuss broader political division.

white
The word *white* refers to a socially constructed and historically fluid category of identity in which people, systems of power, and wealth are invested. This is not a biological or unchangeable category, but neither is it neutral. We struggle with the question of whether to capitalize this word and urge further conversation. We choose not to capitalize *white* in these pages in keeping with current style guidelines.

white power movement, white supremacist extremist movement
see Terrorism

white supremacist *(current entry a subsection of "alt-right")*
In the current configuration of the *Stylebook*, *white supremacist* appears as a subsection of the "alt-right," implying first that not all of the "alt-right" is white supremacist and second that white supremacist is a smaller category. Neither is true. The "alt-right" is a small and largely faded component of the broader white power movement, which itself represents only one part of the larger group of people who identify as overtly white supremacist.

We propose the following definition of white supremacy:

Both individual belief that white people are inherently better than others *and* the broad systems of inequality that insure racial disparity of health, income, life, and freedom. Please note that systems can produce white supremacist outcomes without individual belief or racial animus.

.   .   .   .   .

gender *(additions and modifications to existing section)*

gay

We propose that the *Stylebook* urge reporters not to use *homosexual*, even in clinical contexts or references to sexual activity, as this term refers to a long history of pathologizing this population.

gender identity

We understand this to be one's internal concept of self as male, female, a blend of both, or neither. It includes how individuals perceive themselves and what they call themselves. One's gender identity can be the same or different from their sex assigned at birth. For many transgender people, their birth-assigned sex and their own sense of gender identity do not match. (Human Rights Campaign recommendation)

they

Use as a singular pronoun where preferred in self-identification and in stories about people who identify as neither male/man nor female/woman (which can include some transgender people and nonbinary, genderqueer, or gender nonconforming people).

transgender person

A transgender person *(not "transgendered")* is someone whose sex assigned at birth is different from who they know they are on the inside. It includes people who have medically transitioned to align their internal knowledge of their gender with their physical presentation. But it also includes those who have not or will not medically transition as well as nonbinary or gender-expansive people who do not exclusively identify as male or female. (Human Rights Campaign recommendation)

Always use the name with which the person self-identifies.

"preferred"

When referencing a person's pronouns or name explicitly, do not add the modifier "preferred," e.g., "preferred name" or "preferred" pronouns. Instead, simply refer to their "name" or their "pronouns."

pronouns

Pronouns should always match self-identification.

sexual orientation
This term refers to emotional, romantic, sexual, and relational attraction to someone else, whether you're gay, lesbian, bisexual, straight, or use another word to accurately describe your identity. Refrain from using *sexual preference, lifestyle, homosexuality,* or *heterosexuality*. In addition, be mindful that some people are transgender and straight, while others are transgender and gay. (Human Rights Campaign recommendation)

woman/women
We encourage journalists to avoid using *female* and *woman* as interchangeable terms. Female refers to the genitals present at birth. Woman includes anyone who identifies as a woman.

·   ·   ·   ·   ·

political extremism
We propose a new section correcting inaccuracies in the current *Stylebook*.

terrorism
This term refers to violent action designed to bring about political change and/or to create fear that limits civic life. Do not give detail for Islamist terrorism or left-wing terrorism and then omit similar detail for right-wing, white power, or white nationalist terrorist activity. Always consider comparative casualty rates when dedicating newsroom resources, beat reporting, and story placement related to types of terrorism (for instance, white power terrorism has recently caused more death, damage, and injury than Islamist terrorism, and far more than "antifa").

accelerationism
Accelerationism is an extreme philosophy that aims to hasten the demise of current economic and political systems and create a new one, using political violence as a primary mechanism. The goal is to accelerate what is seen as an inevitable collapse of political and economic systems and start anew. Accelerationism has strong components of apocalyptic fantasies and conspiracy theories, and also overlaps significantly with the beliefs of white power, survivalist, and extreme prepper groups, along with doomsday cults and Islamist extremism.

white power movement, white supremacist extremist
movement *(no current entry)*
This is the preferred terminology for the broad affiliation of Klansmen, neo-Nazis, sovereign citizens, Three Percenters, posse comitatus members, some skinheads, some militia groups, and similar groups who seek the violent overthrow of the United States through race war.

local groups and chapters

White power and antigovernment groups have historically changed their names, slogans, and identifying symbols to avoid description. Investigate claims of neutrality with experts, scholars, and watchdog groups rather than taking them at face value.

Local group and chapter names, as well as symbols and insignia, change more rapidly than a style guide can track. Journalists should refer to watchdog organizations and scholars to understand the relative size, prominence, and ideologies of local groups and chapters. These include paramilitary networks like The Base, casual and meme-driven affiliations like Boogaloo Boys, and small, cell-style operational movements like Atomwaffen Division in addition to organized groups with clear and public activities like Identity Evropa / American Identity Movement. We urge journalists to consult reputable tracking organizations like the Southern Poverty Law Center and the Center for Democratic Renewal regularly.

> **Atomwaffen Division**
> **The Base**
> **Boogaloo Boys**
> **Identity Evropa / American Identity Movement**
> **Oath Keepers**
> **Proud Boys**
> **Three Percenters/III%**

Major ideologies:

alt-left *(current entry inaccurate)*
False terminology, do not use.

"alt-right" *(current entry inaccurate)*
A subsegment of white power and white nationalist activism most active in 2016–17, now fractured. We urge journalists not to use this word to describe present-day activism, as this is an outmoded term.

antifa
Current entry is accurate.

antigovernment
Many militia groups, Three Percenters, sovereign citizens, and other groups are first and foremost antigovernment in their orientation and driven primarily by baseless conspiracy theories about the government disarming citizens and imposing martial law. Some, but not all, of these groups also identify with white power.

white nationalist *(current entry a subsection of "alt-right")*
Use sparingly or in quotation marks as this term often masks violent ideology and intent.

Christian Identity, Odinism

These and other white supremacist religious belief systems may be most precisely referred to as "political ideologies." Each of these posits that non-white persons are less than human or not valuable compared to white people.

Ku Klux Klan

Part of the white power movement, the Ku Klux Klan is an organized terrorist group dating from the post–Civil War era. Membership surges have aligned with the aftermath of every American war. The Klan has, since the 1920s, had representation in every region of the United States. The Klan is classically anti-Black and antisemitic but has used opportunistic targeting of other groups when convenient.

neo-Nazi

Part of the white power movement, neo-Nazism uses the symbols and ideology of Nazi Germany to imagine a white ethnostate.

skinhead

May refer to neo-Nazism, or to other belief systems. It is occasionally necessary to specify *racist skinhead*, but most skinhead groups in the United States are white power affiliates.

militia movement

A militia is an extralegal paramilitary group that trains, dresses, and prepares for combat, sometimes as part of a movement and sometimes as an unaffiliated group. Militias are extralegal in every state. The militia movement has largely opposed the government and upheld white supremacy. (National Guard units, which incorporated legal militias in the early twentieth century, still occasionally use the word *militia* without referring to the militia movement.)

lone wolf *(no current entry, widely used incorrectly)*
Do not use. Ideologically motivated violence should be identified as such. Violence with no motivating ideology should be treated as individual.

manifesto

A manifesto is a document laying out a political ideology, often to explain or incite violence. We urge journalists and editors not to reprint or hyperlink these documents, but rather to seek expert commentary to read, decode, and understand them. The word *manifesto* should not be misunderstood as an endorsement of quality or validity.

radical

This term refers to a person whose critique of society goes to its roots, whether on the far left or far right.

Radicalization is an active process and should not be referred to in passive voice.

white wellness, white wellness advocate, white well-being, "pro-white," white rights advocate, and similar terms

These are synonyms for white power / white supremacist activism; do not use.

Introduction

Kathleen Belew and Ramón Gutiérrez

This *Field Guide to White Supremacy* illuminates the long and complex career of white supremacist and patriarchal violence in the United States, ranging across time and across impacted groups, in order to provide a working volume for those who wish to recognize, understand, name, and oppose it. We focus here not only on the most catastrophic incidents of white supremacist domestic terrorism—like the 1995 bombing of the Oklahoma City federal building and more recent mass shootings at stores and places of worship, and the January 6, 2021, storming of the U.S. Capitol—but also on the manifold ways that overt and covert white supremacy, supported by often-violent patriarchy and gender norms, have shaped American law, life, and policy.

A field guide is meant to train observers to notice a particular phenomenon—here, white supremacy—and its distinctions. This manual will help observers to notice and name variant forms of white supremacy, ranging from systems to laws, from hate crimes to quiet indifference, from the everyday interactions that comprise white supremacist society to the movements that demand something else.

A Field Guide to White Supremacy, in other words, is meant as a resource for journalists, activists, policymakers, and citizens who wish to

In this April 6, 1942, photo, a boy sits on a pile of baggage as he waits for his parents, as a military policeman watches in San Francisco. More than 650 citizens of Japanese ancestry were evacuated from their homes and sent to Santa Anita racetrack, an assembly center for the forced internment of alien and American-born Japanese civilians. (AP Photo)

understand the history, sociology, and rhetoric of this phenomenon. It also offers a sampling of some of the best writing and most recent scholarship on these subfields, to spark broader conversations between journalists and their readers, teachers and their students, activists and their communities.

As this volume took final form, between the summer of 2020 and the first weeks of January 2021, our planet and nation faced multiple crises. A devastating COVID-19 pandemic had left more than two million dead, with numbers mounting. The United States witnessed massive protests against systemic racism, a hard-fought presidential election, the U.S. House of Representatives voting articles of impeachment against President Donald J. Trump for the "Incitement of Insurrection," and the inauguration of President Joseph Biden. A new chapter of the racial justice movement began on May 25, 2020, when George Floyd, a forty-six-year old Black Minneapolis resident, was arrested for purchasing cigarettes with a counterfeit $20 bill. His arrest turned lethal when Officer Derek Chauvin pinned Floyd to the ground, placing his knee on Floyd's neck for more than eight minutes, long enough to kill him. A long summer of peaceful mass protests against racist policing and systemic racism followed, escalating into rioting and looting in some cities. At many of these riots, militant-right activists ranging from antigovernment to white power militants delivered bombs, incendiary devices, and weapons to escalate peaceful demonstrations into confrontation with the militarized police forces. They assassinated law enforcement officers, plotted attacks on civil protests, and launched a major and coordinated attack on American communities. President Trump responded with a "law and order" campaign slogan and deployed federal forces from the Department of Homeland Security, the Bureau of Prisons, and elsewhere—sometimes without name badges or identifying insignia—to subdue the streets, to "dominate" protesters, and to energize the white supremacist segment of his supporters.

Beginning several years before the 2020 presidential election, President Trump had constantly warned his loyalists that Democrats were determined to steal the election from him. Without corruption, he claimed, he, Trump, would easily win. When Joseph Biden beat Donald Trump by more than seven million votes, winning the electoral college by 306 to 232, Trump refused to acknowledge the results and instead contested his defeat with lawsuits alleging widespread voter fraud. Neither the suits nor the intimidation of state election officials changed the tally, and court after court rejected his claim. Trump's final salvo over the "stolen election" was to call his supporters to a "Save America March"—part of "Stop the Steal" campaign—in Washington, DC, on January 6, 2021, the day Congress would certify Joseph Biden's election as president. The motley assemblage, which included white power armed militants, disgruntled military veterans, QAnon conspiracy proponents, radical evangelicals, and fervent members of the Trump base, arrived by the thousands. At the Ellipse, a park just south of the White House, President Trump roiled those gathered: "We will stop the steal . . . we can't let this happen . . . We fight like hell, and if you don't fight like hell, you're not going to have a country anymore . . . We're going to walk down, and I'll be there with you . . . to take back our country." They marched to the Capitol but without Trump. He retired to a White House television set to watch the mob violently attack the building and its occupants for several hours, vandalizing and desecrating the building, injuring numerous Capitol guards, leaving five dead behind in the mayhem. The Federal Bureau of Investigation soon discovered that among the heavily armed insurrectionists were members of white power neo-fascist militias. They had conspired to plan the attack, intending to take prisoners, among them then Vice President Mike Pence and Speaker of the House Nancy Pelosi, to "stop the steal." Two pipe bombs at the Democratic National Committee and Republican Nation Committee headquarters did not detonate, and the activists used neither their Molotov cocktails nor their military-grade weapons, but the body count was stunningly low, considering their preparation. Once the Capitol building was again under federal control that night, Congress certified the election of Joseph Biden as the forty-sixth president of the United States.

This was, make no mistake, a domestic terror attack on U.S. democracy, aimed at derailing free elections through the use of violent force. It was a show of force that used old texts like the white power novel *The Turner Diaries* to script its action and paved the way for recruitment and radical violence to come.

The House of Representatives voted to impeach President Donald Trump on January 13 for "high crimes and misdemeanors" for inciting an insurrection against the federal government at the U.S. Capitol. On the eve of Biden's inauguration, Senator Mitch McConnell, the Senate's leader, concluded: "The mob was fed lies . . . They were provoked by the president and other powerful people. And they tried to use fear and violence to stop a specific proceeding of the first branch of the federal government which they did not like."[1] Though threats had been made by Trump's loyalists that they would disrupt the inauguration of the forty-sixty president of the

United States on January 20, it occurred relatively peacefully, guaranteed only by the massive presence of National Guard troops and police and an increasing recognition of clandestine, extensive networks of organized, armed, antigovernment domestic terrorists espousing insurrectionist variants of white power.

It became clear to many Americans on January 6 that white power and white supremacy are yet live wires in our politics, in our relationships, and in our conversations with one another. As social media companies deplatformed Trump and various groups involved in the insurrection, then pulled hosting from alternative sites like Parler, people grasped for context to understand what they had just seen. But to scholars who have trained their eyes on the study of race and racism, these events did not represent a surprise or a moment of disconnect from "who we are." Instead, they flow clearly from a long and fraught history, one now urgent to understand.

What is white supremacy? White supremacy is a complex web of ideology, systems, privileges, and personal beliefs that create unequal outcomes along racial lines across multiple categories of life including wealth, freedom, health, and happiness. It is not a matter of argument among the vast majority of scholars, but of demonstrable fact. White supremacy includes both individual prejudice *and*, for instance, the long history of the disproportionate incarceration of people of color. It describes a legal system still predisposed towards racial inequality *even when* judge, counsel, and jurors abjure racism at the individual level. It is collective and individual. It is old and immediate. Some white supremacists turn to violence, but there are also a lot of people who are individually white supremacist—some openly so—and reject violence. Others have seen the ugliness of their personal racism and renounced its manifestations large and small.

But white supremacy operates through a collection of misunderstandings. It requires public officials like George Wallace, Patrick Buchanan, and Donald Trump who engage and encourage it in volumes ranging from dog-whistles to overt shouts. It requires a body politic that is not curious about its own history, doesn't understand the long and deep roots of its inequalities, and doesn't recognize its own culpability in the failure to confront its massive injustices.

This story goes back to the founding of the nation. Historians sometimes argue over precise dates and the relative importance of key events, but the overwhelming majority agree that the colonies that eventually formed America were defined through violent articulation of the political identity that would become "whiteness." From Christopher Columbus's 1492 ill-fated settlement on Hispaniola, to the North American outposts the French and Dutch established before the foundation of Jamestown, the goal of these settler colonialists was the denigration of Indigenous peoples and the violent appropriation of their labor, natural resources, and even their lives. The loss of Indian labor quickly gave rise to the African slave trade. The founding documents of the United States promised life, liberty, and pursuit of happiness not for all, but for white, property-owning men. A long series of contestations has gradually opened citizenship to those previously excluded: non–property owners, women, people of color, "Indians not taxed," and more—but this project has been incomplete, characterized by steps forward and back and by massive resistance to the extension of voting and civil rights to subordinated groups.

The historical moments when America saw more people incorporated as democratic subjects came not from goodwill or perfection of the American experiment, but through the actions and organizing of those people themselves. Women worked tirelessly for their own suffrage, for instance. And recent scholarship has highlighted the role of enslaved persons in fighting for their own freedom.

Whiteness itself is a socially constructed category that has changed dramatically over the course of United States history. In early America, whiteness worked as a political affinity among different ethnic groups. Not until the nineteenth century did racial pseudoscience introduce the idea of "white" as a biological marker. Even this whiteness changed over time, expanding to include previously excluded groups like Irish, Jewish, Italian, and Polish immigrants in the early twentieth century. And all along the way, whiteness was determined at the local level largely by individual bureaucrats, who variously held the line on strict standards or allowed passing and mutable boundaries as the local context required.[2]

As the bright line around whiteness changed and intensified, immigration restriction and anti-immigrant animus came to delineate large numbers of persons from Latin America and the Caribbean as nonwhite. Anti-Indian violence defined whiteness in early America. Slavery and Asian exclusion defined it in the nineteenth century. The twentieth century brought the mass forced deportations of Mexican Americans, the internment of Japanese Americans, the durability of Jim Crow segregation in the South and de facto segregation nationwide, and heightening immigration restriction at the U.S.-Mexico border. After intensifying measures born of terrorist threats at the end of the twentieth century, cross-border migrations had become more difficult and much more deadly, with vigilante enforcement of immigration restriction quite regular and, at the time of writing, even condoned by the state.

One need look no farther than basic disparities across medical care, incarceration, life expectancy, maternal mortality, and even incidence of coronavirus infection—which at the time of writing had a death toll twice as high among people of color as among white people—to see that America hasn't fulfilled the promise of equality for women, people of color, LGBT and gender-nonconforming persons, and others. Nor has it reckoned with the legacy of settler colonialism—the process of taking and populating the nation through violence against, forced assimilation of, and legal exploitation of first peoples.

As with many social ills, at least part of this continued injustice has to do with failure to understand these problems as part of an overlapping system of race and gender disparity. Even in the scholarship, specialists often delve deep into one area of the problem—hate crimes against a particular group, for instance, or state violence to the exclusion of individual prejudice or vice versa. This *Field Guide* proposes that a better understanding of hate groups, white supremacy, and the ways that racism and patriarchy have become braided into our laws and systems can help people to tell, and understand, better stories.

To read the intertwined histories of hate crimes against Black Americans, women, Muslim Americans, Latina/o immigrants, Jews, and Asian migrants is to see the large patterns of exclusion and policing that have made possible the continued rule of white supremacy in the twenty-first century. It is to begin to inventory the injustices, past and present, with which the nation would have to reconcile to truly fulfill its democratic promise.

The *Field Guide* opens with a set of recommended changes to the *Associated Press Stylebook*. These are meant to directly engage journalists and other storytellers in a conversation around the ways in which language has contributed to, or failed to directly confront, white supremacy in our society. Here, we mean to begin a conversation, rather than to prescribe arbitrary changes.

Then, Section I, "Building, Protecting, and Profiting from Whiteness," introduces the reader to the broad archaeology of exclusion that constituted United States law from early America to the present, spanning analysis of different racial and religious groups and their comparative access to, or denial of, full citizenship. These essays focus both on the history and mechanisms of exclusion and removal, and on the state violence integral to those processes even in the recent past. Together they argue that the construction and defense of whiteness rests on a plurality of discriminatory and violent systems that have worked to remove people of color from the American body politic.

In "Iterations of White Supremacy," we closely examine groups who have borne the brunt of racist, patriarchal, and homophobic violence. Looking carefully at the casualties attributable to sources ranging from individual domestic violence cases to mass shootings of women; from mob lynching to government incarceration and execution of Black Americans; from harassment of Asian Americans, to homophobic mass murder, to the intersectional risks of trans persons of color; we can discover that the long history of vigilante perpetration of hate crime has gained a degree of implicit state approval. We can read as much in its continued presence in American life.

The next section moves to consider the "Anti-Immigrant Nation," focusing specifically on the violent enforcement of immigration policy at the U.S.-Mexico border, the architecture and enforcement of deportation, and the way that anti-immigrant action groups have shaped a larger political consensus about what sorts of immigrants should be seen as deserving or criminal. These essays reveal the many ways that the nation is constituted by its borders and border-keeping practices.

In "White Supremacy from Fringe to Mainstream," we seek to excavate the relationship between radical manifestations of white supremacist and nativist politics and their continued durability in mainstream political discourse. Spanning the recent career of white supremacy, we focus here on the legacy of the culture wars, the emergence of movements like the "alt-right" and Blue Lives Matter as new articulations of white identity, and the persistence of the white power movement as a violent undercurrent in American politics.

Finally, we ask, where do we go from here? What could knowledge and reporting look like with the context of the *Field Guide* in hand? If we can recognize and name the many variants of white supremacy around us, might we imagine a world that is not so permeated with them?

SECTION ONE Building, Protecting, and
Profiting from Whiteness

Over the last few decades, two new ideas which focus on the origins, legacies, and persistence of white supremacy in the United States and other settler societies around the globe have reshaped the telling of American history. One is *settler colonialism*, which names and documents contact and colonization by a nation that wishes to populate the encountered land, rather than, for instance, *extract colonialism*, in which the colonizers seek only to take wealth and resources back to their home country. The other is *racial capitalism*, the idea that capitalism and white supremacy have been intertwined since their inception.

Settler colonial accounts of the United States study the nature of first contacts between Indigenous peoples and European colonists. Though some of these encounters began as "peaceful conquests" directed by missionaries, they were always supported by force of arms, were routinely violent, and, ultimately, had genocidal results. Following in the wake of the Columbian voyages throughout the Americas, colonial settlers from Spain, England, and France imposed their dominance, systematically exploiting Native Americans, demanding their labor and their bodies, driving them off of ancestral planting and hunting grounds, then declaring those "vacant," the rightful property of the settlers. These lies were compounded when European colonists asserted that the "Indians" were culturally inferior. They were said to worship false gods and had doggedly resisted Christianization and domination, behaviors the settlers racialized as "Red." The Natives were "savages" who required "civilizing" by their white colonial lords and ladies, who claimed superiority of faith and genteel birth. Broken peace treaties and the loss of territorial sovereignty followed. Then came removal onto reservations and intentional exposure to diseases by agents of the U.S. government to quicken the vanishing of the "Red race." For the children who survived this holocaust, it meant separation from their parents and cultures for placement in "Indian" boarding schools, where they were to forget their homelands, seeking an aspirational equality always denied, never fully Americans, ever Natives without rights. Settler colonialism featured two prominent mechanisms of genocide: one through direct violence, the other through forced assimilation. One does not have to look too far to witness the

legacies of settler colonialism still present in Indigenous poverty, segregation, lapses in medical care, and victimization by predators ever intent on
exploiting their natural resources without recompense.[1]

American history relies on two racial dichotomies—white/Black and
white/nonwhite—to tell the story of African slavery and colonial territorial
expansion. James Madison offered one of many possible explanations for
how these distinctions were born. In 1826, by then a former president of
the United States, Madison wrote the U.S. Superintendent of Indian
Affairs, Thomas L. McKenney, expressing a foreign policy concern. "Next to
the case of the black race within our bosom, that of the red on our borders
is the problem most baffling to the policy of our country."[2] African slavery
by then was a long-established, rapidly growing, profitable institution. For
Madison slaves were property of their white masters, in the very "bosom" of
the body politic and unproblematic, while Native Americans were outsiders and threats to the nation's boundaries. Two decades later as the United
States negotiated its spoils at the end of the Mexican War in 1848, John C.
Calhoun rose before his Senate colleagues objecting to the incorporation of
any Mexicans because they were mostly Indians. "Ours is the Government
of the white man ... [of] the Caucasian race," Calhoun vaunted. The
United States had never considered integrating Indian tribes. He reminded
his listeners that they had been driven into the forests by force.[3]

As these quotations illustrate, this section of the *Guide* brings together
authors who combine the insights of settler colonialism with those who
chronicle the history of racial capitalism, two literatures long deemed distant and distinct. Settler colonialism interrogates anew how the United
States managed its foreign policy with Indigenous nations. Racial capitalism reveals the relationship between slavery and development of capitalism as more than just distinct modes of deriving value from the exploitation of racialized human labor in the American South before the Civil War.
It posits instead that slavery's cotton production in the South fueled the
industrialization of Northern cotton mills, its exports monetizing capitalism's global reach, birthing America as its quintessential exemplar of capitalism. To the present it has continued to exploit and marginalize racial
"others" to maintain white supremacy.[4]

Racial capitalism illuminates the historical lineages of our collective past
and present, focusing on a white supremacist legal order and government

public policies related to anti-Blackness and the denigration of nonwhite migrant and immigrant labor. It asserts that whiteness has a value today, and has always had such a value. Africans held in slavery were only three-fifths of a person under the Constitution; despite their hard labor as immigrants and model behavior as residents, Muslims were denied access to citizenship because they were not considered white. Until 1967, antimiscegenation laws prohibited interracial marriages between Blacks and whites and between nonwhites and whites. Simply calling a white person Black in the past was ruled a defamation by judges, requiring monetary compensation. Homer Plessy, of the famous 1896 *Plessy v. Ferguson* Supreme Court case that upheld "separate but equal" as the rule of law, insisted that his seven-eighths whiteness was "the most valuable sort of property . . . the master-key that unlocks the golden door of opportunity." Unfortunately for Homer Plessy, he was not allowed to ride in railroad cars reserved for whites only. He was an octoroon. By laws derived by the idea that even one drop of Black blood contaminated his whiteness, he was Black.[5]

Today, in response to the murders of George Floyd, Breonna Taylor, Rayshard Brooks, Daniel Prude, and more than 160 Black women and men were killed by police in 2020, our streets have boiled over with protest. From the Black Lives Matter movement and others protesting against state violence, mass incarceration, and the lack of opportunities for those racialized as Black and Brown, one constantly hears demands that racial capitalism be abolished for a more equitable economic system. Militant voices were raised after the Great Depression when New Deal government programs created safety nets for American citizens but excluded domestic and agricultural workers without using racist language to target Blacks and Mexicans.[6] Between 1944 and 1971, the U.S. government spent over $95 billion in what was called the GI Bill of Rights for veterans of World War II. It helped millions of men buy homes, move into the suburbs, attend college, gain small business loans, and obtain government job. The benefits mainly reached whites.[7]

Here, then, we begin with Doug Kiel's essay, which studies the Oneida Nation's loss of some sixty thousand acres in northern Wisconsin in the years following the Dawes General Allotment Act of 1887. Ever since, the nation has tried to reestablish its territorial sovereignty, only to have it contentiously stalled and litigated by the white residents of Hobart, who own

A wagon train in honor of the nation's bicentennial crosses the Allegheny River in downtown Pittsburgh, Pennsylvania, headed for Valley Forge and the nation's two hundredth birthday celebration on June 14, 1976. The Bicentennial Wagon Train began on the West Coast and traveled east, reversing the course of settler colonialism to commemorate the nation's history. (AP Photo/Harry Cabluck)

land within the reservation's boundaries. In "A Culture of Racism," Keeanga-Yamahtta Taylor delves into more recent iterations of white supremacy in government programs. Time after time, federal public policy architects have blamed poor Blacks for their lack of access to opportunities as rooted in their cultural pathologies and family structures, when in fact they are due to systemic racism. Juan A. Perea offers us a sweeping historical overview of the legal development of the plenary powers of the United States president and Congress used to manage African slave protest, remove Native Americans from their ancestral lands, and since 1882 to exclude Asians from entering the country and to deport millions of unauthorized immigrants. Finally, Khaled A. Beydoun turns our attention to the long history of Islamophobia in American law, starting with the 1790 Nationalization Act, which denied Muslim immigrants access to naturalized citizenship as non-whites, a prejudice that continues, evident particularly after the terrorist attacks of 9/11 and the more recent Muslim entry bans.

1 Nation v. Municipality

INDIGENOUS LAND RECOVERY, SETTLER RESENTMENT,
AND TAXATION ON THE ONEIDA RESERVATION

Doug Kiel

In 2002 Oneida Nation citizen Hugh Danforth saw the coming trouble with Hobart, a majority non-Native Wisconsin municipality located entirely within the treaty boundaries of the Oneida Reservation.[1] As the wealthy suburban town of Hobart formally became a village, it gained a greater degree of autonomous home rule. Danforth took to the pages of the tribal newspaper, *Kalihwisaks* ("She Looks for News"). "Hobart is an urban cancer that will destroy our reservation, our adopted homeland, and our sovereignty if we don't do something about it," he warned.[2] Writing on another occasion, Danforth urged, "It will be harder for the Oneida Nation to buy back land and it will be harder for the Oneida Nation to put land into trust if Hobart becomes a village."[3] He was right. Within a few years, the historically strained relations between the Oneida Nation and the municipal government of Hobart erupted into an ongoing legal battle over the future of their shared territory.

Hobart was born amid a set of competing goals. The Oneida people lost ownership of all but a couple thousand acres of their more than sixty-five-

This chapter is reprinted from *NAIS: Journal of the Native American and Indigenous Studies Association* 6, no. 2 (Fall 2019).

thousand-acre reservation following the implementation of the Dawes General Allotment Act (1887).[4] As the *Daily State Gazette* noted in 1890, an Oneida general council voted unanimously to pursue the creation of towns on the reservation.[5] A decade later, when land speculators began gradually encroaching within the reservation, Wisconsin state assemblyman J. F. Martin proposed that the Oneida Reservation be divided into two townships. Joseph C. Hart, the federal Indian agent at Oneida, purportedly favored Martin's vision for the reservation's future. One local newspaper declared that "up to the present time the Indians have escaped taxation, but under the township system of government, they will be obliged to pay their fair share of the burdens."[6]

The proponents of creating the two towns argued that they would bring much-needed resources for infrastructure improvements that would benefit the Oneidas. Moreover, according to the *Post-Crescent*, published in nearby Appleton, establishing town governments that could collect taxes "would speedily mean the building of roads and opening the reservation for white settlers."[7] With a small but growing number of non-Native property owners within the reservation boundaries, the newly established governments of the town of Hobart (1908) and the town of Oneida (1910) were both led by tribal members.[8] As Oneidas gradually became the minority within their own treaty territory, however, they lost political control of Hobart.

When the towns were established, nobody—Native or non-Native—imagined that a century later the Oneida Nation would be in a position to buy back so much of the reservation that its white neighbors would feel under assault by a tribal government whose land base was rapidly growing. The Oneida Nation had reacquired ownership of tens of thousands of acres by the early 2000s, and each acre of reservation land it placed back into federal trust meant one fewer acre from which the nation's neighboring municipal governments could draw tax revenue. With Hobart being heavily dependent upon property taxes, transitioning to a village government was an important first step toward enacting its own long-term vision for the land. In Wisconsin, village governments have greater authority than town governments to create tax incremental districts (TIDs) as a mechanism to support development projects that help raise property values. "The village of Hobart Board is mainly interested in growth," Hugh

Danforth remarked, and that stood in contrast to the Oneida Nation's vision of preserving the reservation's rural character.[9]

Beginning in the late 1990s and early 2000s, the Oneida Nation had signed service agreements with several other neighboring governments whose jurisdiction overlaps the nation's: Brown County, the city of Green Bay, and the village of Ashwaubenon. In light of a complex and checker-boarded reservation map that contains both taxable property in fee simple and numerous nontaxable parcels held in federal trust, these service agreements have provided a reasonable solution for compensating local governments for services such as road improvements and fire services that are made available to tribal members residing on trust land.[10] As Ho-Chunk Nation chairman John Greendeer remarked in an address to the Wisconsin State Assembly, "Payments in lieu of taxes, those are taxes."[11] The Oneida Nation and village of Hobart had reached an impasse in negotiating a service agreement. "Why can't the Village of Hobart officials establish a working relationship with the Oneida Nation?" a frustrated Hobart resident wrote in *Kalihwisaks*. "Having overlapping jurisdiction with the Oneida Nation is a tremendous opportunity for Hobart but it's been treated as a liability," he continued, perhaps referring to the nation's having long been one of the biggest employers in the Green Bay area.[12]

By 2008 the tensions over taxation had escalated, and soon Hobart not only challenged the legitimacy of the Oneida Nation's sovereignty but also called into question the basic tenets of federal Indian law and policy writ large. This dispute between the Oneida Nation and its white neighbors provides a case study for how indigeneity, property rights, and settler colonialism all collided in a moment of Wisconsin and U.S. history characterized by economic anxiety and the politics of resentment. Amid the Great Recession and embattled governor Scott Walker's antagonism against public employees, the village of Hobart's leaders set their sights on a tribal government they regarded as greedy and bloated with federal aid and tax exemptions.[13] Although struggles for Indigenous sovereignty are most often viewed through the lens of nation-to-nation relationships with the U.S. federal government, tribal relationships with local municipal governments are also crucial sites for understanding the realization of Indigenous autonomy and recovery.[14] Anthropologist Thomas Biolsi has astutely argued that the system of federal Indian law and policy indeed creates such intergovernmental conflict, pitting the interests of Indigenous nations and their neighbors against one another.[15]

The path to reacquiring ownership of reservation land is full of barriers. The intergovernmental conflict between the Oneida Nation and the village of Hobart is a story about what happens when Indigenous power jeopardizes settler authority on a local scale.

Allotment was catastrophically effective at dispossessing Indigenous people of title to ninety million acres of reservation homelands; when the Indian Reorganization Act (1934) formally halted allotment, it empowered the secretary of the interior to place reservation lands back into tax-free federal trust.[16] For decades, the acreage that tribes, including the Oneida Nation of Wisconsin, bought back and placed back into trust status amounted to a trickle. For some Indigenous nations, the growth of casino gaming following the landmark decision *California v. Cabazon Band of Mission Indians* (1987) and the resulting Indian Gaming Regulatory Act (1988) opened the door to much more rapid land reacquisition.[17]

The Oneida Nation of Wisconsin eagerly pursued the recovery of land ownership within its reservation, having adopted an ambitious goal in 1998 to reacquire 51 percent of the land inside its boundaries.[18] These efforts transformed the Oneida Nation's relationship with its non-Indigenous neighbors who had become the majority of the reservation's residents in the decades that followed allotment.[19] In fact, one way to assess the extent of the Oneida Nation's success in nation rebuilding is to observe how defensive its non-Native neighbors became as the nation's political and economic clout grew. The village of Hobart's leaders rallied around defending their diminishing tax base, seeing themselves as losing ground to vindictive, expansionist Indians.[20]

In November 2004 the Oneida Nation and the village of Hobart signed a three-year agreement regarding the services provided on trust lands located within the village. In signing the document, the Hobart officials recognized that "under the laws of the State of Wisconsin and the United States of America, [the village] is required to provide certain services to the Oneida Nation properties regardless of fee or trust status of the land." However, the two parties affirmed one another as "good neighbors ... [that] desire the spirit of cooperation to continue between the two governments."[21] The village agreed to provide primary fire protection and backup police, ambulance, and first-responder services, as well as street improvements. Likewise, the tribe agreed to provide the village with backup services, took on primary responsibility for most of its people's own emergency services, and consented to pay the village an agreed-upon amount for those services. By 2007 the tribe had paid over $491,000 to the village under the terms of the agreement.[22]

As part of the 2004 service agreement, however, the village agreed that it would not "oppose the Oneida Nation's attempt to place fee land into trust," including properties owned by the tribe when the agreement became effective.[23] In October 2007, however—one month before the agreement was set to expire—the president of the village of Hobart, Richard Heidel, wrote to the Bureau of Indian Affairs Midwest Regional Office to oppose the fee-to-trust applications for parcels that the tribe had purchased in 1995, 1999, and 2001. Heidel characterized the Oneida Nation's actions as "an aggressive ongoing effort" to recover its reservation lands. Noting that the tribe had already reclaimed ownership of 32 percent of the land within the village, Heidel expressed concern that "the amount and pattern of land acquisition and trust status have a cumulative impact on the Village that is eroding its tax base, its ability to extend public utilities, and its ability to manage land use. In short, the Village's ability to remain an effective local government is being jeopardized as the Village finds itself being annexed from within." Heidel remarked that legal action was straining the possibilities of a productive long-term relationship between the two governments. "The Tribe is not merely acquiring large amounts of land," he wrote, "but they are doing so in a pattern, which results in isolating portions of the Village from other portions of the Village and disrupting road utility corridors."[24]

Hobart's tax revenue was draining away due not only to the Oneida Nation's casino-financed land buy-backs but also to annexation by the neighboring city of Green Bay and village of Ashwaubenon. Hobart's leaders used the centennial of the town's founding in 1908 as an occasion to stake their own vision of the future. The village of Hobart purchased 350 acres of farmland in 2008 to create a TID and a downtown where one did not presently exist. Village officials dubbed the new downtown the "Centennial Centre at Hobart, to honor its launch in our centennial year, to honor the founders and settlers of this community, and to ensure the economic sustainability of Hobart's next 100 years."[25] In a promotional brochure that labeled the Centennial Centre "a developer and land buyer's dream" and "a location with staying power," village officials advertised that they would fast-track developer approval.[26] The Centennial Centre would feature retail businesses, light manufacturing, a village square, parks and trails, and single-family and multifamily residential areas. According to *Marketplace Magazine* (a publication based in Oshkosh, Wisconsin), in 2010 it was "expected to bring $43 million to $45 million in residential and commercial development to the village within the next eight years."[27]

The Oneida Nation attempted to block the development of the Centennial Centre. "About the time the ink dried on the acquired Village property," a Hobart newsletter noted, the tribe purchased a seventeen-acre, L-shaped parcel that prevented the village from extending infra-structure, including a sewer line, to the site it had just acquired.[28] When the village attempted to exercise eminent domain over the lands recently acquired by the tribe, the Oneida Nation sued Hobart in federal court. The tribe lost. In March 2008 Judge William C. Griesbach ruled that "the fee land within the original boundaries of the Tribe's reservation which was allotted pursuant to federal law, transferred to the third parties, and subsequently acquired by the Tribe in fee simple on the open market, is subject to the Village's power of eminent domain."[29]

With the development of Centennial Centre underway and a legal victory against the Oneida Nation, the rhetoric emerging from the village of Hobart intensified. In a community forum in early 2008, the village sponsored a lecture by Elaine Willman on the topics of, according to the advertisement in the village newsletter, "Homeland Security and the 2010 Census, as they both relate to Hobart and the borders we share with the Oneida Tribe."[30] According to tribal attorney Rebecca Webster, however, "instead, Ms. Willman advocated for the abolition of tribal governments, with specific reference to the [Oneida] Tribe."[31] That came as no surprise, as Elaine Willman was once the chairperson of the most influential antisovereignty organiza-tion in the United States, the Citizens Equal Rights Alliance (CERA). The Wisconsin-based CERA has attracted the attention of the Southern Poverty Law Center, which monitors hate groups and has criticized CERA's "implicit white nationalism," labeling the group "anti-Indian."[32] As the leaders of the village of Hobart laid plans for their future, they recruited Elaine Willman, the matriarch of CERA, as a full-time employee to lead their efforts.

Willman's reputation as a prominent antisovereignty organizer preceded her, and the news of her hire sent a clear signal to the tribal government that the village was squaring off for a protracted battle. In February 2008, merely a month after her arrival in Wisconsin, the tribal government passed a resolution that ceased all negotiations with the village: "NOW THEREFORE BE IT RESOLVED, that the Oneida Tribe of Indians of Wisconsin will not enter into service agreement negotiations with the Village of Hobart until such time as the Village Board formally recognizes the right of the Oneida Tribe to maintain its own government and exercise jurisdiction within its Reservation, and the Village Board abandons assimilationist rhetoric and attempts to change federal Indian policy to the detriment of the Oneida Tribe."[33] The resolution signaled a complete collapse in diplomacy between the tribal government and the village, and from that point forward both parties became increasingly antagonistic toward one another.

Prior to 2000, Willman had no knowledge of federal Indian policy, but the opening of a tribal casino sparked her interest. In 1992, Willman began working as a community development coordinator for the city of Toppenish, Washington, which lies in the middle of the Yakama Indian Reservation. Upon the opening of the tribe's casino, life inside the Yakama Reservation changed dramatically. "It was like a different day there," Willman remarked. Shortly thereafter, the tribal government began expressing an interest in banning alcohol on the reservation, gaining control of a power utility, and taking over and breaching a dam. "And all of a sudden this quiet, complacent, compliant, and cooperative tribal government was really worrying people," Willman stated. "[Federal Indian policy] had never concerned me," Willman recalled during our interview, "until I was about to be taxed by a government that didn't represent me, and that got my attention." She soon became involved in CERA, becoming its chair in 2002. She left Toppenish and her position as CERA chair to become director of community development and tribal affairs for the village of Hobart. "I came here for a reason," Willman remarked, "[and] part of the reason was the Oneida Tribe itself." Willman noted that the Oneida Nation is among the most successful tribes in the United States and not only economically savvy but also politically influential. Consequently, addressing the conflict between the tribe and Hobart could set a precedent for other municipalities with non-Indian majorities located within Indian reservations to curtail tribal sovereignty.[34]

Now that Willman was leading Hobart's campaign against the tribe, the village leaders' arguments increasingly emphasized what they saw as the limits of the Oneida Nation's jurisdiction and also called into question the very existence of the tribe as a valid legal entity. Hobart leaders offered a competing narrative of Oneida history, which held that the tribe had been gradually phased out of existence during the late nineteenth and early twentieth centuries, the same period in which tribal members first launched a conscious movement to rebuild the reservation following allotment and assimilation. The village also maintained that the tribe, acting under the terms of the Indian Reorganization Act of 1934, had restored a system of self-governance that was completely defunct. Willman and the Hobart government thus argued that the Oneida Nation did not exist until it became a chartered incorporation in 1937. Hobart's claim is an important one in light of *Carcieri v. Salazar* (2009), which ruled that lands cannot be placed back into trust for tribes that were not under federal jurisdiction when the Indian Reorganization Act was enacted in 1934.[35]

Willman argued that because tribal members voted to implement the Dawes Act on their reservation and subsequently even celebrated their U.S. citizenship, they were no longer tribal members. "The day they received their allotment they became Wisconsin citizens," Willman remarked, "and part of that process involved walking away from any tribal government, foreswearing their tribal government."[36] Carol Cornelius, former area manager of the Oneida Tribe's Cultural Heritage Department, refuted the claim that the majority of Oneidas ever supported allotment. "Proposals to allot the reservation were highly contentious for the Oneidas," Cornelius wrote in an affidavit. "People walked out on meetings discussing allotments because they were so disgusted with the allotment proposal, so early votes did not accurately reflect the level of Oneida opposition to allotment," according to Cornelius.[37] Even if the majority of Oneidas had supported allotment, however, to do so would not have meant "walking away" from their self-government.

A point of particular importance in Willman's argument is that as early as the 1890s, some Oneidas expressed interest in creating two Wisconsin municipalities within the bounds of the reservation, and after the formal creation of the town of Hobart in 1908, many Oneidas held elected positions within the new town.[38] Tribal members endorsing the creation of municipalities within the reservation, however, did not signify the end of their self-governance as a federally recognized Indigenous nation. In 1906 the Oneidas created a new committee—the Business Committee—which, according to Cornelius, sought to "protect the interests of the Oneida people with respect to the sale of inherited lands, and repair of roads and bridges and to advocate for the Tribe for money owed by the federal government." At that time, the tribe also created several new elected positions, which included clerks, ballot clerks, and inspectors. Tribal self-government continued after the creation of the towns on the reservation, as evidenced by the fact that in 1911 the Oneidas rejected the federal government's offer of a lump-sum payment to abrogate the annuity obligation under the Treaty of 1794.[39]

Furthermore, it is unclear why gaining U.S. citizenship would have entailed the loss of tribal citizenship. If the federal government no longer considered the Wisconsin Oneidas a recognized sovereign entity, then why did the Bureau of Indian Affairs (BIA) maintain continuous government-to- government relations with the Oneidas before, during, and after the reservation's allotment? And if Wisconsin Oneida sovereignty had already been extinguished, why did the BIA target the Oneidas for termination in the 1950s? In *The Third Space of Sovereignty,* Kevin Bruyneel argues that the U.S. Supreme Court, along with groups like CERA, "increasingly views tribal sovereignty as a political expression that is out of (another) time."[40] That is fundamentally true in regard to Hobart and Willman: they envision the Oneida Nation as an anachronism that has no place in the present despite an abundance of evidence demonstrating its political continuity.

The village and the tribe have each made sincere efforts to reach out to individuals on both sides of the conflict in the hope that better understanding would lead to better relations. The pages of the Hobart newspaper, however, reveal that for village and tribal officials alike, good-neighbor rhetoric was little more than lip service. On June 24, 2011, Elaine Willman's lead article in the *Press* expressed hope for friendly, non-political relations, noting that a small group of Oneidas and non-Indians had recently been gathering at the Oneida Community Library "to encourage interaction, understandings and future social activities that will remind us that we are all Hobart residents regardless of our ethnicities."[41] Meanwhile, on the opposite page, representatives of the village and tribe launched virulent attacks against one another.

Questions of temporality (i.e., it is too late to reverse history and disrupt the status quo) along with the color-blind rhetoric of equality feature centrally in calls for dismantling Indigenous sovereignty.[42] Tribal members have often charged that Hobart's actions against the Oneida Nation have been racially motivated. In an effort to skirt such claims, Heidel stated, "The Village does not see 'tribe' or 'race' or any other institutionalized distinction between people or groups when it comes to dispatching the Village's responsibilities or exercising its authority."[43] Heidel's attempt to articulate a policy of fairness only reveals that he envisions "tribe" as a category with no legal significance whatsoever, a proposition that challenges the U.S. Constitution, numerous Supreme Court decisions, and centuries of federal Indian law. Like Heidel, Willman would also exclude race from the legal dispute. In an apparent attempt to evade accusations of racism, Willman readily identifies her husband as a Shoshone Indian and claims that she herself is eligible for Cherokee citizenship, though she has chosen not to enroll.[44] Willman has never demonstrated any evidence of Cherokee kinship. While the argument that the legal dispute was not initially motivated by race has some credence, it would be naive to overlook how the intense rivalry devolved into a racially defined "us" versus "them" mentality. Moreover, CERA and Willman have deep ties to the overtly racist organization Protect America's Rights and Resources (PARR), which organized protests against Ojibwe people exercising their spearfishing rights in northern Wisconsin during the late 1980s and early 1990s. As can be seen in the documentary film *Lighting the Seventh Fire* (1995), PARR protests frequently featured signage with slogans such as "Save a Walleye . . . Spear an Indian" and shouts of "Timber ni**er!" directed at Ojibwe fishermen.[45] CERA was founded in 1988 at the PARR annual convention, Willman has been a regular columnist for PARR publications, and Heidel has been a speaker at CERA gatherings.[46]

Willman joined a local struggle between Oneidas and non-Natives in Hobart, but ultimately her concern is with Indigenous rights as a whole, not merely those of the Oneida Nation. As tribes exert more jurisdictional power, Willman expresses deep concern that they could potentially hold authority over white people in Indian Country. "To the extent that a tribal government thinks for thirty seconds it has authority over a non-tribal American citizen, it poses a threat," Willman remarked. Tribal rights, she believes, "have gone too far, and they've been abused . . . It's almost like a parent that just gives their child absolutely everything and ruins them . . . and the child says 'more, more, more' and never knows how to say enough or thank you." In this statement, Willman characterizes Indigenous sovereignty as a privilege, even a gift, that can and ought to be revoked by the settler state when tribal self-governance comes too close to actually existing. In the view of the antisovereignty movement, the entire concept of a nation within a nation is unconscionable, and Willman condemns the "loose usage" of the terms *nation* and *sovereignty* when they are applied to tribal communities.[47]

Moreover, Willman and her CERA associates pit Indigenous governments as takers acting as a drain upon the U.S. economy. American conservatives popularized the pithy rhetoric of takers versus makers shortly after the advent of the 2007–8 global financial crisis and the United States' plummet into the Great Recession. Mainstream members of the Republican Party and radical Tea Party activists alike each began deploying the language of takers to disparage the beneficiaries of so-called entitlement programs such as unemployment insurance and food stamps. In time, the ideology of takers versus makers became a core principle of Mitt Romney and Wisconsin congressman Paul Ryan's 2012 Republican presidential campaign.[48] Echoing this increasingly familiar economic binary, Willman characterized the treaty-making process as an institution that disproportionately favored entitled Native peoples. "Since the execution of treaties," Willman claimed, "American Indians have always been given resources that no other citizens were." After all, she argues, in the nineteenth century, western migrants embarked upon their journeys with no government aid, yet "with the Indian treaties [Native people] were given land, houses, blacksmiths, doctors, schools."[49] Not only are her historical claims entirely inaccurate, since most U.S. treaties with Indigenous nations are land cessions in which Americans took territory, but also American westward migrants who went in pursuit of a piece of "free" (i.e., taken) Indigenous land certainly did receive considerable federal aid, a trend that persists into the twenty-first century in some western states.[50]

CONCLUSION

In October 2013 the Oneida Nation won a lawsuit against the village of Hobart and an ordinance attempting to levy a stormwater tax on tribal trust land. The court held that "because federal law prohibits states and local authorities to tax Indian lands, the tribe can't be forced to pay the assessment decreed by the challenged ordinance if the assessment is a tax."[51] In April 2014 the U.S. Supreme Court refused to hear the village of Hobart's appeal, upholding the Oneida Nation's victory. Just over a year later, after spending seven years in Hobart, Elaine Willman accepted a new position in Montana, where she soon began to warn, "We have a growing national epidemic but the impacts first strike locally, in one zip code after another, one town after another, one county after another. It is coming to your front porch." Moreover, she has pursued a new tactic. During a moment of U.S. anxiety over the potential acceptance of Syrian refugees, she appealed to Islamophobic fears, asserting, "Domestic tribalism and Middle Eastern tribalism have shared cultural norms (communalism) and a common adversary: the United States."[52] Such a turn reveals that, for Willman, Indigenous nations mirror what is broadly wrong with America, and they become localized sites for grappling with these broader anxieties.

While American opposition to Indigenous sovereignty is nothing new, the reacquisition of reservation land has reignited old debates and conflicts. The Oneida Nation has the resources to gradually buy out white landowners and create an uninterrupted block of tribally owned land. To view the Oneida Nation's conflict with Hobart as simply a matter of land tenure and taxes would be to overlook the complicated responses to a local reversal of the colonial relationship between Indigenous people and settlers.

The Oneida Nation defies many American expectations of Native people. In the American popular imagination, Native people are often incapable of succeeding in a competitive market. While some critics would characterize tribal casinos as "greedy," that label would hardly describe the behavior of Indigenous nations in light of merely reclaiming fragments of what once belonged to them and doing so on the open market. As one scholar notes, some Americans have worried that "the Indians' wealth has caused them to lose their soul."[53] The expectation of poverty not only essentializes (and even dehumanizes) Native people as striving for bare survival but also implies that Native communities are not suited for competition in the marketplace.[54] Perhaps, then, what stings the antisovereignty advocates at Hobart more than anything else is that even during the challenging conditions of the Great Recession in the small-town Midwest, the Oneida Nation still thrived and its landholdings continued growing.

In some of the most fortunate Native communities, tribal members are prospering and even enjoying a higher standard of living than many of their white neighbors. As a result, the Indian reservation—a system founded upon the American goals of Indian containment, submission, obedience, and assimilation—has surprisingly come to be seen as a site of unfair ethnic advantage.[55] The argument that wealthy tribes should be stripped of their sovereignty is a form of what one scholar has labeled "rich Indian racism."[56] As Jessica Cattelino argues, the double bind of need-based sovereignty is that although Native governments require economic resources to exercise their sovereignty, settlers often contest the legitimacy of tribes that exert economic power.[57]

The intergovernmental conflict between the Oneida Nation and the village of Hobart highlights the long afterlife of allotment: 130 years since its implementation, allotment's legacies remain at the heart of some of the most vexing dilemmas in Indian Country. Attempting to reverse the effects of allotment further highlights the ways in which Indigenous resurgence and resentful backlash go hand in hand. The antisovereignty movement is driven by a zero-sum calculus of rights, that is, the perception that the exercise of Indigenous rights inherently takes from rights of non-Indigenous Americans.

The village of Hobart is now one of the fastest-growing municipalities in Wisconsin and has recently been successful in development.[58] "A decade ago, Centennial Centre was nothing but empty fields," the *Press Times* reported.[59] The new development has since exceeded expectations, having led to the construction of nearly $130 million in taxable property, bringing total property values in Hobart to $975 million.[60] Moreover, the population of the village of Hobart has jumped 53.5 percent (from 6,182 to

9,496) since 2010, according to the U.S. Census Bureau's 2018 estimates.[61] The village also recently claimed an important victory against the Oneida Nation, with the U.S. District Court for the Eastern District of Wisconsin having ruled the reservation boundaries formally "diminished" by allotment. That is, the Oneida Nation cannot broadly assert its jurisdiction over all lands within the reservation but only those lands that are currently held in federal trust.[62]

The nation subsequently prevailed in the U.S. Seventh Circuit Court of Appeals, with the support of amicus briefs from the U.S. government, the State of Wisconsin, and the National Congress of American Indians (NCAI).[63] The nation remains undeterred in its effort to reacquire 75 percent of the land within the reservation by 2033.[64] During a previous hearing in the U.S. Seventh Circuit Court of Appeals in 2013, *Kalihwisaks* reported that Judge Richard A. Posner, the most cited legal scholar of the twentieth century, remarked that "Hobart doesn't seem to like Indians."[65]

2 A Culture of Racism

Keeanga-Yamahtta Taylor

Negro poverty is not white poverty. Many of its causes and many of its cures are the same. But there are differences— deep, corrosive, obstinate differences—radiating painful roots into the community, and into the family, and the nature of the individual.

These differences are not racial differences. They are solely and simply the consequence of ancient brutality, past injustice, and present prejudice. . . . For the Negro they are a constant reminder of oppression. For the white they are a constant reminder of guilt.

Nor can we find a complete answer in the experience of other American minorities. They made a valiant and a largely successful effort to emerge from poverty and prejudice.

The Negro, like these others, will have to rely mostly upon his own efforts. But he just cannot do it alone. For they did not have the heritage of centuries to overcome, and they did not have a cultural tradition which had been twisted and battered by endless years of hatred and hope-lessness, nor were they excluded—these others—because of race or color—a feeling whose dark intensity is matched by no other prejudice in our society.

Nor can these differences be understood as isolated infirmities. They are a seamless web. They cause each other. They result from each other. They reinforce each other.

President Lyndon Johnson, Howard University commence-ment speech, June 4, 1965

This chapter is reprinted from Keeanga-Yamahtta Taylor, *From #BlackLivesMatter to Black Liberation* (Haymarket, 2016).

I understand there's a common fraternity creed here at Morehouse: "Excuses are tools of the incompetent used to build bridges to nowhere and monuments of nothingness." Well, we've got no time for excuses. Not because the bitter legacy of slavery and segregation have vanished entirely; they have not. Not because racism and discrimination no longer exist; we know those are still out there. It's just that in today's hyperconnected, hypercompetitive world, with millions of young people from China and India and Brazil— many of whom started with a whole lot less than all of you did—all of them entering the global workforce alongside you, nobody is going to give you anything that you have not earned. Nobody cares how tough your upbringing was. Nobody cares if you suffered some discrimination. And moreover, you have to remember that whatever you've gone through, it pales in comparison to the hardships previous generations endured—and they overcame them. And if they overcame them, you can overcome them, too.

President Barack Obama, Morehouse University commencement speech, May 20, 2013

On the same day that the Ferguson Police Department finally revealed the name of Darren Wilson to the public as the police officer who killed Mike Brown, police chief Thomas Jackson simultaneously released a grainy video that appeared to depict Brown in the act of stealing cigarillos from a local convenience store. Jackson later admitted that Wilson did not know that Brown was suspected of having stolen anything. But the real work of the tape had already been done. Brown had been transformed from a victim of law enforcement into a Black suspect whose death was probably justified.[1]

Brown's depiction as a possible criminal did not derail the fight to win justice for him, but for the mainstream media and other political elites who had stuck their toes in the waters of social justice, Brown's possible involvement in a criminal act in the moments before his murder cast doubt on his innocence. The *New York Times* ran an unwieldy story about Brown's interest in rap music and reported that he had occasionally smoked marijuana—hardly alien activities for youth of any color, but the *Times* declared that Brown was "no angel."[2] Months later, *Times* columnist Nicholas Kristof tweeted that twelve-year-old Tamir Rice, killed by police in Cleveland, was a better face for the movement because his death was more "clearcut [sic] and likely to persuade people of a problem."[3] The attempt to differentiate between "good" and "bad" Black victims of state violence tapped into longstanding debates over the nature of Black inequality in the United States. Was Brown truly a victim of racist and overzealous police, or was he a victim of his own poor behavior, including defying police? Was Brown deserving or undeserving of empathy, humanity, and ultimately justice?

There are constant attempts to connect the badges of inequality, including poverty and rates of incarceration, to culture, family structure, and the internal lives of Black Americans. Even before emancipation, there were relentless debates over the causes of Black inequality. Assumptions of biological and cultural inferiority among African Americans are as old as the nation itself. How else could the political and economic elite of the United States (and its colonial predecessors) rationalize enslaving Africans at a time when they were simultaneously championing the rights of men and the end of monarchy and establishing freedom, democracy, and the pursuit of happiness as the core principles of this new democracy? Thomas Jefferson, the father of American democracy, spoke to this ironically when advocating that freed Blacks be colonized elsewhere. He said of the Black slave:

> His imagination is wild and extravagant, escapes incessantly from every restraint of reason and taste, and, in the course of its vagaries, leaves a tract of thought as incoherent and eccentric, as is the course of a meteor through the sky. . . . Upon the whole, though we admit him to the first place among those of his own color who have presented themselves to the public judgment, yet when we compare him with the writers of the race among whom he lived, and particularly with the epistolary class, in which he has taken his own stand, we are compelled to enroll him at the bottom of the column. . . .
>
> The improvement of the blacks in body and mind, in the first instance of their mixture with the whites, has been observed by every one, and proves that their inferiority is not the effect merely of their condition of life. . . . It is not their condition then, but nature, which has produced the distinction.[4]

This naked racism flattened the contradiction between enslavement and freedom and, in doing so, justified slavery as a legitimate, if not natural, condition for African Americans. This, of course, was not driven by blind hatred but by the lucrative enterprise of forced labor. Historian Barbara Fields reminds us that "the chief business of slavery," after all, was "the production of cotton, sugar, rice and tobacco," not the "production of white supremacy."[5] The continuing pursuit of cheap and easily manipulated labor certainly did not end with slavery; thus, deep-seated ideas concerning the inferiority of Blacks were perpetuated with fervor. By the twentieth century, shifting concepts of race were applied not only to justify labor relations but more generally to explain the curious way in which the experiences of the vast majority of African Americans confound the central narrative of the United States as a place of unbounded opportunity, freedom, and democracy. This observation challenges the idea that race operates or acts on its own, with only a tangential relationship to other processes taking place within our society.

Ideologically, "race" is in a constant process of being made and remade repeatedly. Fields explains the centrality of ideology in making sense of the world we live in:

> Ideology is best understood as the descriptive vocabulary of day-to-day existence, through which people make rough sense of the social reality that they live and create from day to day. It is the language of consciousness that suits the particular way in which people deal with their fellows. It is the interpretation in thought of the social relations through which they constantly create and re-create their collective being, in all the varied forms their collective being may assume: family, clan, tribe, nation, class, party, business enterprise, church, army, club, and so on. As such, ideologies are not delusions but real, as real as the social relations for which they stand. . . . An ideology must be constantly created and verified in social life; if it is not, it dies, even though it may seem to be safely embodied in a form that can be handed down.[6]

The point is that explanations for Black inequality that blame Black people for their own oppression transform material causes into subjective causes. The problem is not racial discrimination in the workplace or residential segregation: it is Black irresponsibility, erroneous social mores, and general bad behavior. Ultimately this transformation is not about "race" or even "white supremacy" but about "making sense" of and rationalizing poverty and inequality in ways that absolve the state and capital of any culpability. Race gives meaning to the notion that Black people are inferior because of either culture or biology. It is almost strange to suggest that Black Americans, many of whose lineages as descendants of slaves stretch back to the first two centuries of the beginning of the American colonies, have a culture separate and distinct from other Americans. This framework of Black inferiority politically narrates the necessity of austere budgets while sustaining—ideologically at least—the premise of the "American dream." The Black experience unravels what we are supposed to know to be true about America itself—the land of milk and honey, the land where hard work makes dreams come true. This mythology is not benign: it serves as the United States' self-declared invitation to intervene militarily and economically around the globe. Consider President Obama's words in September 2014, when he declared a new war front against the Islamic State in the Middle East. He said, "America, our endless blessings bestow an enduring burden. But as Americans, we welcome our responsibility to lead. From Europe to Asia—from the far reaches of Africa to war-torn capitals of the Middle East—we stand for freedom, for justice, for dignity. These are values that have guided our nation since its founding."[7] What an utterly absurd statement—but that, perhaps, is why the U.S. political and economic leadership clings so tightly to the framework of Black inferiority as the central explanation for Black inequality.

Finally, ideologies do not work when they are only imposed from above. The key is widespread acceptance, even by the oppressed themselves. There are multiple examples of African Americans accepting some aspects of racist ideology while also rejecting other aspects because of their own experiences. At various times, African Americans have also accepted that "culture" and "personal responsibility" are just as important in understanding Black oppression as racism and discrimination are. But the Black freedom struggle has also done much to confront explanations that blame Blacks for their own oppression—including throughout the 1960s and into the 1970s. The Black Lives Matter movement has the potential to shift this again, even as "culture of poverty" politics remain as entrenched as ever and Black inequality remains a fact of American life.

A CULTURAL TAILSPIN

Why are ideas about a defective Black culture so widespread when there is so much evidence for material causes of continued Black inequality? One reason is the way that the political system, elected officials, and the mainstream media operate—sometimes in tandem and sometimes independently of each other—to reinforce this "common sense" view of society. The hearty shouts of "culture," "responsibility," and "morality" come with reckless abandon when politicians of all stripes explain to the world the problems in Black America. Representative Paul Ryan used a commemoration of the fiftieth anniversary of Lyndon Johnson's War on Poverty programs as an opportunity to explicate what he considers their failures: "We have got this tailspin of culture, in our inner cities in particular, of men not working and just generations of men not even thinking about working or learning the value and the culture of work, and so there is a real culture problem here that has to be dealt with." Ryan did not need to invoke "race" explicitly. The code is well known, not only because white conservatives like Ryan readily invoke it but also because liberals both normalize and legitimize the same language.

For example, when Democratic Party leader and Chicago mayor Rahm Emanuel tried to garner support for his plan to curb gun violence, he focused on what he likes to describe as the "four Ps: policing, prevention, penalties, and parenting."[8] Here Emanuel parrots conventional wisdom about juvenile crime: that it requires better parenting and, perhaps, some preventative programming, but if those fail, there are always policing and penalties to fall back on. At other times Emanuel has been less charitable, simply saying, "It's not about crime, it's about values."[9] President Obama also linked youth gun violence in Chicago to values and behavior when he said, "We have to provide stronger role models than the gangbanger on the corner."[10] The problem, according to these examples, is that crime and poverty in cities are not products of inequality but of a lack of discipline. Black youth need better values and better role models to change the culture that produces their dysfunctional and violent behavior, which, of course, is the real obstacle to a successful and meaningful life. Mayor Emanuel made the distinction between his own kids' lives of privilege and luxury and those of Chicago's Black and Brown children clear when, after an extravagant South

American vacation, he quipped to a local newspaper, "Every year, we try to take the kids to a different part of the world to see. When you . . . grow up . . . you want to be an Emanuel child. It's unbelievable."[11]

It is not just in the world of politics that elected officials blame poor Black children for their own hardships. The mainstream media provides a very public platform for these ideas—from the seemingly innocuous to the very serious. For example, the mainstream media made an enormous ruckus about the antics of professional football player Marshawn Lynch, who ignored the press during the Super Bowl in 2015. It was quite the topic of discussion during much of the week leading up to the game, but the media attention shifted when another African American football player, Larry Foote, chastised Lynch for sending the "wrong message" to kids from an "urban environment." He ranted,

> The biggest message he's giving these kids . . . is "The hell with authority. I don't care, fine me. I'm gonna grab my crotch. I'm gonna do it my way." . . . In the real world, it doesn't work that way. . . . How can you keep a job? I mean, you got these inner-city kids. They don't listen to teachers. They don't listen to police officers, principals. And these guys can't even keep a job because they say "F" authority.[12]

In other words, police violence against and higher rates of unemployment among Black youth exist because Black kids do not respect authority—and because Marshawn Lynch is a poor role model.

In a much more serious reflection on these issues, *New Yorker* columnist Jonathan Chait and *Atlantic* columnist Ta-Nehisi Coates debated in a series of articles whether a "culture of poverty" actually exists. According to Chait, some African Americans' lack of "economic success" is directly related to the absence of "middle-class cultural norms." The combination of the two can be reduced to the presence of a Black culture of poverty: "People are the products of their environment. Environments are amenable to public policy. Some of the most successful anti-poverty initiatives, like the Harlem Children's Zone or the KIPP schools, are designed around the premise that children raised in concentrated poverty need to be taught middle class norms."[13]

Chait blithely links Black success to programs promoting privatization—charter schools and "empowerment zones," which have hardly been proven to end poverty. This old argument disintegrates when we try to make sense of the Great Recession of 2008, when "half the collective wealth of African-American families was stripped away," an economic free fall from which they have yet to recover.[14] The "middle-class norms" of home-ownership could not stop Black people's wealth from disappearing into thin air after banks fleeced them by steering them toward sub-prime loans. Nor do "middle-class norms" explain why Black college graduates' unemployment rate is well over twice that of white college graduates.[15] Coates responded with an argument that does not often elbow its way into mainstream accounts of Black oppression:

> There is no evidence that black people are less responsible, less moral, or less upstanding in their dealings with America nor with themselves. But there is overwhelming evidence that America is irresponsible, immoral, and unconscionable in its dealings with black people and with itself. Urging African-Americans to become superhuman is great advice if you are concerned with creating extraordinary individuals. It is terrible advice if you are concerned with creating an equitable society. The black freedom struggle is not about raising a race of hyper-moral super-humans. It is about all people garnering the right to live like the normal humans they are.[16]

AMERICAN EXCEPTIONALISM

While the rest of the world wrestles with class and the perils of "class envy," the United States, according to the legend of its own making, is a place where anyone can make it. Much earlier, colonial leader John Winthrop famously described it as "a city upon a hill," adding that "the eyes of all people are upon us."[17] On the night he won the presidency in 2008, President Barack Obama said, "If there is anyone out there who still doubts that America is a place where all things are possible, who still wonders if the dream of our founders is alive in our time, who still questions the power of our democracy, tonight is your answer."[18] Former secretary of state Madeleine Albright has called the United States the "indispensable nation,"[19] while Ronald Reagan, years earlier, spelled out the specific metrics of the American dream:

> One-half of all the economic activity in the entire history of man has taken place in this republic. We have distributed our wealth more widely among our

people than any society known to man. Americans work less hours for a higher standard of living than any other people. Ninety-five percent of all our families have an adequate daily intake of nutrients—and a part of the 5 percent that don't are trying to lose weight! Ninety-nine percent have gas or electric refrigeration, 92 percent have televisions, and an equal number have telephones. There are 120 million cars on our streets and highways—and all of them are on the street at once when you are trying to get home at night. But isn't this just proof of our materialism—the very thing that we are charged with? Well, we also have more churches, more libraries, we support voluntarily more symphony orchestras and opera companies, non-profit theaters, and publish more books than all the other nations of the world put together . . . . We cannot escape our destiny, nor should we try to do so. The leadership of the free world was thrust upon us two centuries ago in that little hall of Philadelphia . . . . We are indeed, and we are today, the last best hope of man on earth.[20]

American exceptionalism operates as a mythology of convenience that does a tremendous amount of work to simplify the contradiction between the apparent creed of U.S. society and its much more complicated reality. Where people have failed to succeed and cash in on the abundance that American ingenuity has apparently created, their personal failures or deficiencies serve as the explanation.

But there is something more pernicious at the heart of this contradiction than a simple morality tale about those who try hard and those who don't. The long list of attributes that Reagan proudly recites is wholly contingent on the erasure or rewriting of three central themes in American history—genocide, slavery, and the massive exploitation of waves of immigrant workers. This "cruel reality" made the "soaring ideals" of American exceptionalism and American democracy possible.[21] From the mutual foundation of slavery *and* freedom at the country's inception to the genocide of the Native population that made the "peculiar institution" possible to the racist promulgation of "manifest destiny" to the Chinese Exclusion Act to the codified subordinate status of Black people for a hundred years after slavery ended, they are all grim reminders of the millions of bodies upon which the audacious smugness of American hubris is built. Race and racism have not been exceptions; instead, they have been the glue that holds the United States together.

Historian James Adams first popularized the concept of the American dream in his 1931 book *Epic of America*. He wrote:

But there has been also the *American dream,* that dream of a land in which life should be better and richer and fuller for every man, with opportunity for each according to his ability or achievement. It is a difficult dream for the European upper classes to interpret adequately, and too many of us ourselves have grown weary and mistrustful of it. It is not a dream of motor cars and high wages merely, but a dream of social order in which each man and each woman shall be able to attain to the fullest stature of which they are innately capable, and be recognized by others for what they are, regardless of the fortuitous circumstances of birth or position.[22]

This powerful idea has lured immigrants to this country and compelled internal migrants to other parts of the country. But it is rife with contradictions, just as it was in the 1930s, when the failures of the American economy produced widespread insecurity and poverty, despite the personal intentions or work ethic of those most affected. At the same time, the Russian Revolution in 1917 cast a long shadow, and the threat of radical and revolutionary activity loomed over Europe. In this context, the mythology of the United States as different and unaffected by class tensions and dynamics took on new urgency. The New Deal legislation and the reorganization of capital was a reflection of this. As Hal Draper pointed out about the 1930s, "The New Deal liberals proposed to save capitalism, at a time of deep going crisis and despair, by statification—that is, by increasing state intervention into the control of the economy from above."[23]

Indeed, Roosevelt referred to himself as the "savior" of the free-market system. In his bid for reelection, he said: "It was this Administration which saved the system of private profit and free enterprise after it had been dragged to the brink of ruin by these same leaders who now try to scare you. The struggle against private monopoly is a struggle for, and not against, American business. It is a struggle to preserve individual enterprise and economic freedom."[24] In an era when revolution was perceived not as idealistic but as a possibility, it was absolutely necessary to introduce new regulatory measures to create equilibrium in the system. But "preserving" the system was not only about change at an institutional level, it was also a political contest over collective ownership, for which socialists and communists organized, versus private enterprise, the lifeblood of capitalism. There were two significant shifts in the American political economy toward this aim. The turn to Keynesian economics and the bolstering of demand-based consumption helped to underpin perceptions of economic stability. In turn, the development of state-sponsored social welfare—Social Security, aid to mothers with children, public housing—created a bottom through which the vast majority of ordinary people could not fall. These, combined with the U.S. entrance into World War II, revitalized the American economy and gave rise to the longest economic expansion in American history.

The robust postwar economy put flesh on the ideological scaffolding of the American dream. Massive government subsidies were deployed in ways that hid the state's role in the development of the American middle class, further perpetuating the mythology of hard work and perseverance as the key ingredients to social mobility.[25] This was especially true in housing. The private housing lobby and its backers in Congress denounced publicly subsidized housing as creeping socialism. The federal government therefore subsidized home-ownership, not through direct payment, but through interest-rate deductions and government-guaranteed mortgages that allowed banks to lend with abandon. Not only did it rebuild the economy through these measures—and on a sounder basis than the unregulated capitalism of the previous period—but it reinforced and gave new life to the idea of American exceptionalism and the good life. As David Harvey has explained,

> The suburbanization of the United States was not merely a matter of new infrastructures . . . . it entailed a radical transformation in lifestyles, bringing new products from housing to refrigerators and air conditioners, as well as two cars in the driveway and an enormous increase in the consumption of oil. It also altered the political landscape, as subsidized home-ownership for the middle classes changed the focus of community action towards the defense of property values and individualized identities, turning the suburban vote towards conservative republicanism. Debt-encumbered homeowners . . . were less likely to go on strike.[26]

But the fruits of these new arrangements did not fall to African Americans. Political scientist Ira Katznelson describes the uneven distribution of postwar riches in his well-known book *When Affirmative Action Was White*, including the initial exclusion of African Americans from Social Security collection and other New Deal benefits. When it came to home-ownership, for example, federal mortgage guarantees were contingent on the recipients living in new, suburban housing, from which most African Americans were excluded. This meant that while the federal government subsidized suburban development, urban living spaces were an afterthought.[27] As businesses began to relocate their firms and entire industries to suburban areas because of lower land costs and taxes, the urban disinvestment dynamic was exacerbated, leaving cities bereft of the jobs that had initially lured millions of people to them in the first place.[28] Meanwhile, real-estate interests and their backers in government ensured that neither Black renters nor Black home buyers could participate in the developing suburban economy.[29]

COLD WAR CONFLICT

The aftermath of World War II introduced a new dynamic into American "race relations." The war itself created a new, bipolar world in which the United States and the Soviet Union were the "superpowers" that competed with each other for influence and control over the rest of the planet. The war also unleashed massive upheaval among the colonial possessions of the old world order. As the colonized world went into revolt against European powers, the superpowers made appeals to newly emerging independent countries. This made discrimination against American Blacks not only a domestic issue but also an international one.[30] How could the United States present itself as a "city upon a hill" or as the essential democratic nation when its Black citizens were treated so poorly?

Black migration out of the South picked up at an even greater speed than before the war. The postwar economic expansion offered Black laborers their chance at escaping the grip of Jim Crow. One hundred and twenty-five thousand Black soldiers had fought in World War II and were returning to cities across the North—to the most serious housing shortage in American history. Competition over jobs and housing in cities was an old story in the postwar period, but a renewed sense of militancy among African Americans created a palpable tension. One army officer in the Morale Division reported that "the threats to the nation were 'first Negroes, second Japs, third Nazis'—in that order!"[31] A Black GI from Tennessee asked, "What I want to know is how in the hell white folks think we are going to fight for the fascism under which we live each moment of our lives? We are taught to kill and we are going to kill. But do you ask WHO?"[32] White violence directed at Blacks continued, especially when Blacks attempted to breach the boundaries of segregation. Southern whites' "massive resistance" in defense of Jim Crow is well integrated into American folklore, but this attempt at racist mob rule was not regional. In Chicago and Detroit, in particular, thousands of whites joined mobs to terrorize African Americans who attempted to move into white areas.[33] In both the North and South, white police either joined the attacks on African Americans or, as they had done so many times before, passively stood aside as whites stoned houses, set fires, destroyed cars, smashed windows, and threatened to kill any Blacks who got in their way.

The ideological battlefield on which the Cold War was fought compelled Northern political and economic elites to take progressively more formal stances against discrimination and to call for more law and order. This especially became necessary when African Americans began to mobilize against racial injustice and actively tried to bring international attention to it, greatly aware of the country's vulnerability in racial politics given its vocal demands for democracy and freedom. The Nazi genocide of Jews in the 1930s and 1940s had deeply discredited racism and eugenics; the United States had characterized World War II as a battle between democracy and tyranny. It was therefore increasingly concerned about international perceptions of its treatment of African Americans. Mob violence and physical threats against Black people collectively threatened its geopolitical positioning. The developing Black militancy, fueled by political dynamics within the United States as well as the global risings of Black and Brown people against colonialism, set the U.S. state on a collision course with its Black population. African Americans had certainly campaigned against racial injustice long before the civil rights era, but the confluence of several overlapping events brought Black grievances into sharper focus. These factors combined to push the United States toward emphasizing its political commitment to formal equality for Blacks before the law; they also emboldened African Americans to fight not only for formal equality but for social and racial justice as well.

The United States' commitment to formal equality in the context of the Cold War was not only intended to rehabilitate its reputation on racial issues; it was also an effort to bolster its free-market economy and system of governance. The government and its proponents in the financial world were making a global claim that the United States was good to its Black population, and at the same time they were promoting capitalism and private enterprise as the highest expressions of freedom. American boosters sustained the fiction of the "culture of poverty" as the pretext for the persisting inequality between Blacks and the rest of the country. In some ways, this was even more important as the United States continued its quest to project itself as an economic and political empire. Cold War liberalism was a political framework that viewed American racial problems as existing outside of or unrelated to its political economy and, more importantly, as problems that could be fixed within the system itself by changing the laws and creating "equal opportunity." Themes of opportunity, hard work, resilience, and mobility could be contrasted to the perceptions of Soviet society as being impoverished because of its planned economies, prison labor, and infringement of freedom.

President Johnson, for example, described the contest between East and West as "a struggle" between two distinct "philosophies": "Don't you tell me for a moment that we can't outproduce and outwork and outright any communistic system in the world. Because if you try to tell me otherwise, you tell me that slaves can do better than free men, and I don't believe they can. I would rather have an executive vice president . . . than to have a commissar!"[34]

Upholding American capitalism in the context of a bitter Cold War had multiple effects. Elected officials in both parties continued to demonize social welfare as socialism or communism and an affront to free enterprise, as did private-sector actors who had a financial interest in seeing the American government shift its functions to private institutions. As scholar Alexander von Hoffman explains:

> From the 1930s onwards, private housing financiers, real estate brokers, and builders denounced the idea of the government directly helping Americans of modest means to obtain homes. It was, they cried, not only a socialistic plot, but also an unjustified give-away to a select undeserving group of people. It soon became evident, if it was not already, that self-interest, as much as ideology, fueled the hatred of the leaders of private industry for public housing.[35]

Historian Landon Storrs argues that anticommunism—the "Red Scare"—had an even more profound impact on public policies because it weeded out "employees deemed disloyal to the U.S. government." Between 1947 and 1956, "more than five million federal workers underwent loyalty screening," and at least twenty-five thousand were subject to a stigmatizing "full field investigation" by the FBI.[36] An estimated twenty-seven hundred federal employees were dismissed and about twelve thousand resigned.

Those most affected, according to Storrs, "were a varied group of leftists who shared a commitment to building a comprehensive welfare state that blended central planning with grassroots democracy." The impact was indelible: "The power of these leftists was never uncontested, but their expertise, commitment, and connectedness gave them strength beyond their numbers. Before loyalty investigations pushed this cohort either out of government or toward the center of the political spectrum, the transformative potential of the New Deal was greater than is commonly understood."[37] Of course, McCarthyism's impact reached beyond liberal public policies; it was generally destructive for the entire Left. The state specifically targeted leading activists and intellectuals involved in the fight against racism; antiracist campaigns were dismissed out of hand as subversive activity. As Manning Marable observes, "The purge of communists and radicals from organized labor from 1947 through 1950 was the principal reason for the decline in the AFL-CIO's commitment to the struggle against racial segregation."[38] More generally, anticommunism and the complicity of Black and white liberals in its witch hunts "retarded the Black movement for a decade or more."[39]

The volatile politics surrounding who should be eligible for public welfare also aided in creating the political categories of "deserving" and "undeserving." These concerns overlapped with the growing popularity of "culture" as a critical framework for understanding the failure to find the American dream. This political context, as well as the deepening influence of the social sciences as an "objective" arbiter in describing social patterns (sponsored by the Ford Foundation, among others), helped to map a simplistic view of Black poverty that was largely divorced from structural obstacles, including residential segregation, police brutality, housing and job discrimination, and the systematic underfunding of public schools in Black communities. The problem was described as one of "assimilation" for Blacks migrating from South to North. This fit in with a developing global perspective on U.S. poverty that was shaped by the Cold War as well as the social sciences.[40]

In 1959, liberal anthropologist Oscar Lewis coined the term "culture of poverty" to describe psychological and behavioral traits in poor people in underdeveloped countries and "to understand what they had in common with the lower classes all over the world."[41] Lewis wrote, "It seems to me that the culture of poverty has some universal characteristics which transcend regional, rural-urban, and even national boundaries." He identified these cultures in locations as disparate as "Mexican villages" and "lower class Negroes in the United States."[42] The shared traits he identified included resignation, dependency, present-time orientation, lack of impulse control, weak ego structure, sexual confusion, inability to delay gratification, and sixty-three more.[43] These were overwhelmingly psychological descriptions, highly malleable and certainly not endemic to the condition of the people themselves outside of any larger economic context. Lewis was not a political conservative—he was a left-wing liberal who linked this "culture of poverty" to "class-stratified, highly individuated capitalistic societies." But, as Alice O'Connor notes, "the problem was that Lewis made very little attempt to provide direct evidence or analysis that actually linked behavioral and cultural patterns to the structure of political economy as experienced by the poor." The "culture of poverty" in its original incarnation was viewed as a positive pivot away from "biological racism," rooted in eugenics and adopted by the Nazi regime. Culture, unlike biology, was mutable and capable of being transformed. Finally, O'Connor argued, "by couching the analysis so exclusively in terms of behavior and psychology, the culture of poverty undercut its own radical potential and deflected away from any critique of capitalism implicit in the idea."[44]

LOCATING THE SOURCE

As insightful as Lewis's original iteration of the "culture of poverty" may have been, it did not account for the profound racial terrorism that confronted Black people in the North as well as the South. The movement against state-sponsored racism and violence across the South exposed to the world—and, more importantly, to the rest of the United States—the racially tyrannical regime under which African Americans were living. The 1963 March on Washington was the first national display of the breadth of the Southern civil rights movement. It focused on the many manifestations of racial discrimination and gave clear and definable contours to the constraints imposed on African Americans. In doing so, the march also communicated that the movement's understanding of freedom extended beyond simply repealing unjust laws in the South.

A portion of King's much-memorialized "I Have a Dream" speech speaks to the relationship between economic and racial injustice:

> There are those who are asking the devotees of civil rights, "When will you be satisfied?" We can never be satisfied as long as the Negro is the victim of the unspeakable horrors of police brutality. We can never be satisfied as long as our bodies, heavy with the fatigue of travel, cannot gain lodging in the motels of the highways and the hotels of the cities. We cannot be satisfied as long as the Negro's basic mobility is from a smaller ghetto to a larger one. We can never be satisfied as long as our children are stripped of their self-hood and robbed of their dignity by signs stating: "For Whites Only." We cannot be satisfied as long as a Negro in Mississippi cannot vote and a Negro in New York believes he has nothing for which to vote. No, no, we are not satisfied, and we will not be satisfied until "justice rolls down like waters, and righteousness like a mighty stream."[45]

Here King also links the codified racial discrimination of the Jim Crow South to the informal but equally pernicious de facto segregation of the urban North. In both cases, King clearly located the Black condition in public and private institutional practices throughout the United States. Of course, King was not the first to do this, but the scale, scope, and ultimate influence of the march elevated these arguments to a national level.

As early as the 1930s, and certainly throughout the postwar era, Blacks engaged in campaigns for "better jobs, an end to police brutality, access to new housing, representation in government, and college education for their children."[46] Malcolm X considered it "ridiculous" that civil rights activists were traveling to the South to fight Jim Crow when the North had "enough rats and roaches to kill to keep all of the freedom fighters busy."[47] In a speech given at the founding of his new Organization of

Afro-American Unity, in the year before his death, Malcolm described the political economy of Black poverty in the North:

> The economic exploitation in the Afro-American community is the most vicious form practiced on any people in America. In fact, it is the most vicious practiced on any people on this earth. No one is exploited economically as thoroughly as you and I, because in most countries where people are exploited they know it. You and I are in this country being exploited and sometimes we don t know it. Twice as much rent is paid for rat-infested, roach-crawling, rotting tenements.
> This is true. It costs us more to live in Harlem than it costs them to live on Park Avenue. Do you know that the rent is higher on Park Avenue in Harlem than it is on Park Avenue downtown? And in Harlem you have everything else in that apartment with you: roaches, rats, cats, dogs, and some other outsiders disguised as landlords. The Afro-American pays more for food, pays more for clothing, pays more for insurance than anybody else. And we do. It costs you and me more for insurance than it does the white man in the Bronx or somewhere else. It costs you and me more for food than it does them. It costs you and me more to live in America than it does anybody else and yet we make the greatest contribution.
>
> You tell me what kind of country this is. Why should we do the dirtiest jobs for the lowest pay? Why should we do the hardest work for the lowest pay? Why should we pay the most money for the worst kind of food and the most money for the worst kind of place to live in?[48]

His influence and wide appeal across the Black North helped to articulate a different understanding of Black poverty and hardship as the products not of bad behavior but of white racism.

The passage of the 1964 Civil Rights Act and the 1965 Voting Rights Act removed the last vestiges of legal discrimination across the South. It was a surprising accomplishment that could not have been imagined even ten years before it happened. Its success was an amazing accomplishment by the ordinary men, women, and children of the civil rights movement, and it forced a monumental shift in the political and social order of the American South. But almost before the ink could dry on the legislation, its limits were displayed. Ending legal segregation and disenfranchisement in the South did not necessarily guarantee free and unfettered participation in the public and private spheres of employment, housing, and education. This was also true in the North. The civil rights movement had much clearer targets in the South; the means of discrimination in the North, such as housing and job discrimination, were legal and thus much harder to change. Black children went to overcrowded schools in shifts in Chicago and New York—all perfectly legal.

Five days after the Voting Rights Act was signed into law, the Watts Rebellion exploded in South Central Los Angeles. Cries of "Selma" could be heard above the chaos of rebellion.[49] The civil rights movement had hastened the radicalization of many African Americans. There had been smaller uprisings in New York City, Philadelphia, Rochester, and other cities the previous summer, in 1964, but the Watts Rebellion was on an entirely different scale. For six days, an estimated ten thousand African Americans battled with police in an unprecedented rebellion against the effects of racial discrimination, including police brutality and housing discrimination. Thirty-four people were killed, hundreds more injured. Four thousand people were arrested and tens of millions of dollars in property damage occurred.[50]

The fires in Los Angeles were evidence of a developing Black radicalization rooted in the incongruence between America trumpeting its rich abundance as proof of the superiority of free enterprise and Black people suffering the indignities of poverty. After the passage of civil rights legislation, Black suffering could no longer be blamed only on Southern racism.

The Black freedom movement of the 1960s fed the expansion of the American welfare state and its eventual inclusion of African Americans. Though the New Deal had mostly excluded African Americans, Johnson's War on Poverty and Great Society programs were largely responses to the different phases of the Black movement. In 1964, Johnson reminded his supporters in the Chamber of Commerce of the consequences of not backing social welfare:

> Please always remember that if we do nothing to wipe out these ancient enemies of ignorance and illiteracy and poverty and disease, and if we allow them to accumulate . . . . If a peaceful revolution to get rid of these things— illiteracy, and these ancient enemies of mankind that stalk the earth, where two-thirds of the masses are young and are clamoring and are parading and are protesting and are demonstrating now for something to eat and wear and learn and health—[then] a violent change is inevitable.[51]

The War on Poverty and Great Society programs reflected Cold War antipathy toward total government control by emphasizing public-private partnerships and "equal opportunity," as opposed to economic redistribution. Nevertheless, Black protests polarized the political debates concerning the nation's welfare policies and the course of action needed to remedy the growing Black Power revolt—and debates over the nature of Black poverty reemerged.

Presidential consultant Daniel Patrick Moynihan penned a controversial report, titled *The Negro Family: The Case for National Action,* that blamed the problems endured by Black people on a "tangle of pathology." The Moynihan report, as it came to be known, claimed to ground the problems experienced in Black communities in theory and research. Instead, it was a more sophisticated recycling of stereotypes infused with an air of science that located social problems in the supposed behaviors of poor Black families. Moynihan claimed that the heart "of the deterioration of the fabric of Negro society is the deterioration of the Negro family."[52] This deterioration was rooted, he said, in the historic way that American slavery had broken up Black families. Moynihan blamed Black women for emasculating Black men, who then shirked their role as the head of the family. The result was antisocial behaviors experienced far beyond the borders of Black families. At one point, the report casually suggests that "it is probable that at present, a majority of the crimes against the person, such as rape, murder, aggravated assault are committed by Negroes"— then concedes in the next sentence that there is, of course, "no absolute evidence" for this claim. Moynihan identified these problems as the outcome of Black families led by single women.

It is important to note that Moynihan was a liberal serving with the Johnson administration. He viewed his ideas as progressive because he located the "root causes" of Black social pathology in family structure, which could be overcome by "equal opportunity" and other government action. This is where liberal and conservative thought converge, however: in seeing Black problems as rooted in Black communities as opposed to seeing them as systemic to American society. Moynihan offered little description of contemporary manifestations of racism. Instead, he emphasized the role of slavery in explaining the many problems that developed from the overwhelming poverty that most Black families were trying to survive. But the Black rebellion produced other explanations for entrenched Black poverty.

Over the next three years, violent and furious explosions of Black rage in American cities punctuated every summer. They shocked the nation. The triumphalism of the American dream withered with each convulsion. Black protests forged an alternative understanding of Black inequality. Black psychologist Kenneth Clark dislodged the Harlem rebellion from Moynihan's "tangle of pathology" in his book *Dark Ghetto*. Though Clark would later be accused of promoting his own theories about Black pathology, his descriptions of the Harlem rebellion could very easily describe the dynamic underlying all of the Black uprisings in the 1960s:

> The summer of 1964 brought violent protests to the ghettos of America's cities, not in mobilization of effective power, but as an outpouring of unplanned revolt. The *revolts* in Harlem were not led by a mob, for a mob is an uncontrolled social force bent on irrational destruction. The revolts in Harlem were, rather, a weird social defiance. Those involved in them, were in general, not the lowest class of Harlem residents—not primarily looters and semi-criminals—but marginal Negroes who were upwardly mobile, demanding a higher status than their families had. Even those Negroes who threw bottles and bricks from the roofs were not in the grip of wild abandon, but seemed deliberately to be prodding the police to behave openly as the barbarians that the Negroes felt they actually were . . . . [There was] a calm within the chaos, a deliberateness within the hysteria. The Negro seemed to feel nothing could happen to him that had not happened already—he behaved as if he had nothing to lose. His was an oddly controlled rage that seemed to say, during those days of social despair, "We have had enough. The only weapon you have is bullets. The only thing you can do is kill me." Paradoxically, his apparent lawlessness was a protest against the lawlessness directed against *him*. His acts were a desperate assertion of his desire to be treated as a man. He was affirmative up to the point of inviting death, he insisted upon being visible and understood. If this was the only way to relate to society at large, he would rather die than be misunderstood.[53]

Clark's description of how, at least, the Black male psyche was essentially repaired through the course of fighting against racism reflected the widespread growth of Black political organizations in response to every conceivable issue. But it was not just Black men who were being "repaired" through fighting racism; Black women were also at the forefront of many of the most important struggles in the 1960s. From tenant unions to welfare-rights organizations to Black public-sector workers demanding union recognition, ordinary African Americans organized to both define and combat racial injustice.[54]

Lyndon Johnson's administration churned out legislation in an effort to stay in front of the mounting protests and "civil disorder." The most obvious way to keep up was by expanding the American welfare state.[55] The limits of the American welfare state have been the subject of intense debate, but Johnson's Great Society programs included job training, housing, food stamps, and other forms of assistance that inadvertently helped to define Black inequality as primarily an economic question. The greater emphasis on structural inequality legitimized Black demands for greater inclusion in American affluence and access to the benefits of its expanding welfare state. Theresa Vasta spoke for many women on welfare when she said that she had "no time for games. My children are hungry and my oldest one is missing school because I have no money to send her . . . . I am American born. I think I deserve the right treatment. Fair treatment, that is."[56]

The expansion of the welfare state, the turn to affirmative action practices, and the establishment of the Equal Employment Opportunity Commission (EEOC) by the end of the 1960s reinforced the idea that Blacks were entitled to a share in American affluence. The development of Black struggle over the course of the decade, from the protest movement based in the South to the explosion of urban rebellions across the country, changed the discourse surrounding Black poverty. Johnson noted this in his well-known commencement address at Howard University:

> The American Negro, acting with impressive restraint, has peacefully protested and marched, entered the courtrooms and the seats of government, demanding a justice that has long been denied. The voice of the Negro was the call to action. But it is a tribute to America that, once aroused, the courts and the Congress, the President and most of the people, have been the allies of progress. . . . But freedom is not enough. You do not wipe away the scars of centuries by saying: Now you are free to go where you want, and do as you desire, and choose the leaders you please. You do not take a person who, for years, has been hobbled by chains and liberate him, bring him up to the starting line of a race and then say, "you are free to compete with all the others," and still justly believe that you have been completely fair. . . . Thus it is not enough just to open the gates of opportunity. All our citizens must have

the ability to walk through those gates. . . . We seek not just freedom but opportunity. We seek not just legal equity but human ability, not just equality as a right and a theory but equality as a fact and equality as a result.[57]

The phrases "freedom is not enough" and "equality as a result" pointed to structural inequality and affirmed the demand for positive or affirmative action on the part of the state to cure impoverished conditions brought on by centuries of discrimination.

Hundreds of thousands of Black Americans drew even more radical conclusions about the nature of Black oppression in the United States as they were drawn directly into the radicalizing movement; hundreds of thousands more sympathized with the rebellions. The struggle broke through the isolation and confinement of life in segregated Black ghettos and upended the prevailing explanation that Blacks were responsible for the conditions in their neighborhoods. Mass struggle led to a political understanding of poverty in Black communities across the country. Black media captured stories of injustice as well as the various struggles to organize against it, feeding this process and knitting together a common Black view of Black oppression while simultaneously providing an alternative understanding for white people. A Harris poll taken in the summer of 1967, after major riots in Detroit and Newark, found 40 percent of whites believed that "the way Negroes have been treated in the slums and ghettos of big cities" and "the failure of white society to keep its promises to Negroes" were the leading causes of the rebellion.[58] Many, including Martin Luther King Jr., began to connect Black oppression to a broader critique of capitalism.

King began to make those connections in his politics, especially when his organizing brought him in direct confrontation with northern ghettos and residential segregation. At a Southern Christian Leadership Conference convention in the summer of 1967, he gave a speech that raised broader questions about the economic system:

Now, in order to answer the question, "Where do we go from here?" which is our theme, we must first honestly recognize where we are now. When the Constitution was written, a strange formula to determine taxes and representation declared that the Negro was sixty percent of a person. Today another curious formula seems to declare that he is fifty percent of a person. Of the good things in life, the Negro has approximately one-half those of whites. Of the bad things of life, he has twice those of whites. Thus, half of

all Negroes live in substandard housing. And Negroes have half the income
of whites. When we view the negative experiences of life, the Negro has a
double share. There are twice as many unemployed. The rate of infant mortality among Negroes is double that of whites and there are twice as many
Negroes dying in Vietnam as whites in proportion to their size in the
population.[59]

The Black Panther Party for Self-Defense (BPP) went even further when
it declared its intent to rid the United States of its capitalist economy
and build socialism in its place. The Black Panthers were not a fringe
organization—far from it. FBI director J. Edgar Hoover declared the party
the "greatest internal threat" to the security of the United States. Formed
in Oakland, California, directly in response to the crisis of police brutality,
the Panthers linked police brutality to the web of oppression and exploitation that entangled Black people across the country. Not only did they link
Black oppression to its material roots, they connected it to capitalism
itself. Panther leader Huey P. Newton made this clear:

> The Black Panther Party is a revolutionary Nationalist group and we see a
> major contradiction between capitalism in this country and our interests.
> We realize that this country became very rich upon slavery and that slavery
> is capitalism in the extreme. We have two evils to fight, capitalism and rac-
> ism. We must destroy both racism and capitalism.[60]

The Panthers were not a mass party, but they had appeal that stretched far
beyond their actual numbers. At its high point, the BPP was selling an
astonishing 139,000 copies of its newspaper, the *Black Panther,* a week.[61]
In this paper, readers would have seen multiple stories about police brutality in cities across the country. They would have also read the Panthers'
Ten-Point Program, a list of demands intended to explain the aims and
goals of the party, which linked capitalist exploitation and the American
political economy to Black poverty and oppression. In doing so, the party
audaciously made demands on the state to fulfill its responsibility to
employ, house, and educate Black people, whose impoverished condition
had been caused by American capitalism.

The Panthers were a regular topic of discussion in Black mainstream
media. For example, in 1969, *Ebony,* the most popular weekly magazine in
Black America, allowed Newton to pen an article from jail to articulate the

Panthers' program in his own words. The article included a detailed discussion on the relationship between capitalist exploitation and racism. It read, in part, "Only by eliminating capitalism and substituting it for socialism will all black, *all* black people, be able to practice self-determination and thus achieve freedom." This was not just the observations of a marginal Left: this was the most well-known Black revolutionary organization making a case to a much broader Black population about their oppression. The Panthers, who were deeply inspired by Malcolm X, linked the crisis in Black America to capitalism and imperialism. Racism could not be separated from the perpetual economic problems in Black communities. In fact, the economic problems of Black America could not be understood without taking account of racism. Blacks were underemployed, unemployed, poorly housed, and poorly schooled *because* they were Black.

Identifying structural inequality or institutional racism was not just of scholastic interest; linking Black oppression to structural and institutional practices legitimized demands for programs and funding to undo the harm that had been done. This logic underlined calls for what would become "affirmative action" but also much broader demands for federal funding and the enforcement of new civil rights rules to open up the possibility for greater jobs, access to better housing, and improvement in Black schools.

The entire dynamic of the Black struggle pushed mainstream politics to the left during this period, as evidenced by the growth of the welfare state and the increasing number of mainstream voices that identified racism as a problem. The Black struggle also heightened an already intense political polarization. Of course, racists and conservatives had always existed and dominated politics, but the growing movement now put them on the defensive. The political establishment was split over how to respond. Where some liberals gravitated toward including more structural arguments about Black inequality, conservatives clung to stereotypes about Black families. The more ghetto inhabitants rebelled, the more conservative politicians' ideas about the ghetto and the people who lived there hardened.

Generally speaking, however, the positive impact of the struggle could be measured by shifting opinions among the public regarding social programs. There was a nuanced public response to the riots in the late 1960s, not just a backlash. The emphasis on backlash by historians and political figures has simplified the multiple factors that contributed to a conserva-tive shift in formal politics by the end of the decade and into the 1970s. To be sure, there was resentment against the uprisings, the tone of which can be captured by a liberal *New York Times* editorial, written only a few weeks after the riots in Detroit, that read in part, "The riots, rather than develop-ing a clamor for great social progress to wipe out poverty, to a large extent have had the reverse effect and have increased the cries for use of police force and criminal law."[62] Yet the totality of that perspective did not appear to correspond with a number of polls taken ten days later that showed wide-ranging support for expanding social programs aimed at mitigating the material deprivation that many connected to the spreading violence. In a *Washington Post* poll of African Americans published in 1967, Blacks linked deteriorating conditions in their communities with the uprisings. Fully 70 percent of Blacks "attributed rioting to housing conditions." Fifty-nine percent of Blacks said they knew someone living in rat-infested hous-ing. In the same poll, 39 percent of whites said they believed the condition of Black housing was responsible for the ongoing riots. In another poll of African Americans and whites, strong majorities came out in support of antipoverty programs. A *Washington Post* headline read, "Races agree on ghetto abolition and the need for a WPA-style program." Sixty-nine per-cent of *all* Americans supported federal efforts to create a jobs program. Sixty-five percent believed in tearing down ghettos. Sixty percent sup-ported a federal program to eliminate rats, and 57 percent supported summer-camp programs for Black youth.[63]

In some ways, these findings prefigured the coming results of a federal investigation into the regularly occurring Black rebellions. In the spring of 1967, Johnson impaneled a federal commission to investigate them. The Kerner Commission, named after Illinois governor Otto Kerner, inter-viewed Black people in every city that had experienced urban uprisings over the previous three years. The findings were a damning embarrass-ment for the Johnson administration. The report's introduction was quite clear in assigning blame for the discord in American cities. It read, in part:

> We have visited the riot cities; we have heard many witnesses. . . . This is our basic conclusion: Our nation is moving toward two societies, one black, one white—separate and unequal. Segregation and poverty have created . . . a destructive environment totally unknown to most white Americans. What

white Americans have never fully understood—but what the Negro can never forget—is that white society is deeply implicated in the ghetto. White institutions created it, white institutions maintain it, and white society condones it. Social and economic conditions in the riot cities constituted a clear pattern of severe disadvantage for Negroes compared with whites, whether the Negroes lived in the area where the riot took place or outside it.[64]

The top three grievances it found in Black communities were police brutality, unemployment and underemployment, and substandard housing.

Johnson was angered by the report because it indicated that, even after his administration had spent tens of millions of dollars, hundreds of millions more were still needed to respond adequately to the depth of the "urban crisis." Despite Johnson's disappointment and his refusal even to mention the report during the first week of its release, more than two million copies were sold to the public, making it one of the most widely distributed government reports in history. The Kerner Commission, like most liberal bodies by the late 1960s, espoused both structural critiques and cultural arguments about Black families. In the end, though, the report called for massive investment in existing welfare programs to undo segregation and poverty in the United States.

CONCLUSION

A concerted effort continues to link Black poverty to Black culture and the Black family. As always, both conservatives and liberals make these arguments. It is not hard to understand why. There can be significant political disagreements between them, but the shared limits of their political imagination follow the same parameters as the existing society. They cannot see beyond that which exists. To really address the systemic and utterly destructive institutional racism throughout the country would have two immediate consequences, both of which would be unacceptable to liberals and conservatives alike.

The first would be to fundamentally undermine America's continual efforts to project itself as the moral leader of the world. Addressing institutional racism is not the same as firing a racist cop or punishing some other individual for a racist transgression. It is also not the same as blaming slavery or history for the continuation of racial discrimination. It would require a full accounting of the myriad ways that racial discrimination factors in and shapes the daily lives of African Americans, in particular working-class and poor African Americans. The second consequence would be a massive redistribution of wealth and resources to undo the continuing damage.

Instead, the political establishment clings to cultural explanations for the frightening living conditions in places as varied as West Baltimore, Oakland, North Philadelphia, and Overtown in Miami, because such explanations require them to do very little. When social and economic crises are reduced to issues of culture and morality, programmatic or fiscal solutions are never enough; the solutions require personal transformation. This is why Black neighborhoods get police, not public policy—and prisons, not public schools. For example, in the raging debates over the future of public education, corporate education-reform advocates deny that poverty has any bearing on educational outcomes.[65] Instead, they describe Black children as being uninterested in education because to be smart is to pretend to be white. (Former president Obama once argued that this explains why Black students do poorly.)[66] All that remains is an overwhelming focus on charity and role modeling to demonstrate good behavior to bad Black youngsters as opposed to offering money and resources. Obama organized a new initiative, My Brother's Keeper, specifically aimed at young Black and Brown boys and teenagers, whose problems, it says, exceed the capacity of government policy to address. It relies on corporate philanthropic donations, role models, and willpower. Obama, in introducing the measure, was quick to clarify that "My Brother's Keeper is not some big, new government program . . . [but] a more focused effort on boys and young men of color who are having a particularly tough time. And in this effort, government cannot play the only—or even the primary—role."[67]

The widespread and widely agreed-upon descriptions of Black people as lazy cheats rationalizes the social and economic disparities between African Americans and the rest of the population and absolves the economic and political systems from any real responsibility. This is not only a problem for African Americans. It also helps to disguise the greater, systemic inequities that pervade American capitalism. So, even while the ranks of the white poor continue to grow, their poverty is seen as somehow distinct from "generational" Black poverty. The growing ranks of the white incarcerated are distinguished from Black incarceration, which is supposed to be an outgrowth of Black irresponsibility. In the DOJ report on the Ferguson Police Department, released in March 2015, "several" officials told investigators that the reason Blacks received a disproportionately large number of citations and tickets was a "lack of personal responsibility."[68] Pathologizing "Black" crime while making "white" crime invisible creates a barrier between the two, when solidarity could unite both in confronting the excesses of the criminal justice system. This, in a sense, is the other product of the "culture of poverty" and of naturalizing Black inequality. This narrative works to deepen the cleavages between groups of people who would otherwise have every interest in combining forces. The intractability of Black conditions becomes seen as natural as opposed to standing as an indictment of the system itself, while the hard times befalling ordinary whites are rendered almost invisible. For example, the majority of poor people in the United States are white, but the public face of American poverty is Black. It is important to point out how Blacks are overrepresented among the poor, but ignoring white poverty helps to obscure the systemic roots of all poverty. Blaming Black culture not only deflects investigation into the systemic causes of Black inequality but has also been widely absorbed by African Americans as well. Their acceptance of the dominant narrative that blames Blacks for their own oppression is one explanation for the delay in the development of a new Black movement, even while police brutality persists.

There is, however, reason for hope. This chapter has tried to show the fluidity of political ideas and the conditions under which they can be challenged and ultimately changed. Public perceptions about poverty changed in the 1930s when it became clear that the actions of bankers had sent the economy into a tailspin—not the personal character of workers. The connections between capitalism, corruption, and the condition of the working class were made even clearer by communists and socialists, who linked the living conditions of the working class to an economic system rather than just bad luck. The political and economic elite responded by burying the Left and its critiques of capitalism—while honing and deploying the "culture of poverty" theory to explain poverty in the "land of plenty." But this state of affairs was not etched in stone. The political uprisings of the

1960s, fueled by the Black insurgency, transformed American politics, including Americans' basic understanding of the relationship between Black poverty and institutional racism—and, for some, capitalism. Ideas are fluid, but it usually takes political action to set them in motion—and stasis for the retreat to set in.

3 Policing the Boundaries of the White Republic

FROM SLAVE CODES TO MASS DEPORTATIONS

Juan F. Perea

> The determining feature of race relations is not prejudice
> toward blacks, but rather the superior position of whites
> and the institutions—ideological as well as structural—
> which maintain it.
>
> David T. Wellman

> Our duty to expel alien races is as clear as the duty to
> exclude them.
>
> Carlyle McKinley

Hate has many forms. Former president Trump launched a war of hate against undocumented immigrants, characterizing them as criminals, rapists, and unwelcome invaders. Most of us have seen the images of children torn apart from their parents, mothers and children tear-gassed at the border, and armed border guards aiming rifles at unarmed migrants and refugees. Trump and his administration spent great energy and money arresting and deporting undocumented immigrants and pursuing an ineffective but symbolically potent wall to block further immigration and to reassure anxious whites that he will protect them. But how it is that the president had so much power to unleash this hate upon otherwise innocent undocumented people and refugees? Where did the president, and more generally the government, get such power?[1]

Exclusion and deportation through law have been crucial management techniques for the maintenance of white supremacy over the society.[2] Whites established their dominance in part by enacting laws that restricted the conditions and movements of enslaved and free Blacks and Indigenous people subject to colonial jurisdiction. As they restricted the freedom of nonwhites, they simultaneously grew their own, greater freedom from such restrictions and so enshrined white supremacy in American law and culture. This essay examines the deep historical roots of the government's powers to deport and exclude unwanted, racialized nonwhite populations. Colonial and state powers used to exclude undesirable free Blacks eventually became federal plenary powers used to remove Native Americans, to exclude Asians and, today, to deport millions of undocumented immigrants.

COLONIAL MANAGEMENT OF BLACKS AND NATIVE AMERICANS

In colonial America, the establishment and success of white British colonies depended on their ability to control successfully two nonwhite populations: Black slaves and Native Americans. Once large-scale agriculture became a principal feature of colonial survival and success, the importation of enslaved Blacks for labor demanded means for controlling the risks posed by these slaves. The gradual expansion of the colonies westward also required organized means of dealing with Native Americans intent on remaining on their lands.

The regulation of nonwhites in the colonies was through the state's police power, a broader concept than usually understood. The police power is the state's inherent power to protect "the security of social order, the life and health of the citizen, the comfort of an existence in a thickly populated community, the enjoyment of private and social life, and the beneficial use of property." This broad mandate is the source of a "vast expanse of legislation and regulation at all levels of governance." It is "the most expansive, least definite, and yet least scrutinized, of governmental powers."[3]

Slave codes were clear examples of police power in the colonies. These were elaborate statutes that managed the threats posed by Black slaves, mulattoes, and Natives to the order of colonial society, and particularly to their white owners. Enslaved persons threatened revolts and the possibility of violent retribution against whites. Slaves also threatened escape, which meant the loss of property, wealth, and labor. As described by Jonathan Bush, colonial slave codes addressed

> slave criminality, flight and resistance, black-white daily interaction, and manumission. At their core, the codes determined who was a slave and how slaves could be kept unfree and unthreatening. . . . They were police measures. Granted, they went well beyond criminal policing to address public law, broadly defined. That is, the codes were concerned with such seemingly private matters as a master's right to forego punishing, educate, or manumit his slave, or a slave's right to sell produce, precisely because the codes assumed these behaviors implicated the safety of whites and the political etiquette between whites and others (Native Americans, black, and mulatto). The codes defined the public boundaries between free and slave and between non-white and white.[4]

Law, written and executed by whites, defined the boundaries between whites and nonwhites and both reflected and produced the meanings of white supremacy and presumed nonwhite inferiority. As whites migrated west, law was also instrumental in facilitating and justifying white possession and control of former Indigenous land.

Managing Blacks

As whites began consolidating their own racial identity, they began increasing legal control over Blacks, slave and free, as a national phenomenon not restricted to the South. All of the colonies allowed slavery. Though the northern states abolished slavery earlier than the southern, there was widespread agreement on the superiority of whites and the inferiority of Blacks.

British colonists created slave codes to manage potentially dangerous slaves. Enacted in response to a slave revolt earlier that year, the caption of New York's slave code of 1712 read: "An Act for preventing Suppressing and punishing the Conspiracy and Insurrection of Negroes and other Slaves."[5] The fear of the growing Black population is apparent in the preamble of South Carolina's slave code of 1714: "whereas, the number of negroes do extremely increase in this Province, and through the afflicting providence of God, the white persons do not proportionably multiply, by reason wherof, the safety of the said province is greatly endangered."[6]

Throughout the colonial and antebellum eras, and throughout the North and the South, the increasing number of free Blacks provoked similar fears, resulting in restrictions on their behavior and travel. Their mere presence in slave societies threatened the slave regime by providing an example of Black freedom, which might inspire slaves to want their freedom too. Whites also feared the possibility of collaboration between free and enslaved Blacks. Thus the New York slave code of 1712 penalized free Blacks who harbored slaves without permission and forbade free Blacks from owning land.[7]

One of the important devices for the maintenance of white domination was control over free Blacks through restrictions on their migration and through their expulsion. "Blacks' presence was tolerated in the colonies as long as they were slaves," notes legal scholar Kunal Parker. "When they became free they could be ordered to leave. It was the moment of freedom . . . that made them excludable and removable from the community."[8] An early Connecticut statute, probably enacted in 1717, prohibited free Blacks from living in any town in the colony and made them subject to an order "to depart and leave."[9] Virginia's slave laws of 1806 required an emancipated slave to leave the colony within twelve months or face reenslavement.[10] South Carolina's slave code of 1822 stated that "no free negro or person of color, who shall leave this state, shall be suffered to return."[11] The same statute contained the Negro Seaman's Act, which required that any free Blacks employed on a sea vessel entering a South Carolina port "shall be liable to be seized and confined in [jail] until said vessel shall clear out and depart from this state."[12]

Midwestern and Western states excluded free Blacks by preventing their migration. Article 14 of the Illinois Constitution of 1848 states: "The general assembly shall . . . pass such laws as shall effectually prohibit free persons of color from immigrating to and settling in this state; and to effectually prevent the owners of slaves from bringing them into this state for the purpose of setting them free."[13] Article 13 of the Indiana Constitution of 1851 stated clearly that "No negro or mulatto shall come into or settle in the State, after the adoption of this Constitution."[14] "No free negro or mulatto ... shall come, reside or be within this state," announced the Oregon Constitution of 1857; the legislature "shall provide by penal laws for the removal . . . of all such negroes and mulattoes."[15]

In addition to exclusion from physical presence in these states, at the federal level Blacks were excluded from the possibility of naturalized citizenship. In an early act highly symbolic of the national wish for whiteness, Congress enacted the Naturalization Act of 1790. This act restricted naturalization to "free white person[s]."

These legislative and constitutional exclusions of free Blacks were supplemented by popular proposals to colonize free Blacks outside the United States. The American Colonization Society, founded in 1817, sought to remove free Blacks from the United States by deporting them to Africa. Historian George Frederickson has argued that such calls for the removal of free Blacks revealed "the persistence in the white imagination of the impossible dream of absolute racial homogeneity."[16]

Managing Native Americans

Prior to the importation of large numbers of Africans, Native Americans were probably the earliest slaves in the Americas. Accordingly, enslaved Natives were subject to many of the same regulations as enslaved Blacks. New York, for example, regulated the activities and movements of "Negro, Indian, or Mulatto" populations. White perceptions of Native Americans' dark skin and their rejection of European "civilization" led to their racialization as "red" and inferior to whites.[17]

While whites sought to extract uncompensated labor from Blacks, their principal concern in relation to Indigenous people was to secure ownership of their lands. The cession of lands occupied by Native Americans was largely accomplished through treaties and removal, backed by actual or threatened military force. Legal reasoning, therefore, was pivotal in supplying justifications for the dispossession and management of Native peoples.

Federal control over Native Americans was first justified by the Supreme Court in the case of *Johnson v. McIntosh* (1823). In his decision, Chief Justice Marshall described Native Americans as racial inferiors:

The character and habits of the people whose rights have been wrested from them provide an apology for considering them as a people over whom the superior genius of Europe might claim an ascendancy. . . . The tribes of Indians inhabiting this country were fierce savages, whose occupation was war, and whose subsistence was drawn chiefly from the forest. To leave them in possession of their country was to leave the country a wilderness; to govern them as a people, was impossible, because they were as brave and as high spirited as they were fierce, and were ready to repel by arms every attempt on their independence.[18]

This "discovery doctrine," as articulated in *Johnson v. McIntosh*, became the ultimate source of federal authority over Native Americans and their lands: "but [Native] rights to complete sovereignty, as independent nations, were necessarily diminished, and their power to dispose of the soil at their own will, to whomsoever they pleased, was denied by the original fundamental principle, that discovery gave exclusive title to those who made it."[19] Though Native nations retained nominal rights of occupancy, the federal government claimed and exercised exclusive rights of ownership to purchase, sell, and otherwise dispose of former Native lands.

Later, in *Cherokee Nation v. Georgia* (1831), Marshall was even more definitive in describing the summary federal control over Native Americans. He concluded that Native American nations were not sovereign foreign nations, but rather "domestic dependent nations." The United States asserted "a title independent of their will. . . . Meanwhile they are in a state of pupilage. Their relation to the United States resembles that of a ward to his guardian."[20] Because they were not sovereign foreign nations, the Supreme Court lacked jurisdiction over their claims: "If it be true that the Cherokee nation have rights, this is not the tribunal in which those rights are to be asserted. If it be true that wrongs have been inflicted, and that still greater are to be apprehended, this is not the tribunal which can redress the past or prevent the future."[21] Marshall essentially abandoned the Cherokee to their fate at the hands of the president, Congress, Georgia, and private plunderers. The United States was a most dangerous guardian, exercising power and force over a people with no rights and, increasingly, no legal recourse.

The Indian removal of 1828–38, although often understood as a single episode, provides an example of mass deportation of Native people.[22]

The federal government had negotiated earlier removals through treaties that ceded Indigenous lands to the government and pressured Natives to move westward. Between 1828 and 1838, over eighty thousand Native Americans were forcibly relocated to reservations in the far West. Though the relocations were made to appear voluntary through negotiated treaties, Native Americans who resisted faced the threat and reality of military violence. When the Cherokee were finally removed, "the soldiers began rounding them up and confining them in the forts. Troops quickly captured most Cherokees."[23]

In one particularly violent incident, the military decided to make an example of Black Hawk, the leader of a group of about five hundred Sac and Fox Natives who refused to leave the Michigan Territory in 1832. Black Hawk's people were cornered at the intersection of the Bad Axe River and the Mississippi. An American military gunboat fired cannons into the Native Americans, killing many. A militia numbering about thirty-eight hundred troops massacred women and children attempting to cross the water. Three hundred of the remaining Native Americans under Black Hawk were slaughtered.[24] Thousands more Native Americans eventually died from the diseases they contracted and the hardships they experienced during their "voluntary" relocation.

POSTBELLUM MANAGEMENT OF NONWHITES THROUGH FEDERAL PLENARY POWER

During and after the Civil War, several constitutional developments effectively ended state powers to exclude persons of color and portended the development of plenary federal powers to control the deportation and exclusion of nonwhite persons. The Thirteenth Amendment formally abolished slavery. The Fourteenth Amendment overruled the *Dred Scott* (1856) decision and unequivocally created birthright citizenship, both state and federal, for all native-born Blacks.

The Reconstruction era, roughly between 1865 and 1876, witnessed a transition from state-based immigration regimes to a centralized federal regime. Several Court decisions undermined the powers of states to regulate immigration across their borders. In *Crandall v. Nevada* (1867), the

Supreme Court held that national citizenship included the right to travel from state to state without interference, allowing free Blacks to migrate freely, at least in theory.[25] In *In re Ah Fong* (1874), the Court reasoned that states could no longer exclude persons, like free Blacks, who were deemed a threat to the welfare of the state. The Court stated: "We cannot shut our eyes to the fact that much which was formerly said upon the power of the state . . . grew out of the necessity which the southern states, in which slavery existed, felt of excluding free negroes from their limits. . . . But at this day no such power would be asserted, or if asserted, allowed in any federal Court."[26] Finally, in 1887, the Supreme Court declared the death knell of state immigration regimes and ruled them unconstitutional.[27]

But the end of state regulation over immigration did not mean the end of statutes and codes targeting Blacks. The abolition of formal slavery meant only that states could not regulate slaves as such. States still retained the police powers that had earlier justified the slave codes. States used these powers, supported by mob violence, to oppress Blacks through criminal law, voter suppression laws, and Jim Crow laws.

At the end of the nineteenth century, broad federal powers to exclude and to deport developed to replace the now-defunct state powers. Eventually the Court described these powers as "plenary," the broadest, least constrained form of federal power. Plenary power, as Kunal M. Parker explains, is "an inherent, sovereign [power,] one not grounded in any portion of the constitutional text, not limited by any particular provision of the U.S. Constitution, and largely immune from substantive judicial review."[28] As we shall see, plenary federal power exists over immigration, naturalization, Native American affairs, and territories. In these areas, plenary power is used to control the exclusion, citizenship status, and deportation of mostly nonwhite people.

Managing Chinese

The plenary power to exclude and expel immigrants developed primarily through the struggles Chinese immigrants waged to resist their exclusion from the West Coast during the late nineteenth century. Chinese immigrants began arriving in California in the wake of the gold rush, becoming miners and other sorts of laborers. Unable to compete with the Chinese because of the much lower wages at which they were contracted, white laborers grew to hate them and organized violent anti-Chinese hate groups. One commentator wrote, "The Chinese are, morally, the most debased people on the face of the earth . . . Their touch is pollution . . . They should not be allowed to settle on our soil."[29] A labor organizer stated his disdain for the Chinese:

> Before you and before the world we declare that white men, and women, and boys and girls, cannot live as the people of the great republic should and compete with the single Chinese coolie in the labor market. We declare that we cannot hope to drive the Chinaman away by working cheaper than he does. None but an enemy would expect it of us; none but an idiot would hope for success; none but a degraded coward and slave would make the effort. To an American, death is preferable to life on a par with the Chinaman.[30]

White working-class Californians sought federal laws to protect their status and standard of living by ending Chinese immigration. Congress obliged by passing a number of Chinese Exclusion Act between 1882 and 1892 which barred the importation of Chinese laborers, provided for the removal of any Chinese person lacking proper identification, and forbade the return of any Chinese worker who had departed from the United States. Chinese laborers were forced to choose either abandoning their families in China or abandoning their families in the United States.

In decisions upholding these statutes, the Supreme Court described the contours of plenary federal powers over immigration. In *Chae Chan Ping* (1889), the Court declared that Congress wielded absolute power to exclude aliens:

> The power of exclusion of foreigners being an incident of sovereignty belonging to the government of the United States, as a part of those sovereign powers delegated by the Constitution, the right to its exercise at any time when, in the judgment of the government, the interests of the country require it, cannot be granted away or restrained on behalf of any one. . . . To preserve its independence and give security against foreign aggression and encroachment, is the highest duty of every nation, and to attain these ends nearly all other considerations are to be subordinated. It matters not in what

form such aggression and encroachment come, whether from the foreign nation acting in its national character, or from vast hordes of its people crowding upon us.[31]

Beyond powers of exclusion, Congress's plenary power expanded to include the deportation of aliens. The Court subsequently wrote, "The right of a nation to expel or deport foreigners who have not been naturalized, or taken any steps towards becoming citizens of the country, rests upon the same grounds, and is as absolute and unqualified as the right to prohibit and prevent their entrance into the country."[32] Interestingly, despite these Court assertions, there is no power to exclude foreigners among the "sovereign powers delegated by the Constitution." Only the states had the power to exclude foreigners, free Blacks, and others during the antebellum period. Until the *Chae Chan Ping* case (1889), no such power was granted to Congress before or after the ratification of the Constitution. The Supreme Court, as Parker observes, invented a power "grounded in an inherent 'sovereignty' essentially unrestrained by the Constitution."[33]

Managing Native Americans

The development of plenary power over Native Americans coincided roughly with its development over immigrants. Native Americans had been pointedly excluded from the birthright citizenship promised by the Fourteenth Amendment because, as "domestic dependent nations," they were treated as citizens of foreign sovereigns not "subject to the jurisdiction" of federal and state governments.

Several Supreme Court and legislative judgments made clear that, like immigrants, Native Americans were subject to congressional plenary power. In 1870, the Supreme Court ruled that Congress had the ability to unilaterally abrogate treaties with Native tribes simply by enacting subsequent legislation.[34] In 1871, an act of Congress abolished the independent status of tribes, stating that no Native nation or tribe "shall be recognized as an independent nation, tribe or power, with whom the United States may contract by treaty." In *Kagama v. United States* (1886), the Supreme Court grounded congressional plenary power over Native Americans in national sovereignty:

But this power of congress to organize territorial governments, and make laws for their inhabitants, arises, not so much from the clause in the constitution in regard to disposing of and making rules and regulations concerning the territory and other property of the United States, as from the ownership of the country in which the territories are, and the right of exclusive sovereignty which must exist in the national government, and can be found nowhere else.[35]

The Court described congressional power in broad terms, stating that "the power of the general government over these remnants of a race once powerful, now weak and diminished in numbers, is necessary to their protection, as well as to the safety of those among whom they dwell. It must exist in that government, because it never has existed anywhere else."[36] As was the case with the plenary powers over immigrant exclusion and deportation, the Court's analysis relied on sovereignty alone, ignoring "any reliance on the Constitution as the basis for national authority."[37]

In *Lone Wolf v. Hitchcock* (1903), the Supreme Court offered another statement of congressional plenary power over Native Americans: "Plenary authority over the tribal relations of the Indians has been exercised by Congress from the beginning, and the power has always been deemed a political one, not subject to be controlled by the judicial department of the government."[38] This decision had a major impact, one still in force. One senator named it "the Dred Scott decision no. 2, except that in this case the victim is red instead of black. It practically inculcates the doctrine that the red man has no rights which the white man is bound to respect, and that no contract made with him is binding."[39]

Managing Puerto Ricans

Puerto Rico became the next realm for the United States' assertion of plenary power over nonwhite people. As a result of the Spanish-American War, Spain transferred dominion over Puerto Rico to the United States. In the Treaty of Paris (1898), Congress reserved to itself a great degree of control over Puerto Rico and other possessions. This was the first time a territory had been acquired by the United States with neither an implicit nor an explicit promise of statehood.[40]

White concerns over the incorporation of mixed-race Puerto Ricans dominated decisions about whether or not to include Puerto Ricans as full citizens of the United States. In *Downes v. Bidwell* (1908), the Court stated: "The power over the territories is vested in Congress without limitation, and that this power has been considered the foundation upon which the territorial governments rest."[41] According to the Court, this plenary power was important for managing the threats posed by nonwhite people resident in newly acquired territories:

> No construction of the Constitution should be adopted which would prevent Congress from considering each case upon its merits, unless the language of the instrument imperatively demand it. A false step at this time might be fatal to the development of what Chief Justice Marshall called the American empire. . . . If [territorial] possessions are inhabited by alien races, differing from us in religion, customs, laws, methods of taxation, and modes of thought, the administration of government and justice, according to Anglo-Saxon principles, may for a time be impossible; . . . We decline to hold that there is anything in the Constitution to forbid such action.[42]

Based on these concerns, the Court concluded that Puerto Rico was an unincorporated territory, "not a part of the United States" and therefore subject to plenary federal control.[43]

Because of this broad plenary power over them, Puerto Rican island residents are uniquely vulnerable to presidential and congressional discretion exercised over them. Still subject to *Downes v. Bidwell*, Puerto Rico remains unincorporated today, a form of exclusion with profound consequences for the island and its residents. Because it is not a state, it has no voting representatives or senators in Congress. Though residents of Puerto Rico are United States citizens, they are not eligible to vote for president or vice president. Puerto Ricans are subject to federal law, but have no representation in the formulation of the law. For this reason, Puerto Ricans receive fewer benefits and statutory protections than citizens of states. Their lack of representation and inability to vote made it easier for President Trump to respond inadequately to the devastating damage and loss of life caused by Hurricane Maria in 2017.

Managing Immigrants

We have seen how Congress and the Supreme Court used their respective powers to exclude nonwhite peoples. Interestingly, during the early twentieth century, Congress used its plenary powers to exclude relatively fair-skinned immigrants who, at the time, were deemed nonwhite. Responding to popular concerns about increasing immigration from southeastern Europe, Congress used its plenary powers to engineer the numeric balance between whites and nonwhites. The Immigration Act of 1924 imposed numerical quotas on immigrants based on their countries of origin. These quotas were initially based on the 1890 census, before large-scale immigration from southeastern Europe had occurred. The national origins quotas allocated 84 percent of the immigration slots to northern and western Europe and only 16 percent to southern and eastern Europe, thereby advancing the aims of white nativists. The law excluded all aliens ineligible for citizenship from immigration, which effectively ended the immigration of Japanese farm laborers. As stated by Mae Ngai, "At its core, the law served contemporary prejudices among white Protestant Americans from northern European backgrounds and their desire to maintain social and political dominance."[44]

CONTEMPORARY DEPORTATION AND EXCLUSION

Managing Mexicans and Central Americans

Since the U.S.-Mexican War, waged from 1846 to 1848, the prospect of bringing mixed-race Mexicans into the white republic of the United States has ignited fears of the degradation of white supremacy and concerns about the survival of American democracy. Senator John Calhoun, a prominent southern Democrat, opposed annexing Mexican territory at war's end because of its racial implications:

> We have never dreamt of incorporating into our Union any but the Caucasian race—the free white race. To incorporate Mexico, would be the very first instance of the kind of incorporating an Indian race; for more than half the Mexicans are Indians, and the other is composed chiefly of mixed tribes. I protest against such a union as that! Ours, sir, is the Government of a white race. The greatest misfortunes of Spanish America are to be traced to the fatal error of placing these colored races on an equality with the white race. That error destroyed the social arrangement which formed the basis of society.[45]

Though not explicitly stated as such, much of the justification for today's massive deportations of undocumented Mexicans and Central Americans stems from a similar need to protect whites from the threat of racial impurity associated with nonwhite undocumented immigrants. The plenary powers to prevent entry and to deport are the basis for both past and present mass deportations of Mexicans and Central Americans.

Mexican immigrants have long been used as a reserve labor pool, imported when necessary, then expelled when the need ends. Because southwestern agriculturalists since the late nineteenth century have relied extensively on Mexican workers, Mexicans were exempted from the 1924 national origins quotas and were allowed free entry and return. As described by Professor Michael Olivas:

> Most crucial to the agricultural growers was the need for a reserve labor pool who could be imported for their work, displaced when not needed, and kept in subordinate status so they could not afford to organize collectively or protest their conditions. Mexicans filled this role perfectly, especially in the early twentieth century Southwest, where Mexican poverty and the Revolution forced rural Mexicans to come to the United States for work. . . . [Mexican laborers were] cynically employed to create a reserve pool of temporary laborers who had few rights and no vesting of equities.[46]

Between 1929 and 1936, when the Great Depression reduced the need for Mexican labor, approximately one million Mexicans and Mexican-Americans were forcibly expelled from the United States during the so-called "Mexican repatriation." About 60 percent of these were American citizens, including the U.S.-born children of Mexican immigrants. For them, this was no repatriation. It was the forcible deportation of American citizens with no regard for or review of their citizenship or constitutional rights.

During the early 1950s, and culminating in 1954, the federal government conducted Operation Wetback, which has been called "the largest mass deportation of undocumented workers in American history."[47] Over one million persons of Mexican origin, again including many U.S. citizens, were deported to the interior of Mexico. According to INS commissioner John Swing, mass deportation was necessary because an "alarming, ever-increasing flood tide" of undocumented immigrants threatened "an actual invasion of the United States." Resembling a full military operation, hundreds of Border Patrol agents and immigration personnel launched "a direct attack ... upon the hordes facing us across the border."[48] One observer described the operation as "pounding away on these 'wets,'" so known because they were presumed to have entered the United States by swimming across the Rio Grande.[49]

Analogous to Congress's powers, the President has very broad powers to enforce immigration law. In its recent decision enforcing President Trump's anti-Muslim travel ban, the Supreme Court described the breadth of the president's discretion and the limits on judicial review of his actions: "'Any rule of constitutional law that would inhibit the flexibility' of the President 'to respond to changing world conditions should be adopted only with the greatest caution,' and our inquiry into matters of entry and national security is highly constrained."[50]

Recent presidential administrations have been engaged in deportations and border control enforcement strategies of massive scale. Because of changing enforcement priorities under different administrations, it is helpful to define *deportation* here. There are two categories of deportation: removals and returns. Removals refer to persons deported from the United States under a formal order, with administrative or criminal consequences such as penalties or prison sentences. Returns refer to persons deported from the United States without a formal order of removal, who are allowed to leave voluntarily. Accordingly, the best estimate of the total number of deportations in any given year is the sum of both removals and returns.

Increasingly aggressive deportation and vigorous border control enforcement has been the hallmark of recent presidencies. In 1996, President Clinton signed legislation expanding the grounds for deportation and mandating detention for deportable undocumented persons. During the Clinton presidency (1993–2001), the total number of deportations was 12.3 million, including about 870,000 formal removals.[51]

Clinton also initiated Operation Gatekeeper, which sought to deter migrants from entering the country by making it more difficult to successfully cross the border. Operation Gatekeeper provided for additional fencing along the southern border with Mexico and militarized the zone by increasing the number of Border Patrol officers in the most easily traversed regions. Rather than accomplishing deterrence, however, it forced migrants to cross the border in more dangerous desert and mountainous areas, leading to a large increase in migrant deaths, which continue today.

In the wake of the attacks on the World Trade Center and the Pentagon of September 11, 2001, security measures along the country's southern border increased, despite the fact that *there was, and is, little or no evidence that any terrorist activity has ever resulted from crossing that border.* During the Bush presidency (2001–9), the total number of deportations was 10.3 million, while the number of formal removals increased to over 2 million. The Bush presidency also was notable for highly visible raids at workplaces, which resulted in thousands of arrests of undocumented persons.

When President Obama entered office, he inherited a large and well-funded deportation machinery. The total number of deportations under Obama (2009–17) was 4.8 million, less than half the number of deportations during the Bush administration. The number of formal removals, however, increased dramatically to 3.1 million, leading critics to label him the "deporter in chief." Both the number of removals and returns decreased in the final years of Obama's presidency. In 2014, the Obama administration narrowed its priorities for enforcement, prioritizing deportations of criminals and persons who had crossed the border recently.

President Trump's administration sought to expand enforcement at all levels, prioritizing the removal of a broad population of undocumented persons, including persons without criminal records who posed no threat to society. Trump increased the removal of noncitizens from the interior of the country, a process that resulted in the deportation of long-term residents, breaking apart families and disrupting entire communities. During the period between his January 20, 2017, inauguration and September 2017, the number of removals from the interior increased by 37 percent and arrests increased by 42 percent over the same period in 2016.[52] The Trump administration implemented a "zero tolerance" policy, calling for the criminal prosecution of every unauthorized person crossing the border. One result of this policy was the forcible separation of children from their parents when adults were taken into custody. The Trump administration also made it much harder for refugees to qualify for asylum.

Construction of President Trump's loudly proposed and quintessential symbol of exclusion, the border wall, was begun with no evidence that it would actually stem the flow of immigrants. Despite all of these increased enforcement efforts, the level of deportations under Trump's administration was smaller than under the peak years of the Obama administration.[53] This was because fewer persons were entering illegally and because of resistance to these enforcement efforts in sanctuary states like California.

Compared to the "Mexican repatriation" and Operation Wetback, the number of deportations since 1996 is astonishing. Taken together, the "Mexican repatriation" and Operation Wetback accounted for at most about 2.8 million deportations of undocumented Mexicans. During the Clinton, Bush, and Obama presidencies the total number of deportations was about 27.4 million, roughly ten times more. In sixteen out of the combined twenty-four years of these presidencies, between 1 and 1.8 million deportations occurred each year, amounting to regularized massive "repatriations."

These deportations occurred under both Democratic and Republican presidents, who justified them as necessary due to the threat posed by immigrant criminality and the need to protect the nation's security at its borders. President Clinton, during his 1995 State of the Union address, said, "All Americans . . . are rightly disturbed by the large numbers of illegal aliens entering our country. . . . That's why our administration has moved aggressively to secure our borders more by hiring a record number of new border guards, by deporting twice as many criminal aliens as ever before, by cracking down on illegal hiring, by barring welfare benefits to illegal aliens."[54] President Obama described his immigration enforcement as targeted at "Felons, not families. Criminals, not children. Gang members, not a mom who's working hard to provide for her kids."[55] The statistics show, however, that most of the people expelled during the Obama administration had committed minor traffic and drug offenses or were labelled "criminal" merely for crossing the border without documentation.[56]

President Trump showed no restraint in portraying immigration negatively, vilifying and dehumanizing undocumented persons. He also employed the most lavish vocabulary among recent presidents, calling immigrants and refugees "rapists," "gang members," "animals," an "infestation," and "terrorists." He characterized nonwhite immigrants and refugees as emanating from "shithole countries," while expressing his preference for migrants from predominantly white countries like Norway. Reflecting an eclectic mix of medieval, antediluvian, and military influences, Trump also fantasized about constructing a "border wall with a water-filled trench, stocked with snakes or alligators," or an electrified wall "with spikes on top that could pierce human flesh," together with trigger-happy soldiers ready to "shoot migrants in the legs to slow them down."[57]

The consistency and scale of recent mass deportations demonstrates the existence of a national consensus on the deportability and expendability of huge numbers of Mexican and Central American immigrants. Both Democratic and Republican administrations have overseen massive deportations, while Congress has enacted legislation funding ever-increasing border control, thus implicitly agreeing that these immigrants pose a serious threat to the republic. A national consensus also becomes evident when we realize that, notwithstanding record-breaking numbers of deportations, the American public has remained mostly undisturbed by these events. While advocates for immigrants have been sounding alarms for years, the general public expressed serious concern only when the Trump administration's border policies resulted in the forcible separation of young children from their families, a sorry spectacle that recalled the sale and separation of Black families during slavery.

One wonders why the national reflex is to further punish and burden undocumented people. According to a 2015 analysis by the Migration Policy Institute, undocumented Mexicans and Central Americans account for 71 percent of all persons who enter the country without inspection.[58] According to 2015 data, however, persons of these national origins constitute *96 percent* of deportees, an overrepresentation of 25 percent.[59] Mexicans and Central Americans constitute 90 percent of persons detained for immigration violations and 94 percent of persons removed as "criminal aliens," also disproportionately high.[60] By contrast, persons from white-majority countries, such as Poland, Russia, and Ireland, among others, constitute about 4 percent of unauthorized immigrants but only .5 percent of deportees, an underrepresentation of 87.5 percent. Chinese immigrants constitute 14 percent of the unauthorized population, the third-largest after Mexicans and Central Americans. Yet the proportion of Chinese deportees is only .014 percent, a vast underrepresentation of 714 percent.

None of the dangers often associated with undocumented persons, such as increased criminality, violence, welfare fraud, and job theft, are borne out by evidence.[61] Contrary to the prevailing rhetoric, evidence shows that immigrants are no more apt, and may be less apt, to engage in criminality than the native-born citizen population.[62] The number of undocumented persons in the United States has been decreasing, from a peak of 12.2 million in 2007 to 10.5 million in 2017, a 14 percent decrease.[63] The proportion of undocumented immigrants in the United States has been shrinking since 2007, decreasing from 4 percent to 3.2 percent.[64] So why exactly is a diminishing problem so widely interpreted as a serious threat?

Defending the Borders of White America

The southern border with Mexico is not just any border. Most people agree: it is "*the* border."[65] It is the focal point of public and political attention, the line in the sand whose security requires the greatest public concern and anxiety, and whose defense requires billions of dollars, the latest technology, and many thousands of armed guards. This border has grown into the principal symbolic line of defense against real and imagined threats to the United States. The most sober commitments to national security are articulated through promises to enforce the border to protect the safety and security of citizens. Today, as before in American history, the threat is a "Brown scare," a threatened invasion of undocumented migrants and refugees lying just beyond the border.

Immigrants on the southern border threaten the prevailing conception of the United States as a country controlled and dominated by whites and their culture. This perceived threat has been articulated clearly by prominent nativists in recent decades. Describing the views of "new white nationalists," political scientist Samuel P. Huntington wrote:

> The shifting racial balance in the United States means a shifting cultural balance and the replacement of the white culture that made America great by black or brown cultures that are different, and in their view, intellectually

and morally inferior. This mixing of races and hence cultures is the road to national degeneration. For them, to keep America America, it is necessary to keep America white.[66]

In *Alien Nation*, anti-immigrant journalist Peter Brimelow argued that Americans should change immigration law to protect America's white ethnic core from Latino immigration: "Race and ethnicity are destiny in American politics . . . The American nation has always had a specific ethnic core. And that core has been white."[67] Dr. John Tanton, the anti-immigrant founder of a broad network of organizations, which include U.S. English, the Federation for American Immigration Reform, the Social Contract Press, and ProEnglish, expressed grave concerns about the threat that Latinos pose to the white Anglo dominance of American society:

> How will we make the transition from a dominant non-Hispanic society with a Spanish influence to a dominant Spanish society with non-Hispanic influence? . . . As Whites see their power and control over their lives declining, will they simply go quietly into the night? Or will there be an explosion?[68]

The fear and resentment of demographic change remains strong today. The white anger that significantly fueled the election of Donald Trump remains potent, notes Barbara Ehrenreich:

> The maintenance of white privilege, especially among the least privileged whites, has become more difficult and so, for some, more urgent than ever. Poor whites always had the comfort of knowing that someone was worse off and more despised than they were; racial subjugation was the ground under their feet, the rock they stood upon, even when their own situation was deteriorating.[69]

Conservative Fox Television news commentators like Tucker Carlson and Laura Ingraham express and stoke these fears of demographic change.[70] Ingraham stated recently:

> In some parts of the country, it does seem like the America that we know and love doesn't exist anymore. Massive demographic changes have been foisted upon the American people, and they are changes that none of us ever voted for, and most of us don't like. From Virginia to California, we see stark examples of how radically, in some ways, the country has changed. Now, much of this is related to both illegal, and in some cases legal immigration.[71]

The mass deportations of Mexicans and Central Americans can best be understood as the presidential and congressional response to this perceived threat to white identity and white supremacy. The response to this "Latino threat" at the border is itself an assertion of white supremacy and control.[72] Increased militarization of the southern border and funding for more border agents, technology, and a wall send a message that the government is powerful, well armed, and determined to defend the white nation from the Latino "threat." In Leo Chavez's essay in this volume, the Latino threat narrative is explored more extensively.

The very public spectacle of Latino arrests and expulsions reassures the concerned public, consciously or unconsciously, that their government remains a strong, potent guardian of their white identity. We witness regularly the visible, public deployment of police force to arrest and deport millions of Latinos, producing and reinforcing an image of Latinos as "criminal aliens" who are dangerous. Televised coverage shows "perp walks" of undocumented persons being led away in handcuffs by Immigration and Customs Enforcement (ICE) agents. We see images of heavily armed ICE agents conducting raids at workplaces, private homes, courthouses, and public spaces, often with dozens of "criminal aliens" in tow. We see images of a militarized border, with border guards shooting tear gas at migrants and refugees, including women and children.

The public imagery of undocumented illegality stigmatizes and undermines the citizenship of Latino citizens. Legal scholars have described the relationship between the treatment of Latino immigrants and the discriminatory treatment of Latino citizens. Kevin Johnson writes:

> Racial exclusion of noncitizens under the immigration laws, be they express or covert, reveals to domestic minorities how they are viewed by society. The unprecedented efforts to seal the U.S.-Mexico border combined with the increased efforts to deport undocumented Mexicans, for example, tell much about how a majority of society views Mexican Americans and suggests to what lengths society might go, if permitted under color of law, to rid itself of domestic Mexican Americans. . . .
>
> By barring admission of the outsider group that is subordinated domestically, society rationalizes the disparate treatment of the domestic racial minority group in question and reinforces that group's inferiority. Exclusion in the immigration laws must be viewed as an integral part of a larger mosaic of racial discrimination in American society.[73]

Whites enjoy a higher quality of rights and citizenship than Latino citizens because of the visible mistreatment of undocumented Latinos. Because the racial profiling of undocumented persons of "Mexican appearance" is constitutional, Latino-looking citizens have effectively lost their Fourth Amendment rights to be free from unreasonable searches and seizures. Professor Jennifer Chacon has argued:

> Citizens who are perceived to look and speak like foreign nationals and who live in immigrant communities are, in fact, subjected to the very same practices of enforcement that are aimed at their foreign national counterparts. They are racially profiled in ways that produce heightened law enforcement surveillance of their lives, they are questioned about their citizenship and required to prove their belonging in ways that individuals who are identified as "white" are not, and they are sometimes erroneously detained and deported.[74]

In the eyes of enforcement officers, Latino looks and Spanish-language use signal presumptive illegality. For example, Ana Suda and Mimi Hernandez went to the gym together and stopped at a convenience store to pick up groceries on the way home. The two friends, who are bilingual, spoke to each other in Spanish while waiting in line to pay for their food. A Border Patrol agent listened to their interaction and then intervened. As their story was reported by the American Civil Liberties Union:

> He demanded to know where Ana and Mimi were born. After they said they were born in Texas and California, he forced them to turn over their driver's licenses. He detained them by his patrol car, in full view of neighbors, for an extended period before finally letting them return to their homes and families. Ana and Mimi walked away from the interaction humiliated and afraid that they might again be stopped, detained, and interrogated at any time.[75]

Such indiscriminate racial profiling also extends to anti-immigrant violence. For example, the El Paso mass shooter intended to attack Latinos when he entered a Walmart, killed twenty-two persons, and wounded twenty-four more. The shooter stated that he was targeting Mexicans. Echoing white nativists, the shooter intended to do his part to thwart a "Hispanic invasion" of the United States. It is both sad and ironic that most of his victims, thirteen, were United States citizens. Among his other victims, seven were Mexican citizens, one was a German citizen, and one person was of undetermined nationality.[76]

The proper, authorized white national identity of the United States is defined and reinforced by implication when we see forcible arrests and expulsions of undocumented Latinos. We do not see whites subjected to arbitrary detentions, raids, and deportations. Whites live free of the consequent fear and humiliation. Many Latino citizens lose their undocumented parents to arrest and deportation, which breaks up their families and puts their emotional and financial welfare at serious risk. White citizens, in contrast, can feel more secure in their family relationships and welfare as the government wantonly disrupts the families of nonwhites. Sociologist Douglas Massey describes well the message sent by the border wall and other current border enforcement efforts: "Mexico and Mexicans are a threat to the nation, Latino immigrants are unfit for inclusion in US society, and our neighbors to the south are not and will never be accepted as 'real Americans.'"[77]

The recent mass deportations of Latino migrants and refugees are only the most recent examples of the use of the government's plenary powers in the defense of whiteness. As we saw earlier with the expulsion and exclusion of free Blacks, the removal of Native Americans and the exclusion of Chinese persons, the prerogatives of the white state have often required the expulsion of presumed threatening nonwhites. The cyclical ousting of Mexicans and Central Americans shows the continuing "persistence in the white imagination of the impossible dream of absolute racial homogeneity."[78] It shows the brute governmental force—police, military, economic, legal—that Americans continue exerting in the service of whiteness.

CONCLUSION

This history reveals an important truth about the use of American power: as soon as people of color are perceived as a threat or as an inconvenience to white rule, federal power is used to expel and exclude them to reinforce white dominion. When leaders invoke immigrant criminality and depravity to justify heightened immigration enforcement, we should understand terms like "national security" and "law and order" to mean a continuing, undisturbed state of white supremacy.

Deportation and exclusion have been effective in preserving white-majority rule. Absent Chinese exclusion and national origins quotas, our population would have been more Asian and nonwhite. Absent cyclical mass deportations of Mexicans and Central Americans, our population would be numerically more Latino, with many more Latino citizen voters. It is profoundly disturbing to consider the breadth and scope of governmental powers arrayed against nonwhites. As we witness today, this power results in the gross denial of basic human rights. And there is little or no redress in American courts for these abuses.

The failure to recognize the history and scope of the government's powers to exclude and to expel has serious consequences. We risk underestimating seriously the force of state power dedicated to controlling nonwhite people. We also risk not recognizing the deep roots of the nation's commitment to white supremacy.

4 The Arc of American Islamophobia

FROM EARLY HISTORY THROUGH THE PRESENT

Khaled A. Beydoun

> It is well known that [Arabs] are a part of the
> Mohammedan world and that a wide gulf separates their
> culture from that of the . . . Christian people.

Judge Arthur J. Tuttle, December 15, 1942

On December 7, 2015, then Republican presidential frontrunner Donald Trump proposed a "total and complete shutdown" of entry into the United States by Muslim immigrants.[1] This proposed ban, which instantly became known as the "Muslim Ban," marked a new high point in America's fear of Muslims. This proposal was echoed over and again, and even broadened after the Republican National Convention in Cleveland, Ohio. On August 15, 2016, Trump broadened the ban even further, calling for "extreme vetting" of all Muslim immigrants coming into the United States.[2] Far more than a fringe or aberrant policy position, Trump's proposal delivered him the Republican nomination and developed into a cornerstone of a campaign that won him the White House. The Supreme Court ultimately found Trump's Muslim ban constitutional,[3] and as the 2020 presidential election roared forward, the polarizing president expanded the executive order to include six additional countries.[4]

Roundly condemned by a broad gamut of critics, Trump's ban targeting Muslim immigrants was framed as politically deviant, "a relatively new phenomenon," or an ideological break from "everything we [Americans] stand for and believe in."[5] Islamophobia, as the liberal media seemed to understand it, was a novel phenomenon that clashed with established norms and entrenched American values. Closer examination of American legal history, however, reveals otherwise.

Trump's Muslim ban is not unprecedented, nor is his brazen Islamophobia new. Rather, it harkens back to a 154-year period (from 1790 through 1944) when U.S. immigration laws banned the naturalization of Muslim immigrants.[6] This period, referred to by legal historians as the "Naturalization Era," links current anti-Muslim rhetoric with foundational American immigration laws codified as the Alien and Sedition Acts of 1798, which demanded heightened scrutiny for the conferral of citizenship and made it easier for the country to deport immigrants deemed dangerous. These laws preceded the blatant anti-Muslim fear and animus that drove the Trump administration and, more deeply, the built-in suspicion of Islam that has guided prevailing counterterror and immigration policy in recent years. Indeed, they are the very seeds of the phenomenon widely known today as Islamophobia.

ISLAMOPHOBIA AND THE LAW

I define Islamophobia as "the presumption that Islam is inherently violent, alien, and unassimilable . . . [combined with] the belief that expressions of Muslim identity are correlative with a propensity for terrorism."[7] Rooted in antiquated tropes and mischaracterizations of Muslims and Islam, Islamophobia is undergirded by the theory of *Orientalism,* a master discourse articulated by postcolonial scholar Edward Said that simultaneously caricatures Islam as a faith, a people, and an imagined geographic sphere—as the civilizational foil of the West.[8] These bodies of misrepresentations and mischaracterizations amplify Western images, ideas, and ideologies about Islam and Muslims, thereby feeding the blatant Islamophobia that Trump and his supporters peddled during the 2016 presidential campaign.

Islamophobia, as a recognizable term and a distinct form of bigotry, became more widely recognized following the terrorist attacks of September 11, 2001, materially driven by the discursive, political, and legal "redeployment of . . . Orientalist tropes" that followed.[9] After 9/11, Muslim Americans were thought to be loyal to transnational terror networks, like Al Qaeda, and on grounds of religion and race, categorically profiled as terror suspects. In short, Muslim identity became a proxy for violence and terror. Therefore, while the term *Islamophobia* became prominent in political discourse after 9/11, its essence is firmly rooted in the images, ideas, and epistemology of its precedent system, Orientalism. As law scholar Leti Volpp observed, "Historically, Asia and the Middle East have functioned as phantasmic sites on which the U.S. nation projects a series of anxieties regarding internal and external threats to the coherence of the national body." The national identity of the United States has been constructed in opposition to those categorized as "foreigners," "aliens," and "others."[10]

Thus, Islamophobia collectively and collaterally affects all Muslims—as well as non-Muslims. As illustrated by Trump's brash rhetoric during his 2016 presidential campaign and since, such language also acutely impacts and stigmatizes America's eight million Muslim citizens, particularly those living in concentrated and cognizable "Muslim American" communities. Like other forms of bigotry, "Islamophobia is not fixed or static, [but] a fluid and dynamic system whereby lay actors and law enforcement target Muslim Americans based on irrational fear and hatred."[11] Islamophobia is formal law and policy, but also a political language strategically deployed to target, defame, and discriminate.

In practice, the laws and politics that shape Islamophobia do not unfold on separate tracks. Rather, the dialectic between law and political rhetoric is a synergistic and symbiotic one, whereby the former endorses and emboldens the latter. The expansion of "structural" Islamophobia spurs anti-Muslim political rhetoric and incites "private" animus or violence.[12] Structural Islamophobia is manifest in the laws, policies, and actions taken by the state, while private (or popular) Islamophobia is the animus and violence inflicted by individuals unconnected to the state. Further, political rhetoric is itself, first, an expression of prevailing law, and, second, an aspirational expression of laws candidates vying for political power are poised to implement. The brazen disparaging of Islam and Muslims on the campaign trail, then, is far more than just "mere rhetoric": it is an expression of desired law. It is also a narration of American Islamophobia, retooled as an electoral strategy with renewed populist fervor. The campaign message justifies Islamophobia by framing it as a necessary step toward countering radicalization, defeating ISIS, or "protecting American values."

More than two centuries before a "Muslim ban" headlined the *New York Times* or was breaking on Fox News, Muslims were statutorily barred from becoming American citizens. From 1790 through 1944, Muslims were deemed alien, unassimilable, and a threat to American society and thus were banned from becoming naturalized. The Naturalization Act of 1790 mandated that only "free white persons" so declared by a civil court could undergo the process to become naturalized citizens.[13] This law functioned as a ban on Muslim citizenship long before 9/11 and President Trump's repeated attempts to ban immigrants from Muslim countries.

Throughout the existence of the United States as a sovereign nation, whiteness and citizenship have been legally conflated. In short, one had to be white to become a naturalized citizen. The Naturalization Act of 1790 codified whiteness as a prerequisite for citizenship, thereby marking it as the dividing line between inclusion and exclusion, and access to a range of privileges and benefits associated with formal membership. The 1790 law was reformed in 1795, and again in 1798, in an effort to "establish a uniform rule of Naturalization," quickly extending the requisite residency period to qualify for naturalization from two to five, to fourteen years.[14] The objective was clear: make it as difficult as possible for nonwhites, and non-Christians, to become naturalized citizens.

Immigration law scholar Hiroshi Motomura observes that the Naturalization Act "entailed no obligation to naturalize, though many immigrants did take that next step and became citizens."[15] Fearing a negative judicial ruling, many settlers opted not to take this step toward citizenship. This was especially true for immigrants from East and South Asia, the Middle East, North Africa, and other parts beyond Europe. For these persons, living as noncitizen residents, or "Americans in waiting,"[16] and flying under the radar until the whiteness mandate was lifted, was preferable to receiving a negative naturalization judgment by a court.

The task of interpreting the statutory meaning of whiteness fell on the country's civil courts. Employing a number of rotating "racial" tests, some judges emphasized the importance of physical appearance, framers' intent, the commonsense understanding of whiteness, and, in the case of immigrants from the Muslim world, religion. Whiteness was not merely a category of race under the Naturalization Act, notes scholar John Tehranian, but a "material concept imbued with rights and privileges."[17] The greatest prize, citizenship, was inscribed into it, which, considering the deeply embedded narrative of a rivalry between Orient and Occident, Muslims and Christians, drove a Muslim naturalization ban that stood in place for 164 years.

If Islam was equated with nonwhiteness, then Christianity functioned as a gateway toward citizenship even for immigrants from Muslim-majority states. During the first naturalization case involving a petitioner from the "Muslim World," in 1909 George Shishim declared before Judge Hutton of the Los Angeles Superior Court: "If I am Mongolian, then so was Jesus, because we come from the same land."[18] Thus, Shishim not only asserted that his Christian identity merited a finding of whiteness, but also that his hailing from the very same land as Jesus—Christianity's foundational figure and Son of God—compelled such a finding. Therefore, Shishim argued that because Jesus's image served as *the* archetype of whiteness in America—showcased in households, courts, and other halls of power—then he too should be classified as white. In doing so, Shishim's appeal was both geographic and pointedly religious in nature, illustrating how the racial identity rested heavily on the religious identity of Arab petitioners and, specifically, how Muslim identity served to disqualify one from becoming a citizen.

Judge Hutton was skeptical of Shishim's Christian bona fides because of his Lebanese, or Middle Eastern, origins.[19] Again, *Arab* and *Muslim* and *Middle East* were all understood to be synonymous. Shishim's appeal tying his geographic origins to that of Jesus, however, rebutted the legal presumption that he was Muslim, leading Hutton to rule that Shishim fit within the statutory definition of whiteness. Shishim was able to overcome the presumption (or suspicion) that he was Muslim by persuasively demonstrating that he was in fact Christian. Thus, Shishim's twofold demonstration of Christianity (as religion and race) functioned as his pathway toward whiteness and citizenship, thereby enabling him to circumvent the standing Muslim naturalization ban.

For subsequent immigrant petitioners from the Muslim world, *Shishim* established the precedent that Arabs could only become citizens if they overcame the presumption that they were not Arab. Again, during this period, Arab was conflated with Muslim identity, which tasked immigrants from the region to persuade civil court judges that their geographic origins did not necessarily make them Muslim. Shishim, for immigrants from the region who came after him, established that Christianity offered the optimal pathway toward whiteness and the citizenship that came along with it. One year later, in 1910, Costa George Najour overcame the Muslim naturalization ban by demonstrating to a Georgia court that he too was Christian. Subsequently, both a Massachusetts and an Oregon court also found a Syrian Christian and Lebanese Christian white by law. In both instances, the presumption of Muslim identity, based on the geographic origins of the petitioners, was overridden by their in-court performance of Christianity, which again was often interpreted by Naturalization Era judges as a hallmark and harbinger of whiteness.

However, not every immigrant Christian petitioner from the Muslim world overcame the naturalization ban. A 1913 case involving an immigrant petitioner from modern-day Lebanon, *Ex parte Shahid*, illustrates how Muslim identity was acutely racialized under the Naturalization Act.[20] Shahid invoked his Christian faith to rebut the presumption that he was a Muslim. Judge Smith of the South Carolina court, however, viewed his dark skin as evidence of miscegenation with Muslims. Smith described the immigrant petitioner to be "about [the color] of a walnut, or somewhat darker than is the usual mulatto of one-half mixed blood between the white and the Negro races."[21]

Persuaded more by his physical appearance than his faith, Smith denied Shahid's petition. Again, like in *Shishim* and a notable precursor case involving an Armenian petitioner, the court framed religion as much along racial terms as it did faith, pushing Smith to opine: "What is the race or color of the modem inhabitant of Syria it is impossible to say. No geographical area of the world has been more mixed since history began. Originally of Hittite or non-Semitic races ... then again followed by another Semitic conquest in the shape of the Arabian Mahometan

[Muslim] eruption."[22] Smith's framing of Ottoman rule as the "Mahometan eruption" illustrates an aversion to Islam, which today would be characterized as an example of structural Islamophobia. More than a century before the Muslim identity of Syrian refugees fleeing civil war and persecution from the Islamic State of Syria and Iraq (ISIS), the South Carolina court viewed Islam with the very same suspicion and fear gripping immigration officials, politicians, and pundits today. Fears of Muslims in 1913, in 2016, and 2021 share a common thread and kindred orientation of Islam as a national security threat.

The Muslim naturalization ban continued until 1944. While a 1915 Fourth Circuit decision narrowly established that Syrian Christians "were to be classed as white people," bona fide Muslim immigrants were still categorically barred from a pathway to citizenship. This had the effect of suppressing Muslim migration into the United States, encouraging religious conversion on the part of many who did, and branding Islam with the seals of foreignness and fear for those who practiced it stateside. More than merely a stigma, Muslim identity functioned to preclude immigrants from the prospect of citizenship and the spoils that came along with it.

The Muslim naturalization ban lasted until American geopolitical interests shifted, specifically when the need for Saudi Arabian oil facilitated the ban's judicial dissolution in 1944.[23] Even after its repeal, however, the Immigration Act of 1924 instituted immigration quotas against African, Asian, and Arab regions—home to significant Muslim populations. Repealed in 1965, the 1924 Immigration Act effectively extended the Muslim naturalization ban by severely limiting the entry of Muslim immigrants for an additional twenty-one years.

The Muslim naturalization ban persisted for at minimum 162 years, and at maximum, 183 years. By either measure, this long-standing ban was firmly in place for over a century before presidential candidate Donald Trump's December 7, 2015, proposed Muslim ban, thereby illustrating that there was nothing novel or unprecedented in his proposal. Moreover, and conflicting with the assessments of alarmed pundits and politicians, it was consistent with American legal tradition.

Historical prohibitions against granting citizenship to Muslims root modern law and policy that similarly profile Muslims as unassimilable and threatening. Indeed, a close examination of the Arab naturalization cases noted above reveals in lurid and lucid fashion that the polemical and bellicose rhetoric that gained national attention during the 2016 presidential campaign, and still is robust today, is substantively identical to the pronouncements of judges presiding over cases involving immigrant-petitioners for citizenship from the Muslim world. Contemporary laws, particularly policy and programming rolled out after 9/11, restricted Muslim immigrants beyond American borders and closely monitored Muslim citizens and communities with them; both fronts were prompted by structural Islamophobia.

ISLAMOPHOBIA IN THE MODERN ERA

Certainly, whenever a terrorist attack takes place in America, many quickly turn to tropes of an "Islamic menace," "violent foreigner," and increasingly "homegrown terrorist." While these tropes have taken on new forms and frames, they are conceptually and substantively based on much older formative stereotypes.[24] These very stereotypes underlie the state suspicion of Muslims and Islam that steers modern state counterterror policy. Fear of Islam and Muslims took on prolific proportions after 9/11 as restrictive immigration policy and domestic surveillance served as the foundation of a new War on Terror that fixated on every sphere of Muslim life. Sweeping legislation centering on religious and racial "profiling," combined with structural reform of the government to deal with the heightened national security threat, were instituted after the 9/11 terror attacks. The "War on Terror" unleashed after 9/11 continues today.

The Islamophobic laws enacted after 9/11 harvested rife anti-Muslim hatred and hysteria on the ground. Government agencies and laws, such as the Department of Homeland Security and the PATRIOT Act, deemed Muslim Americans a dangerous "fifth column," and private citizens followed suit and mimicked that violence against a subset of the polity designated as an enemy group. As a result of these policies, private violence toward Muslim Americans, and those stereotyped as such, skyrocketed after 9/11. The FBI reported a 1,500 percent increase in hate crimes against "people of Middle

Eastern descent, Muslims, and South Asian Sikhs, who are often mistaken for Muslim" from 27 in 2000 to 481 in 2001.[25]

Still today, Muslim Americans are caught between an intensifying Islamophobic climate and state expansion of counterterror strategies that disproportionately focus on them. Twenty years after 9/11, the extending tentacles of American Islamophobia are, perhaps like never before, "haunt[ing] their ability to enjoy citizenship as a matter of rights,"[26] concludes legal scholar Leti Volpp. Systematically framed as unassimilable, foreign, and threatening by politicians, and monolithically classified as criminally suspicious by the state, Muslim Americans rank among the most misrepresented and maligned members of the American polity. This discursive ignorance, coupled with the escalating fear drummed up by political rhetoric and state policy, facilitates the hate crimes and violence inflicted on Muslim Americans today.

The blatant public Islamophobia freely wielded by President Trump has emboldened a frightening degree of private Islamophobia, used as a covert and overt strategy to garner votes, particularly among disaffected segments of the electorate who take to bigoted and xenophobic messaging. Whether intended or not, the hateful rhetoric emanating from the Republican Party, and even the latent fear-mongering delivered by Democrats, has the effect of endorsing private Islamophobia and facilitating the current spike in hate crimes against Muslim Americans.

Islamophobia, in both its structural and private forms, inflicts enhanced injury upon Muslim American bodies, communities, and geographies. Mirroring the post-9/11 moment, Islamophobia has cast Muslims as disloyal outsiders and noncitizens.[27] While they are citizens, the demonization of Islam and political and legal suspicion of Muslims has enabled the subordination of Muslim Americans. In turn, this deepens their second-class citizenship, denying the "enjoyment of rights" that flow from "social membership."[28] Immigration law scholar Linda Bosniak surmises that "[Muslim Americans] may now enjoy nominal citizenship status, but their members are, in fact, afforded less in the way of substantive citizenship than others in society."[29]

This denial or diminishment of "substantive citizenship" rights is enabled by the convergence of the legal and political Islamophobia illustrated above, which sow the seeds for the rising incidence of hate and violence taking place on the ground today in America.

A number of recent events illustrate the frightening uptick in Islamophobic violence in America. For instance, the February 15, 2015, vandalization of the Islamic School of Rhode Island with Islamophobic graffiti, the targeted arson of a Houston mosque days later, the February 10, 2015, murder of four Muslim American students in Chapel Hill, North Carolina, and the frightening range of armed and unarmed anti-Muslim rallies are all evidence that Islamophobia is exceeding the degree of anti-Muslim bigotry immediately after 9/11. In addition to private Islamophobia, the continued introduction of anti-Sharia bills in states across the country combined with a protracted War on Terror manifest that the government, on the federal and state levels, are invested in state-sponsored Islamophobia.

Beyond mere hate violence, the structural Islamophobia prevailing today has immense unseen repercussions on Muslim life. During the War on Terror, it has become more common for Muslim women to remove their headscarves, for Muslim men to shave their beards and abstain from wearing traditional garb, and for young Muslim professionals to Anglicize their names and seek to "pass" as non-Muslim in the public sphere. This process of "acting less Muslim," although undetected by most and unaccounted for in hate-crimes statistics, ranks among the greatest set of Islamophobic injury.[30]

CONCLUSION

Although a novel term, Islamophobia is hardly a new phenomenon. Through early legal decisions and political pronouncements, the culture of Islamophobia was sown deep into American institutions and even deeper into the popular imagination. The vast and embedded memory of anti-Muslim sentiment facilitated the Islamophobia that ripped through the country after the 9/11 terror attacks and roared loudly during the 2016 presidential campaign.

New generations of Muslim Americans cannot recall a world without a War on Terror. The demonization of their faith by the state, along with the popular Islamophobia it incites, is deeply entwined with their daily out-look and worldview. This perspective, while bleak, has mobilized a broad framing of Islamophobia that connects it to other struggles for racial jus-tice, in turn enabling important and unprecedented connections with other social justice movements and mounting a formidable front against the ominous tide of Islamophobia that prevails today.

SECTION TWO Iterations of White Supremacy

White supremacy, as a web of belief, ideology, history, and systems that perpetuate racial inequality, relies on not one, but manifold structures of power. Racism, overt and covert, is one of these. But white supremacy also relies on patriarchy, the power of men over women. White supremacy and patriarchy have intertwined through American history to create conditions of inequality—and violence—for both women and people of color. Well after the abolition of slavery, women's partial citizenship persisted. They received the vote in 1920 and many basic rights of citizenship later, or not at all. In all regions of the United States, furthermore, the claim of sexual violence against white women was used to lynch racial others—including, and perhaps most iconically, Black men in the South. But this narrative of threat against white women was often invented, as the path-breaking reporting of Ida B. Wells showed even in the 1890s. Lynching, as scholars have firmly established, happened in a lot of places, with per capita lynching of Mexicans and Mexican Americans exceeding that of Black men in the South for a brief period in the early twentieth century. So, too, did lynching appear as a mode of violence against labor organizers, women who refused to marry, social outsiders, and prostitutes over the course of U.S. history.[1]

In other words, not just in the South, but everywhere, violence against women and violence against people of color have interwoven. Scholars refer to *intersectionality* to recognize the way that people could be doubly or triply implicated by multiple identities, such that Black women might be victimized by both race and gender, and Black queer women by sexuality, too.[2]

So, too, did the machine of white supremacy employ white women—though they lacked full citizenship and remained sublimated by white men—as agents of violence in their own right. Historians have found that white women's violence on plantations, and false claims of sexual aggression in the Jim Crow years that fueled lynching, were sufficiently widespread to be considered part of the mechanism of white supremacist rule.[3]

So, too, do patriarchy and white supremacy often come together in moments of violence and hate crime, often interweaving with long and

Protesters gather at the Grand Park in Los Angeles for a Women's March against sexual violence and the policies of the Trump administration on January 20, 2018, as the #MeToo movement marked the third year since it received global recognition. (AP Photo/Jae C. Hong, File)

durable conspiracy theories like those promoted by antisemitism. In ideologies of outright racist groups like the Ku Klux Klan, the interweaving of racism, antisemitism, antifeminism, and homophobia is clear and evident; to see the place of these ideas in our broader society requires the study of moments of violence. Here, they make themselves known.

5 The Longest War

RAPE CULTURE AND DOMESTIC VIOLENCE

Rebecca Solnit

I wrote this at the beginning of a wave of renewed feminist vigor, fueled in part by a new kind of coverage of the same old kind of horror stories. That coverage demonstrated that feminism had already slowly shifted who told the story and how such stories were told, in part because of a Greek chorus of feminist voices on social media, deconstructing and decrying old sexist frameworks and offering both firsthand experience and broad critique, and because of the rise of a new youth-led intersectional feminism. Rereading this piece published in January of 2013, I find it striking how significant it seemed just to state the pervasiveness of violence against women at that point in history. Almost five years later, in October 2017, the wave of news stories about sexual crimes by famous men would be called #MeToo and treated as a beginning rather than a culmination of years and decades of work to dismantle impunity for perpetrators and inaudibility for victims. Because this piece was published online, most of the news stories it cited originally came with links.

This chapter is reprinted from "A Rape a Minute, a Thousand Corpses a Year," *Guernica,* January 25, 2013.

Here in the United States, where there is a reported rape every 6.2 minutes and one in five women will be raped in her lifetime, the rape and gruesome murder of a young woman on a bus in New Delhi on December 16, 2012, was treated as an exceptional incident. The story of the alleged rape of an unconscious teenager by members of the Steubenville High School football team was still unfolding, and gang rapes aren't that unusual here either. Take your pick: some of the twenty men who gang-raped an eleven-year-old in Cleveland, Texas, in 2010, were sentenced in November, while the instigator of the gang rape of a sixteen-year-old in Richmond, California, in 2010 was sentenced in October, and four men who gang-raped a fifteen-year-old near New Orleans in 2008 were sentenced in April, though the six men who gang-raped a fourteen-year-old in Chicago in fall of 2008 are still at large. Not that I actually went out looking for incidents: they're everywhere in the news, though no one adds them up and indicates that there might actually be a pattern.

There is, however, a pattern of violence against women that's broad and deep and horrific and incessantly overlooked. Occasionally, a case involving a celebrity or lurid details in a particular case get a lot of attention in the media, but such cases are treated as anomalies, while the abundance of incidental news items about violence against women in this country, in other countries, on every continent including Antarctica, constitute a kind of background wallpaper for the news.

If you'd rather talk about bus rapes than gang rapes, there's the rape of a developmentally disabled woman on a Los Angeles bus in November 2012 and the kidnapping of an autistic sixteen-year-old on the regional transit train system in Oakland, California, on November 27, 2012—she was raped repeatedly by her abductor over two days that winter—and there was a gang rape of multiple women on a bus in Mexico City around the same time. Another female bus rider was kidnapped in India in 2013 and gang-raped all night by the bus driver and five of his friends, who must have thought what happened in New Delhi was awesome.

We have an abundance of rape and violence against women in this country and on this Earth, though it's almost never treated as a civil rights or human rights issue, or a crisis, or even a pattern. People are eager to discuss violence in terms of race or class or religion or nationality, but gender is habitually glossed over—or, it is so constant a factor it goes unseen and unstated.

Here I want to say one thing: though virtually all the perpetrators of such crimes are men, that doesn't mean all men are violent. Most are not. In addition, men obviously also suffer violence, largely at the hands of other men, and every violent death, every assault is terrible. But the subject here is the pandemic of violence by men against women, both intimate violence and stranger violence.

WHAT WE DON'T TALK ABOUT WHEN WE DON'T TALK ABOUT GENDER

There's so much of it. We could talk about the assault and rape of a seventy-three-year-old in Manhattan's Central Park in September 2012, or the rape of a four-year-old in November 2012 and an eighty-three-year-old in Louisiana in January 2012, or the New York City policeman who was arrested in October 2012 for what appeared to be serious plans to kidnap, rape, cook, and eat a woman, any woman, because the hate wasn't personal (though maybe it was for the San Diego man who actually killed and cooked his wife in November and the man from New Orleans who killed, dismembered, and cooked his girlfriend in 2005).

Those are all exceptional crimes, but we could also talk about quotidian assaults, because though a rape is reported only every 6.2 minutes in this country, the estimated total is perhaps five times as high—which means that there may be very nearly a rape a minute in the United States. It all adds up to tens of millions of rape victims.

We could talk about high school and college athlete rapes, or campus rapes, to which university authorities have been appallingly uninterested in responding in many cases, including that high school in Steubenville, Notre Dame University, Amherst College, and many others. We could talk about the escalating pandemic of rape, sexual assault, and sexual harassment in the U.S. military, where secretary of defense Leon Panetta estimated that there were nineteen thousand sexual assaults on fellow soldiers in 2010 alone and that the great majority of assailants got away with it, though four-star general Jeffrey Sinclair was indicted in September of that year for "a slew of sex crimes against women."

Never mind workplace violence, let's go home. So many men murder their partners and former partners that we have well over a thousand homicides of that kind a year—meaning that every three years the death toll tops 9/11's casualties, though no one declares a war on this particular terror. (Another way to put it: the more than 11,766 corpses from domestic-violence homicides since 9/11 exceed the number of deaths of victims on that day *and* all American soldiers killed in the "war on terror.") If we talked about crimes like these and why they are so common, we'd have to talk about what kinds of profound change this society, or this nation, or nearly every nation needs. If we talked about it, we'd be talking about masculinity, or male roles, or maybe patriarchy, and we don't talk much about that.

Instead, we hear that American men commit murder-suicides—at the rate of about twelve a week—because the economy is bad, though they also do it when the economy is good; or that those men in India murdered the bus-rider because the poor resent the rich, with other rapes in India explained by how the rich exploit the poor; and then there are those ever-popular explanations: mental problems and intoxicants. The pandemic of violence always gets explained as anything but gender, anything but what would seem to be the broadest explanatory pattern of all.

Someone wrote a piece about how white men seem to be the ones who commit mass murders in the United States, and the (mostly hostile) commenters only seemed to notice the white part. It's rare that anyone says what this medical study does, even if in the driest way possible: "Being male has been identified as a risk factor for violent criminal behavior in several studies, as have exposure to tobacco smoke before birth, having antisocial parents, and belonging to a poor family."

Still, the pattern is plain as day. We could talk about this as a global problem, looking at the epidemic of assault, harassment, and rape of women in Cairo's Tahrir Square that has taken away the freedom they celebrated during the Arab Spring—and led some men there to form defense teams to help counter it—or the persecution of women in public and private in India from "Eve-teasing" to bride-burning, or "honor killings" in South Asia and the Middle East, or the way that South Africa has become a global rape capital, with an estimated six hundred thousand rapes yearly, or how rape has been used as a tactic and "weapon" of war in Mali, Sudan, and the Congo, as it was in the former Yugoslavia, or the pervasiveness of rape and harassment in Mexico and the femicide in Juárez, or the denial of basic rights for women in Saudi Arabia and the myriad sexual assaults on immigrant domestic workers there, or the way that the Dominique Strauss-Kahn case in the United States revealed what impunity he and others had in France, and it's only for lack of space that I'm leaving out Britain and Canada and Italy (with its ex–prime minister known for his orgies with the underaged), Argentina and Australia, and so many other countries.

WHO HAS THE RIGHT TO KILL YOU?

But maybe you're tired of statistics, so let's just talk about a single incident that happened in my city in 2013, one of many local incidents in which men assaulted women that made the local papers around the same time:

> A woman was stabbed after she rebuffed a man's sexual advances while she walked in San Francisco's Tenderloin neighborhood late Monday night, a police spokesman said today. The 33-year-old victim was walking down the street when a stranger approached her and propositioned her, police spokesman Officer Albie Esparza said. When she rejected him, the man became very upset and slashed the victim in the face and stabbed her in the arm, Esparza said.

The man, in other words, framed the situation as one in which his chosen victim had no rights and liberties, while he had the right to control and punish her. This should remind us that violence is first of all authoritarian. It begins with this premise: I have the right to control you.

Murder is the extreme version of that authoritarianism, where the murderer asserts he has the right to decide whether you live or die, the ultimate means of controlling someone. This may be true even if you are "obedient," because the desire to control comes out of a rage that obedience can't assuage. Whatever fears, whatever sense of vulnerability may underlie such behavior, it also comes out of entitlement, the entitlement to inflict suffering and even death on other people. It breeds misery in the perpetrator and the victims.

As for that incident in my city, similar things happen all the time. Many versions of it happened to me when I was younger, sometimes involving death threats and often involving torrents of obscenities. The fury and desire come in a package, all twisted together into something that threatens to turn eros into thanatos, love into death, sometimes literally.

It's a system of control. It's why so many intimate-partner murders are of women who dared to break up with those partners. As a result, it imprisons a lot of women, and though you could say that the attacker on January 7, 2013, or a brutal would-be-rapist near my own neighborhood on January 5, or another rapist here on January 12, or the San Franciscan who on January 6 set his girlfriend on fire for refusing to do his laundry, or the guy who was sentenced to 370 years for some particularly violent rapes in San Francisco in late 2011, were marginal characters, rich, famous, and privileged guys do it, too.

The Japanese vice consul in San Francisco was charged with twelve felony counts of spousal abuse and assault with a deadly weapon in September 2012, the same month that, in the same town, the ex-girlfriend of Mason Mayer (brother of Yahoo CEO Marissa Mayer) testified in court: "He ripped out my earrings, tore my eyelashes off, while spitting in my face and telling me how unlovable I am . . . I was on the ground in the fetal position, and when I tried to move, he squeezed both knees tighter into my sides to restrain me and slapped me." According to the newspaper, she also testified that "Mayer slammed her head onto the floor repeatedly and pulled out clumps of her hair, telling her that the only way she was leaving the apartment alive was if he drove her to the Golden Gate Bridge 'where you can jump off or I will push you off.'" Mason Mayer got probation.

In the summer of 2013, an estranged husband violated his wife's restraining order against him, shooting her—and six other women—at her spa job in suburban Milwaukee, but since there were only four corpses the crime was largely overlooked in the media in a year with so many more spectacular mass murders in this country (and we still haven't really talked about the fact that, of sixty-two mass shootings in the United States in three decades, only one was by a woman, because when you say *lone gunman*, everyone talks about loners and guns but not about men—and by the way, nearly two-thirds of all women killed by guns are killed by their partner or ex-partner).

What's love got to do with it, asked Tina Turner, whose ex-husband Ike once said, "Yeah I hit her, but I didn't hit her more than the average guy beats his wife." A woman is beaten every nine seconds in this country. Just to be clear: not nine minutes, but nine seconds. It's the number-one cause of injury to American women; of the two million injured annually, more than half a million of those injuries require medical attention while about 145,000 require overnight hospitalizations, according to the Center for Disease Control, and you don't want to know about the dentistry needed afterwards. Spouses are also the leading cause of death for pregnant women in the United States.

"Women worldwide ages 15 through 44 are more likely to die or be maimed because of male violence than because of cancer, malaria, war and traffic accidents combined," writes Nicholas D. Kristof, one of the few prominent figures to address the issue regularly.

THE CHASM BETWEEN OUR WORLDS

Rape and other acts of violence, up to and including murder, as well as threats of violence, constitute the barrage some men lay down as they attempt to control some women, and fear of that violence limits most women in ways many have gotten so used to they hardly notice—and we hardly address. There are exceptions: back in 2012, someone wrote to me to describe a college class in which the students were asked what they do to stay safe from rape. The young women described the intricate ways they stayed alert, limited their access to the world, took precautions, and essentially thought about rape all the time (while the young men in the class, he added, gaped in astonishment). The chasm between their worlds had briefly and suddenly become visible.

Mostly, however, we don't talk about it—though a graphic has been circulating on the Internet called *Ten Top Tips to End Rape*, the kind of thing young women get often enough, but this one had a subversive twist. It offered advice like this: "Carry a whistle! If you are worried you might assault someone 'by accident' you can hand it to the person you are with, so they can call for help." While funny, the piece points out something terrible: the usual guidelines in such situations put the full burden of prevention on potential victims, treating the violence as a given. Colleges spend more time telling women how to survive predators than telling the other half of their students not to be predators.

Threats of sexual assault now seem to take place online regularly. In late 2011, British columnist Laurie Penny wrote, "An opinion, it seems, is the short skirt of the Internet. Having one and flaunting it is somehow asking an amorphous mass of almost-entirely male keyboard-bashers to tell you how they'd like to rape, kill, and urinate on you. This week, after a particularly ugly slew of threats, I decided to make just a few of those messages public on Twitter, and the response I received was overwhelming. Many could not believe the hate I received, and many more began to share their own stories of harassment, intimidation, and abuse."

Women in the online gaming community have been harassed, threatened, and driven out. Anita Sarkeesian, a feminist media critic who documented such incidents, received support for her work, but also, in the words of a journalist, "another wave of really aggressive, you know, violent personal threats, her accounts attempted to be hacked. And one man in Ontario took the step of making an online video game where you could punch Anita's image on the screen. And if you punched it multiple times, bruises and cuts would appear on her image."* The difference between these online gamers and the Taliban men who, in October of 2012, tried to murder fourteen-year-old Malala Yousafzai for speaking out about the right of Pakistani women to education is one of degree. Both are trying to silence and punish women for claiming voice, power, and the right to participate. Welcome to Manistan.

THE PARTY FOR THE PROTECTION OF THE RIGHTS OF RAPISTS

It's not just public, or private, or online either. It's also embedded in our political system, and our legal system, which before feminists

---

* *A note from 2021:* This of course was early in the years-long barrage of threats, lies, harrassment, and denigration that would become known as Gamergate, targeting Sarkeesian and other women. Gamergate is often seen as a key moment in coalescing what would become known as the alt-right, with consequences we could not see in early 2013.

fought for us didn't recognize most domestic violence, or sexual harassment and stalking, or date rape, or acquaintance rape, or marital rape, and in cases of rape still often tries the victim rather than the rapist, as though only perfect maidens could be assaulted—or believed.

As we learned in the 2012 election campaign, it's also embedded in the minds and mouths of our politicians. Remember that spate of crazy pro-rape things Republican men said in the summer and fall of that year, starting with Todd Akin's notorious claim that a woman has ways of preventing pregnancy in cases of rape, a statement he made in order to deny women the right to terminated pregnancies resulting from rape. After that, of course, Senate candidate Richard Mourdock claimed that rape pregnancies were "a gift from God," and shortly after, another Republican politician piped up to defend Akin's comment.

Happily, the five publicly pro-rape Republicans in the 2012 campaign all lost their election bids. (Stephen Colbert tried to warn them that women had gotten the vote in 1920.) But it's not just a matter of the garbage they say (and the price they now pay). In March of 2013, many congressional Republicans voted against reauthorizing the Violence against Women Act, because they objected to the protection it gave immigrants, transgender women, and Native American women. (Speaking of epidemics, one of three Native American women will be raped, and on the reservations 88 percent of those rapes are by non-Native men who know tribal governments can't prosecute them.)

And they're out to gut reproductive rights—birth control as well as abortion, as they've pretty effectively done in many states over the last dozen years. What's meant by "reproductive rights," of course, is the right of women to control their own bodies. Didn't I mention earlier that violence against women is a control issue?

And though rapes are often investigated lackadaisically—there is a backlog of about four hundred thousand untested rape kits in this country—rapists who impregnate their victims have parental rights in thirty-one states. Oh, and in 2013, former vice-presidential candidate and congressman Paul Ryan (R-Manistan) reintroduced a bill that would give states the right to ban abortions and might even conceivably allow a rapist to sue his victim for having one.

ALL THE THINGS THAT AREN'T TO BLAME

Of course, women are capable of all sorts of major unpleasantness, and there are violent crimes by women, but the so-called war of the sexes is extraordinarily lopsided when it comes to actual violence. Unlike the last (male) managing director of the International Monetary Fund, the current (female) head is not going to assault an employee at a luxury hotel; top-ranking female officers in the U.S. military, unlike their male counterparts, are not accused of any sexual assaults; and young female athletes, unlike those male football players in Steubenville, aren't likely to urinate on unconscious boys, let alone violate them and boast about it in YouTube videos and Twitter feeds.

No female bus riders in India have ganged up to sexually assault a man so badly he dies of his injuries, nor are marauding packs of women terrorizing men in Cairo's Tahrir Square, and there's just no maternal equivalent to the 11 percent of rapes that are by fathers or stepfathers.

No major female pop star has blown the head off a young man she took home with her, as did Phil Spector. No female action-movie star has been charged with domestic violence, because Angelina Jolie just isn't doing what Mel Gibson and Steve McQueen did, and there aren't any celebrated female movie directors who gave a thirteen-year-old drugs before sexually assaulting that child, while she kept saying "no," as did Roman Polanski.

IN MEMORY OF JYOTI SINGH

What's the matter with manhood? There's something about how masculinity is imagined, about what's praised and encouraged, about the way violence is passed on to boys that needs to be addressed. There are lovely and wonderful men out there, and one of the things that's encouraging in this round of the war against women is how many men I've seen who get it, who think it's their issue too, who stand up for us and with us in everyday life, online and in the marches from New Delhi to San Francisco this winter.

Domestic violence statistics are down significantly from earlier decades (even though they're still shockingly high), and a lot of men are at work crafting new ideas and ideals about masculinity and power. But the rampages continue.

The lives of half of humanity are still dogged by, drained by, and sometimes ended by this pervasive variety of violence. Think of how much more time and energy we would have to focus on other things that matter if we weren't so busy surviving. Look at it this way: one of the best investigative journalists I know is afraid to walk home at night in our neighborhood. Should she stop working late? How many women have had to stop doing their work, or been stopped from doing it, for similar reasons?

One of the most exciting new political movements on Earth is the Native Canadian Indigenous rights movement, with feminist and environmental overtones, called Idle No More. On December 27, 2012, shortly after the movement took off, a Native woman was kidnapped, raped, beaten, and left for dead in Thunder Bay, Ontario, by men whose remarks framed the crime as retaliation against Idle No More. Afterward, she walked four hours through the bitter cold and survived to tell her tale. Her assailants, who have threatened to do it again, are still at large.

The New Delhi rape and murder of Jyoti Singh, the twenty-three-year-old who was studying physiotherapy so that she could better herself while helping others, and the assault on her male companion (who survived) seem to have triggered the reaction that we have needed for a hundred, or a thousand, or five thousand years. May she be to women—and men—worldwide what Emmett Till, murdered by white supremacists in 1955, was to African Americans and the then-nascent U.S. civil rights movement.

We have far more than eighty-seven thousand rapes in this country every year, but each of them is invariably portrayed as an isolated incident. We have dots so close they're splatters melting into a stain, but hardly anyone connects them, or names that stain. In India they did. The pattern spells out that this is a civil rights issue, it's a human rights issue, it's everyone's problem, it's not isolated, and it's never going to be acceptable again. It has to change. It's your job to change it, and mine, and ours.

6 The Pain We Still Need to Feel

THE NEW LYNCHING MEMORIAL CONFRONTS THE
RACIAL TERRORISM THAT CORRUPTED AMERICA—AND
STILL DOES

Jamelle Bouie

On April 26, 2018, the National Memorial for Peace and Justice opened in Montgomery, Alabama, to remember the thousands of Americans who were hanged, burned, or otherwise murdered by white mobs. The memorial sits just a short drive from the state capitol building, where three days earlier, the state of Alabama had celebrated Confederate Memorial Day, an official state holiday. It's a city where slave traders once sold children for profit, and where slave owners would later launch a rebellion, and form a government, on the conviction that slavery was necessary, inviolable, and good. It's the same city where, in living memory, a sitting governor pledged his total commitment to segregation in the face of an unprecedented civil rights struggle, and where—in the present—more than 30 percent of Black people in the area live under the poverty line.

The central structure of the memorial is a looming cloister where eight hundred steel columns hang from the roof. On each column is a state, a county, and the names of everyone lynched there, along with the dates of their deaths. The columns start at eye level, but as you walk through the memorial, the floor descends and the structures hang like so many

This chapter is reprinted from *Slate*, May 1, 2018.

"Raise Up," a sculpture by Hank Willis Thomas, sits on the grounds of
The National Memorial for Peace and Justice in Montgomery, Alabama, built to
commemorate the Black victims of lynching in the United States. Photo by Michael
Innis-Jiménez.

victims. You, the visitor, become a kind of witness to the ritualistic murders that claimed at least four thousand Black Americans between 1877 and 1950: from the collapse of Reconstruction to the beginning of the end of Jim Crow. The scale of that killing becomes clear in an adjacent room, where replicas of those hanging steel structures are placed like coffins on the ground, arranged in alphabetical order for visitors who want to find the one that marks their town or county.

For me, two markers mattered: Ware County, Georgia, and Gadsden County, Florida, where my mother and father are from, respectively. Four people were lynched in Ware and four people in Gadsden—the earliest in 1881, the latest in 1941. Walter Wilkins, killed on June 27, 1908, in Ware County's seat of Waycross, had been accused of assaulting a young white girl. It is difficult, for me, to express the feeling of finding the columns that mark your origins—seeing the names of the victims and imagining the terror and fear that must have coursed through those communities. And thinking, too, that the most recent killings happened within living memory of people you knew, or who knew your parents and grandparents.

Racial hierarchy and inequality still exist today, but Jim Crow is gone and the public, socially sanctioned violence that defined the lynching era has largely disappeared. Which may lead some to ask *why?* Why dwell on this painful period of American history? Why fight to bring this unspeakable violence into the national consciousness? And why work to integrate it into public memory when lynching remains an incredibly fraught metaphor for racial conflict, with heavy symbolic baggage that weighs on any conversation around the subject?

The answer is straightforward. We live in a moment when racism—explicit and unapologetic—has returned to a prominent place in American politics, both endorsed by and propagated through the Oval Office. And in that environment, a memorial to racial terrorism—one which indicts perpetrators as much as it honors victims—is the kind of provocation that we need, a vital and powerful statement against our national tendency to willful amnesia.

The victims of lynching and racial terrorism deserve a memorial that makes plain the scale of the offense and the magnitude of the crime. The communities in question deserve a chance to reckon with the weight of their history. And Americans writ large need an opportunity to grapple with this period as we struggle to understand a present that contains disturbing echoes of our not-too-distant past.

Neither the memorial nor the museum shies away from calling lynching what it was—"racial terror violence." *Terrorism* is a loaded term, but Bryan Stevenson, whose nonprofit Equal Justice Initiative organized and built the memorial and the accompanying Legacy Museum, embraces it and its implications. "When a black person was lynched, they were not just lynching that person, they were targeting the entire African-American community," said Stevenson. "Nobody thinks that the 9/11 perpetrators were just trying to kill only the people who worked at the World Trade Tower. They were trying to terrorize the rest of us, and that's the reason why we felt justified in fighting a war. I look at the exodus of 6 million people who flee the American South during this period as victims of lynching, even though they weren't strung up. And in that respect, you have to use the word *terrorism* to characterize this violence."

Both the memorial and museum show how widespread and wanton this campaign of violence could be. "Elbert Williams was lynched in Brownsville, Tennessee, in 1940 for working to register black voters as part of the local NAACP. Reverend T. A. Allen was lynched in Hernando, Mississippi, in 1935 for organizing local sharecroppers. Jack Turner was lynched in Butler, Alabama, in 1882 for organizing black voters in Choctaw County." By highlighting "offenses" like labor and political organizing in addition to alleged sexual violence against white women—the most remembered casus belli for lynching—the memorial reminds us that this violence was first and foremost a form of social control, a way to preserve race hierarchy against the claims and actions of Black Americans. Many were killed with the approval of state authorities. Few committed any real crime. The murderers themselves escaped punishment or accountability. Some participants, like future senator Ben Tillman of South Carolina, would go on to Washington.

The terror wasn't just for Blacks accused of supposedly unacceptable conduct in their contact with whites. In her investigation of the lynching of three Memphis grocers—Thomas Moss, Calvin McDowell, and William Stewart—pioneering journalist and antilynching activist Ida B. Wells concluded that their alleged offense was simply success. The lynching had been "an excuse to get rid of Negroes who were acquiring wealth and property and thus keep the race terrorized." An April 1919 edition of the *Chicago Defender* records a lynching in Blakely, Georgia, where Private William Little—a soldier returning from the war in Europe—was accosted by whites who demanded he remove his uniform. Several weeks later, after warnings that he had worn his Army garb for "too long," he was found dead, beaten by a mob.

These murders weren't driven by a small group of virulent racists but were embraced by most white communities in which they occurred. They were communal acts that imparted meaning to spectators and participants alike. What is made clear in the museum is that the history of lynching is for white Americans as much as it is Black ones. It is a history of how the white South constituted itself through communal violence, creating and policing the borders of its racial identity. Lynching wasn't just a way to enforce caste relations between Blacks and whites, it was also a tool white Southerners used to define the meaning of their whiteness.

You can see what this looked like in the large body of lynching photographs, some of which are presented in the museum as evidence of lynching's broad acceptance among white Southerners. The pictures had a purpose: they were circulated by perpetrators as mementos, souvenirs, and propaganda, meant to warn Blacks of the danger of stepping out of line, no matter how innocuous the offense. A 1935 photograph from the lynching of Rubin Stacy, a young homeless tenant farmer, shows the perpetrators and their families in comfortable, seemingly well-constructed clothing. The men are wearing slacks; the women and girls are in dresses. At their center is Stacy's lifeless body, hanging from a tree, his hands cuffed. One of the girls is smiling. A 1930 photograph from the lynchings of Thomas Shipp and Abram Smith, both nineteen, shows a crowd that is large, well-dressed, and visibly interested in the grim spectacle. Another photograph—from the 1916 lynching of seventeen-year-old Jesse Washington in Waco, Texas— shows a crowd of thousands watching as his body burns and smolders.

White communities celebrated these lynchings in the local press, as documented in *100 Years of Lynchings,* a collection of contemporaneous news accounts. "Zachariah Walker, a negro desperado, was carried on a cot from the hospital here last night and burned to a crisp by a frenzied mob of men and boys on a fire which they ignited about a half mile from town," crowed the *Montgomery Advertiser* in a story dated August 15, 1911. Politicians were often enthusiastic supporters of these efforts. Commenting on a recent lynching in his state, Governor Cole Blease of South Carolina told crowds that he would rather have "resigned the office," and "led the mob" himself, than deter any white man from punishing "that nigger brute."

This was more than gruesome titillation or curiosity. The age of lynching emerged at a time when much of the country was preoccupied with the decline of traditional morality, represented by urbanization and the growing autonomy of women. This larger context is outside the scope of the museum—which turns its attention to the victims—but it is an important part of understanding the lynching era and why it matters for the present. In the white South, that preoccupation blended with patriarchal norms, evangelical religion, and white supremacy to produce a noxious brew where, as historian Amy Louise Wood writes in *Lynching and Spectacle: Witnessing Racial Violence in America, 1890–1940,* "white southerners . . . conceptualized the threat of black enfranchisement and autonomy as . . . a dire moral threat to white purity, literally a physical assault on white homes and white women." And in this vision, "black men came to personify the moral corruption that they believed to be the root cause of social disorder."

Lynchings served two purposes: they both preserved white dominance against the prospect of Black equality *and* restored the presumed moral status of white communities by eliminating threats to white purity and virtue as well as white authority. These killings often took a ritualistic cast. "Lynch mobs at times gave their victims time to pray and, more frequently, wrought confessions from them," writes Wood. Likewise, lynch mobs paid close attention to torment and suffering, "practices that publicly rehearsed narratives of human sin and divine judgment"—well known in an age of public, deeply held Christianity. It is not without meaning that lynching defenders condemned victims as "demons," "fiends," and "brutes," nor is it coincidence that, in her defense of lynching, prominent temperance activist, suffragette, and future U.S. senator Rebecca Latimer Felton thundered that if "there is not enough religion in the pulpits to organize a crusade against sin . . . nor manhood enough in the nation to put a sheltering arm about innocence and virtue" then "lynch a thousand times a week if necessary."

With brutal, unspeakable violence, white men affirmed their manhood, white communities affirmed their virtue, and the white South, as a whole, affirmed its power. To murder with impunity, in full view of the public, is to claim total authority. On the other side, both Black men and Black women were shown their essential powerlessness in Southern society. And the extent to which Black women were lynched—Mary Turner, for instance, was killed with her unborn child for complaining about the lynching of her husband—served to underscore the scant value attached to their lives and "womanly virtue." If the master-slave relations of the antebellum South were shattered by the Civil War and Reconstruction, then lynching helped recreate them, albeit on more "democratic lines," as all white Southerners—and not just a select, propertied few—could claim the right to kill. Lynching dramatized the South's emerging caste system at the same time that it defined its terms.

That rigid caste system may be gone, but the central narrative of lynching—the lie of inherent Black criminality—still shapes public life. In November of 2018, fourteen-year-old Brennan Walker was shot at after knocking on a door in the predominantly white Rochester Hills, Michigan. The woman at the door thought he was there to rob them, and her husband, who heard her screams, ran down with his shotgun. Walker had simply stopped, on his way to school, to ask for directions. He was lucky. In 2013, nineteen-year-old Renisha McBride knocked on a door in a Dearborn Heights neighborhood, seeking help after a car crash. The homeowner, Theodore Wafer, opened his door and fired his shotgun, killing her. Compare both incidents to a lynching account presented at the memorial: "A black man was lynched in Millersburg, Ohio, in 1892 for 'standing around' in a white neighborhood."

The specter of the Black criminal continues to weigh on our justice system. Stevenson is quick to note that the most reliable predictor of a death penalty sentence is still the race of the victim, not the perpetrator. Black killers of white victims are far more likely to receive a death sentence than Black killers of Black people.

Lynching echoes in other ways. Our politics are in the grip of a backlash defined, in large part, by deep racial entitlement on the part of many white Americans. Indeed, racial violence—or the promise of such—remains a potent tool for defining the boundaries of white racial community. As a candidate for president, Donald Trump promised state action against Hispanic immigrants and Muslim refugees—not as punishment, but as defense: a way to keep America free of people who, in his view, cannot assimilate. How did he describe these groups? As "rapists," criminals, and drug dealers—dangerous gang members who defile and kill innocent American women. Far from repelling voters, this language primed and activated racial fear and resentment among many white voters, supercharging its electoral potency. Trump wasn't just defining an enemy, he was speaking a language of racial threat—of purity and morality—that has its roots in the lynching era.

Perhaps, had white Americans in particular possessed a better understanding of the lynching era and what it entailed, they would have viewed Trump's message of past greatness with appropriate skepticism. "I think about the history, and I realize we've never said, 'Never again,'" Stephenson said. "We didn't say, 'Never again' at the end of enslavement. We didn't do it at the end of lynching, at the end of segregation. And because we haven't actually articulated the commitment, things keep happening. We keep replicating new forms of bigotry and discrimination that get applied to people of color and to African Americans in particular, that ideology of white supremacy survives."

The National Memorial for Peace and Justice forces Americans into a difficult but necessary confrontation over the depths of our racial divide. It's a rebuke to the whitewashed history of "Make America Great Again" as well as the naive "post-racialism" of the recent past. And it tries to push the story forward. A statue titled "Raise Up" shows a row of men, their heads and shoulders coming out of stone, their hands raised above their heads. You don't need a guide to know what they're saying. *Hands up, don't shoot.* Placed after the central monuments of the memorial, it connects the racial violence of the past to the racial violence of the present, challenging the triumphant narratives that make today's America—and today's Americans—fundamentally different from those who lived before.

It's reminiscent of journalist Isabel Wilkerson's comparison between lynchings and police shootings, following the unrest in Ferguson, Missouri, in 2014. "The rate of police killings of black Americans is nearly the same as the rate of lynchings in the early decades of the 20th century," wrote Wilkerson, placing those events on a continuum with the violence that drove the "Great Migrations" of the twentieth century. "The haunting symmetry of a death every three or four days links us to an uglier time that many would prefer not to think about, but which reminds us that the devaluation of black life is as old as the nation itself and has yet to be confronted."

There are other potent connections between the past and the present. The public nature of lynching echoes in the ubiquitous videos of police assaults and police killings. Like lynching photographs, they have sparked outrage and galvanized activists, building political will for criminal justice reform. But they also turn trauma into endlessly repeated spectacle, rehashing the initial injury and reminding Black people of their tenuous place within American society.

There is some danger in the directness of these comparisons. To use lynching too much as a metaphor is to wear it down, robbing it of its specificity and meaning. A phrase like "high-tech lynching"—or rhetoric that compares harsh criticism to a "lynch mob"—obscures far more than it illuminates. Still, there's reason to keep lynching as a metaphor and analytical tool; as the Legacy Museum shows, there are too many parallels between that era of racial terrorism and the current struggles against police brutality and white racial backlash to ignore.

But what do we do with those connections? The memorial and museum suggest one approach. Both are interactive in a sense. Individual communities can claim one of the individual monuments that make up the memorial. They can remove it to their town or county and erect it as a memorial to *their* particular victims of lynching. Over time, visitors will be able to see who has taken a marker and who hasn't, who is reckoning with their history and who isn't. Stevenson also hopes that after experiencing the monuments and exhibits, individuals are primed to act. He wants the country to look at racial terrorism and say, "Never again," and in pursuit of that end, the Equal Justice Initiative will provide information to help visitors register to vote or sign petitions relating to racial justice and reform.

It's both a powerful gesture—connecting this history to the politics of today—and one that doesn't quite fit the sheer radicalism of this project. The National Memorial for Peace and Justice isn't just a memorial. It is an indictment of the United States and its ongoing commitment to racial hierarchy. It argues, explicitly, that white supremacy is fundamental to the structure of this society. And it suggests that our only option for uprooting those evils is a radical correction from our present course.

The National Memorial of Peace and Justice and The Legacy Museum: From Enslavement to Mass Incarceration, both in Montgomery, Alabama, were opened to the public on April 26, 2018, commemorating the racial terror African Americans and other racialized groups faced from the birth of the republic to the present. Lynching was execution by violent mob justice, without recourse to formal courts of law, usually by hanging and the mutilation of the victim's body. The presumption that one was innocent until proven guilty by a jury of one's peers did not apply. Those interested in the history of lynching in the United States as it affected African Americans, Native Americans, Asian American, and Mexican Americans should consult the following sources. Equal Justice Institute, *Lynching in America: Confronting the Legacy of Racial Terror* (https://lynchinginamerica.eji.org/report-landing); Manfred Berg, *Popular Justice: A History of Lynching in America* (Lanham, MD.: Ivan R. Dee, 2011); William D. Carrigan and Clive Webb, *Forgotten Dead: Mob Violence against Mexicans in the United States, 1848–1928* (New York: Oxford University Press, 2013); Nicholas Villanueva, *The Lynching of Mexicans in the Texas Borderlands* (Albuquerque: University of New Mexico Press, 2017); Monica Muñoz Martinez, *The Injustice Never Leaves You: Anti-Mexican Violence in Texas* (Cambridge, MA: Harvard University Press, 2018); Scott Zesch, *The Chinatown War: Chinese Los Angeles and the Massacre of 1871* (New York: Oxford University Press, 2012); Daniel F. Littlefield, *Seminole Burning: A Story of Racial Vengeance* (Jackson: University Press of Mississippi, 1996).

7 Anti-Asian Violence and U.S. Imperialism

Simeon Man

On March 19, 2020, days after U.S. president Donald Trump began referring to the coronavirus as the "Chinese virus," Asian American civil rights groups in San Francisco launched the Stop AAPI Hate reporting center to document the growing numbers of racist acts targeting Asian people in the United States. Within two weeks, the website reported over eleven hundred incidents, including acts of verbal and physical assaults that were often laced with taunts like "go back to China" and profanities linking Asian bodies to disease. Commentators have been quick to point out that this is not a new phenomenon. Russell Jeung, a co-organizer of Stop AAPI Hate, remarked, "We have seen time and again how dangerous it is when leaders scapegoat for political gain and use inflammatory rhetoric to stir up both interpersonal violence and racist policies. As we've seen throughout American history—from the Chinese Exclusion Act of 1882 to Japanese American wartime incarceration and most recently, immigration bans—Asians have been targeted with such vehement hate."[1]

Anti-Asian violence indeed has a history, and this essay offers one interpretation of this historical phenomenon. Its argument is simple: that anti-Asian violence is a part of the violence of the United States itself, that is, U.S. imperialism, and that ending one requires the dismantling of the

other. The essay concludes by examining some of the activist efforts leading the way, tackling the roots of "anti-Asian" violence in solidarity with
those fighting U.S. militarism and state racial terror on a global scale.

ASIANS ARE NOT IMMIGRANTS

Anti-Asian violence is a feature of settler societies like the United States
that are founded on Native dispossession and the freedom of individuals
to own property. The violence takes a pattern. It emerges in moments of
crisis, when the capitalist economy predicated on the seizure of Native
lands, the extraction of resources, and the exploitation of labor fails to
generate profit, threatening the individual worker-consumer and his
imagined sense of safety that is itself derived from the security of his property claims. This insecurity is expressed through a violence directed at
those deemed "alien," a figure who occupies a space of illegality and threatens "order," or the governance of property relations, and thus exists to be
contained, expelled, or eliminated.[2] In the nineteenth century, "The
Chinese Must Go!" became the rallying cry of the "workingman," a racialized and gendered figure aspiring for inclusion into U.S. market society. In
other words, anti-Asian violence has served as a stabilizing force amidst
structural inequality, producing a sense of belonging and shoring up the
belief in capitalism and white supremacy from unlikely adherents, while
foreclosing other economies not premised on the theft of labor and
Indigenous lands.[3] In this view, anti-Asian violence recurring throughout
U.S. history should not be seen merely as episodic, arising in periods of
xenophobia, but rather as a structure sustaining racial divides. Indeed, it
is intrinsic to capitalism, or racial capitalism—a relation of property accumulation that distributes unequal life expectancies and advantages based
on group differentiation—and its twin condition, settler colonialism, a
system of conquest dependent upon laws, ideologies, and other state institutions to buttress property claims on stolen land.[4]

To understand anti-Asian violence on these terms requires restating an
unorthodox premise: Asians were not "immigrants." In the nineteenth and
early twentieth centuries, Chinese, Japanese, Koreans, Filipinos, and South
Asians arrived in North America as a result of capitalist and imperial

expansion that radically altered relationships within households and villages, destroyed working and rural people's homes and lives, and generally made those lives unlivable. A more accurate term is "migrant labor," which denotes that Asians' sole function within the capitalist economy was as labor, their value derived from their ability to extract profit.[5] Unable to naturalize as citizens, they were made to be mobile and replaceable through the enactment of laws that controlled and criminalized their social relations, that ensured the maximization of their labor and not their lives. For example, the California Supreme Court in 1854 determined in *People v. Hall* that the race of the Chinese was "not white," thereby depriving them of the right to testify against a white person in legal proceedings, and hence leaving them unable to protect themselves from violence. Here, and repeatedly throughout the nineteenth and early twentieth centuries, the law buttressed lawless violence; the two worked in tandem to discipline Chinese labor. They also worked to confer value on whiteness itself, such that being white held a property value articulated over and over again in court and defended violently throughout the expanding U.S. settler empire.[6]

VIOLENCE OF INCLUSION

Participation in the culture of anti-Asian violence in the nineteenth century provided a means for those who were themselves differentially marginalized, excluded, and dispossessed under capitalism to assert their belonging in the nation. Put differently, violence against Asians was one means by which European immigrants became Americans. The culture of violence entailed the acts, their public spectacle, and the casual circulation of the imagery of brutality in the form of postcards and snapshots.[7] Lynch mobs and "driving out" campaigns targeting Chinese people were ceremonial occurrences on the U.S. frontier. On October 24, 1871, a mob of nearly five hundred attacked Chinese residents in Los Angeles, dragging them from their homes and hanging seventeen victims in what became the largest mass lynching in U.S. history.[8] On September 2, 1885, white coal miners at Rock Springs, Wyoming, killed at least twenty-eight Chinese miners, an organized brutality that included scalping and castrating some victims before driving the rest of the Chinese workforce out of the camps.[9]

Two months later, in Tacoma, Washington, hundreds of armed men descended on two Chinese neighborhoods and violently expelled all eight hundred to nine hundred Chinese residents from the city.[10] These campaigns and sadistic rituals were fueled by the popular tropes of the "yellow peril" that depicted the Chinese (and later the Japanese) as a threat to white men's property, including "their" jobs, women, and family. The ritualistic violence did more than accomplish the stated aim of driving out the Chinese. They were at heart inclusionary processes for participants and observers to forge community in the assertion of white identity and the maintenance of the color line.

This process extended beyond U.S. "domestic" territory. During the Philippine-American War at the turn of the twentieth century, soldiers seasoned in these campaigns and wars of extermination on the frontier encountered a foreign landscape they likened to "Indian country" and an enemy they called "niggers." The application of these terms to new peoples and places did not signal merely the export of racial idioms but rather demonstrated the racializing processes at the heart of U.S. imperialism, by which entire populations were made enemy and the military's exterminist tactics justified as necessary to the "civilizing" mission.[11] The seizure of distant lands and markets that resulted from the crisis of capitalism in the late nineteenth century required a violence to make "Indians" out of newly occupied peoples. It was a violence that regenerated whiteness and masculinity, the fragile possessions that offered tangible forms of security in precarious times.

U.S. imperialism, scholar Dean Saranillio argues, emerges historically from positions of weakness, not strength. In this view, the annexation of the Philippines and other island territories including Hawai'i, Guam, Puerto Rico, American Samoa, and Wake Island in 1898–99 secured new lands and markets for the United States in order to resolve capitalism's inherent failures. This "fail forward" pattern of U.S. imperialism continued in subsequent decades.[12] In 1924 Congress established the Border Patrol to further consolidate U.S. sovereignty on stolen land in the Southwest and to control Mexican migrant labor that made the land profitable, mobilizing the promise of whiteness to motivate the force.[13] The pattern continued in the 1940s, when the federal government reorganized the nation's manufacturing, resource-extraction, and knowledge industries for warmaking, bringing the country out of the Great Depression. World War II and the subsequent land and aerial wars in Korea (1950–53) and Southeast Asia (1954–75) ushered in a permanent war economy in the United States, one in which war no longer served only as the means to acquiring markets but became a profit enterprise itself. This economy was geared around making industrial killing more efficient and wars more "humane," a claim of preserving life that relied on the introduction of the atomic bomb and modes of chemical and psychological warfare developed in tandem with academic disciplines, universities, and think tanks.[14]

The expansion of racial capitalism on a global scale during this period required a shift in the management of U.S. racial populations. Indeed, the period from the 1940s through the 1960s witnessed the inclusion of racial minorities into U.S. national life in unprecedented ways. Racial restrictions to citizenship and immigration bans were lifted, allowing Chinese, Filipinos, South Asians, Japanese, and Koreans to become naturalized citizens and an exceptional few to enter the United States once again. And, for the first time since the end of Reconstruction in 1876—which we might better think of as a failed revolution, when an experiment in radical democracy led by Black workers after the Civil War was brutally replaced with a vicious system of white supremacy under Jim Crow—the government enacted civil rights laws to protect Black citizens' freedom from violence. Racial violence continued, to be sure, particularly directed at returning soldiers, antiracist activists, and others who transgressed the racial order, but that violence was seen increasingly as fringe and unsanctioned by a government that officially disavowed white supremacy, now understood as a (foreign) malice and detrimental to government conducts abroad.

Scholars have referred to the post–World War II period as the "era of inclusion," but that needs qualification. If we understand white supremacy not simply as acts of racial terror enacted by racist white people but as a structure of racial capitalism, we can see this period as a continuation of the past rather than a break from it. Indeed, even as Asian Americans and African Americans enjoyed new freedoms as valued—even valorized—members of the nation-state, their value was derived from their participation in the permanent war economy that for some included the work of killing and dying. National inclusion was premised on the very notion that their lives were expendable in order to safeguard the freedoms promised by the nation-state. It also required the making of new racial enemies as targets of U.S. perpetual war. "The Oriental doesn't put the same high price on life as does a Westerner," the commander of U.S. forces William Westmoreland had remarked during the Vietnam War. "Life is plentiful. Life is cheap in the Orient."[15] It may be tempting to interpret the blatant racism of this statement as a contradiction of the era's mandate of formal equality and disavowal of white supremacy, but it would be more accurate to view them as inescapably entwined. Under racial capitalism, deadly racism formed the underside of liberal inclusion, a contradiction that Asian Americans and other racial minorities helped to stabilize through their recruitment into the military.

FIGHTING NEOLIBERAL AUSTERITY

A deep economic recession hit the United States and much of the industrialized world in the 1970s, unraveling the preceding decades of relative prosperity as corporate profits tanked and unemployment climbed to a level not seen since the 1930s. The period also saw the renewal of labor migrations from Asia and Latin America, facilitated by the Hart-Celler Act of 1965. The act abolished the immigration quota system based on "national origins" and reunified families separated by exclusionary policies; in broader terms, it absorbed into the United States populations that were idled or unsettled by economic policies and state violence under U.S.-backed undemocratic regimes. These outcomes, as seen before, were the result of capitalism's intrinsic unsustainability that required continual state intervention. Along with the U.S. military defeat in the Vietnam War in 1975, these compounding realities exacerbated the vulnerabilities of people across race and class, including those whose identity in whiteness had reaped them much of the material and ideological rewards of the preceding decades of the "golden age." Not coincidentally, the period witnessed a resurgence of anti-Asian violence. In 1979, white fishermen in Galveston, Texas, enlisted the Ku Klux Klan to wage a campaign of intimidation to drive out the Vietnamese refugees who had resettled there, viewing them as an economic, even communist, threat, abetted by the federal government. They saw themselves as continuing a war against the "Viet Cong" that had been abandoned by the military and the government, now waged on the "home" front, reasserting the scripts of settler violence and white supremacy.[16]

Anti-Asian violence in the United States, which had never let up since the time Asians first entered the profit calculus in the nineteenth century, came into the U.S. national spotlight in 1982 with the brutal slaying of Vincent Chin by two Detroit autoworkers. Detroit's failing auto industry at the time had reactivated a deep-seated anti-Japanese racism in U.S. culture. And once again, the vulnerability of white working men had grave consequences for the lives of others. On the night of June 19, Ronald Ebens and Michael Nitz bludgeoned Chin to death with a baseball bat after a confrontation at a nightclub in which Ebens said, "It's because of you little motherfuckers that we're out of work." The shock of the murder was compounded by the tragic realization that the post–civil rights age of ostensible color-blindness would offer no reprieve from racism's deadly consequences. The murder case and subsequent acquittal of the killers ignited a grassroots movement led by Asian Americans calling attention to the spate of racially motivated hate crimes against people of Asian descent and demanding justice for Vincent Chin. Spearheaded by the group American Citizens for Justice, which comprised Chinese, Japanese, Korean, and Filipino Americans, the movement was deliberately panethnic and crossed class lines, and it spanned coast to coast.[17]

What has gone unnoticed in most historical accounts of this movement, however, is that many activists understood anti-Asian violence in broad terms, seeing it not as a result of "discrimination" or "scapegoating" but as symptomatic of the capitalist system itself, including the violence of criminalization and policing. Indeed, the spike in anti-Asian violence in the 1980s coincided with the rise of punitive governance in the United States that targeted a host of marginalized peoples, including undocumented migrants, queer and trans people of color, the workless and the houseless poor. This was the dawn of the neoliberal era, in which the government's answer to social and economic precarity was to further dismantle the welfare state by slashing and privatizing public services, while ramping up policing to protect the propertied class. Seen as a malignancy of disordered families and households and an index of crime to-be-committed, poverty itself became criminalized, deflecting attention away from capitalism's failures.

Grassroots movements such as the Coalition against Anti-Asian Violence (CAAAV) made these connections explicit. Founded in New York City in the summer of 1986, CAAAV pulled its members from other civil rights and labor groups including the Asian American Legal Defense and Education Fund, Korean-Americans for Social Concern, the New York Asian Women's Center, and the Japanese American Citizens League—New York Chapter, among others. Observing a rise in hate crimes against Asians throughout the country, CAAAV sought to diagnose and tackle the problem at the roots. Its statement of purpose read: "The recent series of attacks on Asian Americans is neither a new phenomenon nor an aberration in an otherwise just and peace-loving society." Rather, it is a function of "the American economy that is based on . . . confiscated lands and 150 years of institutionalized slavery."[18] This broad view enabled organizers to see "police brutality" as part of the organized violence of neoliberal accumulation by dispossession. In early 1987, CAAAV won its first campaign to defend the Wong and Woo family, Chinese immigrants who were beaten by New York City police officers after they had broken down the door of their Chinatown apartment and entered without warrant, arresting them for allegedly bootlegging cable television services. Recognizing that such police conduct occurred regularly in impoverished Black and Brown communities—an institutionalized practice later termed as "broken windows policing," which criminalized the behavior of the racialized poor—CAAAV organized with other "Third World groups" in an effort to hold the police officers accountable.[19] On July 28, 1987, CAAAV mobilized two hundred Chinatown residents to deliver a community indictment of the NYPD's 5th Precinct, condemning its racist violence.[20]

In its approach to organizing, CAAAV built on already-existing organizational forces set into motion through struggles that came before, specifically those that sought to make New York City's Chinatown a livable place for residents. In the early 1980s, in response to new zoning laws passed by the city that paved the way for the construction of luxury apartments in Chinatown, the Chinese Progressive Association (CPA) organized low-income tenants to stop evictions and to fight for better and more affordable housing. "A dangerous trend is under way," a CPA Housing Committee pamphlet declared, as the government facilitated the incursion of capital into the historic neighborhood through urban renewal projects, displacing longtime residents and fracturing communities.[21] The people fought back. In 1983, in response to the latest city plan to rebuild the dilapidated White Street jail in the neighborhood, thousands of Chinatown shop owners, workers, tenants, and students descended on City Hall to demand a halt to the plan. The protests resulted in a major concession by the city government, the Chung Park Project, a three-floor building slated for senior housing and community use. As the development of the project got under way, residents mobilized once again, this time to push back against the developer's nefarious plans to promote real estate speculation and to attract corporate businesses to the space. Residents signed petitions and showed up for public hearings to demand accountability to the community, including keeping rents affordable to incentivize small shopkeepers and making space for a daycare center.[22]

Movements against anti-Asian violence in this period were multifaceted, and they were long term. Throughout the country, in Los Angeles, San Francisco, Seattle, and New York City, these movements were struggles for affordable housing, health care, and other basic needs, and they were sustained through collaboration with other movements fighting for the same things, out of a shared recognition that violence against any one group was violence against others. This Third World consciousness, a legacy of the global anticolonial revolts of the late 1960s, allowed activists to extend their analysis beyond the boundaries of their own communities and to draw connections to antiracist and anticapitalist struggles around the world. In particular, the movement to end apartheid in South Africa in the mid-1980s mobilized many of the housing activists in New York Chinatown. In June 1986, organizers from the Chinese Progressive Association, the New York Chinatown Senior Citizens Coalition Center, the Alliance for Filipino Concerns, Young Koreans United, and the Japanese American Citizens League–New York Chapter formed an Asian contingent to march in the citywide antiapartheid rally. Rocky Chin of CPA spoke on its behalf: "In [P. W.] Botha's martial law measures, we see the parallels with [Ferdinand] Marcos' regime in the Philippines and Chun Doo Wan's repressive Korean regime."[23] These fascist states were not exceptional, he insisted, but parts of a globe-spanning neoliberal regime rooted in histories of colonialism and the economy of permanent warfare. The people's struggles were connected throughout the globe.

ABOLITIONIST FUTURES

This brief snapshot of antiracist organizing in the 1980s shows that the crisis we confront today is not entirely new, and that in confronting it we need not dream up entirely new solutions. For while we have inherited the crisis in the form of a growing carceral state, we have also inherited a tradition of radical activism that set its sights on dismantling racial capitalism and imperialism and building something new in its wake. Today we call these forms of radical activism *abolitionist,* a term that is applied to anti-prison organizing specifically but that at its core is about imagining a society that does not thrive on punitive governance and doing the slow work of getting us there, pulling from already-existing movements and capacities.[24] An abolitionist framework explains why many of the movements that were activated in the 1980s are finding space to make their mark in the current conjuncture of the COVID-19 pandemic and state racist violence.[25] CAAAV is one example. In the 1990s, CAAAV shifted from anti–hate crimes advocacy to organizing immigrant communities to fight for safe and affordable housing and healthcare, counteracting the criminalization of immigrants and the organized abandonment of the Clinton era. To mark this shift, it changed its name to CAAAV: Organizing Asian Communities. In 2005 it founded the Chinatown Tenants Union to empower tenants to fight for greater protections from predatory landlords and unjust evictions. In the midst of the COVID-19 pandemic, organizers activated these capacities to launch a mutual aid effort to assist vulnerable senior citizens, demanding that landlords repair dilapidated and unsafe housing units and clean and disinfect common areas. CAAAV also joined housing justice advocates statewide in calling for rent cancellation and a moratorium on evictions.[26]

The mounting death toll from the pandemic and the crackdown on protests throughout the country in response to the police murders of George Floyd, Breonna Taylor, Tony McDade, Rayshard Brooks, and many more Black people lays bare the violence of a system that cares for profit over people. Asian American activist groups formed in the time of neoliberal multiculturalism have been among those on the front lines combatting the government's deadly negligence and racist violence. At a time when civil rights advocates were condemning Donald Trump's racist rhetoric and the spike in hate crimes against people of Asian descent, others are reminding us yet again that "anti-Asian violence" has deep roots. They see the racism of the Donald Trump administration as part of the calculated cruelty of the United States itself, linking the COVID pandemic to the violence of U.S. empire. Nodutdol is one such organization. Formed in 1999 among diasporic Koreans in New York City united by a struggle to end war and militarism on the Korean peninsula and here in the United States, Nodutdol called for the lifting of U.S.-backed sanctions that prevented life-saving medical equipment from entering North Korea, Venezuela, Iran, and other countries. The pandemic has not slowed the U.S. drive to build borders, prisons, and other war infrastructures, its organizers noted. The struggle therefore must be expansive. Its statement on COVID reads: "We encourage collective struggle and solidarity, as the capitalist system collapses, to provide relief for the unhoused, the incarcerated, the unemployed, the undocumented, the immune-compromised, the uninsured, and for all workers in the US and around the world."[27] The slow work of dismantling U.S. imperialism, Nudotdol argues, calls for the implementation of radical forms of aid as well as the eradication of anti-Black racism, which required nothing short of efforts "to abolish police and prisons and to undo the United States for our collective liberation."[28]

This is ultimately why the fight against anti-Asian violence is one with the struggle for all Black lives. In New York City, Seattle, Los Angeles, and other places throughout the country ravaged by the COVID pandemic and by the violence of capitalism, groups are uniting and fighting for the lives of those left to die. Alongside demands to defund and dismantle the police, people are modeling other ways of living through mutual aid and practices of transformative justice. They are showing that the time for decolonization is now and that, when this moment passes, another world will be more possible.

8 Homophobia and American
Nationalism

MASS MURDER AT THE PULSE NIGHTCLUB

Roderick A. Ferguson

On June 12, 2016, a gunman by the name of Omar Mateen opened fire in the Pulse nightclub, a gay bar and dance club in Orlando, Florida. With forty-nine people killed and fifty-three people injured, it was the second worst mass shooting by a lone gunman in U.S. history. While he professed allegiance to the Islamic State of Iraq and Syria, commonly referred to as ISIS, Mateen is an Afghan American, born on Long Island and raised in the United States.

The most common interpretations of Mateen's behavior explained it in terms of a hatred that apparently emanated from his declared allegiance to ISIS and the homophobia presumed from that allegiance. The *New York Times* reported: "It was the worst act of terrorism on American soil since Sept. 11, 2001, and the deadliest attack on a gay target in the nation's history." President Barack Obama seemed to endorse this interpretation as well, stating, "In the face of hatred and violence, we will love one another . . . We will not give in to fear or turn against each other. Instead we will stand united as Americans to protect our people and defend our nation, and to take action against those who threaten us." Donald Trump, then still a candidate for the Republican nomination for the presidency, used the occasion to argue that Muslims should be barred from entering the country's borders. Hillary Clinton, the presumptive Democratic nominee, called for a "redoubling" of efforts to stop terrorism in the United States and abroad.[1] All of the comments assumed not only the exceptional but also the foreign nature of homophobia within this country. They did so by presuming that Mateen's supposed hatred of LGBTQ+ people was based on a personal dislike that was nurtured in his parents' country of origin.

The narrative of Mateen as an ISIS terrorist who "disliked" queer men was undermined by a man who claimed to be Mateen's lover and by men who said that Mateen had messaged them via the dating apps Grindr and Jack'd. According to this narrative, what was advertised originally by Mateen and others as an attack in the name of ISIS was, in fact, the result of a man rejected by potential and actual lovers at the Pulse.

One way of explaining Mateen's behavior would be to locate it in the histories of anti-LGBT hate crimes such as those committed against Matthew Shepherd and the lesser-known Black and Latinx victims of homophobic and transphobic violence. However, framing the violence against LGBTQ+ people as simply one about hate can individualize what is in fact a social issue of national and global ramifications. It can too easily make the solution into one about changing people's hearts and less about changing ideologies. Moreover, it also personalizes matters that implicate not only individuals but social institutions like nation-states. Using hate to explain Omar Mateen also too readily conflates an Islamophobic narrative that misnames Islam as a religion of hate. The violence at the Pulse nightclub cannot then be understood as the contempt of a lone individual but the result of a heteropatriarchal ideology that cannot be relegated to the predations of a particular religious community or region in the world. In this way, this chapter is in dialogue with Rebecca Solnit's piece in this volume. In it, she insists that we confront sexual violence as a phenomenon that is social rather than personal in origin. She cautions us away from explanations that locate violence within a particular social group: "Violence doesn't have a race, class, religion, or nationality."[2]

Whether Mateen was motivated by unrequited queer love and whether he was driven by religious radicalism are questions that may never be settled and are not the point of this essay. I am interested instead in the explanations of Mateen's behavior that don't rely on individualizing the reasons that people were murdered at the nightclub. I am more interested in those explanations that tried to get at the social reasons for what happened that night and how those explanations turn us back to social entities such as nations (particularly the United States) and their investments in racial, gender, sexual, and ethnic violence.

The explanations that do not condition Mateen's acts on whether or not he belonged to ISIS or whether or not he was gay are particularly significant. These responses focus alternatively on the social aggression that led him to kill the clubgoers in the first place. For instance, in his blog post Jack Halberstam wrote, "In other queer clubs, on other nights, other bodies have fallen victim to the toxic masculinities that imagine violence as the solution to shifts in the status quo that might shake up hierarchies of sex and gender. But on this night, in this club, the target of steroid fueled, militaristic, narcissistic, deeply conflicted masculinity was a group of mostly Latino gay men."[3]

In his article about the killings, the novelist Justin Torres located that toxicity within the borders of the United States. "Outside, there's a world that politicizes every aspect of your identity," writes Torres. "There are preachers, of multiple faiths, mostly self-identified Christians, condemning you to hell. Outside, they call you an abomination. Outside, there is a news media that acts as if there are two sides to a debate over trans people using public bathrooms. Outside, there is a presidential candidate who has built a platform on erecting a wall between the United States and Mexico—and not only do people believe that crap is possible, they believe it is necessary. Outside, Puerto Rico is still a colony, being allowed to drown in debt, to suffer, without the right to file for bankruptcy, to protect itself. Outside, there are more than 100 bills targeting you, your choices, your people, pending in various states."[4] Torres and Halberstam both account for the murders at the nightclub not in terms of Mateen's pathologies or external terrorist threats but by locating them in social forces that are at work within this nation. By turning to the long history of toxic masculinities' relationships to homophobia, Halberstam disrupts the narrative that displaces homophobia onto Muslim communities and refutes the myth of American exceptionalism. And in contrast to the narrative that tried to suture Mateen's actions to his identifications with ISIS, Torres places the violence of that night within the everyday poisons of homophobia, racism, colonialism, and xenophobia.

For many of us, the horror of the killings was followed by the curious presumption that homophobia was a foreign hatred. It was curious because many of us had seen this violence before. We knew that it did not require an allegiance to ISIS in order to express itself. Rather than being monopolized by a single national or religious formation, homophobia—as Torres suggests—extends to them all. In a moment in which there was every effort to sustain an Islamophobic narrative, the most critical versions of queerness arose to bear witness to the breadth of homophobic aggression, which extends way beyond national and religious boundaries.

Bearing witness to the extent of that aggression and other hatreds like it is more crucial than ever. The increase in the number of white nationalist groups in the United States during Donald Trump's candidacy and subsequent election, the burning of mosques, and the desecration of Jewish cemeteries suggest that what happened at the Pulse was not an isolated event. It is part of a larger wave of violence that implicates not only ISIS but American society as well. In his study of international socialist movements and their response to the global growth of fascism, the British historian G. D. H. Cole argued, "Before Hitler, Mussolini had built Italian Fascism round the cult of the nation, conceived as essentially an assertive power group, activated by a collective 'social egoism' in its dealings with the rest of the world, and inspired by a cult of 'violence' that exalted violence and cruelty into virtues when they were manifested in the cause of the nation so conceived of."[5] We see the versatility and destructiveness of this social egoism as it attempts to make virtues out of transphobia, homophobia, antisemitism, xenophobia, Islamophobia, settler colonialism, anti-Black racism, and ableism. Rather than relegating a social problem to one region of the world, the killings seem to call attention to how varieties of nationalism around the globe are providing the ground on which fascism might have a brand new and multirouted run.

9 Wounds of White Supremacy

UNDERSTANDING THE EPIDEMIC OF VIOLENCE AGAINST BLACK AND BROWN TRANS WOMEN/FEMMES

Croix A. Saffin

One of the most egregious realities that many trans persons encounter is that of violence. From verbal abuse, street harassment, sexual and physical assault, to brutal murder, transgender people are the targets of many of the most vicious and blatant forms of violence. The National Coalition of Anti-Violence Programs (NCAVP) reports that in 2017 transgender or gender-nonconforming people represented 39 percent of the hate violence committed against LGBTQ persons nationally.[1] Since 2013, when the Human Rights Campaign began collecting data, over two hundred transgender people have been killed in the United States, and more trans people were killed in 2020 than in any other recorded time in U.S. history.[2] This transphobic and cissexist violence is not random, nor is it an aberrant act committed by a handful of hateful individuals. It represents a systemic pattern of dehumanization and oppression within the larger U.S. society that sends a message not only to the immediate trans victim but to the larger communities who bear witness: you are not welcome, you are not safe, you are not valued, you are disposable, and you do not matter.

Unfortunately, these hate-violence statistics do not come close to capturing the true number of crimes committed against transgender persons. Even though the Matthew Shepard and James Byrd Jr. Hate Crimes

Prevention Act was passed in 2009, expanding the 1969 U.S. federal hate-crime law to include crimes motivated by a victim's actual or perceived gender or gender identity, reporting hate crimes to the FBI is not mandatory.[3] In 2019, only 2,172 law enforcement agencies out of about 15,000, or less than 15 percent, reported hate-crime data.[4] Furthermore, many trans persons do not report experiences of harassment or violence due to distrust and fear of revictimization by police. The National Center of Transgender Equality found that in 2019, 58 percent of transgender people who interacted with law enforcement within the last year reported harassment, abuse, or other forms of mistreatment by police.[5] Thus, because of mistreatment, dehumanization, and abuse by a largely transphobic and cissexist criminal justice system, transgender people often risk additional harm and trauma if they report. Moreover, there is extensive misgendering of trans people by police and media outlets when reporting does occur. According to an analysis by Media Matters for America, almost two out of every three transgender murder victims in 2020 were misgendered by police, major U.S. news organizations, or both.[6] In total, 23 out of 37 transgender people who were killed in the United States in 2020 were misgendered or "deadnamed." And of the 139 news articles written about these deaths, only 18 were updated or corrected to reflect the victim's gender identity or to remove language that misgendered them.[7] Due to these cumulative factors, violence against trans persons is significantly underreported and unaccounted for.

But trans people do not occupy one homogenous category of identity. Race, class, sexual orientation, gender presentation, occupation, nationality, religion, ability, and age all factor into a trans person's overall safety (or lack thereof) in society. And while data is incomplete and incidents of violence against trans people are underreported, what the statistics do show over and over again is that Black and Brown trans women/femmes are disproportionately targeted for violence. In 2020, 68 percent of trans murder victims were Black or Latinx women/femmes, and since 2013, two-thirds of all known trans victims of fatal violence have been Black women.[8] A war is being waged against Black and Brown trans women/femmes in the United States. And this war is caused by systemic white supremacy that fuels racism, economic inequality, and transmisogyny.[9] It is important to understand how these systems of dehumanization and oppression operate together in order to more accurately understand and combat societal violence. Black and Brown trans women/femmes deserve safety and protection. They deserve the freedom to walk and live and work without harassment and harm. They deserve justice, liberation, affirmation, love, and joy. Black and Brown trans women/femmes deserve a world where they can thrive, not just survive.[10]

#SAYHERNAME

In July 2018, Sasha Garden, a twenty-seven-year-old Black trans woman who lived in Orlando, Florida, was found dead from traumatic injuries in a parking lot behind an apartment complex. Mulan Montrese Williams, an advocate for transgender women and outreach coordinator for the HIV/AIDS organization Miracle of Love, knew Sasha and was asked by police to identify the body. Williams stated that Sasha was a sex worker who was saving money to transition and become a hairstylist and believed that Sasha was likely working when she was killed.[11] Despite Montrese Williams correcting deputies on her own identity as a trans woman (not a transvestite, as they were calling her) and informing the Orange County Police that the body she was identifying was of a trans woman whose name was Sasha, in the official report police described Sasha as a twenty-seven-year-old man from Jacksonville, who "was wearing a wig and was dressed as a female."[12] Orlando television stations followed suit with headlines that described her as a "man in a wig" and a "man dressed as a woman."[13] Local LGBTQ groups described the media and police reports as a "desecration of her memory," and several of Sasha's close friends gathered to demand justice; however, no charges or arrests were ever made in Sasha's murder.[14]

Like Sasha's, several other recent antitransgender deaths from hate violence reveal glaring similarities. For example, Celine Walker, a thirty-six-year-old Black transgender woman, was found fatally shot in a hotel room in Jacksonville, Florida. Celine was repeatedly misgendered by police and in initial media reports, even after loved ones reached out numerous times to request corrections.[15] Sasha Wall, a twenty-nine-year-old Black transgender woman, was found dead in the driver's seat of a still-running car, shot multiple times at close range, in a rural area of Chesterfield County,

South Carolina. Sasha was misgendered in initial media reports.[16] Diamond Stephens, a thirty-nine-year-old Black transgender woman, was killed in Meridian, Mississippi, after suffering a gunshot wound to the head. Family members said Diamond was driving home to get ready for work when she was killed. Meridian police report that she was found dead in the driver's seat of her van, and investigators suspect that one or two other individuals may have been present in the vehicle when she was shot. Diamond was misgendered in initial media reports, delaying advocates' awareness of the incident.[17] Londonn Moore, a twenty-year-old Black trans woman, was found shot to death in a remote area of North Port, Florida. Police investigators tracked down Moore's missing vehicle in nearby Port Charlotte and believe that the suspect may have driven the car there from the crime scene. Moore was misgendered in initial reports, delaying awareness of her death until it was reported to transgender advocates.[18] Ciara Minaj Carter Frazier, a thirty-one-year-old Black transgender woman, was found fatally stabbed on the West Side of Chicago. According to officials, Ciara was killed and her body left in an abandoned building. Transgender advocate Monica Roberts stated that Ciara's body was mutilated before she was discovered by authorities.[19] These are just a handful of the transgender people who experienced fatal violence recently, and the vast majority of these murders remain unsolved.

The disproportionate rates of violence committed against Black, Indigenous, and Latinx trans women / trans femmes are a result of systems of oppression—white supremacy, racism, cissexism, transmisogyny, and sexism—working concurrently.[20] These systems of oppression impede access to social, economic/material, and emotional resources. White supremacy, racism, and sexism in lesbian, gay, bi, and trans communities lead many trans women/femmes of color to not feel supported, whole, valued, seen, or accepted in the queer community. Coupled with the structural realities of racism and possible rejection from their own racial/ethnic communities due to cissexism/transphobia, many BIPOC trans women/femmes have limited social and economic support systems in place.[21] Without these support systems, some trans folks may turn to criminalized work, such as sex work, out of economic necessity. Many experience unstable housing because they have left home due to emotional/physical violence from family members or are struggling to find *any* job as a trans woman/femme, much less a job that pays a livable wage. Poverty, houselessness, and stigma for being trans, which are exacerbated by racism and sexism, lead to increased vulnerability, instability, dehumanization, and oppression. And the result of all of these systems of oppression working together is violence.

This systemic, patterned violence against Black and Brown trans women/femmes should merit a public outcry. But it doesn't. In fact, even within the queer community, few, if any, LGBTQ persons are familiar with these names or stories. They may be "remembered" by queer groups and communities on Transgender Day of Remembrance (November 20) or included in a hashtag, but there is little in the form of active mobilization efforts. And while racism in the queer community, cissexism/transphobia in communities of color, economic inequality, and transmisogyny/sexism all operate together to exacerbate violence and harm against Black and Brown trans women/femmes, the source fueling these systems is white supremacy.

QUEER WHITE SUPREMACY

Many Black and Brown trans women/femmes cannot seek refuge in the larger LGBT community because of pervasive racism and white supremacy. From the white-run gay bars and clubs of the 1950 and '60s, where queers of color were not welcome, to the multiple forms of identification more recently asked of Black queer patrons for entrance into gay bars in the Castro, racism, both historical and contemporary, abound within the queer community.[22] Of late, there has been strident criticism from many white gay men about the addition of black and brown colors to the rainbow flag (which were added to be more inclusive of LGBTQ folks of color). Some gay white men are opposed to the addition because the rainbow stripes were historically chosen to reflect the spectrum of color in nature, not skin color.[23] Additionally, a blatant whitewashing of history recently occurred with the release of the film *Stonewall*. In the film, a white, masculine gay male was featured as the main protagonist throwing the first brick to incite the Stonewall riots, instead of Marsha P. Johnson, a Black trans woman/femme, erasing the significant presence Black trans women/

femmes have had as historical actors and activists in the queer community. Moreover, numerous Black queers have reported discriminatory policies in gay bars across the country. For example, in Washington, DC, reports document cover charges only occurring on nights with predominately Black patrons, and glassware as well as certain liquors, like Hennessy, are removed when events cater to Black customers.[24] Furthermore, queer folks of color are often discriminated against, fetishized, stereotyped, and/or objectified on gay dating sites like Grindr and Tinder, and in the broader queer dating culture. Statements like "no Blacks, no Asians" or "no chocolate, no curry, no rice, no spice" are pervasive and couched as a "sexual preference" (not racism) by white gay folks.[25] And, many white queers fail to recognize the need for all-Black or -Brown spaces within the queer community. The lack of presence, visibility, participation, and leadership of BIPOC within the LGBT community is a result of racism. Whiteness is normalized within the community. For example, during the 2020 Pride month in North Carolina, white queers stated that a Black pride was "not necessary" because Pride is "inclusive," stating their support for Black Lives Matter as "proof" of their inclusivity.[26] White queers may think they are being inclusive, but many Black and Brown queers feel, think, and say differently. Accounts such as these are all too familiar to queers of color, and many feel excluded, exploited, and patronized by the dominant white gay organizations.

The white-dominated queer community, like white U.S. society in general, has taken a colorblind approach to conceptualizing race since the civil rights movement of the 1960s. Within this approach, racism gets equated with legal de jure segregation (and hence racism becomes a phenomenon of history's past), and acts of racism are committed by "bad" individuals who intentionally, consciously, and maliciously cause harm to other persons because of their race.[27] Most white people will cite their friend, neighbor, coworker, or partner of color as "proof" that they are inclusive (not participating in racial segregation) and thus are not racist. And most whites do not see themselves as individuals who actively, consciously, and intentionally discriminate against BIPOC or wish to cause harm to people of color. Instead, they are "good" people who "do not have a racist bone in their body." Racists, then, get typified as extremist, white supremacists who actively hate BIPOC and seek to threaten or harm them.

And since the vast majority of white people do not fall under that category, racism, then, is thought of as an aberration.

White queer folks are not immune from this colorblind thinking, and this fuels oppression and marginalization of queer BIPOC within the community. When white queer people employ colorblindness, we act as though racism is an anomalous experience for BIPOC in our community. In doing so, we fail to take responsibility for our own white supremacy and we fail to see the ways that institutional oppression, whiteness, and power function. In the queer community, whiteness is normalized and the white gay experience stands for the universal queer experience. Whites run most queer organizations, white cis gay men define LGBTQ political agendas, and white queers are visibly represented and their voices centralized in queer movements. Organizing around experiences of oppression due to sexual orientation without also taking into account race (or class, gender, ability) results in more oppression to BIPOC who are queer. Colorblindness is a form of white supremacy and racism, and the queer community is largely failing to acknowledge, name, and address this. As queer Black author and activist George Johnson states as he reflects on the fiftieth anniversary of the Stonewall riots in 2019:

> We watch violence occurring at alarming rates in the Black queer community while rainbow capitalism continues to dominate an "inclusion" conversation that never seems to *include* us . . . While Black queer people are still fighting for survival, white queer people were fighting for marriage equality. This is not to say that marriage equality isn't important, but it is certainly not the only fight. Although we all share the same oppressors, white queer folks must come to terms with the fact that they play a role in the harm experienced by Black and Brown queer folks—a problem they could stop if they acknowledge the privilege they have, this month and every month.[28]

When racism is relegated to the periphery of a white-dominated gay political agenda and race is minimized as a salient component shaping one's lived experiences, finding safety, belonging, and empowerment as a person of color in the queer community is typically bleak. This is especially true for Black and Brown trans women/femmes who, in addition to experiences of racism from the queer community and larger U.S. society, also experience institutionalized cissexism/transphobia, sexism, and marginalization by BIPOC communities.

ANTI-QUEERNESS IN COMMUNITIES OF COLOR

Many Black and Brown trans women/femmes are also rejected from their biological families or racial/ethnic communities because of cissexism/transphobia. Cissexism permeates all communities, and communities of color are no more cissexist/transphobic than white communities. What is different is that because of hundreds of years of persecution, violence, marginalization, discrimination, unequal opportunity, and hatred in a white supremacist and systemically racist society, BIPOC communities have organized around race in order to resist oppression. And if race and a shared experience of racism become *the* major uniting factors for the community to organize around, other identities or issues, such as sexual orientation or gender, become either secondary or seen as a threat to community solidarity because attention is taken away from discussions of and mobilization around race and racism. So, many queers of color face an identity bind: be out as who you are as a queer person and face possible rejection, hostility, or neglect from the racial/ethnic community that you lean on for support to help you navigate and cope with racism/white supremacy or keep your sexuality or gender identity hidden and invisible, oftentimes having to then lead a secret double life, but maintain the community connection. Both options leave queers of color hurt and their identities fragmented.

Religion, particularly Christianity, has been used by many communities of color to strengthen community ties, find solace in racial oppression, and organize. For example, much political organizing and resistance during the civil rights movement came out of the Black church. The church is also a space where many BIPOC communities have the ability to lead and govern themselves outside of the presence of whiteness. Religious leaders of color tend to community needs, listen, mentor, guide, and provide material, spiritual, and emotional support. The church provides a ritualized space for bonding as a community and sharing emotions: celebrating major life events, like a marriage or birth of a child, grieving the loss of a community member at funerals, or even processing major current events that impact the community. The church is also a space that is often financially dependent on community donations and tithing, meaning, economically, the BIPOC community invests and fiscally sustains it. Financially controlling and owning something within your own community is particularly powerful in a society where so many folks of color lack access to property, home, or business ownership. For all of these reasons, religion and the church play a foundational role in communities of color.

But with these strong ties to religion and the church also comes antiqueer rhetoric. Queerness, according to most Christian teachings and beliefs, is perceived as immoral and sinful. Across many Christian sects, biblical interpretations are used to condemn queerness, which can elicit intense feelings of shame, guilt, and self-hatred amongst many queer people. In communities already experiencing oppression, such as BIPOC communities, queerness can be perceived as a threat to the heterosexual family and the community as a whole because queer relationships and queer sex are outside of dominant cis-het norms. Queers who challenge or play with gender scripts and roles, who do not identify with the sex they were assigned at birth, who have sex for pleasure (not just procreation), who use sex toys, engage in kink, who identify as neither boys nor girls, who desire folks of the same gender, or who redefine relationships outside of heterosexual, monogamous marriage go against the idealized image of the "proper," "upstanding," "moral," and "respectable" nuclear family/partnership. The cis-het nuclear family/partnership is often used as a political strategy (called respectability politics) by BIPOC communities for gaining acceptance in and by white society. The premise of respectability politics is that in order for communities of color to be treated better and gain more opportunities and acceptance in a white supremacist society, you must conform to the standards maintained by dominant mainstream white society.[29] Queers of color, then, because they operate outside of this "respectability" standard, can be seen as a threat to potential racial uplift, which can result in ostracism and rejection from friends, family, and/or community members of color.

Consequently, many queers of color feel they have to hide their queerness in order to be accepted within their larger racial or ethnic community. Hiding a core part of oneself inevitably has damaging and poor mental health outcomes. There are very few studies that document and measure the impacts of social oppression on queer people of color's mental health.[30] What can be surmised, though, is that queers of color face barriers to accessing mental health resources and that, for a queer person of color, there are heightened forms of stress, depression, and suicidal ideations coupled with feelings of internalized shame, fear, rejection, guilt, isolation, and loneliness. In part, the stress, shame, and fear of rejection come from the pressure of being forced to choose between primarily identifying with one's race or with one's sexuality/gender expression (and not feeling that one can be whole). For some queer BIPOC, this fear may drive them to feeling that leaving home is their only way to survive as who they are. For Black and Brown trans women/femmes, leaving or being expelled from home and from the racial/ethnic community means losing support while facing the realities of white supremacy and racism. It means not being able to find consolation in the queer community. It often results in Black and Brown trans women/femmes finding one another to build a chosen family and supportive community with.

RACIALIZED ECONOMIC INEQUALITY

White supremacy and systemic racism result in race-based class inequality. For Black, Indigenous, and Latinx folks, differences in wealth, income, home ownership, and joblessness are stark in comparison to whites. In fact, over the last three decades, the racial wealth divide for Black and Latinx families compared to whites has grown.[31] Racialized inequalities result in a disproportionate number of Black, Indigenous, and Latinx folks living in poverty. According to the 2018 U.S. Census data, the poverty rate of BIPOC was drastically higher than—and in fact, double that of—whites. Blacks had a poverty rate of 21 percent, "Hispanics" 18 percent, and Native Americans 25 percent, compared to whites and Asians, whose poverty rate was 10 percent.[32] These numbers demonstrate that gross economic disparities exist for Black, Indigenous, and Latinx communities, resulting in food, housing, and employment hardships and less access to economic/material resources and stability.

Racialized economic inequity and less access to economic and material resources are compounded for Black and Brown trans women/femmes. According to the National LGBTQ Task Force, Black trans people have a 26 percent unemployment rate, which is twice as high as the unemployment rate for transgender people of all racial/ethnic backgrounds, and four times as high as the unemployment rate in the general population.[33] The study also found that 41 percent of Black trans people have been homeless (more than five times the general population), 34 percent of Black trans people have household incomes less than $10,000 (more than eight times the general population), and nearly half of the Black trans population have attempted suicide.[34] The National Center for Transgender Equality also reports that 38 percent of Black trans people report living in poverty, compared to just 12 percent of the U.S. population and 29 percent of transgender people overall.[35] Fifty-one percent of Black trans women also reported experiencing homelessness/houselessness at some point in their life.

Moreover, harassment and violence against trans persons of all racial and ethnic backgrounds are rampant in schools, and many drop out or are kicked out before finishing. This leads to less opportunity in a job market that already severely discriminates against trans persons. Many trans folks are fearful of applying to jobs because their legal documents, driver's license/state-issued ID, or other paperwork reflect their deadname or show a differing gender than they identify as. Up until the Supreme Court's recent landmark *Bostock* decision in June of 2020, transgender people were not granted any federal antidiscrimination protections in employment and could be fired for transitioning on the job or when a trans person's gender identity came to the attention of a supervisor.[36] These fears, coupled with transphobia in employment, leave many trans persons with few opportunities to live economically secure lives.

In addition to food, housing, and employment inequities, transgender folks also face barriers to getting the health care that they need, placing them in a more vulnerable position. One of five transgender adults is uninsured.[37] Trans people often skip health care because of cost: nearly half (48 percent) have postponed medical care when sick or injured and avoided preventive care (50 percent) because they couldn't afford it.[38] Trans people often hide their gender identities from health providers out of fear of discriminatory treatment and harassment. Only 40 percent of trans people report being out to all their medical providers, 28 percent of trans people report experiencing verbal harassment in a medical setting, and 19 percent report having been refused medical care by providers because of their gender identity. Because of stigmatization and harassment, 28 percent of trans people report avoiding care altogether.[39] These inequities in health care have a disproportionate impact on Black,

Indigenous, and Latinx trans women/femmes who are already mistreated and discriminated against by the healthcare industry.[40]

Attacks on transgender access to health care and homeless services/shelters were perpetuated by the Trump administration in 2020. In June, the Trump administration sought to eliminate transgender protection as part of the Affordable Care Act, which would allow healthcare providers/insurers to refuse treatment to trans folks on religious grounds.[41] Similarly, in September of 2020, the Trump administration also proposed a rollback of the Equal Access Rule created in 2016 by the U.S. Department of Housing and Urban Development (HUD), which ensured emergency housing and homeless shelters be open to all eligible individuals and families regardless of gender identity, sexual orientation, or marital status.[42] This Trump administration proposal permitted sex-segregated shelters to discriminate against transgender people based on religious grounds and stated that shelter placement determinations should be based solely on biological sex and not gender identity, eliminated self-identification from its definition of gender identity, and allowed shelters to demand evidence of biological sex if they had a "good faith belief" that a person seeking access is not of the sex the shelter serves.[43] While it is unlikely that the Biden administration will uphold these rollbacks on gender identity protections, religious exemptions continue to be subject to interpretation based on who is in office.[44]

White supremacy and racism cause vast wealth and income gaps, less access to home or business ownership, greater rates of poverty and houselessness, and discrimination in employment and healthcare for BIPOC. These inequities are exacerbated for Black, Indigenous, and Latinx trans women/femmes who have limited avenues of economic support and stability. And poverty, coupled with racism and cissexism, leads to greater vulnerability, oppression, and potential experiences of violence.

TRANSMISOGYNY/TRANSMISOGYNOIR AND SEXISM

Like cis women, trans women/femmes experience individual and systemic levels of oppression, ranging from physical and sexual objectification and discrimination at all levels of society to routine harassment, assault, and violence by cis men. Gender-based violence is rooted in patriarchal gender norms where men are socialized into and rewarded for conforming to masculine traits associated with superiority and dominance, such as being aggressive, strong, powerful, independent, invulnerable, and controlling. Women are socialized into feminine traits associated with inferiority and submission, such as being passive, weak, dependent, emotional, and powerless. This socialization results in unequal power between men/masc and women/femme and fuels sexism. Because patriarchal society devalues the traits of femininity and normalizes (even glorifies and celebrates) violence as a legitimate expression of masculinity, violence against women/femmes is pervasive.

But in a cis-het, patriarchal society, trans women/femmes experience an exacerbated form of sexism, often manifesting through violence, because they are both trans and feminine. The Human Rights Campaign has estimated that trans women are 4.3 times more likely to become homicide victims than cis women.[45] And trans women are more likely than cis women to experience sexual violence.[46] Violence occurs because trans women/femmes are seen as "choosing" (even desiring and valuing) femininity in a society that says being femme is inferior. Violence, then, is used to punish trans women/femmes for this transgression and to assert male/masculine dominance. Trans women/femmes also call attention to the fact that gender is changeable. Many trans women/femmes report that their visible transgender status makes them particularly vulnerable to male violence.[47] For example, Tiffany Mathieu, a Black trans woman living in New York, states that she has been assaulted at least one hundred times: on the subway, walking down the street, in her own home, and by NYPD officers.[48] She contends that violence is not just physical, but forms of verbal harassment (mostly transphobic slurs) "follow her wherever she goes."[49] So much of our society organizes itself around the rigid, mutually exclusive categories of male/female or man/woman. The presence and visibility of trans (and nonbinary) folks shows how false this binary actually is, and because that threatens dominant cis society, violence can result. Transmisogynistic violence can also be a reaction by threatened cis-het men. More than half of all trans people experience intimate partner violence in their lifetimes, and the most common perpetrators of violence against trans women/femmes are intimate partners.[50] If a cis-het man is attracted to a trans woman/femme person and does not know that the other person is trans, many cis-het men feel they are being "deceived" or "tricked" and thus can engage and justify transmisogynistic violence.[51] This is so pervasive that an offensive slur, "trap," is often applied to trans women/femmes who are thought to be presenting as women in order to intentionally deceive men. Furthermore, as trans activist Alyssa Pariah, states, "Most of the trans women I know who've been murdered by men are murdered by men they were dating who knew they were trans. You're dealing with secondhand transphobia—maybe someone in [his] life found out that the woman that [he's] seeing and loving is trans, and it makes [him] nervous. And they're killing our friends and family." Because toxic masculinity is deeply rooted in homo/transphobia and sexism, a cis-het man's heterosexuality and masculinity are called into question if they are dating a trans woman/femme, usually by other cis-het men. Cis-het men can feel shamed for loving a trans woman/femme by other cis-het men, and because their heterosexuality and masculinity are threatened, they respond with violence.

Systems of white supremacy and racism interlock and function concurrently with transmisogyny and cissexism/sexism, causing disproportionate amounts of violence directed toward Black and Brown trans women/femmes. While the overall murder rate for the U.S. is 1 in 19,000 per year, the murder rate for Black trans women/femmes is 1 in 2,600, more than seven times as high as that of the general population.[52] According to the National Center for Transgender Equality, Black and Latinx transgender women are more likely to be physically attacked because of being transgender compared to Black/Latinx non-binary people and transgender men.[53] And many trans folks do not seek help with violence from police, who routinely harass, abuse, assault, or mistreat Black and Brown trans women/femmes.[54] In responding to the murder of two Black trans women in Dallas in 2018, Rev. Louis Mitchell, an African American trans man, outlines, "There's a number of reasons black trans women are disproportionately affected by violence. The combination of racism and misogyny and the disregard for black women has always been a factor, so I'm not surprised it's landing on this population. There's not a lot of mystery, when you're stacking up oppression, its gonna hit black trans women the hardest."[55]

Black trans women/femmes are most often killed by Black cisgender men.[56] While on the surface this statistic may look as if white supremacy is not causing transmisogynistic violence, white supremacy is playing a foundational role in several ways. Every race is likely to be killed by their own race due to racial segregation and who is in close proximity to you, which is a direct result of white supremacy.[57] Focusing on "Black-on-Black" crime, without examining the causes of crime to start with (such as poverty, inequitable school funding, segregation, housing/employment discrimination, systemic incarceration, and police violence), is also a way to decenter conversations away from race and white supremacy. Black cis men's violence toward Black trans women/femmes is about asserting dominance and power in a white supremacist system that systematically denies Black men power that they feel they should be entitled to as men. If patriarchal white society defines traditional masculine gender roles and manhood as being tough, hard, dominant, in control, a leader, provider/breadwinner, aggressive, competitive, and self-reliant, but because of racism/white supremacy, Black men, on average, are not able to provide economically for their families, protect themselves or their families from violence or crime if they live in poverty, experience discrimination and disproportionate punishment in schools, and are under constant surveillance through racial profiling and/or threats from police and citizens, Black men can respond with violence to regain masculinity. When cis men's masculinity is threatened, anger and potential violence follow to regain dominance and control. We see this currently with the Coronavirus pandemic. Amid an increase in financial instability, unemployment, and stress, rates of intimate-partner violence around the globe have spiked.[58] Many men are angry, frustrated, depressed, and scared. All of those emotions are in opposition to what men are "supposed to" be and feel, so there is a crisis of masculinity. And the result is directing violence toward those you can exert power over: women. For Black and Brown trans women/femmes, violence is pronounced. As Beverly Tillery, executive director of the NYC Anti-Violence Project, states, "Not only are members of this community trans, but they are also black, women and often poor. All of the discrimination results in people often living lives that are just more vulnerable to violence. You have a job that is more tenuous, you live in places that are more tenuous. And in addition to all that, people look at you and they don't care about your existence and they don't value your life."[59]

SEX WORK: WORKING ON THE MARGINS

In the United States, buying and selling sex is criminalized (illegal) everywhere except for a few counties in Nevada. Despite no federal law banning sex work, states and cities craft their own regulations and penalties for engaging in sex work. In some states, such as Arizona and Florida, repeated arrests for doing sex work can result in a felony conviction and prison time.[60] In other states, like New York, sex work–related offenses are misdemeanors, punishable with fines and other penalties.[61] But even then, people arrested on sex work charges may be jailed until trial if they can't make bail. Authors Molly Smith and Juno Mac maintain in their book *Revolting Prostitutes: The Fight for Sex Workers' Rights* that tens of thousands of people are arrested, prosecuted, incarcerated, deported, or fined for sex work–related offenses in the United States every year.[62]

All sex workers are at an increased risk of violence because of criminalization. Criminalization of the commercial exchange of voluntary, consensual adult sexual services makes sex workers more vulnerable to rape, robbery, assault, harassment, intimidation, and stalking by both clients and police. Criminalization results in greater surveillance, scrutiny, and persecution of sex workers by police. Human Rights Watch has conducted research on sex work around the globe, including the United States, and has repeatedly and routinely found that police officers harass, extort, physically and verbally abuse, bribe, rob, coerce, and/or rape sex workers.[63] Criminalization also makes sex workers more vulnerable to violence because they are stigmatized by the larger society and thus regularly dehumanized by clients and police. For example, in recounting her treatment by police, Tamika Spellman, a thirty-year sex worker in Washington, DC, states, "I've had them call me names, tell me that I was stupid, that whatever happened to me out there, I deserved it for being out there." She has been sexually assaulted by officers and says, "This is something that you can find across the board with sex workers . . . [police] take advantage of us."[64] And because sex work is criminalized, sex workers have to work in unsafe locations or structure their work in such a way to avoid police harassment and arrest. This could mean working in more hidden and isolated conditions, which could be more dangerous.

Furthermore, passage of bills like FOSTA (Fight Online Sex Trafficking Act) and SESTA (Stop Enabling Sex Traffickers Act) by the Trump Administration in 2018 makes it more difficult for sex workers to screen clients and prevents sex workers from having a presence/voice on the internet. FOSTA-SESTA makes website publishers like Craigslist, Eros, Google, or Reddit responsible if third parties are found to offer sex work on their platforms. The ostensible goal of these bills is to try to shut down websites that facilitate sex trafficking. But the impact this has on sex workers is that it makes work scarcer and therefore some sex workers may engage in more risk-taking behaviors. Instead of screening clients, negotiating terms, rates, and boundaries online from the privacy of a home, many sex workers now must connect with clients and work on the streets. Prior to FOSTA-SESTA, some websites even offered tools to help sex workers vet potential clients through shared blacklists of dangerous clients, but if sex workers need work in order to live, they may accept clients who have been blacklisted or who have crossed boundaries with workers.[65] New York sex worker Danielle Blunt stated, "Whenever we lose access to internet spaces, there has been a devastating effect on the community and the community's ability to support themselves, to take care of themselves, to make money, and to screen clients and stay safe."[66] Moreover, FOSTA-SESTA limits the ability of sex workers to advertise, which decreases financial stability. While some websites for advertising still remain, most require fees to place ads. FOSTA-SESTA is essentially systematically forcing many sex workers onto the streets, resorting to working with agencies or pimps, and increasing their exposure to violence.

Criminalization of sex work and passage of bills like FOSTA-SESTA has other serious consequences for sex workers. On top of stigma and police violence, many sex workers struggle to secure stable housing. Under the Fair Criminal Record Screening for Housing Act of 2016, it is illegal for landlords to look into an applicant's criminal record before they offer them conditional housing.[67] However, a housing provider can deny an application after the offer is made if the applicant has been convicted of a crime within seven years of the date of application. Given police violence and harassment against sex workers, being arrested and convicted for prostitution, solicitation of prostitution, loitering with the intend to prostitute, or other subjective laws, such as giving a massage without a license, is certainly a reality.[68] Many landlords also ask for proof of employment or pay stubs to show that you will be able to afford rent, and they can inquire into your credit history before offering housing. Most sex workers, then, have to lie or they are denied housing. For other sex workers, economic instability and work scarcity as a result of FOSTA-SESTA or COVID means not being able to afford housing on their own and thus living in motels, exchanging sex for housing, couch surfing with friends, living in shelters, or living on the streets.

Banking discrimination also poses a major hurdle to sex workers. Following the passage of FOSTA-SESTA, the End Banking for Human Traffickers Act of 2019 was passed. This act increases pressure on banks to shut down the accounts of anyone suspected of engaging in trafficking. Since trafficking and sex work are often used interchangeably in legislation and banks are seeking to eliminate any potential liability, sex worker credit cards and banking accounts are being frozen and canceled more frequently and indiscriminately, leaving sex workers in a more perilous place economically. Sex worker Bianca Baker described to the *Huffington Post* that she tried to use her debit card for a purchase and it was declined despite the thousands of dollars she had in her account. After several phone calls and in-person visits to Bank of America, she was told that her account was shut down for "suspicious activity" and, eventually, that it was because she was a sex worker.[69] Furthermore, many banks and institutions include morality clauses in their terms of service allowing them to freeze and terminate sex worker accounts at will.[70] Payment platforms like Venmo, PayPal, and CashApp are currently suspending many sex worker accounts as well.

While there has been an increase in legislative scrutiny and criminalization of sex workers, white supremacy/racism and transmisogyny/cissexism function to disproportionately impact Black and Brown trans women/ femmes who engage in sex work. BIPOC are significantly more likely to be arrested for sex work–related offenses than white people.[71] According to Amnesty International, nearly 40 percent of adults and 60 percent of youth arrested for prostitution in the United States in 2015 were Black, even though Black folks only make up about 12 percent of the U.S. population.[72] Trans women/femmes are also especially likely to be arrested on sex work charges, even if they're not doing sex work and just walking down the street. There have been several instances of Black or Brown trans women/femmes being arrested for carrying condoms.[73] Like New York's "stop and frisk" policies that targeted Black and Latinx folks, subjective loitering or disorderly conduct laws are used by police to target, arrest, and harass trans women/femmes who are BIPOC. This surveillance, harassment, and regulation of Black and Brown bodies is not new: it is a product of centuries of white supremacist racialized stereotypes and a way for white cis men to maintain institutionalized control and power. For trans women/femmes of color, engaging in sex work means navigating, maneuvering, and attempting to survive in a system predicated upon racist, sexist, and cissexist stereotypes and enacting systemic violence through criminalization.

CRIMINAL PUNISHMENT SYSTEM

Currently, 2.3 million people are caged in American prisons or jails.[74] But this statistic doesn't come close to capturing the far-reaching impact of state-sponsored violence inflicted on so many individuals and communities in the United States by an oppressive system of punishment and policing. With 4.9 million people formerly incarcerated in state or federal prisons, 19 million people having a felony conviction on their record, 77 million people having a criminal record, and 113 million adults having an immediate family member in jail or prison, the criminal punishment system is besieging.[75] Incarceration and policing results in physical, emotional, spiritual, and economic devastation to individuals and communities, particularly poor, queer BIPOC, who are terrorized by these oppressive systems of "law and order."

The criminal punishment system targets and harms particular communities in disproportionate ways. Poor people are more likely to be incarcerated. People both incarcerated and in jail have median annual incomes 41 percent (prison) and 54 percent (jail) below nonincarcerated people of similar ages.[76] Poor people are also more likely to be harmed by unjust laws and policies that pervade the criminal punishment system, such as use of cash bail as a form of collateral before criminal trials. Most jurisdictions rely on a cash bail system whereby the court determines an amount of money that a person has to pay in order to be released from jail.[77] Those who cannot afford bail are placed in jail (often for weeks or months) until their trial date. Currently, three out of five people in U.S. jails (nearly a half a million people) are detained without having been convicted of a crime: they are simply too poor to afford bail.[78] Cash bail policies are not only oppressive because they criminalize poverty, but they also fuel economic inequality, because many folks who are detained lose their jobs or homes while sitting in jail. Furthermore, while legal representation is appointed to poor folks who cannot afford a lawyer, public defenders are overburdened with excessive caseloads and often encourage guilty pleas in exchange for lesser sentences and going to trial.[79] This results in an individual having a criminal record, making it, then, more difficult to secure employment upon release, fueling a cycle of poverty.

Black and Brown communities, which experience much greater rates of poverty, are also disproportionately impacted. The Black community, for example, comprises 13 percent of the U.S. population, 35 percent of the imprisoned, 42 percent of those on death row, and 56 percent of those serving life sentences.[80] Anti-Blackness and white supremacy in policing have deep historical roots in the United States. From the white slave patrols who captured Black people escaping slavery to the enforcement of Black Codes and vagrancy laws after slavery, whereby Black folks who did not work would be fined or imprisoned, policing and anti-Black law enforcement have always been woven into the fabric of the American criminal punishment system. Police and police violence were used to enforce racial segregation in housing, travel, and public facilities, restrict Black voting, and suppress Black organizing and protesting for rights. Surveillance, harassment, profiling, and imprisonment of Black and Brown folks is not new. It has taken on new forms, but the outcome is the same: systemic control and containment of BIPOC to maintain white supremacy.

Incarceration rates for queer, particularly trans people, are also disproportionate. Nearly one in six transgender people (including 21 percent of transgender women) have been incarcerated at some point in their lives—far higher than the rate for the general population.[81] In part, high rates of incarceration are driven by poverty, lack of access to full-time employment due to stigma, housing instability, and high costs of trans-related medical care in a for-profit health care system which results in some trans folks turning to criminalized industries to get money, which then increases contact between trans folks and police. Pervasive gender policing in society also contributes to high rates of incarceration for trans folks. Having the police or security called for "bathroom violations" is all too common an experience for trans people. Moreover, traffic stops by police, purchasing alcohol or tobacco, getting through airport security, opening a bank account, renting an apartment, receiving medical care or obtaining health insurance, signing up for a mobile phone contract, registering to vote, and seeking employment all require some administrative agent to review a person's proof of identity.[82] If a trans person's legal identification does not match their gender presentation, police can be called because it is suspected that the trans person is engaging in gender identity fraud. Additionally, many trans women/femmes are unduly incarcerated due to narrow interpretations of laws, like self-defense, when they try to protect themselves from physical, verbal, or sexual assault. Trans women/femmes such as CeCe McDonald, Davia Spain, Ms. Campbell, Alisha Walker, GiGi Thomas, Cyntonia Brown, and many more, especially who are BIPOC, are often deemed outside of the protections of "respectable womanhood" and protection, and thus are often charged with murdering their assailants or abusers.[83] Trans women/femmes, particularly who are Black or Brown, do not fit the "perfect victim" narrative, and thus many juries or judges are not sympathetic to the violence or abuse they are experiencing.[84]

Policing, profiling, criminal punishment, and state-sanctioned violence, then, become all too common for Black and Brown trans women/femmes, who live at the intersections of these disproportionately impacted groups. One in five transgender women/femmes (21 percent) is incarcerated at some point in her life.[85] This is far above the general population, and is even higher (47 percent) for Black transgender people.[86] One major reason for this is pervasive harassment, violence, and arrest by police officers. Policing is founded on violence. The state authorizes police to enforce laws and social control through use of force or the threat of force. Transgender people across the United States experience 3.7 times more police violence than cisgender people and are seven times more likely to experience physical violence when interacting with the police compared to cisgender people.[87] Black transgender people report much higher rates of harassment (38 percent) and assault (15 percent) by police officers.[88] And transgender sex workers report elevated and pervasive levels of police violence—this includes 16 percent of all trans people, 34 percent of Latinx trans people, and 53 percent of Black trans people.[89] Police routinely and aggressively target, question, search, strip search, arrest, detain, and assault trans BIPOC for simply daring to be themselves in public spaces. Police also subjectively apply laws against loitering, jaywalking, panhandling, or solicitation, for example, and in doing so, are incentivized for a "job well done."

Black and Brown trans women/femmes experience abuse after being arrested as well. Most trans women are forced into in men's prison facilities, where they experience extremely high rates of sexual and physical violence. Trans people are five times more likely than their cis peers to be sexually assaulted by staff and nine times more likely to be sexually assaulted by fellow inmates.[90] The U.S. Department of Justice also reports that one in three trans women/femmes is sexually assaulted in prison. In response to pervasive physical, sexual, and verbal assault, prisons place trans women/femmes in solitary confinement to "protect them" from the general cis male population.[91] Many trans women/femmes spend indefinite, prolonged periods of time in isolation with little to no judicial oversight.[92] In 2011, the United Nations deemed solitary confinement a form of torture and stated that "segregation, isolation, separation, cellular, lockdown, Supermax, the hole, Secure Housing Unit . . . whatever the name, solitary confinement should be banned by States as a punishment or extortion technique," but trans women/femmes are regularly placed in solitary confinement.[93] Trans women/femmes are also often placed in solitary confinement for disciplinary reasons related to gender identity, such as wearing a cut-up tank top, being in possession of glitter, or crafting a bra out of t-shirt material, which is considered contraband.[94] Moreover, many trans folks are denied transition-related medical care, which can have devastating effects on mental health.

State-sponsored violence against Black/Brown trans women/femmes takes many forms. From police persecution, profiling, and surveillance to punishing poor people through unjust laws and adjudication, Black and Brown trans women/femmes are disproportionately targeted and harmed. But violence by the criminal punishment system is not the result of "a few bad apples" being racist, cissexist, or discriminatory: It is a system designed to control, manage, regulate, and oppress anyone outside of cishet white maleness. In the criminal punishment system, the only "serving and protecting" that is done is in the name of white supremacy.

TRANSFORMATIVE JUSTICE

The horrors of white supremacy enacted through police killings have captured national attention in recent years, predominately through organized social movements like Black Lives Matter. Video footage has provided "proof" of what Black and Brown people have been saying for centuries about violence and harm committed indiscriminately in BIPOC communities by systems of white supremacy, including police. This "proof" has launched national political conversations about banning choke holds, reallocation of police funding, use of technology to increase police accountability, increase of police training, especially around de-escalation, and many other reform measures. While increased publicity and activism are driving conversations about the need for policy changes, the ubiquity of fear, harassment, persecution, and violence experienced by many Black and Brown trans women/femmes remains largely outside of this national focus. In order for a better future to be created by and for Black and Brown transwomen/femmes where harm and violence is no longer routine and queer trans women/femmes of color have the opportunity to live their lives more freely, collective systems of oppression that are rooted in white supremacy must be dismantled and radically reimagined.

Reforms are not enough. While well-intentioned, policy and legal changes to existing structures of oppression and violence simply mutate oppression and violence into new forms. The Equality Act, for example, is a federal bill that legislators have tried to pass for five years. This act would expand federal civil rights law to prohibit LGBTQ and gender identity discrimination in employment, housing, credit, education, public spaces and services, federally funded programs, and jury service.[95] Essentially, this act will explicitly include sexual orientation and gender identity as protected classes under the Civil Rights Act. In 2021, President Biden, on his first day in office, stated:

I was proud to sign an Executive Order on Preventing and Combating Discrimination on the Basis of Gender Identity or Sexual Orientation. I directed agencies to implement the Supreme Court's Bostock ruling, and fully enforce Title VII of the Civil Rights Act of 1964 and other laws that prohibit discrimination on the basis of gender identity or sexual orientation. Now, it's time for Congress to secure these protections once and for all by passing the Equality Act—because no one should ever face discrimination or live in fear because of who they are or whom they love.[96]

Reforming the Civil Rights Act to add protections for sexual orientation and gender identity is welcomed and would strengthen existing protections for queer folks. But like hate-crime legislation where sexual orientation and gender identity is "protected," it is only enacted after someone is already harmed. The structural roots of violence remain intact, and the result is simply placing more people who are found guilty of committing crimes against queer people behind bars, fueling a racist, classist, cissexist system of criminal punishment where individuals are simply locked up, not actively educated about or engaged in repairing the harm they have created. Punished people are caged, further divided from their families and support networks while incarcerated and, if released, will struggle to find employment and housing. The Equality Act, if passed, would mandate that all prisons house transgender inmates according to their gender identity instead of their sex assigned at birth.[97] While this sounds like a solution to the profuse physical, verbal, and sexual violence experienced by trans women/femmes in today's prisons, and would also potentially result in fewer trans folks being placed in solitary confinement, this does not address why so many trans women/femmes, especially Black and Brown trans women/femmes, are in prison/jail to start with. They are imprisoned because of targeted police persecution, white supremacy and racism, unequal access to economic resources and stability through jobs and housing, criminalization of sex work and drugs, and lack of refuge and support in larger queer and BIPOC communities. Both hate-crime legislation and the Equality Act rely on existing oppressive systems and simply seek modifications to the language of the law. BIPOC folks know all too well that legislating equality or protection does not result in equality or protection. Relying on a punitive and oppressive system steeped in violence does not reduce violence; it generates more harm.

The broader, transformative, and radical reimaginings of existing systems of oppression led by Black and Brown trans women/femmes must be centralized, funded, and supported. Mandating reforms, such as implicit bias training for police officers to help them recognize their unconscious biases and hope for less harmful police behavior, doesn't work: systems of oppression founded on and powered by white supremacy are upheld. What many in BIPOC communities, including trans women/femmes, have for decades advocated for that could result in less systemic violence and oppression is decriminalizing sex work and all drugs; redirecting money spent on policing and prisons into community-led social services that would increase food, housing, education, child care, and job security; providing and ensuring access to universal health care, including mental health care and trans-affirming healthcare; reparations—paying Black and Brown communities for the damage that has been inflicted by white supremacy, including police violence; expanding social services for addiction, domestic/intimate partner violence and sexual violence; and finally, individuals unlearning the oppressive systems that we have unquestioningly internalized in ourselves through critical education. At the heart of all these interlocking systems of oppression and violence is white supremacy. In order for true healing, safety, justice, and freedom to flourish in U.S. society, whereby Black and Brown trans women/femmes are empowered, valued, and liberated, white supremacy, and the capitalist, racist, cissexist systems that are fed by white supremacy, must be acknowledged, reimagined, and completely dismantled.

10 On Antisemitism

Judith Butler

There are many ways to approach antisemitism. A study might be dedicated to understanding what antisemitism is, what forms it now takes, and how best to oppose it. Another might ask why there are conflicts about how best to identify antisemitism and try to situate and understand those conflicts in light of their underlying political aims. Still another might set forward the proposition that any analysis of antisemitism ought to be conceptually and politically linked to other forms of racism. And yet another might ask about how the demography and history of the Jewish people are represented in contemporary arguments about antisemitism, or how the history of antisemitism has changed in various times and places. Still another might ask about the conditions under which the charge of antisemitism is made, who makes it, for what purpose, against whom is it leveled and why, and how best to judge whether the charge is justified.

As one seeks to open up these important intellectual questions, one is invariably asked to respond to the urgent ethical and political questions: Is antisemitism wrong? And should it be opposed in all its forms? The

This chapter is reprinted from *On Antisemitism: Solidarity and the Struggle for Justice* by Judith Butler and Jewish Voices for Peace (Haymarket, 2017).

simple and clear answer is: yes. While it is certainly true to say that everyone in this volume agrees that antisemitism is wrong and must be opposed,
it is not at all clear whether there is more generally a single understanding
of what constitutes antisemitism (which acts, practices, forms of speech,
institutions) or how best to conceptualize its workings. Barring a common
understanding of what antisemitism is, it is not at all clear what is being
claimed when one explicitly opposes antisemitism. If we could arrive at a
single or, at least, a minimal definition of antisemitism, then we would not
only be able to explain what we mean when we say that we oppose it, but
we would also be able to bring that definition to bear on particular cases
in order to distinguish, for instance, between charges that are justified and
those that are not.

In our contemporary world, there is a great deal of conflict about how
to identify forms of antisemitism. First, antisemitism is sometimes cloaked
as something else. It takes a fugitive form when, for instance, a discourse
emerges that presumes that there is a group that owns all the banks, or
that actively makes use of conspiracy theories to explain how political
events take place. The word *Jew* hardly has to be mentioned to be already
nefariously at work in such a discourse. The same can be said about any
reference to the "blood libel"—a scurrilous rumor that has been tena-
ciously circulated against the Jewish people for centuries, justifying
attacks on and murders of Jews in eastern Europe. The more explicit
forms of antisemitism not only subscribe to gross generalizations based on
ostensible anatomical or physiological characteristics, the attribution of a
"Jewish character," concocted histories, or the projection of sexual pro-
clivities, but also engage active forms of legal discrimination, for seques-
tration, expulsion, or active oppression or death. Genocide is the most
extreme version of antisemitism, and boycotts against Jewish businesses,
especially in the history of Germany, are also clearly part of the history of
antisemitism. These are all examples of antisemitism, but they do not,
taken together, give us a single definition that could serve our purposes. In
fact, far more important than a single definition of antisemitism would be
an account of its history and its various forms: the language, the attitudes,
actions and practices, the policies. That is the only way to know what it is,
and that means we cannot expect that a single definition will hold for all
cases. Or rather, if we do establish a single definition, it will of necessity be

so broad that we will not be able to say immediately how and when it should be applied. After all, the charge of antisemitism depends on the ability to identify antisemitism in its various instances, and here is where the matter of interpretation does come into play.

Given the contemporary framework in which the matter of antisemitism is discussed, the conflict about how to identify its forms (given that some forms are fugitive) is clearly heightened. The claim that criticisms of the State of Israel are antisemitic is the most highly contested of contemporary views. It is complex and dubious for many reasons. First: What is meant by it? Is it that the person who utters criticisms of Israel nurses antisemitic feelings and, if Jewish, then self-hating ones? That interpretation depends on a psychological insight into the inner workings of the person who expresses such criticisms. But who has access to that psychological interiority? It is an attributed motive, but there is no way to demonstrate whether that speculation is a grounded one. If the antisemitism is understood to be a consequence of the expressed criticism of the State of Israel, then we would have to be able to show in concrete terms that the criticism of the State of Israel results in discrimination against Jews. Of course, it would be a clearly antisemitic belief to say that "all Jews" share a single political position, or that "all Jews" support the State of Israel, or even that "all Jews" are the same as the State of Israel (either that the State represents "all Jews" or that there is no distinction between Jews and the State—it is all a blur). The latter claim rests on a gross stereotype and fails to acknowledge the various viewpoints and political affiliations of Jewish people who have very different histories, locations, and aspirations.

Distinguishing among the very different historical trajectories of Ashkenazi, Sephardic, and Mizrahi Jews breaks up monolithic understandings of what it is to be a Jew and so deprives antisemitism of its noxious habit of vulgar generalization. It also foregrounds the demographic and racial differences among Jews, and it calls into question the way that Jewish history is so often narrated through the lens of European history alone. That some Jews suffer discrimination on the basis of their Arab origins also foregrounds the way that both racism and antisemitism can operate in tandem, but also how intra-Jewish hierarchies are built. Doing a better job of gathering those various histories will not only disrupt antisemitic generalizations, but also replace forms of inequality with a more diverse understanding of who the Jewish people have been and continue to be. Finally, Jews within the Diaspora and within Israel hold a wide range of views about the State of Israel and Zionism more broadly. Is that diversity of viewpoint to be accepted as part of being Jewish, or does a critical position qualify a person—or his or her utterance—as antisemitic? Just as we assume a diversity of viewpoints among Jewish people, so should we assume it about Palestinians and their allies. Is there only one viewpoint to be ascribed to Palestinians? In any case, the notion that the critique of Israel by Jew or non-Jew is antisemitic only makes sense if we accept that the State of Israel is the Jewish people in some sense. Indeed, that particular identification would have to be very firmly consolidated for the position to take hold that criticism of the State of Israel is hatred for, or prejudice against, the Jewish people in general. Of course, when and where those criticisms are accompanied by explicit stereotypes, there are good grounds for seeing antisemitism at work.

But what about the fugitive forms that antisemitism takes? Could we not say that the criticism is silently fueled by antisemitic hatred? That claim is a complex one, since if we accept that antisemitism has conventionally taken fugitive forms, it is clearly possible that it could provide a motivation for some criticisms. But how would one ground that interpretation? On what basis would anyone argue that they know this interpretation to be true? Is the problem that no motivation besides hatred can be imagined for the person who criticizes the State of Israel? Or is it that only someone deeply insensitive to the historical suffering of the Jews would not "see" clearly that hatred continues and now takes the form of the critique of the Israeli state? Whoever holds that view would have to explain whether every criticism of Israel is a sign of an antisemitic motive, or only some criticisms. What difference does it make whether what is criticized is Israeli policies, the occupation, or the structure and legitimation of the State itself? Are only those who voice the latter criticisms eligible for the charge of antisemitism, or does the charge include members of all three groups?

If modern democratic states have to bear criticism, even criticisms about the process by which a state gained legitimation, then it would be odd to claim that those who exercise those democratic rights of critical expression are governed only or predominantly by hatred and prejudice. We could just as easily imagine that someone who criticizes the Israeli state, even the conditions of its founding—coincident with the Nakba, the expulsion of eight hundred thousand Palestinians from their homes—has a passion for justice or wishes to see a polity that embraces equality and freedom for all the people living there. In the case of Jewish Voice for Peace, Jews and their allies come together to demonstrate that Jews must reclaim a politics of social justice, a tradition that is considered to be imperiled by the Israeli state.

So under what conditions does a passion for justice become renamed as antisemitism? It cannot be that the only way to refute the charge of antisemitism in these debates is to embrace injustice, inequality, and dispossession. This would be a cruel bargain indeed. Similarly, when Palestinians call for an end to colonial rule, administrative detention, land confiscation, and violence done against their communities, are they not motivated by a desire for freedom, equality, and economic and political justice? The shared Palestinian desire to be released from colonial rule is surely a reasonable desire, one that is broadly admired and valued in other decolonization struggles (South Africa, Algeria). For that desire to be renamed as fugitive antisemitism seems then to be part of a strategy to delegitimate that struggle. It would be odd to assume that the main reason why Palestinians seek to be free of colonial rule is that it will fulfill their ostensibly antisemitic desires. The colonizer projects the desire to destroy colonial power onto the colonized, but renames it as the desire to destroy the Jewish people. The founding mandate of Hamas only amplifies this problem—and should be definitively rejected. Still, if the desire to throw off colonial power is renamed as the desire to destroy the Jew, then the Jew is equated with colonizing power (and the equation is made not by the colonized, but by the colonizer!). There is no reason to assume that Jews have to be colonizers, so the desire to overcome colonialism should be, in every instance and on all sides of the conflict, disarticulated from antisemitism. Only then can the Palestinian struggle be grasped as motivated by a legitimately grounded desire to be free of colonial rule.

So to answer the question, why is antisemitism attributed to those who express criticisms of the Israeli state?, we have to change the terms of the question itself. We have been asking, under what conditions can we decide whether or not the charge of antisemitism is warranted? What if we ask: What does the charge of antisemitism do? If the charge operates as a form of power, what role does the charge of antisemitism assume in the political debate about Zionism, the State of Israel, and the Palestinian struggle for freedom? If a critical position can be discounted by calling it antisemitic, then it does not exactly answer the criticism: rather, it seeks to put the criticism out of play. When the charge functions in a spurious way to censor a point of view, it seeks to delegitimate the criticism by claiming that it is a cover for antisemitic passion or motivation. If a criticism is nothing but a fugitive and persistent form of antisemitism, then that criticism has to be censored and expunged in the same way that antisemitism has to be censored and expunged. A great deal depends on this substitution: critique of Israel = antisemitism. Taken together with that other substitution, the State of Israel = the Jewish people, it can then be argued that the critique of the State of Israel is antisemitic. And yet, if neither of those substitutions holds, then the argument begins to fall apart.

When the charge of antisemitism is used to censor or quell open debate and the public exchange of critical views on the State of Israel, then it is not exactly communicating a truth, but seeking to rule out certain perspectives from being heard: so whether or not the accusation is true becomes less important than whether or not it is effective. It works in part through stigmatizing and discrediting the speaker, but also through a tactical deployment of slander. After all, the charge can be enormously painful. It does not roll easily off the back; it does not get quickly shaken off, even when one knows it is not true. For many Jews, there could hardly be anything worse than being told that they are antisemitic, allied with Nazis or right-wing fascists in Hungary, Greece, Belgium, or Germany, or with all those who believe in the poisonous Protocols of Zion. Those who deploy the charge of antisemitism to discount a point of view and discredit a person clearly fear the viewpoint they oppose and do not want it to be heard at all. It is also a tactic of shaming, seeking to silence those for whom identifying with antisemitism is loathsome.

If I am right, then those who accuse those who have criticisms of the State of Israel of antisemitism know that it will hurt Jewish critics of the State of Israel in an emotionally profound way. They know it will hurt because they also know that Jewish critics of the State of Israel also loathe antisemitism, and so will loathe the identification with antisemitism with which they are charged. In other words, those who make use of the accusation for the purposes of suppressing criticism actually know that the person accused is not antisemitic, for otherwise the accusation could not hurt as it does. Indeed, it does not matter whether the accusation is true, because the accusation is meant to cause pain, to produce shame, and to reduce the accused to silence. So my efforts to use reason to show how it is not necessarily justified to attribute antisemitism to those with strong criticisms of the State of Israel will doubtless not persuade. The point of the charge is not to utter what is true, but to do damage to the criticism as well as the person who speaks it. In other words, the charge of antisemitism has become an act of war.

Finally, I wish to point out how important it is that the charge of antisemitism be saved for those situations in which it aptly describes what is going on. If the charge is instrumentalized for other purposes, a general cynicism about the charge is engendered. It is considered a lie or a tactic and it loses credence as a claim. We need the charge of antisemitism to remain a strong and credible instrument against contemporary forms of antisemitism, especially when we note that swastikas have appeared at fraternities (Emory University is a case in point), that the right-wing populist parties with antisemitic agendas have won representation in governments in Poland and Hungary, where the Jobbik party won 20 percent of the vote just a few years ago. One of its leaders claimed that Jews were a threat to national security. Golden Dawn continues to draw popular support in Greece. That party has rallied anti-Roma, antirefugee, and antisemitic sentiment and maintains alliances with Far Right groups in the United Kingdom, Poland, Slovakia, Croatia, Austria, and Bulgaria. A resurgence of fascist ideology is now happening in Austria, reanimating the scourge of Nazism. And the United States has now joined ranks with it. The rise of hate crimes in the immediate aftermath of the Trump election targeted Jews, Blacks, Latinos, and Arabs. Trump's racist discourse emboldened self-avowed white supremacists to take to the streets while the mainstream media normalized this scandal by calling them the "alt-right."

If the charge of antisemitism becomes a tactic to suppress open criticism and debate on the State of Israel, its practices of dispossession and occupation, its founding and the ongoing implications of that founding for Palestinians, then it will lose its claim to truth. It will be understood as a tactic that actually knows the untruth of what it claims. Who will believe the charge when it is used to name and oppose rising forms of fascism or actual ideologies bound up with its actual toxicity? We should not waste our words, the words we need to name and oppose forms of oppression that are on the rise with new forms of nationalism and populism. We should be trying to build a world in which injustice is named and all forms of racism, including antisemitism, are opposed as equally unjust and unacceptable. There is enough hatred circulating in the world that remains unnamed and unopposed, so it makes no sense to wage a war on critical viewpoints whose accommodation is one of the basic obligations of democracy, and when we need to understand the contemporary constellations of racism. When the struggle against antisemitism becomes allied with all struggles against racism, including anti-Black and anti-Arab racism, we will be surely on the way to building a world in which language still means, and justice names, the passion that motivates critique.

SECTION THREE   Anti-Immigrant Nation

In the early years of America's thirteen colonies, immigration and slavery were the only ways to acquire labor. Through recruiters and promotional literature, the Virginia Company attracted indentured servants, promising passage, a year's provisions, a home, tools, a share of production profits, and quick naturalization in return for four to seven years of work. How persons so indentured became citizens was established by the Naturalization Act of 1790: "Any alien being a free white person, who shall have resided within the limits and under the jurisdiction of the United States for the term of two years, may be admitted to become a citizen."[1] The act barred Native Americans, slaves, free Blacks,[2] Muslims, and Asian "coolies" from naturalization as nonwhites, as the essay in this volume by Khaled Beydoun notes.

Federal regulation over immigration was established in 1891, when the Bureau of Immigration set out to construct Ellis Island as a processing station for European immigrants.

The anti-immigrant impulses of the United States between 1881 and 1916 were largely qualitative, excluding alien contract laborers, "lunatics," "idiots," and sick persons likely to become public charges. Concern that the country was being invaded by unsavory sorts who were diluting whiteness and undermining Protestant hegemony culminated in 1882 with the passage of the Chinese Exclusion Act, followed in 1907 with equally severe entry limits on the Japanese. The immigration law of 1917 finally metastasized xenophobic concerns through stricter qualitative and quantitative exclusions. Prejudice against the entry of more Catholics and Jews continued, camouflaged as numeric limits on immigrants from southern and eastern Europe. The concern here was that the continued admission of large numbers of Catholics and Jews would dilute the country's foundational Protestantism and shift the proportion of whites to nonwhites. Immigrants from these parts of Europe at the time were racialized as nonwhite, but in the mid-twentieth century became white.[3] The 1917 law denied admission to residents of the "Asiatic Barred Zone"—India, Indochina, Afghanistan, Arabia, East Indies, and a host of smaller Asian countries. Immigrant admissions numbered 295,403 in 1917. In 1918 only 110,618 were granted entry, a reduction of almost two-thirds.[4]

These quick-fire restrictions failed to satisfy nativists, pseudo-scientific racists, and eugenics devotees, and shortly their concerns led to the National Origins Act of 1924, defining "national origin" as those "persons who descended from the white population of the United States at the time of the nation's founding." Generous numeric quotas were established for them, slashing the number of visas for nonwhites, capping the total number of immigrants admissible yearly at 165,000. The law achieved its goal. Between 1907 and 1924, 862,514 immigrants legally entered the United States; 176,983 from northern and western Europe, 685,531 from southern and eastern Europe representing almost 80 percent of the total. In 1924, the number was reduced to 161,846; 140,999 from northern and western Europe, 20,847 from southern and eastern Europe, now only 13 percent of the total.

The National Origins Act of 1924 won passage as law only because the labor needs of Western farmers were satisfied though the "Western Hemisphere Exception," a provision that allowed Mexicans to enter the country without a numeric quota, but simultaneously establishing the Border Patrol and funding the construction of a networks of border stations to apprehend unauthorized entrants. This is how Mexicans were first demonized as "illegal aliens," a classification that also applied to Chinese, Irish, Russian, and other nationals who skirted major ports of entry, choosing instead the vast, poorly patrolled, and easily breeched southern border of the United States.[5]

By the late 1950s it had become clear that the National Origins Act was racist and religiously discriminatory, something the nations of the world understood and critiqued. In 1960 John F. Kennedy ran for the presidency promising immigration reform. His assassination left it to President Lyndon B. Johnson, who realized it in the 1965 the Hart-Celler Act. The law excised the racial and religious prejudices codified in the 1924 National National Origins Act of 1924, thus, in the words of Johnson, repairing "a very deep and painful flaw in the fabric of American justice. It corrects a cruel and enduring wrong . . . those wishing to immigrate to America shall be admitted on the basis of their skills and their close relationship to those already here."[6] National origins quotas were replaced by country-specific visa allocations, raising the yearly total from 165,000 to 290,000, allocating 170,000 of these to the Eastern Hemisphere (Europe, Africa, Middle East, Asia, Pacific), and 120,000 to the Western.[7]

Mexico in 1964 was supplying the United States with roughly 200,000 authorized agricultural workers yearly through the Bracero Program (*bracero* in Spanish means "one who works using his arms"), a bilateral treaty enacted in 1942 after the start of World War II still in place in 1964, plus another 800,000 unauthorized workers. Yet Mexico's new visa allocation was set at only 20,000, instantly exacerbating what became known as the Mexican "illegal alien problem," or the entry of hundreds of thousands of unauthorized and undocumented migrants to meet the labor demands of the American Southwest.[8]

Here is where Leo Chavez's essay "Fear of White Replacement" takes up subsequent developments, chronicling the threat narratives that began circulating among conservative media pundits, in government reports, and in scholarly publications calling for further immigration reforms. White Americans increasingly felt that their racial and religious heritage was being erased by Latin American and Asian nonwhite immigrants, something that failed to capture media attention when the "illegals" were workers from Ireland and Russia racialized as whites. White Americans railed about "immigrant invasions," "ethnic reconquests," "the racial replacement of whites," and the "racial dilution" of the republic. Much of the blame for the rising numbers of Mexicans and Mexican Americans, as Chavez explains, was pinned on the high fertility rates of Latinas, which were patently false, intensifying demands for the abolishment of birthright citizenship as a potent solution. What white working-class Americans had actually been experiencing since 1970 was deindustrialization, manufacturing capital flight to countries with lower wages and no employee benefits, and repeated economic recessions, particularly the one of 2008, which economically devastated middle- and working-class families of every creed and color. Yet immigrants were blamed for the declension natives felt.

How immigration reform became a burning issue among Washington policymakers and eventually the Trump administration is the story Carly Goodman tells, focusing on the organizational acumen of Dr. John Tanton, an ophthalmologist from northern Michigan. In the 1970s he became intensely concerned about population control and rising fertility rates and set out to solve them. To do so, he founded the Federation for American Immigration Reform (FAIR), the Center for Immigration Studies (CIS), and a number of organizations and publications to upend the Hart-Celler Immigration law of 1965. By the early 1980s Tanton's lobbying network was gaining the attention of presidents and Congress, shaping public opinion through savvy messaging and media saturation advocating for heightened immigration restrictions, slowing the rate of the country's demographic racial change seen as producing bilingualism and ethnic separatism and as hampering immigrant assimilation. Tanton's prescriptions became Donald Trump's agenda, which he vowed to enact if elected president and did.

The plenary powers American presidents enjoy in issuing executive orders that govern the day-to-day activities of the Department of Homeland Security's Immigration and Customs Enforcement (ICE) is the focus of Adam Goodman's piece. He calls the state's enforcement of its sovereignty a "deportation machine," which is not new. It has existed since the late nineteenth century. One presidential administration after another has used formal removals and voluntary departures to rid the nation of unauthorized immigrants. What Donald Trump has added to this machine are heightened level of violence used in apprehensions and removals, separating children from their parents, imposing long periods of detention, underfunding and understaffing immigration courts to lengthen litigation and appeal processes, thus inflicting additional levels of personal familial suffering on immigrants.

Jessica Ordaz gives these detained and deported migrants names and faces. She takes us to the southern parts of California and Arizona's U.S.-Mexico border, chronicling the violence immigrants suffer from the desert's desiccating heat and dehydration, from the "border justice" of vigilantes and other predators, and from racist renegade ICE agents out to punish unauthorized border crossers. The conditions of border apprehension, detention, and deportation for many lead to suicide, medical malpractice deaths, and the sadistic, gratuitous violence that occurs in private detention facilities far from the public eye.

Two U.S. Border Patrolmen walk five people who crossed the border illegally to the holding center in Texas shortly after their apprehension in the desert. Between this image in 1981 and the present moment, border crossings have become much more violent, militarized, and deadly. (AP Photo/Lennox McLendon, file)

11 Fear of White Replacement

LATINA FERTILITY, WHITE DEMOGRAPHIC DECLINE, AND IMMIGRATION REFORM

Leo R. Chavez

During the post-1965 wave of immigration, the reproduction and fertility of Latina and Mexican immigrant women became ground zero in a war waged not just with words but also through public policies and laws.[1] Indeed, anti-immigrant sentiment during the last fifty years has focused specifically on the biological and social reproductive capacities of Mexican immigrant and Mexican-origin (U.S.-born) women (Chavez 2004; Gutiérrez 2008). Their fertility has been represented as "dangerous," "pathological," "abnormal," and even as a threat to national security, as a key component of an "immigrant invasion" (Chavez 2013). In addition, much American nativist rhetoric about the decline of the white race has identified Mexican, and subsequently Latina women more generally, as largely responsible for the demographic changes underway in the United States since 1965.

In this chapter, I examine two prominent parallel narratives in public discourse about Latinos and immigration. The first, which I call the demographic narrative, is found in scholarly studies and U.S. Census reports on fertility, birthrates, and population statistics that show a continuous decline in fertility rates for all U.S. women, including Latinas. Second, the

References are provided at the end of this chapter.

177

immigrant/Latino threat narrative focuses on what it perceives as high Latina/Hispanic fertility and birth rates. This narrative is spread primarily by influential mainstream media pundits, writers, academics, and a host of conservative groups who seek to curtail immigration by invoking tropes of white decline, profound demographic change, and an ongoing Mexican invasion of the United States. I argue that this second narrative propagated anxieties over birthrates (too low for whites, too high for racial others) and notions of "immigrant invasions," "ethnic reconquests," "racial replacement," "racial dilution," and immigrants who refuse to assimilate, which have now become mainstream. I end with a reflection on how these views gained ascendency in President Trump's administration, which helps us understand his administration's immigration policies.

IMMIGRATION AND NATIVIST CONCERNS

The U.S. census began collecting data on nativity in 1850. As figure 11.1 indicates, the 1850 census counted about 2.2 million foreign-born residents, or immigrants, which accounted for about 10 percent of the U.S. population. While the total number of immigrants increased throughout the nineteenth century until it peaked in the 1920s, immigrants as a percentage of the U.S. population stayed relatively constant between 1860 and 1910, from about 13 percent to just under 15 percent, peaking at 14.8 percent in 1890 (Batalova, Blizzard, and Bolter 2020).

The increase in immigration after 1850 corresponds with the emergence of the nativist Know Nothing Party, which viewed Catholic immigrants as a particular threat to the nation (Gerstle 2004). Nativist groups in the late nineteenth and early twentieth centuries often viewed the "new" immigration from southern and eastern Europe as unassimilable and racially different from the old-stock American population of northwestern European origin (Higham [1955] 2002). Eugenicists and nativists believed that the most efficient way to establish ethnic homogeneity and the supremacy of the "white race" was restricting immigration (Grant 1916). The Immigration Act of 1924 did just that, instituting racialized national origins quotas, which severely restricted immigration from southern and eastern Europe in favor of northern and western Europe.

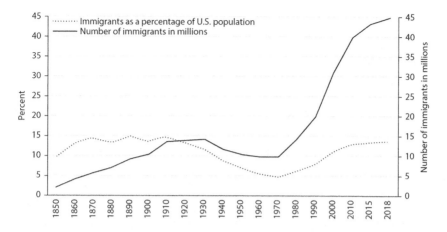

Figure 11.1. Size and share of the foreign-born population in the United States, 1950–2018. Source: Batalova, Blizzard, and Bolter 2020; Migration Policy Institute (MPI) tabulation of data from U.S. Census Bureau, 2010–18 American Community Surveys (ACS) and 1970, 1990, and 2000 Decennial Census, MPI DATA Hub: Immigration Facts, States, and Maps. All other data are from Gibson and Lennon 1999.

Thus, for example, while between 1907 and 1924, 685,531 immigrants had entered the United States from southern and eastern Europe, only 176,983 had originated in northern and western Europe. By 1925 the United States only admitted 20,847 persons from southern and eastern Europe, while 140,999 come from northern and western Europe. The Chinese Exclusion Act of 1882 and the Japanese Gentleman's Agreement of 1907 had already curtailed Asian immigration (Gerstle 2004, 2001).

The Immigration and Nationality Act of 1965 dismantled national origins quotas, instead capping the total number of immigrants admissible yearly at 290,000, allocating 170,000 to the "Old World," and 120,000 to the "New World." Asian and Pacific prohibitions were lifted. A system of preferences based mostly on kin ties, known as "family reunification," was put in place, exempting skilled workers from national numeric caps.

The 1965 immigration law soon fundamentally altered the geographic origins of subsequent immigrants. In 1960, 84 percent of all immigrants originated in Europe and Canada, 10 percent in Central and South America, 4 percent in South and East Asia, and 2 percent from Africa and the rest of the world. By 2017, Europe and Canada accounted for 13 percent of immigrants, Central and South American 51 percent, South and East Asia 27 percent, and about 9 percent from the rest of the world (Radford and Noe-Bustamante 2019).

The 1965 Immigration Act also had a profound impact on the cross-border migration of Mexicans into the United States, mostly as temporary guest laborers. Between 1942 and 1964, approximately two million Mexican workers were entering the United States yearly to meet mostly agricultural labor needs in the American West and Southwest; about a quarter entered under bilateral treaties between Mexico and the United States, the rest without inspection or documentation. Because these regional labor needs remained, while Mexico was allocated only thirty thousand immigrant slots by the 1965 law, which was reduced to twenty thousand in 1976, the natural result was the rhetorical birth of the "illegal alien invasion," which increasingly fueled fears of white racial decline.

Since the passage into law of the Immigration and Naturalization Act of 1965, which abolished the racial quotas that had been put into effect in the 1924 Immigration Act, nativists in the United States have constantly expressed their concerns about "immigrant invasions" and their rising fertility rates, which they fear will soon lead to the decline of the "white race." Such xenophobic views have a long history in America but, because of the demographic and economic changes that have been afoot in the republic since 1965, have grown in intensity and overt violence (Gerstle 2001).

Demographic change has fueled white nationalist movements and populist political campaigns in Europe and the United States, which includes Donald Trump's rise to power in 2016. These populist movements often fan the flames of anti-immigrant sentiment and a fear of white decline (Bangstad, Bertelsen, and Henkel 2019; Mazzarella 2019; Ahmed 2004; Stern 2019; Belew 2019; Shoshan 2016; Mahmud 2020). For example, Brenton Tarrant, the gunman accused of killing fifty-one Muslims attending Friday prayer services at two mosques in Christchurch, New Zealand, on March 15, 2019, issued a manifesto which he titled "The Great Replacement." Therein he railed against "Islamic invaders . . . occupying European soil." The first sentence of the manifesto asked readers to scrutinize "the birth-rates," a phrase he repeated three times (Bowles 2019). Tarrant seemed to be echoing the white nationalists, neo-Nazis, and Klansmen who had gathered for the "Unite the Right" rally that turned lethal on August 11–12,

2017, in Charlottesville, Virginia. Marching through the campus of the University of Virginia carrying torches on Friday night, August 11, the women and men shouted "Jews will not replace us," with placards bearing Nazi symbols and one sign that read "Jews are Satan's children."

Patrick Crusius, the twenty-one-year-old gunman who killed twenty-two persons at a Walmart in El Paso, Texas, on August 3, 2019, posted a manifesto online titled "The Inconvenient Truth," in which he claimed that his actions were to stop the "Hispanic invasion of Texas" (Romero, Fernandez, and Padilla 2019). The words *invasion* and *invaders* appear six times in the manifesto. One does not have to look too far for where Crusius got his inspiration. Between May 2018 and September 2019, President Donald Trump ran some twenty-two hundred Facebook ads using the word *invasion* (Zhao 2019).

A LOOK AT DATA ON FERTILITY RATES, BIRTH RATES, AND POPULATION

Fertility rates are important when considering population dynamics. Fertility rate is an indicator of population growth. It measures the average number of children a female could give birth to over her entire lifetime. Table 11.1 indicates that there has been a dramatic decline in fertility rates among all American women, from 2.48 children per woman in the 1960s to 1.89 in the 2010s ("Total Fertility Rate" 2015). The U.S. population essentially is at zero population growth. Although Hispanic fertility rates have dropped dramatically since the 1960s, these rates must be disaggregated by generation of residence in the United States. Statistics from 2015 show that by the third and higher generations, Hispanic fertility rates were at 1.98 children per woman and projected to equal white women's rates by 2060 ("Total Fertility Rate" 2015).

Emilio A. Parrado and S. Philip Morgan, in their comparative 2008 study of the number of children ever born to U.S. Hispanic and Mexican-origin grandmothers, mothers, and daughters over time, found that fertility differentials between Mexican-origin women in the United States and white women had decreased across generations. Fertility fluctuated in relation to changing socioeconomic conditions:

Table 11.1 Total Fertility Rate for Population Estimates and Projections, by Origin and Generation 1965–70, 2010–15, 2060–65

	Total			First generation			Second generation			Third or higher generation		
	1965	2010	2060	1965	2010	2060	1965	2010	2060	1965	2010	2060
	1970	2015	2065	1970	2015	2065	1970	2015	2065	1970	2015	2065
Total	2.48	1.89	1.90	2.59	2.58	2.06	2.59	1.84	1.88	2.47	1.76	1.85
White	2.37	1.71	1.86	2.31	1.76	2.00	2.43	1.78	1.90	2.37	1.70	1.86
Black	2.94	1.91	1.90	(z)	1.90	2.10	(z)	1.83	1.89	2.93	1.90	1.85
Hispanic	3.10	2.53	1.94	3.13	3.36	2.30	3.33	2.01	1.90	3.06	1.98	1.86
Asian	2.37	1.66	1.88	2.30	1.70	1.90	2.66	1.59	1.90	2.28	1.61	1.76
2 or more races	2.61	1.86	1.86	(z)	2.20	2.00	(z)	1.79	1.90	2.56	1.80	1.82

NOTE: z = Population too small to compute rate. Whites, Blacks, and Asians include people who claim only single-race non-Hispanics. Those who claim two or more races are classified as multiple-race non-Hispanics. Hispanics are of any racial classification. "First generation" is foreign-born; "second generation" is people born in the United States with at least one foreign-born parent; "third and higher generations" are people born in the United States with U.S.-born parents.

SOURCE: PEW 2015.

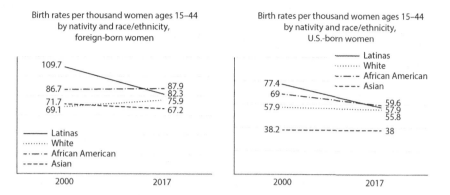

Figure 11.2. Birth rates per thousand women ages 15–44, by nativity and race/ ethnicity. Foreign-born women and U.S.-born women. Note: Latinas are of any race. African Americans, Whites, and Asians include only non-Latinas. Asians include Pacific Islanders. Source: Pew Research Center analysis of National Center for Health Statistics data (Livingston 2019).

Contrary to the idea that Hispanic fertility may be less responsive to improvements in human capital or socioeconomic conditions, either due to a cultural proclivity to high fertility or to blocked opportunities in the U.S., we find a strong negative effect of years of education on the number of CEB [children ever born] among Hispanic women that is actually slighter larger than that found among white women. This is especially the case among the third immigrant generation. (2008, 26–27)

Birthrates are also important for understanding population dynamics. Birthrates indicate the rate at which the births take place in a population and are usually given as "number of births per thousand women" for a specific time, typically a given year. The declining trend in birthrates fell to record lows in 2016 and 2017, according to the National Center for Health Statistics (Tavernise 2018). The Pew Research Center found similar dramatic declines in birthrates for Latinas between 2000 and 2017 compared to Blacks, whites, and Asians (Livingston 2019). As figure 11.2 indicates, foreign-born Latina birthrates declined from 109.7 to 82.3 births per thousand women ages 15–44 between 2000 and 2017. U.S.-born Latina birthrates also declined from 77.4 to 57.9 births per thousand women over that same period. Both foreign-born and U.S.-born

Latinas had birthrates similar to white and Black women in 2017. As this decline in birthrates became more apparent, the state of California revised its population projections because of an "unexpectedly large decline in the Hispanic birthrate" (Kelley 2004; Pitkin and Myers 2012).

THE LATINA/IMMIGRANT THREAT IN PUBLIC DISCOURSE

In contrast to the demographic narrative, there is the immigrant-as-threat narrative. Latinos, especially people of Mexican origin, play a central role in this narrative. This second narrative, too, focuses on Latina/Hispanic fertility and birth rates, which are deemed too high.

Some of the early discussions of the demographic transformation of the United States appeared in *Time* magazine's January 11, 1960, issue. Its cover story presented the world caught in a Malthusian nightmare in which the darker populations of the world would soon biologically reproduce so quickly that they would overwhelm the world's whites.

> Long a hot topic among pundits, whose jargon phrase for it is "the population explosion," the startling 20th century surge in humanity's rate of reproduction may be as fateful to history as the H-bomb and the Sputnik, but it gets less public attention. Today two-thirds of the human race does not get enough to eat. And it is among the hungry peoples of Asia, Africa and Latin America that the population explosion is most violent. In 1900 there was one European for every two Asians; by 2000 there will probably be four Asians for every European, and perhaps twice as many Americans living south of the Rio Grande as north of it. If by then, all that faces the growing masses of what is euphemistically called "the underdeveloped nations" is endless, grinding poverty, their fury may well shake the earth. ("Population" 1960)

This article's alarmist rhetoric was matched by this issue of *Time*'s cover, which depicted fourteen adult women of color and only one white woman, who appears relatively affluent with a shopping cart that also carries her two children and her consumer goods. Asian, African, and Latin American women are in working-class or traditional clothing, or simply naked, indicating a world much less affluent and backward than that of the white woman. These parts of the world would soon supply the immigrants who would enter the United States after 1965. (See image at http://content.time.com/time/covers/0,16641,19600111,00.html.)

Undoubtedly influenced by the 1965 immigration law, Paul Ehrlich, a biologist at Stanford University, in 1968 published his influential book *The Population Bomb*, which boldly asked on its jacket cover, "Population Control or Race to Oblivion?" Ehrlich argued that fertility was a national and worldwide problem that would result in environmental degradation, famines, pestilence, and wars between rich and poor (Ehrlich 1968). "The birth rate must be brought into balance with the death rate or mankind will breed itself into oblivion," he wrote. "We can no longer afford merely to treat the symptoms of the cancer of population growth; the cancer itself must be cut out. Population control is the only answer" (Ehrlich 1968, 12).

A decade later, Ehrlich coauthored *The Golden Door: International Migration, Mexico, and the United States*, which argued that Mexico's population growth was a major problem for both Mexico and the United States because social inequalities and inadequate job creation produced intense pressures that could only be solved by emigration. Mexico's high fertility rate was the result of an "unusually pronatalist cultural tradition," which placed an abnormally high cultural value on having children. Because of machismo and Marianismo, men were dominant and women were submissive, and having more children increased the social status of both men and women, or so they argued. "Motherhood is viewed as the essential purpose for a woman's existence," Ehrlich and his colleagues opined, adding that these pronatalist values were reinforced by the Catholic Church (Ehrlich, Bilderback, and Ehrlich 1979, 235).

In *The Latino Threat: Constructing Immigrants, Citizens, and the Nation* (Chavez 2013), I argued that the media popularized Ehrlich's population projections with alarmist articles about demographic change and high Latina birthrates, even though available data, such as that presented above, did not support their arguments. Mainstream news stories about immigration have reported on academic research and census data. Rather than objective reporting, news stories can evoke alarmist concerns about immigration, population growth, and demographic change, a trend that has continued from the 1970s until more recently (Chavez 2013, 2001; Massey and Sánchez R. 2012). A host of conservative groups (e.g., the alt-right, Federation for American Immigration Reform, the Center for

Immigration Studies, the Tea Party) also invoke the immigrant threat narrative to raise an alarm about white decline, profound demographic change, and an ongoing Mexican invasion of the United States. The immigrant threat also serves to promote their views on curtailing immigration. Into this volatile mix are more fringe groups such as the Ku Klux Klan, border militias, and the Proud Boys (Stern 2019; Belew 2019). At the core of this immigrant threat narrative are anxieties over birthrates (too low for whites, too high for racial others), "immigrant invasions," "racial replacement," "racial dilution," and immigrants who refuse to assimilate.

The mainstream media's representation of undocumented immigration in the 1970s is an example of alarmist journalism that evoked an immigrant-threat narrative. For example, the impact of the 1965 immigration law had barely started to be felt when *U.S. News & World Report* published "How Millions of Illegal Aliens Sneak into the U.S." as its cover story on July 22, 1974. Some six months later it followed up with "Rising Flood of Illegal Aliens: How to Deal with It," as its February 3, 1975, lead article. On April 25, 1977, *U.S. News & World Report* announced on its cover: "Border Crisis: Illegal Aliens Out of Control," followed by "Time Bomb in Mexico: Why There'll Be No End to the Invasion by 'Illegals'" on July 4, 1977. The "time bomb" was the foreign threat of Mexican women's fertility rates that would lead to massive emigration to the United States. On July 5, 1976, *Time* magazine told the nation that "the new immigrants . . . are changing the face of America," by which they meant more non-white faces and fewer white faces (Chavez 2001). These headlines used words such as "millions," "sneak," "flood," "out of control," "no end to the invasion," "time bomb," and "changing face of America," all of which signal threat and alarm. The image that is evoked in these news stories is one of countless uncontrolled immigrants sneaking into the country, or worse, invading, laying waste (flood) to the nation, and pushing the white majority into demographic decline.

These alarmist magazine stories did not go unnoticed by the Ku Klux Klan (KKK), which has been concerned about the rising numbers of non-white immigrants entering the United States for more than a century (Belew 2019). On October 27, 1977, David Duke, then the twenty-seven-year-old Grand Dragon of the KKK, held a press conference to announce Klan Border Watch. His intention was to have the KKK patrol the U.S.-

Mexico border in California, Arizona, New Mexico, and Texas ("That Time David Duke . . ." 2016). A photograph of David Duke, at the border, looking out of a car window with "Klan Border Watch" stenciled on the door circulated widely in the media at the time. Duke said, "We will be here as long as it takes to meet the response of the illegal alien problem" ("Klan's Border Patrols Begin" 1977). Duke's actions did not reduce undocumented immigration, but they did receive a great deal of media attention, underscoring the U.S.-Mexico border as a site of immigration political theatre, while simultaneously harassing and intimidating border crossers. In the next decades, many groups, such as the Minuteman Project, the United Constitutional Patriots, and others would engage in vigilante actions along the U.S.-Mexico border (Chavez 2013; Belew 2019; Gilchrist and Corsi 2006; Romero 2019). (See image at https:// dangerousminds.net/comments/that_time_david_duke_and_kkk_ patrolled_the_mexican_border.)

In addition to the "invasion" trope, news stories in the 1980s increasingly focused on the growth of the U.S. Hispanic population, which was often discussed in relation to the declining proportion of whites in the U.S. population. The stories also told of the decline in European immigrants (Chavez 2001). *Newsweek*'s January 17, 1983, issue reported that between 1970 and 1980, the Hispanic population in the United States grew by 61 percent, largely because of immigration and higher fertility rates and because since 1965 46.4 percent fewer immigrants had entered from Europe. Hispanic fertility again was tied to the "immigration invasion" narrative.

Latina fertility was also a focus of news stories. Both *U.S. News & World Report* (March 7, 1983) and *Newsweek* (June 25, 1984) published covers with photographs of Mexican women being carried across water into the United States. *U.S. News & World Report*'s cover announced, "Invasion from Mexico: It Just Keeps Growing," and *Newsweek*'s title read, "Closing the Door? The Angry Debate over Illegal Immigration: Crossing the Rio Grande." The message was that the invasion carried the seeds of future generations. Women would have babies, create families, and soon communities of Latinos who would remain linguistically and socially separate would be clamoring for a reconquest of the United States (Chavez 2013).

Apprehensions about the changing demographic profile of the U.S. population were newsworthy in the 1990s, with the "browning of America" idea gaining increasing currency in the press. By then, white European immigrants had radically declined in number, accounting for only 12 percent of post-1965 immigration. *Time* magazine mentioned this fact in 1990:

> The 'browning of America' will alter everything in society, from politics and education to industry, values and culture . . . The deeper significance of America becoming a majority nonwhite society is what it means to the national psyche, to individuals' sense of themselves and the nation—their idea of what it is to be American . . . While know-nothingism is generally confined to the more dismal corners of the American psyche, it seems all too predictable that during the next decades many more mainstream white Americans will begin to speak openly about the nation they feel they are losing. (Henry 1990)

In the early 1990s, the conservative magazine *National Review*, which arguably helped build the alt-right, carried essays by Peter Brimelow, John O. Sullivan, Lawrence Auster, and others who regularly railed against multiculturalism and "Third World" immigrants (Auster 1994; O'Sullivan 1994; Brimelow 1992; Nwanevu 2017). Peter Brimelow was at the forefront of these pundits, and his essay "Time to Rethink Immigration?" was a diatribe against the negative ways immigrants, especially Hispanics, were changing America, ideas which he expanded on in his book *Alien Nation: Common Sense About America's Immigration Disaster* in 1995 (Brimelow 1995, 1992). According to Brimelow, "Symptomatic of the American Anti-Idea is the emergence of a strange anti-nation inside the U.S.—the so-called 'Hispanics.' . . . Spanish-speakers are still being encouraged to assimilate. But not to America" (Brimelow 1995, 218–19). While concerned that nonwhite immigrants were changing America for the worse, Brimelow found that Hispanics were particularly troublesome because of biological and social reproduction issues. Brimelow targeted Hispanics as he railed against bilingualism, multiculturalism, multilingual ballots, citizenship for children of illegal immigrants, the abandonment of knowledge of English as a prerequisite for citizenship, the erosion of citizenship as the sole qualification for voting, welfare and education for illegal immigrants and their children, and congressional and state legislative apportionment based on populations that include illegal immigrants.

A number of publications emphasizing similar themes soon followed. For example, books by Arthur Schlesinger Jr., Georgie Ann Geyer, Pat Buchanan, Samuel P. Huntington, Michelle Malkin, Victor David Hanson, and other conservative writers basically promoted a populist anti-immigrant and anti-Latino agenda (Schlesinger 1992; Malkin 2002; Buchanan 2002, 2006, 2011; Geyer 1996). Jeff Maskovsky and Sophie Bjork-James call such entreaties a "politics of rage," which "frame relatively privileged groups, especially those privileged along racial lines—as imperiled" (Maskovsky and Bjork-James 2020, 11). These publications spoke to people, particularly white American men, who felt displaced and resentful at being left behind by the "elites" who run the country in Washington, DC, and who control the media, who they felt often portrayed people like them as "rednecks" and ignorant, ignoring their pain resulting from their experiences of economic decline, government policies favoring the "elites," and perceived job competition from immigrants (Hochschild 2016; Mulligan and Brunson 2020).

THE FUTURE IS NOW

Understanding the appeal of the immigrant/Latino fertility threat to its intended audience requires us to consider a number of key factors. America experienced demographic trends, which began to develop in 1970 but accelerated during the Great Recession of 2008, that showed a decline in the proportion of the country's white population in relation to its total. Whites accounted for 79.6 percent of the U.S. population in 1980, but fell to 61.3 percent in 2016, and the Census Bureau projections indicate that the white population will constitute less than half (47 percent) of U.S. population by 2050 (Sáenz and Johnson 2018; Colby and Ortman 2014). Although Latina birthrates and fertility rates are often blamed, those rates have fallen significantly, as discussed above. But other important factors in white decline are also at play.

Low birthrates and fertility rates among U.S. white women, combined with an aging population, meant that in 2016 white deaths exceeded births for the first time in U.S. history, according to an analysis of National Center for Health Statistics data (Sáenz and Johnson 2018). Whites have been dying faster than they are being born in California, Arizona, Florida, and twenty-three other states. Between 1999 and 2016, white births fell by 10.8 percent and the number of deaths rose by 9.2 percent, trends which influenced the decline of whites in the population (Sáenz and Johnson 2018). As Rogelio Sáenz and Kenneth M. Johnson (2018) noted:

> With significantly fewer white births and a rising number of deaths, natural increase (births minus deaths) actually ended in 2016. In that year, for the first time in U.S. history, data from the National Center for Health Statistics showed more white deaths than births in the United States. The white natural loss of 39,000 in 2016 compares to a natural gain of 393,000 in 1999. Both the growing number of deaths (up 180,000 between 1999 and 2016), and the declining number of births (down 252,000 between 1999 and 2016) contributed to the dwindling white natural increase and more recently to natural decrease. In 2016, whites accounted for 77.7 percent of all U.S. deaths, but just 53.1 percent of births.

An important factor affecting these trends is what some demographers are calling "deaths of despair." These deaths would include deaths by suicide, drug-induced deaths, accidental drug overdoses, and alcohol-related deaths. These deaths of despair have increased significantly among whites over the last decade (Sáenz and Johnson 2018). Drug overdoses, especially from oxycontin, the overconsumption of alcohol and cigarettes, and depression-induced suicides appear to explain part of this trend. But with fewer births than deaths, and an aging population, which means fewer women of child-bearing age, it is easy to see reasons for the decline in the white population. U.S. Census projections forecast that the non-Hispanic white population will shrink by about 19 million people by 2060, from 199 million in 2020 to 179 million in 2060 (Vespa, Armstrong, and Medina [2018] 2020, 3). By 2045, whites may no longer make up the majority of the U.S. population (Vespa, Armstrong, and Medina [2018] 2020, 7).

In addition, Douglas S. Massey and Magaly Sanchez R. (2012) have argued that the dramatic increase in economic inequality in the United States since the 1960s is an important reason for the rise of anti-immigrant sentiments. Figures 11.3 and 11.4 use data from the U.S. Census Bureau to update Massey and Sanchez R.'s tables on household income

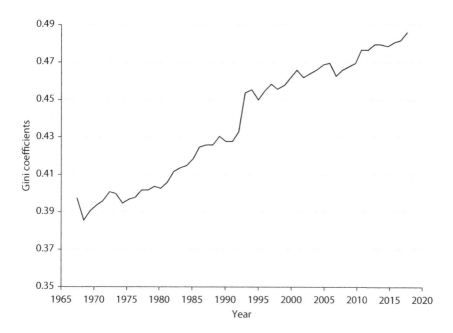

Figure 11.3. Household income inequality in the United States. Source: U.S. Bureau of the Census 2019 (Semega et al. 2019). Note: The Gini coefficient summarizes the distribution of income into a single number. It ranges from zero, which is a perfectly equal distribution, to one, where only one person has all the money. Source: U.S. Bureau of the Census 2019 (Semega et al. 2019).

inequality and the share of income earned by the top quintile and next two quintiles from 1967 to 2018 (their tables stopped at 2006) to show how inequality has continued apace since their important publication (Semega et al. 2019).

The Gini coefficient ranges from 0, which is a perfectly equal distribution of income, to 1, where only one person has all the money. As figure 11.3 indicates, in 1968, the Gini coefficient for income inequality was at a record low of 0.386. It would not be so low again. By 2018, the Gini coefficient had risen to 0.486, a 21 percent increase over five decades. The distribution of U.S. income in 2018 was more unequal than at any time since 1929, the beginning of the Great Depression (Massey and Sánchez R. 2012, 59).

Figure 11.4 presents the share of the income earned by the top quintile and next two quintiles taken together. We often hear that the rich keep

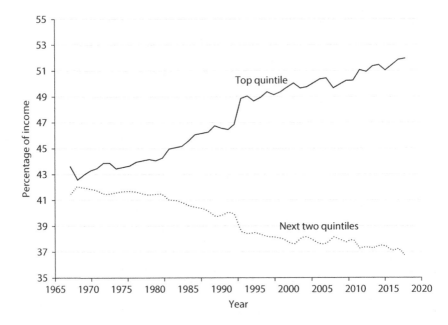

Figure 11.4. Share of income earned by top quintile and next two quintiles. Source: U.S. Bureau of the Census 2019 (Semega et al. 2019).

getting richer, and this table shows that there is much merit to that view. In 1960, the top quintile earned 42.6 percent of the income, which was almost the same as the 42.1 percent of income earned by the next two quintiles. The middle and upper middle classes were not dissimilar to those at the very top at that time. But the fortunes of the top quintile continued to rise inexorably until they earned 52 percent of the wealth in 2018. In contrast, the next two quintiles saw their share of income plummet over the next five decades, to a low of 36.7 percent in 2018. Anti-immigrant rhetoric found its appeal in these wide income disparities. The first two years of the Trump presidency witnessed increases in earnings for the top earners and a decline in earnings for the rest.

Taken together, demographic change, white fertility decline, rising death rates, and economic decline can take their toll and create fertile ground for scapegoating immigrants and Latinos. As MIT political theorist John Tirman opined, these trends were "a key to the accumulating white anger that drives right-wing extremism to ever uglier heights. The prospects for living as well as their parents, or fulfilling the dreams fostered by popular culture begin to unravel in one's forties, and the easy availability of alcohol, opiates, and other drugs is one release. So is fascistic political noise-making" (Tirman 2015).

In her essay titled "Dead, White, and Blue," journalist Barbara Ehrenreich argued that low-income whites perceived that they are losing ground in relation to other ethnic groups. "All of this means that the maintenance of white privilege, especially among the least privileged whites, has become more difficult and so, for some, more urgent than ever. Poor whites always had the comfort of knowing that someone was worse off and more despised than they were; racial subjugation was the ground under their feet, the rock they stood upon, even when their own situation was deteriorating" (Ehrenreich 2015).

Ehrenreich's observations from a left-liberal perspective were echoed from the conservative political Right by Tucker Carlson, the Fox News television program host. On March 19, 2018, he reflected on the demographic transformation that had occurred in Hazleton, Pennsylvania, between 2000 and 2016. Latinos represented 2 percent of the town's residents in 2000, but by 2016 were the majority.

> That's a lot of change. People who grew up in Hazleton return to find out they can't communicate with the people who now live there. And that's bewildering to people. That's happening all over the country. No nation, no society, has ever changed this much this fast . . . How would you feel if that happened in your neighborhood? It doesn't matter how nice the immigrants are. They probably are nice. Most immigrants are nice. That's not the point. The point is, this is more change than human beings are designed to digest. This pace of change makes societies volatile, really volatile, just as ours has become volatile. (Coaston 2018)

MAKING AMERICA GREAT AGAIN

I end this chapter with some reflections on how the immigrant/Latino threat narrative was articulated in immigration-related policies of Donald Trump's presidency. Scholars have argued that Trump's presidential campaign made explicit overtures to white nationalist ideology, that national identity should be built around white ethnicity and white people should maintain a demographic majority, as a way to fire up his political base (Huber 2016; Taub 2016; Kaufmann 2019). Indeed, Trump and his supporters and key members of his staff and cabinet appear to adhere to the idea that immigrants are displacing the white ethnics who claim ownership of the nation that they allegedly founded.

For example, Donald Trump initiated his campaign for the American presidency on June 16, 2015, assailing Mexico and Mexican immigrants: "When Mexico sends its people, they're not sending their best. They're not sending you. They're not sending you. They're sending people that have lots of problems, and they're bringing those problems with us. They're bringing drugs. They're bringing crime. They're rapists. And some, I assume, are good people" ("Here's Donald Trump's Speech" 2015). During the CNN televised debate among the Republican Party's eleven presidential hopefuls on September 16, 2015, Trump emphasized assimilation. "We have a country where, to assimilate, you have to speak English . . . This is a country where we speak English, not Spanish" ("Wednesday's GOP Debate Transcript" 2015). This statement was soon followed up with another: "We also have to be honest about the fact that not everyone who seeks to join our country will be able to successfully assimilate. It is our right as a sovereign nation to choose immigrants that we think are the likeliest to thrive and flourish here" (Trump 2016).

White nationalists embraced Stephen K. Bannon's appointment as chief strategist after Trump's victory. Bannon's views as editor of Breitbart News expressed alt-right thinking, which some have criticized as making white nationalism palatable for mass consumption (Taub 2016). Jefferson Sessions, the former U.S. attorney general under President Donald Trump, offered his opinion that the 1924 National Origins Act, which established racial quotas, had been "good for America" (Bazelon 2017). Steven King, Republican congressman from Iowa and strong supporter of former president Trump, offered a very similar remark on May 12, 2017: "Culture and demographics are our destiny. We can't restore our civilization with somebody else's babies" (Schleifer 2017).

Stephen Miller, who began his Washington career as then senator Jeff Sessions's communications director, moved into the White House in 2016 as President Trump's architect of immigration enforcement and reform policies. Although it had long been suspected that Miller harbored white nationalist sentiments, Miller's emails between 2015 and 2016 to the editors of Breitbart News, which were leaked in November 2019, showed that Far Right websites helped form his thinking on immigration. In his emails, Miller cited Peter Brimelow, founder of VDARE, an anti-immigration website, and whose views of nonwhite Americans, especially Hispanics, are discussed above. He also cited Jared Taylor, editor of *American Renaissance,* a white nationalist magazine, and others as sources for his views (Rogers and DeParle 2019). In his leaked emails, Miller makes arguments against the Deferred Action for Childhood Arrivals (DACA) program, going so far as to indict Jeb Bush's support for DACA during the 2015 presidential campaign as a way to use "immigration to replace existing demographics" (Grenoble 2020). Miller also expressed his opposition to citizenship for the young undocumented immigrants known as DREAMers, as well as his opposition to birthright citizenship for the children of undocumented immigrants (Grenoble 2020).

The influence of the immigrant/Latino threat narrative can be seen in President Trump's relentless pursuit to eliminate undocumented immigration, drastically reduce refugee admissions, and promote the reduction of legal immigration in a way that would at the same time increase immigration from Europe. He also stigmatized the U.S.-born children of undocumented immigrants, whom he called "anchor babies," even to the point of denying them birthright citizenship (Chavez 2017). The goal of dramatically reducing future immigration in favor of Northern and Western Europeans, skilled laborers, and persons fluent in English was pursued vigorously on a number of fronts.

Although an extensive review of the Trump administration's immigration policies is beyond the scope this chapter, a brief list of important policies would include (Boghani 2019):

- banning people from majority-Muslim countries;
- reducing refugee admissions from 110,000 to 50,000, with even fewer in 2020;
- imposing a "wealth test" for immigrants, that denied entry to anyone the State Department believed would become a public charge, that is, might use public assistance or welfare in the United States;

- denying pregnant women temporary visas if the State Department believed they were traveling to give birth, an end run on the Fourteenth Amendment and birthright citizenship;
- adding to the backlog of pending green card applications, extending the processing time; and
- expediting deportations and deporting legal permanent residents who might have made errors in their applications.

The result of such policies was that legal immigration declined under President Trump. Persons obtaining legal permanent resident status fell from 1,183,505 to 1,096,611, a decline of 86,894 (−7.3%) between 2016 and 2018 fiscal years. The countries with significantly lower rates of immigration included Mexico, China, Vietnam, and South Korea (Anderson 2020). President Biden has reversed many of Trump's immigration policies, including the public charge policy that would have dramatically led to a decline in legal immigration from countries with low-income immigrants who might have at some future date relied on welfare assistance (NFAP 2020). Stephen Miller admitted that the Trump administration's temporary ban on immigration during the COVID-19 pandemic, which was to protect citizen workers from foreign competition, was part of a long-term strategy to curb legal immigration. In late April 2020, Miller told Trump supporters that the sixty-day ban was merely a pause, and that further restrictions on temporary workers were under consideration. Miller said, "The most important thing is to turn off the faucet of new immigrant labor . . . As a numerical proposition, when you suspend the entry of a new immigrant from abroad, you're also reducing immigration further because the chains of follow up migration that [sic] are disrupted. So the benefit to American workers is compounded with time" (Miroff and Dawsey 2020). Miller has been critical of the current family preference system for legal immigration, which he says results in chain migration. Miller clearly does not consider family reunification a good thing.

What I am calling the demographic narrative does not appear to have played a major role in recent immigration policies under Donald Trump. A debate over future immigration is possible, but the demographic narrative must be included, as well as the concerns of those who have experienced decades of growing economic inequality. Such a conversation would remind those feeling aggrieved that perhaps the target of their anger is not immigrants and Latinos. Whites still earn more than Hispanics and Blacks at all steps of the income ladder. In 2016, whites in the 90th percentile of earners earned $133,529, compared to $76,847 for Hispanics. At the median percentile, whites earned $51,288 and Hispanics $30,400. And at the bottom 10th percentile, whites earned $15,094 while Hispanics earned $9,900. Between 1970 and 2016, whites gained in relative income compared to Hispanics, thus increasing economic inequality (Kochhar and Cilluffo 2018).

Also included in the conversation would be the importance of immigrant labor when the economy expands in order to continue that expansion. In addition, babies who grow up as educated members of society, with a path to citizenship if undocumented, are the future of the nation, not just the economy. However, immigration policies are often formulated not based on such conversations but on an ideology that values one type of people over others. Such policies could change American society dramatically. At the very least, they will alter who gets to come to America for the foreseeable future. A public discourse around immigration policies that emphasizes the threat narrative will only further stigmatize immigrants, Latina mothers, and children. It will also give license to intolerance and lead to divisive struggles over belonging and citizenship. Should the nation continue down this road, we are in for hard times indeed.

References

Ahmed, Sarah. 2004. *The Politics of Emotion*. New York: Routledge.

Anderson, Stuart. 2020. "New Data: Legal Immigration Has Declined under Trump." *Forbes*, January 13 2020.

Auster, Lawrence. 1994. "Avoiding the Issue." *National Review*, February 21, 1994.

Bangstad, Sindre, Bjørn Enge Bertelsen, and Heiko Henkel, eds. 2019. "The Politics of Affect: Perspectives on the Rise of the Far-Right and Right-Wing Populism in the West." *Focaal—Journal of Global and Historical Anthropology* 83: 98–113.

Batalova, Jeanne, Brittany Blizzard, and Jessica Bolter. 2020. "Frequently Requested Statistics on Immigrants and Immigration in the United States." Migration Policy Institute, last modified Februrary 14, 2020.

www.migrationpolicy.org/article/frequently-requested-statistics-immigrants
-and-immigration-united-states (accessed April 21, 2020).

Bazelon, Emily. 2017. "Department of Justification." *New York Times Magazine,*
March 5, 2017, 36.

Belew, Kathleen. 2019. *Bring the War Home: The White Power Movement and
Paramilitary America.* Cambridge, MA: Harvard University Press.

Boghani, Priyanka. 2019. "A Guide to Some Major Trump Administration
Immigration Policies." *Frontline,* October 22, 2019.

Bowles, Nellie. 2019. "As Birthrates Fall, Fearing 'Replacement' on Far Right."
New York Times, March 19, 2019, A8.

Brimelow, Peter. 1992. "Time to Rethink Immigration?" *National Review,* June
22, 1992, 30–46.

———. 1995. *Alien Nation: Common Sense About America's Immigration
Disaster.* New York: Random House.

Buchanan, Patrick J. 2002. *The Death of the West: How Dying Populations and
Immigrant Invasions Imperil Our Country and Civilization.* New York: St.
Martin's Press.

———. 2006. *State of Emergency: The Third World Invasion and Conquest of
America.* New York: St. Martin's.

———. 2011. *Suicide of a Superpower: Will America Survive to 2025?* New York:
St. Martin's.

Chavez, Leo R. 2001. *Covering Immigration: Popular Images and the Politics
of the Nation.* Berkeley: University of California Press.

———. 2004. "A Glass Half Empty: Latina Reproduction and Public Discourse."
Human Organization 63 (2): 173–188.

———. 2013. *The Latino Threat: Constructing Citizens, Immigrants, and the
Nation.* 2nd ed. Stanford, CA: Stanford University Press.

———. 2017. *Anchor Babies and the Challenge of Birthright Citizenship.*
Stanford, CA: Stanford University Press.

Coaston, Jane. 2018. "Watch: Tucker Carlson Rails against America's Demogra-
hic Changes." *Vox,* March 21, 2018. www.vox.com/2018/3/21/17146866
/tucker-carlson-demographics-immigration-fox-news.

Colby, Sandrea L., and Jennifer M. Ortman. 2014. *Projections of the Size
and Composition of the U.S. Population: 2014 to 2060.* Current
Population Reports, P25–1143. Washington DC: United States Census
Bureau.

Ehrenreich, Barbara. 2015. "Dead, White, and Blue." *Huffpost,* December 1,
2015. www.huffingtonpost.com/barbara-ehrenreich/middle-class-life
-expectancy_b_8687694.html.

Ehrlich, Paul R. 1968. *The Population Bomb.* New York: Ballantine Books.

Ehrlich, Paul, Loy Bilderback, and Anne H. Ehrlich. 1979. *The Golden Door.*
New York: Ballantine Books.

Gerstle, Gary. 2001. *American Crucible: Race and Nation in the Twentieth Century*. Princeton, NJ: Princeton University Press.

———. 2004. "The Immigrant as Threat to American Security: A Historical Perspective." In *The Maze of Fear: Security and Migration After 9/11*, edited by John Tirman, 87–108. New York: The New Press.

Geyer, Georgie Ann. 1996. *Americans No More*. New York: Atlantic Monthly Press.

Gibson, Campbell J., and Emily Lennon. 1999. "Historical Census Statistics on the Foreign-Born Population of the United States: 1850 to 1990." Working Paper no. 29, U.S. Census Bureau, Washington, DC.

Gilchrist, Jim, and Jerome R. Corsi. 2006. *Minutemen: The Battle to Secure America's Borders*. Los Angeles: World Ahead.

Grant, Madison. 1916. *The Passing of the Great Race, or The Racial Basis of European History*. New York: Charles Scribner's Sons.

Grenoble, Ryan. 2020. "Stephen Miller Echoes White Nationalists in Leaked Anti-DACA Emails." *Yahoo! News*, January 14, 2020.

Gutiérrez, Elena R. 2008. *Fertile Matters: The Politics of Mexican-Origin Women's Reproduction*. Austin: University of Texas Press.

Henry, William A. III. 1990. "Beyond the Melting Pot." *Time*, April 9, 1990, 28–31.

"Here's Donald Trump's Presidential Announcement Speech." 2015. *Time*, June 16, 2015.

Higham, John. (1955) 2002. *Strangers in the Land: Patterns of American Nativism, 1860–1925*. New Brunswick, NJ: Rutgers University Press.

Hochschild, Arlie Russell. 2016. *Strangers in Their Own Land: Anger and Mourning on the Amercan Right*. New York: The New Press.

Huber, Lindsay Perez. 2016. "'Make America Great Again!': Donald Trump, Racist Nativism and the Virulent Adherence to White Supremacy amid U.S. Demographic Change." *Charleston Law Review* 10: 215–48.

Kaufmann, Eric. 2019. *Whiteshift: Populism, Immigration and the Future of White Majorities*. New York: Harry N. Abrams.

Kelley, Daryl. 2004. "California Cuts Its Population Projection." *Los Angeles Times*, October 4, 2004, A-1.

"Klan's Border Patrols Begin." 1977. *Desert Sun*, October 27, 1977. https://cdnc.ucr.edu/cgi-bin/cdnc?a=d&d=DS19771026.2.27&e=-------en--20--1--txt-txIN--------1.

Kochhar, Rakesh, and Anthony Cilluffo. 2018. "Income Inequality in the U.S. Is Rising Most Rapidly among Asians." Pew Research Center, July 12, 2018. www.pewsocialtrends.org/2018/07/12/income-inequality-in-the-u-s-is-rising-most-rapidly-among-asians/.

Livingston, Gretchen. 2019. "Hispanic Women No Longer Account for the Majority of Immigrant Births in the U.S." Pew Research Center, August 8,

2019. www.pewresearch.org/fact-tank/2019/08/08/hispanic-women-no-longer-account-for-the-majority-of-immigrant-births-in-the-u-s/.

Mahmud, Lilith. 2020. "Fascism, a Haunting: Spectral Politics and Antifascist Resistance in Twenty-First-Century Italy." In *Beyond Populism: Angry Politics and the Twilight of Neoliberalism,* edited by Jeff Moskovsky and Sophie Bjork-James. Morgantown: West Virginia University Press.

Malkin, Michelle. 2002. *Invasion: How America Still Welcomes Terrorists, Criminals, & Other Foreign Menaces to Our Shores.* Washington, DC: Regnery.

Maskovsky, Jeff, and Sophie Bjork-James. 2020. *Beyond Populism: Angry Politics and the Twilight of Neoliberalism.* Morgantown: West Virginia University Press.

Massey, Douglas S., and Magaly Sánchez R. 2012. *Brokered Boundaries: Creating Immigrant Identity in Anti-Immigrant Times.* New York: Russell Sage Foundation.

Mazzarella, William. 2019. "The Anthropology of Populism: Beyond the Liberal Settlement." *Annual Review of Anthropology* 48: 45–60.

Miroff, Nick, and Josh Dawsey. 2020. "Stephen Miller Has Long-Term Vision for Trump's 'Temporary' Immigration Order, According to Private Call with Supporters." *Washington Post,* April 24, 2020.

Mulligan, Jessica M., and Emily K. Brunson. 2020. "Structures of Resentment: On Feeling—and Being—Left Behind by Health Care Reform." *Cultural Anthropology* 35 (2): 317–43.

NFAP (National Foundation for American Policy). 2020. *The Impact of Administration Policies on Immigration Levels and Labor Force Growth.* Arlington, VA: National Foundation for American Policy.

Nwanevu, Osita. 2017. "How the *National Review* Helped Build the Alt-Right: The Magazine Laid the Foundations for the Movement It Now Opposes." *Slate,* March 23, 2017.

O'Sullivan, John. 1994. "America's Identity Crisis." *National Review,* November 21, 1994, 36.

Parrado, Emilio A., and S. Philip Morgan. 2008. "Intergenerational Fertility among Hispanic Women: New Evidence of Immigrant Assimilation." *Demography* 45 (3): 651–71.

Pitkin, John, and Dowell Myers. 2012. *Generational Projections of the California Population by Nativity and Year of Immigrant Arrival.* Los Angeles: Population Dynamics Research Group, Sol Price School of Public Policy, University of Southern California.

"Population: The Numbers Game." 1960. *Time,* January 11, 1960.

Radford, Jynnah, and Luis Noe-Bustamante. 2019. "Facts on U.S. Immigrants, 2017." Pew Research Center. www.pewresearch.org/hispanic/2019/06/03/facts-on-u-s-immigrants/.

Rogers, Katie, and Jason DeParle. 2019. "The White Nationalist Websites Cited by Stephen Miller." *New York Times*, November 18, 2019. www.nytimes.com /2019/11/18/us/politics/stephen-miller-white-nationalism.html?search ResultPosition=3.

Romero, Simon. 2019. "Militia in New Mexico Detains Aslyum Seekers at Gunpoint." *New York Times*, April 18, 2019.

Romero, Simon, Manny Fernandez, and Mariel Padilla. 2019. "Massacre at a Crowded Walmart in Texas Leaves 20 Dead." *New York Times*, August 3, 2019.

Sáenz, Rogelio, and Kenneth M. Johnson. 2018. "White Deaths Exceed Births in a Majority of U.S. States: A Census Data Brief by the Applied Population Lab." Applied Population Lab, University of Wisconsin–Madison. https://apl .wisc.edu/briefs_resources/pdf/natural-decrease-18.pdf.

Schleifer, Theodore. 2017. "King Doubles Down on Controversial 'Babies' Tweet." *CNN Politics*, March 14, 2017.

Schlesinger, Arthur M. Jr. 1992. *The Disuniting of America*. New York: W. W. Norton.

Semega, Jessica, Melissa Kollar, John Creamer, and Abinash Mohanty. 2019. *Income and Poverty in the United States, 2019*. Report No. P60–266. Washington, DC: U.S. Government Printing Office.

Shoshan, Nitzan. 2016. *The Management of Hate: Nation, Affect, and the Governance of Right-Wing Extremism in Germany*. Princeton, NJ: Princeton University Press.

Stern, Alexandra Minna. 2019. *Proud Boys and the White Ethnostate: How the Alt-Right Is Warping the American Imagination*. Boston: Beacon Press.

Taub, Amanda. 2016. "'White Nationalism,' Explained." *New York Times*, November 21, 2016. www.nytimes.com/2016/11/22/world/americas/white -nationalism-explained.html.

Tavernise, Sabrina. 2018. "U.S. Fertiilty Rate Fell to a Record Low, for a Second Straight Year." *New York Times*, May 16, 2018.

"That Time David Duke and the KKK Patrolled the Mexican Border." 2016. *Dangerous Minds*, December 7, 2016.

Tirman, John. 2015. "The Origins of Intolerance in America." *Huffpost*, December 15, 2015. www.huffpost.com/entry/the-origins-of-intolerance _b_8812476.

"Total Fertility Rate for Population Estimates and Projections, by Race-Hispanic Origin and Generation: 1965–1970, 2015–2020 and 2060–2065." 2015. Pew Research Center. www.pewresearch.org/hispanic/2015/09/28 /modern-immigration-wave-brings-59-million-to-u-s-driving-population -growth-and-change-through-2065/9-26-2015-1-30-23-pm-2/.

Trump, Donald J. 2016. "Donald J. Trump: Address on Immigration" (speech in Phoenix, AZ). *P2016 Race for the White House: Press Releases, Advisories, Statements*, August 31, 2016. www.p2016.org/trump/trump083116sp.html.

Vespa, Jonathan, David M. Armstrong, and Lauren Medina. 2020. "Demographic Turning Points for the United States: Population Projections for 2020 to 2060." U.S. Census Bureau. www.census.gov/content/dam /Census/library/publications/2020/demo/p25–1144.pdf.

"Wednesday's GOP Debate Transcript, Annotated." 2015. *Washington Post,* September 16, 2015. www.p2016.org/trump/trump083116sp.html.

Zhao, Christina. 2019. "Donald Trump Has Run Roughly 2,200 Facebook Ads Using the Word 'Invasion' since May 2018." *Newsweek,* September 30, 2019.

12 Unmaking the Nation of Immigrants

HOW JOHN TANTON'S NETWORK OF ORGANIZATIONS TRANSFORMED POLICY AND POLITICS

Carly Goodman

By 2016, public polling in the United States showed historically high support for immigrants and immigration, while Donald Trump captured the Republican nomination for the presidency with unusually vitriolic anti-immigrant rhetoric.[1] His signature issue elicited intense support from a narrow section of the public and helped land him in the White House. Far from a policy wonk, when he assumed the presidency, he brought a range of professionals into his government to help transform the words that had so animated his rallies into policies.

He drew inspiration and expertise from a handful of organizations that had been at the forefront of the anti-immigration movement for decades, including "FAIR"—the Federation for American Immigration Reform—and the "Center for Immigration Studies" (CIS).

The Trump administration began ticking off boxes on CIS's blueprint for the new administration, bringing both public protests at the cruelty of the policies and a series of injunctions from the courts. But the administration

The author is grateful for the financial support of the Bordin-Gillette Researcher Travel Fellowship at the Bentley Historical Library, University of Michigan, for facilitating research in the papers of John Tanton.

doubled down, transforming the immigration system as dramatically as it could from the executive branch. With a pen and a phone, Trump began to remake the immigration policy landscape.[2] Such swift action was possible because he had the plans, expertise, and support of a small group of well-funded and interrelated organizations that boasted limited grassroots support but deep experience and a powerful media presence.

To understand the anti-immigration movement and its power within the Trump administration, it is critical to understand where these organizations came from and how they gained traction in the 1980s and 1990s: by positioning themselves at the center of the debate, using savvy messaging and media strategies, and steadily transforming the politics of immigration to support greater restrictions, treat immigrants as a threat, and slow the rate of demographic transformation of the country.

John Tanton founded FAIR, CIS, and other groups, and used their apparent independence and related missions to create an anti-immigration ecosystem to challenge the mythic ideal of the "nation of immigrants." Between the late 1970s and early 1990s, his organizations helped shape and exploit the media narratives of immigration-related events to build support for punitive policies and undermine support for humane ones. Fostering a truly grassroots broad-based movement was not Tanton's goal, however, because he understood that the most fervent support for his project came from people and groups that would undermine his claim to the center. By selectively cultivating grass-tops allies while carefully managing the grassroots, Tanton and his organizations claimed a position at the center and defined its terms, eventually making the strident anti-immigration politics of the Trump administration conceivable.

CREATING THE TANTON NETWORK

Between 1924 and 1965, the United States restricted immigration through a quota system that privileged immigrants from northern and western Europe, limited immigration from southern and eastern Europe, and all but excluded immigrants from Asia and Africa. When President Lyndon B. Johnson signed the Immigration Act of 1965 into law, he framed the new legislation as nonrevolutionary but nonetheless transformative. No longer would the United States and its values be "distorted by the harsh injustice of the national origins quota system" that had been in place since the 1920s.[3] Overt discrimination on the basis of national origin and race was no longer acceptable. The act ended the quota system and the racism it had come to represent, while imposing new numerical limits on immigration from the Western Hemisphere.

But Johnson and others had reason to believe that the revised language of the bill would correct a historical wrong—a racist law—without changing the demographic makeup of the country. Basing the system on family reunification and keeping and imposing key restrictions, they imagined that small numbers of mostly Europeans would continue to immigrate to the United States while a decolonizing world would appreciate but be unable to act on changes that made them broadly eligible to immigrate.

They didn't anticipate three changes to immigration: an increase in the number of immigrants, a shift such that a majority came from Asia and Latin America, and the rise of unauthorized immigration, a result of the imposition of limits on Mexican migration.[4]

In the years that followed, policymakers and media reports focused on the border as a site of insecurity, with President Jimmy Carter planning to build new fencing between the countries; objections from both sides of the so-called "Tortilla Curtain" led to a scaling back of the plan.[5] Immigration and Naturalization Service (INS) commissioner Leonard Chapman wrote an alarmist *Reader's Digest* piece in 1976 warning of a "vast and silent invasion of illegal immigrants across our borders . . . fast reaching the proportion of a national disaster."[6] White power activists also focused on border insecurity, including David Duke, who drew media attention when he organized the Ku Klux Klan into an armed Border Patrol in 1977.[7]

But at the time, there was no organized effort to lobby Congress for immigration restriction. Established groups working on Capitol Hill tended to be more interested in liberalizing immigration than restricting it: to ensure a steady labor supply, for humanitarian purposes, and to facilitate family reunification.[8] The 1965 act had repudiated the eugenicist origins of the previous restrictions, and overtly racist arguments for restriction were unlikely to find outspoken proponents on the Hill. Soon filling the void was the Federation for American Immigration Reform (FAIR), founded in 1979.[9]

Lobbying Congress and building the public's support for more restrictionist policies would require carefully avoiding any association with the
restrictionists who had succeeded so powerfully in the 1920s. The man
who took on the challenge was Dr. John Tanton. An unassuming ophthalmologist from Petoskey, a tiny lakeside resort town in northern Michigan,
his interest in immigration grew out of his environmental activism and
interest in population control. He had previously worked on local issues
related to development and environmental degradation, warning neighbors in northern Michigan that their way of life was under attack, threatened by downstate urbanites who had "destroyed" their environments and
now sought to do the same in the pristine "unspoiled" north.[10]

This theme carried into the work that would define the rest of his life:
immigration. "Around 1971 it became apparent to us that immigration
contributed significant amounts to population growth in the United
States," he told a newspaper in 1974. "This is because the native birthrate
is declining and because immigrants are mostly in their twenties and thir-
ties and therefore more fertile than a cross-section would be."[11]

In the 1960s Tanton chaired the Population Committee for his Sierra
Club chapter.[12] But he struggled to get the national organization involved
in immigration policy. As he wrote in 1974, "Because of the role which
immigration has played in American history, and because there is an emotional sensitivity to the issue, very few individuals and no major group has
been willing to begin a vigorous public discussion."[13] He eventually served
as president of the organization Zero Population Growth (ZPG) from
1975 to 1977, chairing its Immigration Study Committee. In 1977,
Melanie Wirken, hired as the project's director, was working with the
Carter administration on immigration issues. And as early as 1977, the
organization was meeting with the INS, the State Department, and White
House staff.[14] Tanton also cultivated relationships with organizations like
the National Border Patrol Union, the Border Patrol's labor union, and the
INS's labor union, to encourage their presence at ZPG meetings and
to find ways to collaborate to address what he called the "illegal alien
problem."[15]

Almost immediately, Tanton put issues of cultural threat front and
center. He suggested that a major problem in the 1970s was the growth of
"bilingualism and its illegitimate child of separatism," and specifically he

was concerned about the concentration of Spanish-speaking people among newcomers. His stated goal was "to end illegal immigration," which had already become the focus of public critique of immigration, but also "to reform policies governing legal immigration, conforming them to today's demographic, resource, political and social realities."[16]

By 1978, Tanton had identified a need he could fill: "an organization on the restrictionist side around which the dominant public opinion can coalesce, providing the strength and visibility needed to push for change . . . A new one must be started for this specific purpose." The plan was to "garner support from all sides of the political spectrum," and to avoid being dismissed as too right-wing, or too similar to 1920s restrictionists. "We plan to make the restriction of immigration a legitimate position for thinking people, and to have FAIR identified in the minds of leaders in the media, academia and government as speaking for a consensus of American thought and opinion," he proposed.[17]

Other than a growing sense that immigration was becoming more politically fraught, it was unclear how the public really felt about immigration restriction. Polling on immigration grew increasingly negative during the 1980s.[18] But FAIR found the public mood muted. As Roger Conner, FAIR's first executive director put it, "We were wrong to think that there was massive, intense concern. We were wrong to be fooled by looking at the opinion polls . . . Our support was broad and thin like the top, warm layer of the Atlantic Ocean and there was nothing underneath."[19]

Deepening that support would require dramatically shifting the terms of the debate.

DEVELOPING MESSAGES THAT WORKED

> In our nation of immigrants, the question naturally arises,
> why can't we help? Overcrowding and underdevelopment
> have been solved by migration before. Why a limit now?
> The answer lies in the numbers.
> FAIR pamphlet

Tanton and FAIR executive director Roger Conner understood that the major hurdle to advancing their cause was "the traditional character of the

United States as a nation of immigrants," as Tanton put it.[20] As Conner noted, "the history of immigration was recalled by Americans as a history of racist exclusion. That's a history we had to overcome if we were going to be influential . . . "[21] FAIR's messaging therefore avowedly avoided any talk of race.

"The issue for the modern immigration debate is not race or ethnicity, it's numbers," said Conner.[22] It was a savvy, if slippery, observation. As immigration increased in the 1970s and 1980s, it became possible to frame the numbers as viscerally overwhelming. Moreover, focusing on numbers rather than individuals' stories distanced the debate from its human component and burnished FAIR's image as neutral and fact-driven. But as those who legislated the 1965 act understood well, one needn't articulate formal racial exclusion in order to try to effect it. "Restricting" immigration by the numbers instead of "excluding" based on race would, in an age of high immigration of nonwhite people, limit and exclude the migration of nonwhite people.

Tanton and FAIR also believed that if immigrants from countries with high fertility rates were limited in coming to the United States, the overall population growth rate could be slowed. As FAIR Board member, donor, and Gulf Oil tycoon Sidney Swensrud put it, "I think we all had an objection to races that had extremely high birth rates, so that if they came into this country they would present greater population problems than if they had birth rates about like our own."[23] The issue of immigrant birthrates was important to Tanton and other FAIR members who came to the issue from population control circles, because of the question of resource depletion and environmental degradation—but also because of assumptions they made about the different birthrates of people of different races. "As our native birthrate falls, immigration will account for an increasing proportion of our growth," Tanton warned.[24]

This framing touched on issues of cultural assimilation and evoked the specter of "white replacement theory," the eugenicist fear about the "passing" of the "great race," as Madison Grant put it in his influential 1916 book. Such ideas echoed in FAIR's messaging: "Though today this flood of illegal immigrants effects [sic] the lives of only a few U.S. citizens, in 20 years it will be an excruciating problem for all of us. In a couple of generations the offspring of these illegal immigrants may have more influence on how our grandchildren live than they do."[25] Without explicitly mentioning race, FAIR affirmed a national identity that centered whiteness.

In 1980, the Select Commission on Immigration and Refugee Policy estimated that year's admissions at 808,000, the "largest annual admission of legal immigrants to the United States since 1921," as FAIR noted.[26] FAIR was deeply concerned about imposing greater limits on legal immigration but found that it was out of step with the mainstream on this issue. The public and policymakers were more interested in addressing unauthorized immigration, which they could do while still upholding the idea of the "nation of immigrants" and the welcoming stance of the Statue of Liberty. So FAIR tended to center the issue of undocumented immigration in its public materials as well.[27]

FAIR helped fuel the narrative that unauthorized immigration was a problem, an "overwhelming influx" that would be "catastrophic." "Polls show that 90 percent of Americans favor shutting off the flow of illegal immigrants," went one FAIR newspaper ad. "As long as this 90 percent of us remain a silent, but overwhelming, majority, America's control of its future will continue to be eroded by illegal immigration."[28] By invoking the idea of the "silent majority," FAIR used masked language to target a white audience, one it expected could be made to feel threatened by immigration if it framed the issue properly: as overwhelming in numbers, likely to have a disproportionate impact on the future because of higher birthrates, and "illegal" and thus immoral or criminal.

SPREADING MESSAGES THROUGH THE MEDIA

FAIR enjoyed its first national media attention after filing a lawsuit in 1979 that argued that the 1980 census should not count unauthorized immigrants.[29]A reporter from the *Christian Science Monitor* covered the lawsuit, and the story was picked up nationally. Conner was invited on the *MacNeil-Lehrer NewsHour*. And then nothing happened, until the next summer, when a refugee "crisis" was "*thrust* upon television" in the Mariel boatlift of 1980.[30]

Initially, the U.S. government supported resettling these Cuban refugees—like previous waves of Cuban refugees, they were fleeing a Communist regime, and the United States had long welcomed Cubans fleeing Castro with open arms. But locally in Florida, the issue had become a hot-button one, with Miami's residents angry about the disorderly arrival of people on boats to the city's shores.

And then, the *Today Show* called. Mariel was becoming a national issue in an election year, and the show decided "they would have someone speak for the view that the Cubans should be stopped." As Conner recalled, "Whoever their reporter was couldn't find anybody who was willing to speak for that view. He then remembered that census case. So he looked up FAIR and called me and said, 'What about coming on the *Today Show* to talk about the need to stop the Cubans?'"[31]

The show went out of its way to find somebody to speak for that "side" of the debate, and in the process set the "center" of the debate markedly closer to exclusion. Conner went on Neal Rogers's radio show in South Florida to discuss the issue and later remembered the famous broadcaster's gratitude. "Thank God I've found you," Rogers told him, according to Conner's oral history. "I've finally found somebody who's rational. I've got the rednecks calling me. I've got the racists calling me. I'm an old-fashioned liberal myself," Rogers reportedly said, "but what's happening right here in Miami is . . . " He trailed off.[32] Unable to find spokespeople who were not "rednecks" to speak against resettling Cubans, media outlets were grateful to—and went out of their way to—put Conner on the air, setting the terms of the debate in the process. Whether this impulse was designed to uphold the FCC's "fairness doctrine" or was just reflected ingrained journalistic practice, it had a major effect on how the public understood this and other issues. Instead of framing the issue in other terms—How should resettlement funding be shared? What agencies can help provide shelter?—the question became: *how can we stop the Cubans?*

Before FAIR, there was no national-level organization to take that position. Locally, the group Citizens of Dade County United was expressing this position in terms that Conner recalled as "simply filled with free-floating anger, hostility and anxiety. They wanted to drive around and blow horns and tell the Cubans to get the you-know-what out."[33] FAIR offered a palatable alternative, putting out messages that framed the Cuban influx as out of control without resorting to racist language or violence.

IMMIGRATION REFORM

Building relationships with media outlets proved fruitful in the fight on Capitol Hill for immigration reform. The Select Commission on Immigration and Refugee Policy had recommended in its 1981 report that the United States address unauthorized immigration by imposing sanctions on employers who hired undocumented workers while beefing up border security. In Congress, Select Commission member Senator Alan K. Simpson, Republican from Wyoming, and Representative Romano Mazzoli, Democrat from Kentucky, began incorporating this recommendation into legislation, which they first proposed in 1982 in a bill that used employer sanctions, border security, and a one-time legalization program to wipe the slate clean on unauthorized immigration.

FAIR supported the bill, working closely with Simpson and members of the Reagan administration. In early April 1982, Roger Conner testified to support the bill, and Mazzoli thanked him for "bringing it to the attention of the American people"—a reference to the tremendous work FAIR was doing to publicize the bill and frame the issue for the public.[34]

The next week, when Simpson wrote to Reagan to urge his support, he was careful to frame the bill as being "without the tinges of nativism and racism which have characterized almost all of our past 'reforms.'" This line, which he used in the hearings as well, signaled how important it was that immigration restriction in the 1980s eschew overt racial prejudice. FAIR had helped provide alternative language for restriction.[35] Simpson enclosed editorials supporting the legislation for the president to consider.

Here too, FAIR had been instrumental. Colorado governor Dick Lamm took Conner to the *New York Times* and to *Time* magazine, and at the same time allies in the administration like Attorney General William French Smith and Simpson were going around and meeting with editorial boards, repeating the same talking points. "These editorial writers,"

Conner explained, "began to respond because they'd met one of us. They'd see that we were rational centrists. We were giving them an inside story about what was going on [with immigration] that their own beat reporters usually didn't give them." Then, FAIR would circulate resulting editorial pieces to all the members of Congress to convey a sense of "growing consensus, a growing concern, among the right thinking people, of 'let's do something before that angry grassroots comes up from behind.'"[36]

Conner met with Jack Rosenthal of the *New York Times*, who won a 1982 Pulitzer for his editorials in support of the Simpson-Mazzoli Act. "A million people are waiting in line to enter the United States legally; millions more are eager to jump the line; and the nation must choose which to let through the door," Rosenthal wrote. The more the system "spins out of control," he warned, "the more Americans lose patience with Government—and perhaps with any immigration at all."[37]

The legislation lagged, failing to pass in the 97th or 98th Congress. The bill had opponents that included agriculture, employers, and organized labor. Liberals like Senator Ted Kennedy, Democrat from Massachusetts, did not support employer sanctions because the policy seemed likely to encourage discrimination in hiring, causing him to withhold support from a bill that also promised to legalize millions of unauthorized immigrants. Behind the scenes, FAIR used its research to prompt a 1985 Government Accounting Office report on employer sanctions outside the United States that showed that the policy was nondiscriminatory.[38] Meanwhile, Rosenthal at the *New York Times* wrote in early 1986 that employer sanctions had become "well within the liberal-conservative consensus that has formed in the last decade."[39] That consensus was built by FAIR, and Ronald Reagan signed the Immigration Reform and Control Act into law in November 1986.

And while IRCA had provisions FAIR didn't support, it created the framework for immigration reform that insisted on restrictionist elements as the basis of any agreement. Increasing border security became a permanent feature of immigration policy debates and central to immigration politics more broadly. And while FAIR was unable to achieve its legislative goal of limiting legal immigration, either in the legislation of the 1980s or in the Immigration Act of 1990, the organization doubled down on its effort to shape the public conversation.

SPREADING INFLUENCE WITHOUT BECOMING
A MASS MOVEMENT

John Tanton had founded FAIR as a policy advocacy organization that would channel grassroots energy and bring it to Washington. On Capitol Hill, special interest groups needed to be seen as representing specific constituencies. In this case, FAIR would be giving a voice to the "average U.S. citizen." "We felt we had to do it, if for no other reason than to have some members behind us," he said, explaining why FAIR launched a direct mail campaign in the early 1980s. "When we were asked the question of whom we represented, we had, in fact, some citizens we represented and people who would write letters, we hoped, when they were asked to do so."[40] Having members "gives you some credibility for your lobbying effort," he said.[41]

But members could be a problem, too, especially for an organization seeking to define "the center."[42] Tanton worried that unvetted people sympathetic to the cause "might go off half-cocked and spoil the whole effort."[43] In Miami in 1980, for example, the only groups that shared FAIR's thinking on immigration did so by, as Otis Graham put it, "speaking in direct ethnic, cultural terms of dislike or conflict."[44] FAIR soon learned that "the way to control the grassroots is to have staff there."[45]

What appealed to supporters seemed "like dangerous territory" to some of FAIR's board members.[46] "I knew that the public could be aroused to go, in a sense, into the streets, but were not going to be chanting slogans like 'We need zero population growth to protect the environment.' There were going to be some other slogans," recalled Roger Conner ominously.[47]

Unable to build up a robust membership program—either because its ideas were unpopular or because of the overt racism required to appeal to people who shared its beliefs—FAIR relied for funding on a few major donors and foundations, most importantly The Pioneer Fund, a eugenicist foundation founded by 1920s immigration restrictionist Harry Laughlin, and Cordelia Scaife May, a reclusive heiress of the Mellon family fortune.[48]

Not having a true grassroots movement, Tanton worked to create the appearance of a broad grass-tops movement, courting thinkers and activists to seed an anti-immigration ecosystem. He founded a publishing company and journal, the Social Contract Press, to help spread his ideas and lend them an air of quasi-academic authority.

He also started other organizations to perform different roles in the movement, from a congressional lobbying organization to an official English organization, to the Center for Immigration Studies, the think-tank-like organization whose innocuous name belies strident positions. Owing to its "research-oriented profile and greater appearance of objectivity," as FAIR president Dan Stein put it, "its reports have been accepted by the media and some members of Congress as authentic research ... it plays a very valuable role, and has continued to develop as an independent organization and perform much of the mission it was originally designed to carry out."[49]

Creating a broad network of interrelated organizations, Tanton was able to produce the appearance of a wide-ranging grassroots movement. Media reports might include quotes from multiple Tanton groups without knowing or noting the links, giving the appearance that they formed a consensus view.

GROWING INFLUENCE IN THE 1990S

When FAIR's press secretary Dan Stein became the organization's executive director in 1988, he channeled more energy than ever into "making the case to the people."[50] In the early 1990s, anti-immigration took off as a grassroots issue.[51] The moment that the winds changed, Stein said, was when a judge issued an injunction against interdicting boats carrying Haitian asylum seekers in 1991. The injunction precipitated a legal battle while thousands of people were held at Guantanamo. But the fight took place in the political sphere, in the middle of an election year in which President Bush was facing a primary challenge by Pat Buchanan, running on a nativist "America First" agenda. FAIR was delighted to draw parallels between the Haitian boat people in 1991 and the Mariel Cubans back in 1980.

In doing so, FAIR's messaging, adopted by journalists and interviewers, drew on and advanced threat narratives and racial scripts about who belonged and who didn't. They didn't need to be explicit about barring

immigrants based on race or nationality. They could speak only about numbers and control, and there were these "TV visuals of crowded leaky boats
that seared the public consciousness and moved the issue higher up onto
the agenda."[52] The images contributed to a crisis narrative, framing
migrants themselves as a problem, shaking the public's support for a com-
passionate response. They echoed FAIR board member Garrett Hardin's
essay about lifeboat ethics, reinforcing the idea that in the 1990s, migration
was a zero-sum game pitting insiders against outsiders, us versus them.
"The issue changed dimensions and dynamics from that point forward and
it has never been the same," said Stein. "It may never be the same."

Other events in the early 1990s provided FAIR with the opportunity to
build its domination of media coverage including the 1993 World Trade
Center bombing—which led to a high-profile episode of "60 Minutes"
where FAIR framed asylum seekers as innately threatening and the system as unaccountably insecure and vulnerable to abuse. The core values
that Tanton had previously highlighted as his main opponent—the idea of
the nation of immigrants—were, in FAIR's telling, quaint qualities better
suited to the distant past. With the threat of catastrophic violence looming, did it make any sense for the United States to continue to welcome
the world's vulnerable?[53] In 1993, Stein said, FAIR had three thousand
press calls, and on average they garnered three to four hundred media
clips each week. The media's framing of immigration thus echoed FAIR's
and helped build support for a series of harsh policies in the 1990s that
caused immigration detention and deportation to skyrocket, in particular
the Illegal Immigration Reform and Immigrant Responsibility Act of
1996. As Stein said, "The acceptance of the issue itself and the recognition
of the basic core problems . . . means that you can now talk about the issue
in ways that you simply could not when I first came to FAIR."[54]

TANTON'S MEMOS

Critics of FAIR charged that the group was advancing policies that would
harm immigrants and communities of color. The pro-restrictionist organization had appeared suddenly on Capitol Hill and had shown immediate
influence, gaining allies in the government and prime media hits. The

Immigration Reform and Control Act in 1986 contained compromises, but it had set the terms of debate. Tanton's wish had come true: restriction was a legitimate, bipartisan position.

Yet in Tanton's writings and the positions adopted by his organizations was evidence that at the heart of this effort was not concern about U.S. sovereignty, national security, or even uncontrolled immigration. For one thing, FAIR and Tanton remained committed to reducing legal immigration, calling in the early 1990s for a "moratorium" on legal immigration.

And Tanton's writers' workshops and Social Contract Press featured thinkers and ideas that were far outside the mainstream discourse on immigration, including Samuel Francis, Wayne Lutton, Larry Auster, Peter Brimelow (the founder of VDARE), and Jared Taylor of *American Renaissance*. The Social Contract Press published an English-language edition of the racist French novel *Camp of the Saints,* a favorite of the Far Right, which portrays white Europe under siege by an armada of non-white refugees.[55] While FAIR avoided being labeled a special interest group for white people, as FAIR board member and historian Otis Graham put it, the inclusion of people "whose chief interest was the implications of a loss of a white majority" in the writers' workshops was warranted because it "struck me as a legitimate position."[56]

In a notorious 1986 memo, Tanton posed a series of questions about what he called "the Latin onslaught." He wondered what would happen to whites' power in a country where they were no longer in the majority: "Will the present majority peaceably hand over its political power to a group that is simply more fertile?" "Can *homo contraceptivus* compete with *homo progenitiva* if borders aren't controlled?" he mused. "Or is advice to limit one's family simply advice to move over and let someone else with greater reproductive powers occupy the space?" He made a crass joke: "Perhaps this is the first instance in which those with their pants up are going to get caught by those with their pants down!"[57] In addition to being "outbred," Tanton worried that if whites were no longer in the majority, it would harm the environmental movement. Conservation, he explained, is a "characteristic of American society" rooted in "Western Civilization." "If we look at the conservation ethic of some of the countries from which large numbers of immigrants are coming, we don't find the same sort of respect for the land and our fellow creatures that has developed here. We certainly don't see this in many of the southeastern Asian cultures or in Latin America."[58]

When the memo was published in a newspaper in 1988, Tanton lost some mainstream supporters, including Linda Chavez, who had been leading one of his organizations, and donor Walter Cronkite. But Tanton's positions didn't soften. He wrote in a 1988 memo of the problem at the heart of the population control movement that would have to be dealt with after immigration was brought under control: "Isn't the problem that the wrong people are having children?"[59] In his personal correspondence, he continued to worry about the "sub-replacement fertility rates" of the developed countries, and express frustration that those responsibly limiting their number of children appeared to be "handing our territory over to the more fertile, and thereby lose the battle."[60] In a 1995 letter he wrote "about what might be done to breath [sic] some life back in the eugenics movement, whether through restarting the American Eugenics Society, or some other means . . . One of the big questions is whether we need to try a new name—some euphemism—or whether we should simply go ahead with the present one and fight the battle for respectability."[61]

Tanton also seeded more extreme, fringe groups through funding, like the American Immigration Control Foundation (AICF). Dan Stein suggested that AICF might be too incendiary in its rhetoric—but "there's always room for all kinds, and there's plenty of opportunities for their mail to be out there educating the public."[62] Tanton donated to Glenn Spencer's organizations American Patrol (and sat on its advisory board) and Voices of Citizens Together.[63] In 1999, FAIR brought Roger Barnett, a border activist in Arizona who later claimed to have captured five thousand migrants to turn over to Border Patrol, to Capitol Hill for "Immigration Awareness Week" to speak with members of Congress. U.S. Inc., the umbrella organization Tanton had created, hired Barnett to spearhead its "Border Defense Coalition," a project largely focused on putting up billboards to advocate for sending the U.S. Army to the border. The initiative included former Border Patrol agent and long-term FAIR board member Bob Park.[64] Park also founded Veterans for Secure Borders, an Arizona billboard project, and the Article IV—Section 4 Foundation, a reference to the federal government's obligation to protect states from "invasion" which Park asserted was happening through immigration, or what he deemed "immivasion."[65] Bringing more radical and extreme voices and methods into the anti-immigration ecosystem helped keep Tanton's groups at the center, a reliable source for support for restrictive legislation on the Hill and the go-to voices to provide a quote in media stories on immigration.

CONCLUSIONS

While FAIR avoided explicit talk of race, an implicit understanding of the United States as a white nation undergirded its arguments about limiting immigration. Too much diversity, Tanton argued, "leads to divisiveness and conflict."[66] National unity is being sacrificed on the altar of diversity," wrote his biographer, echoing the sentiment.[67]

Borrowing from W. E. B. Du Bois, Tanton wrote about the "color line" issue of the twenty-first century. In 1998 he noted the "projection that early in the next century U.S. immigration policy, coupled with high immigrant fertility, will reduce the historic white, European-descended majority in the country to minority status. Whether the current majority group will acquiesce in its disenfranchisement, and how any such transition will be managed, will be one of the chief problems of the twenty-first century," Tanton warned. Noting that Americans of European descent faced increased hostility from nonwhites, he suggested that "the European-derived people of the U.S. would have something very real to fear if they were to become a minority in a country of people who have been taught to hate and fear them."[68] Elsewhere in the issue of *The Social Contract Press*—the last that Tanton edited—Samuel Francis wrote that whites were sacrificing their own future by not fighting harder to halt immigration.[69]

While such explicit white nationalism is often considered a fringe view, with varying power at different moments in history, the visceral sense that Tanton had that immigration threatened an American people he understood implicitly to be majority white was something he perceived was widely shared. These ideas animated his work.

And while the movement he built to sell and deliver those ideas to allies on the Hill and to journalists seeking quotes avoided such explicit talk, it too recognized that the primacy of whiteness was embedded in the mainstream institutions of American life, from the Senate to the *New York*

Times. FAIR and CIS endeavored to position themselves as middle-of-the-road. They found success not because their ideas were hugely popular—if anything, those at the grassroots who agreed with them were small, disorganized, and too openly driven by concerns about ethnicity to help FAIR grow itself into a true social movement. Instead, Tanton's organizations put a respectable face on the prorestriction side of the debate and found eager partners in Washington and in the media—eventually shaping the policy landscape such that border security, enforcement, and the urgent need for control were at the center of all reform legislation proposals after the 1980s.

13 The Expulsion of Immigrants

AMERICA'S DEPORTATION MACHINE

Adam Goodman

Headlines about immigration raids, detention camps, and border walls have dominated the news in recent years. But the deportation machine did not come into being during the presidency of Donald J. Trump. Nor did it first emerge during the administrations of Barack Obama, George W. Bush, or Bill Clinton. The machine's roots are much deeper, dating back to the late nineteenth century, when Congress gave the federal government plenary power over immigration, as described in Juan Perea's essay in this volume. Since then, both Democratic and Republican politicians and private third parties have contributed to its growth, implementing punitive policies and pouring the equivalent of hundreds of billions of dollars into enforcement efforts that have resulted in tens of millions of deportations by whatever means necessary.

To understand immigration enforcement under the Trump administration, we first must understand how the deportation machine works. In reality, we know relatively little about the vast majority of expulsions throughout U.S. history. Most scholars and journalists equate expulsions

Excerpted and updated from Adam Goodman, *The Deportation Machine: America's Long History of Expelling Immigrants* (Princeton, NJ: Princeton University Press, 2020).

with so-called formal deportations, which, until recently, often happened by order of an immigration judge. However, these only represent a small sliver of the total. More than eight of every ten deportations since the 1880s have occurred via a fast-track, administrative removal procedure euphemistically known as "voluntary departure." Countless others have left the country in response to calculated fear campaigns, violence, and anti-immigrant laws and policies meant to make people's lives so miserable they "self-deport" without ever coming into contact with immigration officials. These other means of expulsion have minimized the federal government's expenses and restricted immigrants' rights while achieving the same end: terrorizing communities amid what amounts to mass removals. Although most people have paid scant attention to these coercive mechanisms, any definition of deportation that excludes them is both inaccurate and misleading, as the Trump administration's enforcement actions make clear.[1]

Persistent political economic realities, racial prejudices, and cultural concerns have fueled widespread xenophobia during the past 140 years. The machine's three mechanisms—formal deportations, voluntary departures, and self-deportations—have functioned in unison, though at different levels at distinct moments. Authorities have used them to target Chinese communities across the U.S. West in the nineteenth century; southern and eastern Europeans at the turn of the twentieth century; people deemed immoral or a threat to public health, including women working (or suspected of working) as prostitutes and individuals whom officials considered deviants for being gay or lesbian; Mexicans and Filipinos pressured to repatriate in the 1930s; Japanese immigrants and Japanese Americans forcibly moved to internment camps during World War II; Mexicans vilified as prototypical "illegal aliens," especially after 1965; and Central American asylum seekers accused of being gang members, and Muslims, Arabs, and Middle Easterners stereotyped as potential terrorists in recent years.[2]

The fact that immigration officials have deported so many people, regardless of which party has been in the White House or has controlled Congress, makes it tempting to say that the machine has operated somewhat autonomously. And to an extent it has. But the Trump administration left no doubt that who is in power also matters.

The deportation machine was running on all cylinders under Donald Trump, who waged an all-out war against immigrants and immigration. His brazen anti-Black, anti-Latino, and anti-Muslim xenophobia has played a significant role at every stage of his political career. In a June 2015 speech announcing his candidacy, he referred to Mexican immigrants as criminals, drug smugglers, and rapists, and promised to "build a great, great wall on our southern border" for which Mexico would supposedly pay. In the lead-up to the election, Trump also pushed for more interior enforcement, mandatory detention after apprehension, and an end to sanctuary cities that offered certain protections to undocumented immigrants.[3]

Following his inauguration in January 2017, Trump set out to make good on the draconian campaign promises that had rallied the Republican base around him. During his first week in office, he signed a series of executive orders calling for the construction of a nearly two-thousand-mile wall along the U.S.-Mexico border, the hiring of an additional ten thousand Immigration and Customs Enforcement (ICE) officers and five thousand Border Patrol agents, and a ban on immigration from seven majority-Muslim countries. The orders also threatened to publish weekly lists of crimes immigrants committed and to fine and penalize not only undocumented people but also "those who facilitate their presence in the United States."[4]

Such dramatic policy changes and proclamations further emboldened immigration officers, whose morale skyrocketed in the weeks and months ahead. In a marked departure from Obama-era policies of prosecutorial discretion and preferential categories that offered some semblance of protection in name if not always in practice, officials made clear that all undocumented people were now deportation priorities. Trump, his then–press secretary Sean Spicer explained, "wanted to take the shackles off" immigration agents.[5] During the first eight months of Trump's presidency, apprehensions of immigrants with no criminal record increased, as ICE arrests spiked 42 percent. In the years thereafter, the crackdown on interior enforcement continued as arrests, workplace raids, and neighborhood sweeps spread throughout the nation and the Department of Homeland Security (DHS) reinitiated and expanded federal partnerships with local law enforcement agencies through programs such as 287(g) and Secure Communities.[6]

Private prison companies capitalized on the Trump administration's anti-immigrant rhetoric and enforcement-first mentality. GEO Group and CoreCivic each contributed $250,000 to Donald Trump's inauguration festivities. Between the November 2016 election and late February 2017, their stock prices had increased 140 and 98 percent, respectively. By the end of that year GEO Group's revenue reached an all-time high of $2.3 billion, up more than 250 percent from a decade earlier. During the president's first eighteen months in office, GEO Group and CoreCivic combined to spend more than $3 million on federal lobbying—and DHS granted them a total of $800 million in contracts. In June 2019, the number of migrants detained in public and private facilities—including a makeshift, outdoor camp in El Paso an observer described as "a human dog pound"—reached an all-time high of more than fifty-four thousand.[7]

In addition to ratcheting up enforcement, the Trump administration rolled out radical policies meant to curtail legal immigration. The president sought to end family-based "chain migration" from Latin America, Asia, Africa, and the Caribbean by eliminating key provisions of the 1965 Immigration and Nationality Act. The White House attempted to terminate DACA, for young people brought to the United States as children, and Temporary Protected Status, for people from war-torn or natural-disaster-stricken countries like El Salvador, Haiti, and South Sudan. If authorities had succeeded in ending them, as many as one million people—many of them long-term residents with U.S. citizen relatives—would have found themselves in legal limbo and potentially subject to deportation. Meanwhile, DHS set up a "denaturalization task force" to ferret out people who supposedly made false statements on their immigration petitions and strip them of citizenship. Agents arrested people who showed up for regular immigration check-ins and marriage interviews, and they denied passports to ethnic Mexicans born in the United States along the southwestern border. Officials implemented restrictions on immigrants' eligibility for visas and green cards if they had ever used public benefits such as food stamps or Medicaid, calling to mind restrictions on people "likely to become public charges" going back to the founding of the nation.[8]

Authorities set out to speed up deportations as well. The president took to Twitter to call for denying due process rights to immigrants in order to streamline expulsions: "We cannot allow all of these people to invade our

Country. When somebody comes in, we must immediately, with no Judges or Court Cases, bring them back from where they came. Our system is a mockery to good immigration policy and Law and Order." The Department of Justice, for its part, hired more than one hundred new immigration judges to handle the backlog of cases, which had ballooned to more than one million by the end of August 2019.[9]

The Trump administration also attempted to dismantle the nation's asylum system, drastically reducing the annual refugee quota, from 110,000 during Obama's last year in office to 30,000 in fiscal year 2019 and 18,000 in fiscal year 2020. To cut admissions even further, officials turned people away at the border before they could even request asylum, gummed up the vetting process, suspended the federal refugee resettlement program, and rewrote the rules to exclude victims of gang violence and domestic violence. In fiscal year 2018, the United States only admitted 22,491 refugees, fewer than half of the allotted quota. To justify such actions, Trump has demonized Black and Brown migrants and refugees as "animals," potential terrorists, "thieves and murderers," "snakes," and people from "shithole countries" who pose an existential threat to the United States and Europe. And in the spring and summer of 2020, authorities took advantage of the COVID-19 pandemic to severely restrict all entry into the country and to grant low-level agents the unilateral power to summarily remove anyone who showed up at the U.S.-Mexico border. By continuing to deport migrants and asylum seekers during the global public health crisis, the administration helped spread COVID-19 around the world.[10]

However, no policy change garnered more public attention or condemnation than President Trump's "zero tolerance" strategy. In April 2018, in response to an increase in migration across the southwest border, then attorney general Jeff Sessions declared that anyone entering the country without authorization would be criminally charged and ineligible to apply for asylum. Prosecutors charged migrants with no prior record with a misdemeanor, and judges in South Texas carried out mass hearings of up to eighty people at once and two hundred people per day, which was as many as the overwhelmed government lawyers could handle. Judges usually handed down sentences of time served to first-time offenders, which meant formal deportation was imminent. But people with prior offenses, including those who had been previously apprehended, faced felony convictions that resulted in stiffer prison sentences followed by expulsion and a twenty-year or even lifetime ban from the United States. Zero tolerance's crackdown on all unauthorized entries turned an increasing number of migrants and refugees into criminals in the eyes of the law. By the end of July 2018, the Department of Justice had convicted more than thirty thousand migrants.[11]

The month after zero tolerance went into effect, officials announced a second facet of the policy: the forced separation of detained parents and children, most of them Central American refugees, in hopes of deterring future unauthorized migration. The idea of separating families dated back to the 1950s, if not earlier. U.S. Citizenship and Immigration Services officer John Lafferty had floated it anew in February 2017, just two weeks after Trump's inauguration and more than a year before it gained national notoriety. According to Amnesty International, U.S. officials divided some eight thousand "family units" during 2017 and 2018, even after widespread protests and public pressure forced Trump to sign an executive order supposedly ending the practice. Similar to other prevention-through-deterrence measures, from the treatment of nearly fifty thousand Mexicans as human cargo during the infamous deportation boatlifts across the Gulf of Mexico in the 1950s to the militarization of the border during the last quarter-century, family separation represented an extreme form of state-sponsored violence that traumatized thousands of migrants and refugees.[12]

By June 2018, considerable lasting damage had occurred. The American Academy of Pediatrics warned that the family separation policy could "cause irreparable harm." Although a top ICE official described the detention facilities housing children—more than one hundred of them privately run—as "like a summer camp," photographs showed kids in cages and leaked audio revealed their desperate, inconsolable cries for "Mami" and "Papá." Detained children's days were regimented. At one facility near the Mexican border in South Texas, kids woke up at dawn and proceeded to clean the bathroom, including scrubbing the toilet, before eating breakfast and going on to have some schooling. The rules included no running, no sitting on the floor, no sharing food, and no touching other children, "even if that child is your hermanito or hermanita—your little brother or sister." DHS held some 250 kids and teens at a remote Border Patrol station in Clint, Texas, without adequate food, water, or sanitation. Some of the children had been there for weeks, without showering or changing clothes, even though government regulations require immigration officials to transfer them to the Department of Health and Human Services (HHS) within seventy-two hours. And at federally funded immigrant shelters in Chicago where authorities held minors for months, some tried to escape, undertook hunger strikes, and even contemplated suicide. Between fall 2018 and spring 2019, six children died in federal custody.[13]

Even though a federal court ordered authorities to reunite separated families by set dates, DHS and HHS authorities had no mechanism in place to easily do so since they had purposefully scattered them across the country. More challenging still was reconnecting kids with already-deported parents. Officials coerced some people into dropping their asylum claims and agreeing to deportation under the false pretense that it would expedite their family reunion. Instead, the opposite was true: some of these parents and children may never be reunited. While the Trump administration's zero tolerance policy tore apart families, it did not stop people from coming to the United States.[14]

In many ways, Trump's immigration enforcement policies were a continuation of those of his predecessors. But the administration's heavy reliance on self-deportation campaigns represented an important break from the recent past, even if it was not entirely unprecedented. Trump and administration officials like Stephen Miller deployed concerted fear campaigns, along with nativist policies and virulent anti-immigrant rhetoric, to push people further into the shadows or out of the United States altogether. "Real power is . . . fear," he told two *Washington Post* reporters in the lead-up to the 2016 election.[15] And, to be sure, the administration's scare tactics had a considerable impact on immigrant communities. As Juanita Molina, the executive director of the Tucson-based Border Action Network, told *The Guardian* a month after Trump's inauguration, "It's almost like it's psychological warfare that's being waged against people of color to create a constant feeling of fear and uncertainty."[16] Testifying before Congress a few months later, then acting director of ICE Thomas D. Homan essentially confirmed Molina's assessment. "If you're in this country illegally and you committed a crime by being in this country, you should be uncomfortable, you should look over your shoulder. You need to be worried."[17]

In response, dozens of people sought sanctuary in churches across the country. Jeanette Vizguerra, a forty-five-year-old undocumented immigrant from Mexico, took refuge in the basement of the First Unitarian Church in Denver for nearly three months before receiving a temporary stay of deportation. Forty-year-old Javier Flores García, an undocumented Mexican immigrant with three U.S. citizen children, spent nearly eleven months at the Arch Street United Methodist Church in downtown Philadelphia. He only left after receiving a special U visa for victims of crimes who agree to cooperate with the police.[18]

Other people self-deported. Thirty-six-year-old Miguel Hernández had lived and worked on the same Wisconsin dairy farm for sixteen years when, in June 2017, he, his wife Luisa, and their two U.S.-born sons, five and four, decided it was time to leave. While Luisa and the kids flew back to Mexico from Chicago, Hernández and four coworkers who also chose to return after years in the United States made the 2,300-mile trip to their mountainous town in the state of Veracruz in a Honda pickup truck packed with their possessions—"bags of clothes and shoes, TV sets in boxes and a bucket of children's toys." Explaining the reasoning behind their decision, one of the men told a Wisconsin Public Radio reporter, "It's better to go back home because of the laws—they're coming after us. It's better to go willingly and be with the family rather than getting deported."[19]

But the vast majority of the estimated ten to twelve million undocumented immigrants in the United States stayed. And, for many of them, living in constant fear became commonplace. "There is a dreadful sense of fear," Fred Morris, a United Methodist pastor in a mostly Latino neighborhood in Los Angeles told the Associated Press a few weeks after Trump's inauguration. "It's more than palpable. It's radiating. People are terrified." Some undocumented immigrants stopped going to the grocery store and no longer sought out medical care or public nutrition services. Worried that a run-in with the police might lead to their deportation, the number of immigrant street vendors in New York City plummeted and Latina women made fewer domestic violence reports in cities across the country.[20]

The threat of deportation and family separation weighed heavily on both parents and children. Fear led some people to pull their kids from schools across the country. During the first month of Trump's presidency, enrollments dropped by 43 percent at some Head Start preschool programs in Florida that used to have long waiting lists. The following year, the day after a large ICE raid at a meatpacking plant in eastern Tennessee, five hundred kids stayed out of school. A study of fifty-five counties with active 287(g) partnerships between DHS and local law enforcement agencies found that the agreements reduced the Latino student population by 10 percent in two years. Many children experienced heightened levels of stress and anxiety, had difficulty concentrating, and needed more frequent referrals to specialists. They also struggled with tardiness, absences, and sleep problems, and some got into fights. "The fear is affecting every part of their lives," a counselor with Catholic Charities Archdiocese of New Orleans told *The Atlantic* in March 2017. A Southern California pediatrician elaborated: "Kids are suffering from anxiety about not wanting to leave their parents or being worried [about if] they'll still be there when they get home." As a result, many families put action plans into place, instructing their kids—some of them still in elementary school—what they should do if they ever returned home to an empty house. Still, youths could not help playing out, in great detail, nightmare scenarios in their heads of immigration agents arresting, detaining, and deporting their parents.[21]

The pitched battles over immigration during the Trump years left many to wonder: What kind of nation is the United States? Is it a white Anglo-Saxon Protestant, English-speaking nation, as some people imagine it, or a multiracial, multicultural, multilingual nation? Is it a nation of immigrants, a deportation nation, or some combination of the two?

The Trump administration has made its views on these questions clear, from the president's sympathetic statements about Nazis and white supremacists to the U.S. Citizenship and Immigration Service's decision to remove the phrase "nation of immigrants" from its mission statement.[22] Authorities have drawn hard lines around inclusion and exclusion, both at the border and in the interior, and they have relied on the machine's coercive mechanisms to enforce them. Today, as in the past, streamlining expulsions and promoting self-deportation continue to serve as ways to augment state power while sidestepping legal and financial constraints without regard to individuals, families, and communities' well-being.

At the same time, immigrants and their allies have put forth a very different vision of the country, forming nothing less than a mass solidarity movement in the process. They have taken to the streets, filed lawsuits, descended on airports to protest the Muslim ban, organized know-your-rights workshops and antideportation trainings, and pushed religious institutions, towns, and cities to declare themselves sanctuaries for undocumented people. They have also called for the abolition of ICE and for an end to inhumane policies both fueled by and meant to instill fear. Recognizing the many personal and familial connections between citizens and noncitizens and the impossibility of neatly dividing "us" from "them," activists have insisted that all people are deserving of basic rights, respect, and dignity.

Their struggle did not end when Donald Trump left office. Although racist, fear-mongering politicians share the blame, they are hardly the only ones responsible for creating and perpetuating inhumane immigration policies and enforcement practices during the last century and a half. Numerous others have also propelled and profited from the deportation machine, from employers seeking a steady supply of exploitable labor and consumers only willing to pay rock-bottom prices, to bureaucrats trying to justify annual budgets and investors in private firms eager to make millions of dollars at noncitizens' expense. The diverse stakeholders that benefit from expulsion mean that the relentless targeting and scapegoating of immigrants will likely continue—regardless of which politician or party is in power.

14 The Detention and Deportation Regime as a Conduit of Death

MEMORIALIZING AND MOURNING MIGRANT LOSS

Jessica Ordaz

The United States incarcerates more people than any other country in the world. This massive carceral system includes the largest infrastructure for migrant detention, comprised of over two hundred service processing centers, privately operated detention facilities, local and state jails, and juvenile detention sites. In 2017, Border Patrol agents apprehended a total of 454,001 noncitizens, held 323,591 migrants at detention facilities, and deported 226,119 people from the United States.[1] Examples of injury, declining health, and death exist at all stages of this immigration industrial complex, which involves prisons, detention facilities, asylum processing centers, external border controls, and interior immigration enforcement.[2] My past work has centered on the long history of migrant solidarity and protest, but this essay will instead chart migrant injury and death to examine and document how the U.S. state operates while policing the U.S. southern border.[3] The state disavows stories of antimigrant violence, yet this essay argues that the entrenched and expansive power of the detention and deportation regime is structured as a *conduit of death*. The following examples of loss expose the lack of value the state places on migrant life, show the degree of terror enacted by the state and individuals, and reveal the depth of migrant mourning.

Between 2003 and 2017, U.S. Immigration and Customs Enforcement (ICE, previously INS) officials documented 172 in-custody deaths, including 21 suicides. Yet, neglectful detention conditions and antimigrant violence were common long before this data was collected in 2003. For instance, on July 21, 1983, American Border Patrol agents apprehended Alfredo Serrano Martínez at a Border Patrol checkpoint in San Clemente, California. Although sources do not indicate why Martínez was arrested, his family told the American Friends Service Committee U.S.-Mexico Border Program that agents transported him 165 miles southwest to the El Centro INS Detention Center, an immigration facility located in the Imperial Valley. Three days later, an Immigration and Naturalization Service (INS) official informed Martínez's family of his release, which was soon followed by a telephone call explaining that Martínez had hung himself. Apparently, right before the suicide, INS guards injected him with a sedative.[4] As this essay will show, Martínez's suicide was part of a larger pattern of structural violence that occurred "at the intersection of local, national, and international acts of racialized violence."[5] Martínez ended up in detention because of the economic and political systems that influence migration as well as the racial profiling that results in apprehension. In this context, the very definition of suicide, the taking of one's own life, is not accurate. Martínez might have hung himself but he was not wholly responsible for his death.

Fourteen days later, on August 4, Fidencio Martínez was apprehended while traveling on a Greyhound bus at the same San Clemente checkpoint. Border Patrol agents removed him from the bus and asked that he sign a voluntary departure form, which would have required him to return to Mexico. When Martínez refused, the agents took him inside a restroom, where they "beat and tortured him" by placing needles on his feet.[6] He was so badly hurt that an ambulance had to transport him to the Tri-City Hospital in Oceanside, California. Law enforcement officials identified the agent who tortured Martínez and disclosed that he was connected to multiple cases of abuse. This disclosure suggests that the Border Patrol agent had a history of harming migrants but was allowed to continue working. Tragic incidents such as these permeate the history of immigration enforcement along the U.S.-Mexico border, signifying that this type of violence is state sponsored, constant, and mostly ignored.

Antimigrant state violence has been an integral part of how the United States controls its southern border. Although examples of antimigrant violence can be found across the country, this essay will focus on the periods between 1994 and 2018 and across pivotal migration entry points—California, Arizona, and Baja California, Mexico—as a type of case study. The following stories of migrants attempting to escape economic displacement, intensified border militarization, Border Patrol agents seeking vigilante-type "border justice," horrific detention conditions, migrant suicides, and deportee deaths demonstrate that deportation policy has functioned as a form of violence. Immigration enforcement is part of the larger history of hate in the United States, which includes various modes of power, including vigilantism, white supremacy, and reproductive violence. Organized in four sections—migrant apprehension, detention, removal, and deportation—the succeeding migrant testimonies emphasize the various and often circular junctures of antimigrant violence as well as the inequities of death, grief, and mourning.

THE CROSSINGS: MIGRATION AND APPREHENSION

Mexican migration to the United States increased during the 1990s with the passage of the North American Free Trade Agreement (NAFTA), an agreement signed by leaders in Canada, the United States, and Mexico, which became effective on January 1, 1994. Within thirteen years, or by the year 2007, about twelve million Mexican citizens were living in the United States.[7] The goals of the free trade agreement were to end tariffs, lower or eliminate trade restrictions, and increase business among the three countries. Unfortunately, NAFTA led to the privatization of many of Mexico's collective farms, which displaced rural populations and forced many to migrate north in search of work.[8]

NAFTA allowed corporations to move across national borders with ease, which was not the case for workers displaced by the treaty. Political scientist Peter Andreas argues that because NAFTA said nothing about migrant labor, what resulted was a "borderless economy and a barricaded border," which allowed capital and money to move freely but restricted the mobility of workers.[9]

Migrant crossings from Mexico to the United States became more difficult and dangerous throughout the 1990s.[10] In 1994, the Clinton administration implemented Operation Gatekeeper, a measure to reduce the number of unauthorized border crossings in the San Diego region, modeled after Operation Hold the Line, started in El Paso, Texas, in 1993. Operation Gatekeeper increased the number of Border Patrol agents, doubled the budget of the INS to $800 million, and authorized the construction of more fences, with the hopes that it would deter the number of immigrant entries without inspection.[11] The installation of new and better fencing, along with motion detectors and infrared body heat sensors, made it more difficult to cross undetected. Rather than reducing migration, these measures caused entry points to shift further east, into more isolated and mountainous regions, resulting in more deaths due to hypothermia and dehydration in this desert terrain. According to scholar Bill Ong Hing, in 1994, "fewer than 30 migrants died along the border . . . by 1998, the numbers had risen to 147 [and] 477 by 2012."[12] For Central American migrants, the U.S.-Mexico border was one of several boundaries. They faced potential abuse, injury, sexual assault, and kidnappings before reaching northern Mexico.[13]

State violence at the hands of Border Patrol agents escalated. Migrants from Mexico and Central America spoke out against the "border justice" inflicted by agents who went out of their way to capture them.[14] They were verbally harassed, kicked, stepped on, shoved, fist-punched, and pummeled with flashlights and billy clubs. Often, Border Patrol agents saw the injuries they caused or the results of the migrants' treacherous journey north, but they refused to provide aid or care, displaying a lack of empathy. On October 8, 1994, a deported migrant in Tijuana, Mexico, reported that when he attempted to cross into the United States, he saw a Border Patrol agent on horseback chase a woman while she was holding a child. "He nearly trampled them," leaving the woman's leg badly cut from contact with the horse's hoof.[15] These injuries were not simply the actions of a few individual agents but "socially produced and connected to local and global political and economic structures," which made migration a potentially lethal process.[16]

After the onset of Operation Gatekeeper, the number of dead bodies found throughout the deserts and mountains of the U.S.-Mexico border radically increased, transforming the border region into a mass grave. Between 1994 and 2017, more than eleven thousand migrants perished trying to cross.[17] Operation Gatekeeper increased migrant reliance and dependence on *coyotes* or professional smugglers, who "underplay[ed] [the] dangers [of crossing the border] when they ma[de] their pitch to the migrants," not mentioning that the journey would take up to four days, traveling across very rough terrain and in extreme climate conditions of heat and cold, and without access to natural sources of drinking water.[18] The result of smuggler abuses, dehydration, hypothermia, snake bites, and tarantula stings was an increased number of deaths.

In 1995, Terrace Park Cemetery in California's Imperial Valley became a burial site for hundreds of nameless migrants. The City of Holtville opened the cemetery, which is located eleven miles east of the El Centro Immigration Detention Center, in the 1930s. Holtville is a small town of about six thousand residents.[19] Most of the migrant bodies brought here died of thirst, heat stroke, or drowning in the All-American Canal while attempting to cross the U.S.-Mexico border. An INS Border Patrol memo from 1994 clearly articulated the migrant risks: "Illegal entrants crossing through remote, uninhabited expanses of land and sea along the border can find themselves in mortal danger . . . the prediction is that with traditional routes disrupted, illegal traffic will be deterred, or forced over more hostile terrain, less suited for crossing."[20] If increasing the number of deaths was the goal, the policy was successful. In 1998 alone, twenty-one migrants died from hypothermia in Southern California's Tecate mountains and Mount Laguna region, forty-six died from heat stress near the Salton Sea, and fifty-two drowned in the All-American Canal.[21]

By 2009, the lot behind Terrace Park Cemetery held 280 interred migrant bodies belonging to families who could not pay for gravesites and 240 more whom the coroners had not been able to identify.[22] Visitors to the cemetery pointed out the sharp difference between the graves of migrants with formal immigration documents and those without. The burial sites of anonymous migrants were marked by a brick with words like "John Doe," "Jane Doe," or "Baby Doe." No one notified the families of these migrants due to their anonymity. Entire families continued to live knowing they had a missing relative or friend and were forced to mourn their absence without any information. They would never know how their loved ones died or where they were laid to rest. Instead, like in most disappearance cases, they had to go on in a perpetual state of grief. As Judith Butler has written, "If a life is not grievable, it not quite a life; it does not qualify as a life and is not worth a note. It is already the unburied, if not the unburiable."[23] The unidentifiable nature of the bodies resulted in unacknowledged migrant life, trauma, and grief, a deeply dehumanizing process.

The last year migrants were buried here was 2009.[24] Since then, unidentified bodies have been cremated and their ashes scattered at sea, to save Imperial County the $555 per person interment cost.[25] Immigrant rights activists have argued that cremation is disrespectful because the majority of the dead were Catholic, a religion that frowns upon that practice. Groups like Border Angels, a nonprofit migrant human rights organization, pointed out that cremation makes it impossible to ever identify those who have died for lack of DNA. Enrique Marones, founder and director of Border Angels, notes that "even in death they are marginalized."[26] Members and volunteers have taken onto themselves the visitation of these unmarked migrant graves for the last seventeen years. They have attempted to bring dignity to the migrants by placing wooden crosses with the words "Not Forgotten" on the burial sites.[27] This act of memorializing and collective mourning is of particular significance since the acquaintances of the unidentified migrants cannot visit the gravesite.

Although we have a good understanding of the causes of migrant death, it is harder to comprehend the nature of injuries and their connection to state-sponsored negligence. As anthropologist Wendy A. Vogt has written, "For many migrants, their injuries, ailments and other bodily preoccupations are less apparent. Conditions like intestinal parasites or urinary infections are hidden, but cause discomfort and distress."[28] Migrant testimonies suggest that Border Patrol agents were often inattentive when encountering migrants with life-threatening hazards. Esther Morales originally migrated from Oaxaca, Mexico, to the United States in 1989. Throughout the 1990s, she crossed back and forth, and although these crossings were not easy, she was able to avoid interdiction.[29] But ICE (formerly the Immigration and Naturalization Service) agents apprehended her in 2008 and only deported her back to Mexico after she had served five years at the California Rehabilitation Center in Norco and the Valley

State Prison for Women in Chowchilla, California, for committing an aggregated felony.

During an attempt to reunite with her daughter Elsa in September 2008, Esther came across a swamp. She got stuck in it and thought she was going to die. ICE agents had spotted her and apparently watched her struggle for a long time.[30] They finally pulled her out just moments before she would have drowned, dragging her out by using a log onto which she grabbed.[31] After processing her, ICE agents took her to a hospital, ill and feverish due to the vaginal infection she developed from the muddy water. She was then transferred to the privately run Western Region Detention Facility in San Diego, California. During her six-month stay there, fellow detained migrants spread rumors that she had been hospitalized because she had contracted a communicable disease. Although doctors had given her medication, the infection persisted. Her doctor concluded that it was best to burn and remove her clitoris, a procedure that was performed. Morales's experiences reveal the negligence migrants often face while crossing the border. If the Border Patrol agents had acted more quickly when they saw Morales struggling in the swamp, she might not have developed a life-altering infection.

DETENTION

Overcrowding is a frequent complaint of people held at short-term migrant holding facilities on the American side of the U.S.-Mexico border. Migrants interviewed noted that there were not enough chairs at most detention centers and therefore they had to sit on the floor next to piles of trash.[32] On occasion, INS blasted the air conditioners but limited the number of blankets allocated to detained migrants. A migrant disclosed that when he was in INS custody in the early 1990s, guards forced him to take off all his clothes and stand under the air-conditioning vent,[33] mocking him as he shivered in place. Detained migrants were routinely called offensive names, from *cabrones* (shitheads) to *pinches putos* (fucking whores).[34] Often guards used physical force as a form of amusement, awakening migrants with kicks. As one person declared, "Patean y pegan por gusto" (they kick and hit for the fun of it).[35] These examples suggest that guards often viewed migrants as the target of their jokes and amusement. Migrants had limited access to water and were forced to drink from sink spigots, which were foul smelling. Two women testified that when they requested water, the guard replied, "We are not running a restaurant."[36] These conditions were not unique. Similar treatment occurred at federally run service processing centers such as the detention facility in El Centro.

The El Centro Immigration Detention Center in Southern California's Imperial Valley exclusively detained men "who entered the United States illegally or violated their immigration status" and those awaiting "completion of their deportation case, release on their own recognizance, or pending release." The migrants were from Mexico, Central America, South America, the Caribbean, and Southeast Asia.[37] Overcapacity at a facility known for abusing and neglecting migrants resulted in amplified tensions in 1998.[38] On one March night, guards stormed into one of the dormitories to search for drugs. According to a Jordanian migrant, "When they do a search, we lose legal paperwork, pictures of our families, phone books. They throw them in the trash."[39] One of the detained migrants had enough that night and resisted. The INS guards responded quickly and violently. When the group refused to step out of their dormitory, the facility's tactical team intervened. Dressed in black, wearing riot helmets and ski masks, and armed with pepper spray, billy clubs, and guns loaded with wooden bullets, they closed in on the detained men.

When FBI crisis negotiators arrived to deescalate the situation, they wrote down the protestors' grievances and assured them they would investigate further. The FBI apparently did not follow up, prompting the men to stage a hunger strike.[40] In their memo addressed to "El Centro INS Detention Staff/and Media TV" from "The Whole Detention Camp," they complained that "The officers dressed in army fatigues . . . along with 3-feet wide batons . . . indiscriminately came in numbers of dozens and started hitting inmates in this facility in the face, head, and body . . . without any type of justification."[41] The memo ended by asking why the FBI did not conduct a proper investigation of the events. This example of dissent highlights that the state, in this case the FBI, neglected to address migrant grievances. What does it mean when the state dismisses migrant claims? People in detention face violent, negligent, and unsanitary conditions, and when they attempt to protest these circumstances they are met with silence, disregard, and disavow.

Besides this mistreatment, death lingered inside detention. In May 2007, ICE agents arrested twenty-three-year-old Victoria Arellano during a routine traffic stop. Arellano, a transgender Mexican migrant, was sent to the ICE Detention Center in San Pedro, California, known as Terminal Island. The federal government opened Terminal Island in 1936, located opposite the San Pedro Navy Supply Depot, and next to the U.S. Coast Guard Station there.[42] Armed guards and barbed-wire towers surrounded it. Many of the people held here were accused of engaging in subversive activities. During her initial intake, Arellano informed the staff that she had AIDS and would need access to medication.[43] The clinical director of the facility did not immediately order lab work done and refused to prescribe medication for an entire month. The director claimed there was a prohibition on lab tests for thirty days, which, according to immigration advocates, was clearly "a violation of ICE medical guidelines and medical ethics."[44]

Despite knowing the importance of medication in helping to prevent opportunistic infection among people diagnosed with HIV and AIDS, medical staff at Terminal Island did not make an exception. Arellano's health waned. She became weak and complained about a persistent cough and fever. Within two months, blood appeared in her vomit and urine. Yet, medical personnel continued to ignore her and suggested she take Tylenol and drink lots of water along with the antibiotics they prescribed. Arellano died of meningitis while in ICE custody on July 20, 2007. The very next year, ICE officials reported that denying detained migrants treatment authorization requests saved them $129,713.62 on HIV-related treatments.[45] The lack of response to Arellano's deteriorating health made ICE officials, the detention staff, and medical professionals complicit in her death. Detained migrants who were HIV positive faced similar conditions at detention facilities across the country.

Migrant deaths, including suicides, occurred within an environment that bred and permitted state-sanctioned violence. On April 28, 2013, Elsa Guadalupe-Gonzales, a twenty-four-year-old Guatemalan migrant, hung herself in a cell at the Eloy Detention Center in Arizona,[46] operated by the Corrections Corporation of America (CCA) since its opening in

1994. Guadalupe-Gonzales was apprehended trying to enter the United States near Sasabe, Arizona. She was detained at the Eloy facility on March 20, 2013, where she was assigned to the Bravo housing unit for women, in cell 206. During the initial processing, guards allowed Guadalupe-Gonzales to keep her shoes, which included laces. Despite the nurse's report that claimed she was in good health and did not have any mental health problems, various detained women thought otherwise.[47]

ICE officials scheduled Guadalupe-Gonzales's removal for April 2, 1994. In hopes of avoiding deportation, she applied for asylum. On April 26, Guadalupe-Gonzales participated in a fifty-minute credible fear interview, as part of her asylum application. During the meeting, she disclosed that her family "was involved in a violent property dispute in Guatemala, which caused her to fear for her life."[48] Detained migrants reported that Guadalupe-Gonzales had very mixed feelings on that day. She was ecstatic because ICE was set to release her husband from the Florence Correctional Facility, but also troubled after the interview. One of the women she confided in reported that Guadalupe-Gonzales was afraid of deportation and also worried that if given the choice, she would not be able to afford bail and rejoin her husband. She also missed her son, who lived in Guatemala.[49] After Guadalupe-Gonzales's death, several detained women confessed that they had told her that ICE would deport her regardless of how well her credible fear interview had gone.

On the day that Guadalupe-Gonzales took her own life, her sadness was clear. She skipped breakfast and morning recreation. During lunch, she did not eat. She told a fellow detained migrant that this was her last meal.[50] After lunch, the guard in charge asked her why she was washing her shoelaces. Guadalupe-Gonzales responded that they were dirty and she needed to clean them. She skipped dinner and stayed in her cell with the door locked, as was protocol. After dinner, as one of the detained women approached cell 206, she screamed. Guadalupe-Gonzales was found hanging from a bunk bed with a pair of shoelaces.[51] By the time she was untied and lowered, Guadalupe-Gonzales did not have a pulse. The paramedics arrived at 5:45 p.m. but were unable to revive her. They declared her dead twenty-one minutes later. The acting field office director of Phoenix Enforcement and Removal Operations (ERO) mailed her husband a letter informing him of her death four days later.[52] Guadalupe-Gonzales's death reveals the emotional toll that detention and the asylum process take on migrants. In dire and precarious circumstances, Guadalupe-Garcia was caught in an impasse that was not of her own making.

REMOVAL

Shortly after the announcement of Operation Gatekeeper in 1994, Claudia E. Smith, an immigration lawyer, and Roberto Martínez, director of the American Friends Service Committee U.S.-Mexico Border Program, traveled to Mexican immigration checkpoints at San Ysidro, Otay, and Mexicali to interview migrants released from INS custody. "Everywhere we heard the same litany of complaints. All too often the interview ended with: *'nos tratan como perros'* (they treat us like dogs)," Smith and Martínez reported.[53] Mistreatments included being transported in hand-cuffs and chains despite having no criminal record. They were denied food and water while en route to the Mexican border. After 1994 immigration agents started to separate family members by busing them to different locations.[54]

On February 23, 1995, Smith interviewed the thirty-eight men on bus no. 2005 as it arrived in Mexicali. They were being deported from Stockton, Fresno, Bakersfield, and Los Angeles, California. Several of the men carried gallons of water that they had purchased along the way because the INS did not provide them with any. On March 22, 1995, Border Patrol agents apprehended Antonio Gómez in Stockton, California, who a few days earlier had been treated for a torso gunshot wound. Gómez was still in pain and needed frequent bandage changes when apprehended. INS agents refused to provide him with a clean dressing for the wound and pain killers. The bus driver allowed Gómez to buy aspirin in Chowchilla, but only after several of the men on the bus demanded it.[55] This type of solidarity was common among migrants. By the time Gómez reached Mexico, his bandage was soiled and he needed medical attention.

After a year of advocacy from immigration lawyers such as Smith, the INS created a Western Regional Detention and Deportation Transportation System Plan, which attempted to address such medical concerns in the transport of deportees. The document emphasized the importance of "protecting the lives, safety and welfare of our officers, the general public, and those in INS custody."[56] The guidelines included requiring drivers to complete a bus training program where they were instructed on their responsibilities; inspecting their vehicles, ensuring detained migrants were transported safely, operating vehicles prudently, and obeying traffic laws. The plan stated that migrants should be treated humanely and safely but also specified that security was a top priority, emphasizing that deportation buses were carceral spaces. In regards to seating assignments, the document indicated that "restraining equipment be utilized on any person identified as a high-security risk."[57] Drivers were encouraged to carry extra pairs of handcuffs, flex-cuffs, cutters, batons, pepper spray, and tasers. Herein the INS admitted that its agents had not always followed official policy as "detainees with identified medical problems [should have been] situated in areas that accommodate[d] their medical conditions" or provided with appropriate transportation.[58] Lastly, INS policy now required drivers to provide passengers with meals and plenty of water during all bus transfers, as well as snacks if their transport took more than six hours.

Six months after the plan was published on March 28, 1995, Claudia Smith found that these new rules continued to be ignored.[59] Bus drivers often transported migrants in unsafe conditions. They complained of being forced to sit three to a seat or stand. Some drivers drove so recklessly that passengers arrived in Mexico covered in bruises after being thrown around.[60] On the weekend of July 4, 1997, Smith again interviewed deportees in Mexicali. Despite the summer heat, Border Patrol agents had not provided the passengers with water, life's most basic need. Smith noted that "109 people got off an INS bus with a maximum passenger capacity of 64."[61] Overt violations such as these were difficult to enforce because many INS agents harbored deep-rooted racist ideas about the lack of value of immigrant lives, views evident to Smith as she was bombarded with hate mail for her activism. An anonymous Border Patrol agent wrote, "I was so repulsed at your sympathetic liberal, multiculturalist, anti-American hogwash hatched in hell [toward] dishonest, disgusting, filthy, ignorant, racist, ungrateful, vile, violent people internationally recognized as Mexicans, locally referred to as wets, and, in my occupation, affectionately termed as 'tonks.'"[62] The writer concluded asking Smith if she inquired whether the deported migrants came "over with the intent to commit crimes. Or to fraudulently submit paperwork for the plethora of social hand-outs?"[63] This Border Patrol agent parroted a decades-long discourse that rendered migrants inherently criminal and undeserving. As Luisa Marie Cacho argues, "Certain bodies and behaviors are made transparently criminal while privileged bodies and their brutal crimes are rendered unrecognizable as criminal or even as violent."[64] Thus, the anonymous letter writer viewed crossing the border as a punishable crime while disavowing antimigrant violence enacted by immigration agents, guards, and officials.

DEPORTED

The passage of the Antiterrorism and Effective Death Penalty Act (AEDPA) and the Illegal Immigration Reform and Immigrant Responsibility Act (IIRIRA) in 1996 helped to expand immigration enforcement in the United States by further criminalizing non–U.S. citizens. IIRIRA mandated that individuals classified as national security risks be detained and "criminal aliens," defined as noncitizens guilty of a criminal offense, be apprehended. These offenses included aggravated felonies, criminal convictions with sentences of five years or more, controlled substance violations, drug trafficking, and crimes of moral turpitude.[65] IIRIRA required the indefinite detention of noncitizens who could not be deported to their home countries. It also made offenses committed before IIRIRA retroactive, which increased the number of people deemed detainable and deportable.[66] By the year 2000, the number of people so held totaled five thousand nationwide.[67]

AEDPA further legalized the detention and deportation of legal permanent residents convicted of a crime, including minor offenses, as was the case of Daniel Jáuregui Mariz. He had lived in the United States since the age of three, and although he was a permanent resident, ICE deported him to Tijuana, Mexico, in 2014 based on his criminal record. "All my friends who have been deported, have either died or committed suicide because they just can't find a way of life over here," Mariz lamented.[68] Speaking to the difficulties of being deported, such as the trouble of finding employment and then being forced to acclimate to a new and unfamiliar country, Mariz highlighted its psychological effects. Migrants repeatedly echoed feeling alienated and isolated.

In 2006, ICE agents deported Emma Sánchez de Paulsen to Tijuana, forcing her to leave her husband and three children in Vista, California. In 2013, Paulsen's husband was scheduled to undergo open-heart surgery. She requested special permission to visit him in the hospital, but ICE officials rejected it. Her husband found great irony in the fact that if he died, "she could come and bury me, but she couldn't come to visit me during a major operation of open-heart surgery." Paulsen continued to press immigration authorities for permission to be with her husband during his surgery. She requested humanitarian aid at the San Ysidro border crossing into the United States, but was told again that she could only visit her husband if he was a few hours from death or after he was deceased.[69] Paulsen's anguish at being relatively close to her family, about a one-hour drive, but divided by a man-made border, speaks to a common experience among deportees along the U.S.-Mexico border. Deported migrants live in a constant state of anxiety.

For instance, Jessica Nalbach recounted the toll that deportation had on her mental health. One 2015 evening, ICE agents showed up at her home and apprehended her husband because of a criminal record ten years old. Despite having served his time for the crime, ICE deported him to Mexico. To keep her family intact, Nalbach took her two kids and moved closer to her husband. Already suffering from postpartum depression, she was extremely frustrated and upset at the circumstances she faced. Within the first six months of moving to Mexico, she attempted suicide three times.[70] Nalbach's distress shows that the effects of deportation persist after a person has been legally removed from the United States. Her mental health deteriorated due to the precarity caused by deportation.

Deportation and forced removal are deemed the final step for immigration enforcement agents, but for deportees, this is just the beginning of several more unpredictable threats. ICE agents deported Gerardo Sánchez Pérez to Tijuana after he had lived in the United States for twelve years. He was apprehended during a workplace raid, and agents transported him to a short-term detention facility. When Pérez was finally deported, he lived on the streets because he knew no one in Tijuana and had no money or kin or friendship connection he could ask help from. During an interview, he recounted the tremendous loneliness of being separated from his family in an unfamiliar place. Like many deportees, Pérez was a casualty of the War on Drugs, caught in the crossfire of a *narco* shootout on the streets of Tijuana. Pérez was shot and killed while simply trying to get by working at a homeless shelter.[71] His death shows that antimigrant violence can continue after immigration agents remove deportable migrants. Migrants are often sent to their deaths, caused by the violence they have attempted to flee.

CONCLUSION

The detention and deportation regime is a conduit of migrant death. I have discussed how the state polices the southern border to show that the immigration policies enacted in the 1990s further produced a dehumanizing and violent environment for migrants throughout the immigration industrial complex. Calls for free trade and nativism resulted in policies such as Operation Gatekeeper, which further militarized the U.S.-Mexico border and engendered an atmosphere that made migrant injuries and deaths more probable. From attempts to cross the border to being apprehended, detained, and deported, migrants experienced laws that did not consider their value or humanity, a system that encouraged terror and increased migrant loss and mourning. I have focused on various modes of antimigrant violence, from torture to medical neglect and suicide, to argue that these examples of hate are structural and state sanctioned. While various individuals are complicit in this system, immigration policies and their enforcers have made migration a potentially deadly process.

Although death is difficult to discuss, the stories collected in this essay highlight migrant voices, which the state often silences, dismisses, and disavows. This approach centers on migrant experiences, which have historically been deemed unreliable and biased sources, to chart the increase of migrant death and its connection to criminalization and policing as well as to memorialize and identify migrant loss. This analysis has illuminated the violence migrants face when the enforcers of immigration law do not see value in their lives or deaths. From Border Patrol agents who cause physical injury and deny migrants lifesaving sources of water to bus drivers who transform deportation buses into carceral spaces, this essay has shown the inequalities of migrant life and death. The research presented here can be used to further explore the toll the carceral state takes on migrants' mental health and well-being.

White Supremacy from
Fringe to Mainstream

It's easy enough to see white supremacy in acts of fringe violence, when the people involved often proclaim their racism, misogyny, and hatred outright. To trace the impact of fringe mobilizations on political formations in the mainstream—and vice versa—is more complex. Still, over the last half-century, scholars have not only documented the persistence of white supremacist systems, but have noted significant movement of racist ideas between fringe and mainstream.

Consider, for instance, the recent career of white supremacy, which careened back into the public discourse under President Donald J. Trump. Not only did the Trump administration back a policy program of anti-immigrant and other white supremacist action, but the president himself failed to denounce fringe white supremacist actors and outright welcomed white nationalists and nativists into his staff. There is a relationship between Trump's grandstanding rhetoric on Twitter and at campaign rallies, the policies enacted in his name, and the work of fringe groups who see themselves as furthering several similar social goals. These ties became even clearer during the insurrection at the United States Capitol on January 6, 2021, and the subsequent impeachment trial that sought to prove Trump had incited an extremist mob to storm the building.

Some of this relation becomes clear in the history of how the fringe has impacted the mainstream of American politics. In the history of nativism and the Buchanan campaign and the formation of the alt-right, we can excavate deliberate fringe attempts to shape mainstream belief; in the actions of the white power movement, their deadly consequences are clear. In other words, fringe and mainstream manifestations of white supremacy work together as part of a social structure, enabling the continuation of racist violence and policymaking. To disable them would be to truly understand the widespread culture of racism that defines American life, and the way that those in positions of social trust ranging from politicians to police have been co-opted into the service of this culture.

A protestor holds a "Blue Lives Matter" flag during a rally at the Utah State Capitol Saturday, September 12, 2020, in Salt Lake City. (AP Photo/Rick Bowmer)

15 A Recent History of White Supremacy

Ramón A. Gutiérrez

American men and women of every creed and color marched into battle during World War II to end fascism, to safeguard democracy, and, at war's end, to herald the benefits of capitalism over socialism to the rest of the world. The hot war the United States entered in Europe and Asia in 1941 ended in 1945, soon after Hiroshima and Nagasaki were leveled by atomic bombs on August 6 and 9. What followed was an equally intense Cold War—one in which the Soviet Union critiqued American white supremacy and patriarchy to claim superiority. The Soviets ridiculed the hypocrisy of America's vaunted democratic promise of equality, when not even high-ranking diplomats from Africa, Asia, and the Middle East could buy a meal or rent a hotel room in parts of the United States. This contradiction—between white supremacy and the promise of equality—became fertile ground for propaganda and recruitment.

In 1944, Gunnar Myrdal, a prominent Swedish economist and eventual Nobel laureate, was commissioned by the Carnegie Corporation of New York to assess the state of race relations in the United States and to offer a prescription for a better path forward as the American soldiers returned from war. His report, *An American Dilemma: The Negro Problem and Modern Democracy,* advanced scientific arguments akin to those anthropologist Franz Boas articulated at the beginning of the twentieth century. Racial discrimination was social and cultural, they found, and not biological. It was based largely on the symbolism skin color bore as a sign of subordination and inferiority. Color prejudice originated as a mark of slavery rather than of some innate human difference or claim of eugenic pseudoscience. Myrdal argued that as the war ended, Americans were torn between the ideals of democracy and equal opportunity, what he called the "American Creed," and the festering realities of discrimination and segregation in daily life. "The American Negro problem is a problem in the heart of the American. It is there that the interracial tension has its focus. It is there that the decisive struggle goes on." The dilemma facing Americans was whether they would yield to their irrational, but often economically interested, prejudices. "Practically all the economic, social and political power is held by whites . . . It thus is the white majority group that naturally determines the Negro's 'place' . . . White prejudice and discrimination keeps the Negro low in standards of living, health, education, manners and morals." Myrdal predicted that racial conflict would surely continue because the distance between the ideals of the American Creed and its raw realities was so great.[1]

The promise of democracy and equality was tested and found wanting again as minority soldiers returned home. Though all the soldiers, women and men alike, had put their lives in harm's way to defend these ideals, the rewards for valorous service at war's end and in the years following 1945 were still deeply structured by race, class, and gender. Americans of African, Mexican, Puerto Rican, Asian, and Indigenous ancestry fared poorly, as did lesbian and gay GIs. They returned to places in the South and Southwest still rife with discriminatory practices, prohibiting "colored" war heroes from being buried in white cemeteries, forcing soldiers even in uniform to use segregated facilities, to quench their thirst at "colored" water fountains, to swim in public pools only on the last day of the month before the water was emptied and the pool cleaned. Black and other nonwhite veterans were still denied service at many restaurants and hotels. In short, their place was still very much at the back of the bus, as it had been before the war. Soldiers of color felt this contradiction acutely, and organized around a "Double V" campaign to vanquish fascism abroad and racism at home.

But in the aftermath of the war for democracy, the democratic promise had not yet reached veterans of color. No federal postwar program exemplified this better than the Serviceman's Readjustment Act signed into law by President Franklin D. Roosevelt on June 22, 1944, which became popularly known as the GI Bill of Rights. It was a massive federal investment in programs to help young veterans who had experienced the mental and physical traumas of war to peacefully reintegrate into society through economic, educational, medical, and psychological programs to meet their needs. The U.S. government invested some $95 billion in them between 1944 and 1971. These monies subsidized the purchase of new homes by young men who had no collateral, no down payment, offering them minimal interest rates amortized over thirty years for a new life in segregated white suburbs. Money for education flowed, covering the cost of tuition, books, and living expenses for those veterans eager to attend college or vocational schools. Between 1944 and 1955, 2.3 million GIs availed themselves of these educational benefits, earning degrees and skills that propelled their occupational mobility. Those who wanted to start small businesses got Veterans Administration (VA) start-up loans, eventually realizing the American Dream of economic comfort, married life with a wife and children residing in a new suburban home, educational accomplishment, medical benefits to insure their health, and at death, benefits for their widows. When veterans reflected on the upward mobility they had experienced after World War II, they concluded that it stemmed from their own merit and hard work. In fact, they were beneficiaries of the massive handouts the government gave them explicitly as part of a "model welfare system."[2]

William J. Bennett, who studied the impact of the GI Bill on American postwar prosperity, has argued that it was "America's first color-blind social legislation," an assertion that is technically true but ignores the bill's differential administration.[3] Recent scholarship has also shown that straight men benefited from the GI Bill dramatically more than women or gay men.[4] Right from the program's start, there were concerns voiced by the press that the GI Bill had "completely failed veterans of minority races." African American and Mexican American civil rights organizations came to a similar conclusion. They clearly understood that the benefits were "for white veterans only." When the legislation was first drafted, there were endless debates over whether the program would be federal in scope and administration. By the time the bill was marked up in the Committee on World War Legislation, chaired by Representative John Rankin of Mississippi, he and his allies had authored a bill that indeed created a federal bureaucracy that was national in scope but in the administrative hands of local and state authorities who established eligibility and doled out the monetary benefits. Rankin and his fellow congressmen from the South were determined to reassert white supremacy and segregation—the status quo ante—because war mobilization had so profoundly unsettled local hierarchies and subordination regimes. That could not be. As Rankin noted in correspondence with the head of the VA, "a definite line should be drawn in the schooling on the matter of race segregation." What southern congressmen feared most was that young Black man returning from war might militantly claim their citizenship, demanding access to quality education for themselves and their children, resisting those limited and limiting employment opportunities that only offered poverty with no avenues to class or generational mobility. White Texans, like Professor Edward E. Davis, who served as the dean of North Texas Agricultural College from 1925 to 1946, held similar opinions about educating the children of vets: referring to that "dirty 'greaser' type of Mexican," he held that white and Brown children had to be separated in school. Ramón Rivas, a World War II Army veteran from Charlotte, Texas, recalled exactly how this was done in his youth. Mexicans "would start 1st grade, stay there two or three years, and then go to 2nd grade then stay there." By the time they should have entered the seventh grade, they simply dropped out and never attended high school. Rivas's limited and segregated education as a child hindered his social mobility before, during, and after his military service, as was the case for many Mexican American and Puerto Rican soldiers.[5]

The GI Bill legally discriminated against Black, Mexican American, Puerto Rican, and Native American veterans. It was theoretically egalitarian, excluding only those discharged dishonorably. But the administrative bureaucracies that doled out jobs, medical care, disability pensions, and unemployment benefits and partnered with banks, schools, and realtors to extend VA benefits were nearly all staffed by whites, who sometimes embodied covertly the prejudices John Rankin was known to express overtly, constantly deprecating Blacks, Catholics, and Jews. Raúl Medina attested of his experience, "As far as the Veterans Administration is concerned . . . we were treated just plain goddamm rotten."[6]

Educational subsidies, jobs, and medical care were the three benefits racialized minorities sought with differing levels of success. Educational institutions were still separate and unequal. Thus, 95 percent of those Blacks who availed themselves of VA student loans and stipends attended historically black colleges and vocational schools. A few Mexican American veterans enrolled and graduated from the University of Texas at Austin, but there were two requisites that mostly kept them out: English-language mastery and high school diplomas. Many had become fluent in the English language while in the military, some even finishing high school while on active duty. But like their fellow Black veterans, they were directed to vocational schools as more appropriate for men of color who descended from sharecroppers and agricultural migrant workers. Thus, for example, when David Fuentes was discharged in 1946, he imagined becoming a dentist. His school of choice limited Mexican American enrollments and had "a two year waiting list." In desperate need of a job, Fuentes turned to tailoring and clothes design. Though he never saw fame or fortune, he expressed happiness with his modest state. Raúl Medina on discharge returned to Fresno, California, in 1946. His wife had sold their home and deserted him. "I came home to nothing. I didn't have anything." Through his GI benefits he enrolled in an upholstery training program, a job that ultimately brought him satisfaction because it allowed him to work creatively with his hands.[7] Of the 7.8 million veterans who received educational benefits, the vast majority, 5.6 million, enrolled in vocational schools and on-the-job training apprenticeships because many of them had dropped out of their segregated primary and secondary schools, and thus neither aspired to attend college nor met the requirements for admission. White supremacy enforced through segregated schooling in the South and Southwest had limited their occupation mobility after the war.[8]

Sociologists Harley Browning, Sally Lopreato, and Dudley Poston Jr. studied the income outcomes of Anglo, Black, and Mexican American veterans who served in World War II to understand what impact veteran benefits ultimately had. They concluded that there had been a significant economic advantage in yearly income for Black and Mexican American veterans: a $344 advantage for Blacks and $711 for Mexican Americans (in 1960 dollars). For Anglos the gross mean difference between veterans and nonveterans was slightly over $100 for veterans. An analysis of the occupational niches these veterans occupied in 1960, fifteen years after the war, showed that the majority of Blacks had failed to enter professional and managerial jobs and were employed as craftsmen, clerical and service workers, and manual laborers. Mexican Americans fared slightly better, some making it into the professional and managerial ranks as a result of the GI Bill's educational benefits, but like Blacks, many were still at the bottom of the nation's occupational structure.[9]

The discretion to determine eligibility for VA benefits was left to local administrators, but with federal appeal rights. Soldiers were legally ineligible *only* if dishonorably discharged. Discharges went from honorable to dishonorable, with "undesirable" in an ambiguous middle, originally called "blue" because this discharge order was printed on blue paper. Undesirable discharges mostly targeted homosexuals and African Americans who challenged racial segregation in the armed forces, but they were also used to dismiss drug addicts, alcoholics, and bed wetters. The conflation of these categories was what gave "blue" undesirable discharges their heinous stigma. Veterans with this discharge were immediately suspected of the most nefarious behaviors. Their benefit applications were routinely denied, even when appealed, and these servicemen found themselves haunted by the designation for the rest of their lives, especially if they applied to schools, jobs, or for bank loans.[10] To them, the largest federal transfer of funds systematically reproduced systemic racism through benefits distributions, made palpable through the daily, routine decisions VA workers made about who was worthy of benefits and who was not, which in turn determined to whom banks would loan, realtors would sell, and educational institutions would admit.

Civil rights organizations protested VA abuses starting in 1945. Some of these organizations by then had long histories, some formed in the early 1900s, others after the 1929 Great Depression, and still others at the end of World War II. The National Association for the Advancement of Colored People (NAACP) was created in 1909 "to promote equality of rights and eradicate caste or race prejudice among citizens of the United States; to advance the interest of colored citizens; to secure for them impartial suffrage; and to increase their opportunities for securing justice in the courts, education for their children, employment according to their ability, and complete equality before the law."[11] The League of United Latin American Citizens (LULAC) had its origin in South Texas in 1929 as a group of de jure white citizens determined "to advance the economic condition, educational attainment, political influence, housing, health and civil rights of the Hispanic population of the United States." When the Treaty of Guadalupe Hidalgo was signed ending the U.S.-Mexico War (1846–48), those Mexicans who remained in their homelands were granted full legal citizenship as whites, but rarely enjoyed what that meant in practice. LULAC's first major mobilization was against the forced deportation to Mexico of 1.5 million Mexican American citizens between 1930 and 1934. Those targeted had largely lived in the United States for generations. They may have been poor but were hardly destitute immigrants who had become public charges in need of charity during the worst years of the depression. This was what putatively justified the Border Patrol's forced removals, leading to LULAC's actions.[12]

The American GI Forum was begun in 1948 by Dr. Hector García, who wanted to ensure that Mexican American veterans received all the medical and educational benefits to which they were entitled; as a physician, he could see this was not the case. García and the American GI Forum first gained broad recognition in the Southwest when the body of Private Felix Longoria, who had been killed in combat in the Philippines, was denied burial in his segregated hometown cemetery in Three Rivers, Texas, early in 1949. Mrs. Longoria had made arrangements for the wake and burial at the town's Rice Funeral Home, but the mortuary's owner, Mr. Kenneday, would not allow Longoria's body to be viewed or blessed in the mortuary's chapel. He told her, "Well, Mrs. Longoria, I have lots of Latin friends but I can't let his body rest at this chapel because the whites won't like it . . . They had never let the Latin Americans use the chapel and were not starting now, even if he was a soldier killed in action." Dr. García mobilized the American GI Forum's members—all of them veterans, all of them Americans. Lyndon B. Johnson, the U.S. senator from Texas, quickly intervened. He wrote Mrs. Longoria, "I deeply regret to learn that the prejudice of some individuals extends even beyond this life . . . I have today made arrangements to have Felix Longoria buried with full military honors in

Arlington National Cemetery here at Washington." Mrs. Longoria accepted Senator Johnson's offer, and that is where Felix Longoria's body is still interred.[13]

The most significant civil rights organization grew out of Black churches, coalescing as the Southern Christian Leadership Conference (SCLC) in 1957, when the Reverend Dr. Martin Luther King Jr. invited sixty Black ministers to work together to desegregate bus transport, boldly challenging the white supremacy and segregation enforced in the South by police departments, the Ku Klux Klan, and Citizens' Councils that resisted school integration even after the U.S. Supreme Court's ruling in *Brown v. Board of Education* in 1954. The Councils continued to engage in Black voter suppression, something that still haunts the country today. By 1964, leading a broad coalition through peaceful protest, Rev. Dr. King and his northern allies pressed for the passage of the Civil Rights Act of 1964, the Voting Rights Act of 1965, and the Fair Housing Act of 1968, which guaranteed all Americans federal protection against racial discrimination in education, employment, voting, and housing. Affirmative Action programs followed to eradicate the country's history of racial subordination with the goal of creating a more equitable society.

In 1965, the Hart-Celler Immigration Act also was signed into law by President Johnson, repealing the nativist, eugenics-based, white supremacist–inspired racial quotas enacted in the 1924 National Origins Act. This legislation had limited Catholic and Jewish immigrant entries from southern and eastern Europe, and more generally from Latin America, Asia, Africa, and the Middle East. While Hitler's forces systematically murdered six million Jews between 1933 and 1944, the United States granted immigrant admission to fewer than 250,000, and only 38,056 between 1945 and 1948.[14]

As the Johnson administration was starting to address the legal and political grievances of racialized Americans, Los Angeles, Chicago, Detroit, Newark, and a number of other cities were set ablaze by racial protest in 1965, 1966, and 1967. Johnson mobilized federal forces to establish order and rapidly expanded his signature economic opportunity programs to address the economic needs of African Americans, Mexican Americans, Puerto Ricans, and Indigenous peoples. In hopes of understanding the causes of these incendiary mass rebellions, on July 27, 1967, he appointed a National Advisory Commission on Civil Disorders. The first page of Commission's February 1968 report (popularly known as the Kerner Report) was blunt. "This is our basic conclusion: Our nation is moving toward two societies, one black and one white—separate and unequal . . . Discrimination and segregation have long permeated much of American life; they now threaten the future of every American." The race riots, the report explained, originated in segregation, inadequate housing, poor access to quality education, systematic police violence, and labor market exclusion. "Segregation and poverty have created in the racial ghetto a destructive environment totally unknown to most white Americans . . . White institutions created it, white institutions maintain it, and white society condones it . . . White racism is essentially responsible for the explosive mixture which has been accumulating in our cities since the end of World War II."[15]

Throughout the 1940s and 1950s, the word *racism* was used to describe individual acts of hatred, mostly denominated as *prejudice, discrimination,* and *bigotry.* This is how Gunnar Myrdal and his team of social scientists framed it in their 1944 report. The vocabulary of race began to change in the mid-1960s primarily as racial minorities identified forms of "institutional racism" and the process of "racializing" individuals and groups that ultimately were rooted in society's unequal social and economic arrangements.

The first and fullest articulation of "institutional racism" appeared in Stokely Carmichael and Charles V. Hamilton's 1967 book *Black Power: The Politics of Liberation in America.* Analyzing the ills that afflicted Harlem's ghetto, they concluded that its structure was that of a domestic or internal colony, profitably exploited by outsiders, intensely segregated and surveilled by the police, with barriers to the exercise of the franchise, and often characterized by treachery and betrayal from white political allies. Outlining a "framework" for Black political, economic, and psychological empowerment, they offered a searing critique of "white power" and "white supremacy" differentiating individual and institutional racism (now deemed systemic racism), locating the latter in a host of local and federal policies that produced the immiseration of inner-city ghettoes where the majority of Blacks and Puerto Ricans lived. This came at the same moment that the government, through the GI Bill, subsidized white middle-class mobility, ownership of new suburban homes, and segregated neighborhoods with excellent schools that gained them access to the finest universities and professional careers. If Blacks were to forge their own freedom, they had to overthrow their oppressors and establish community sovereignty and self-determination as part of a larger global movement to end colonialism at home and abroad.[16]

Though Rev. Dr. King was himself becoming more radical around issues of economic justice and racial oppression on the eve of his assassination on April 4, 1968, the language of Black Power profoundly unsettled him. For decades he had rallied allies around the "Freedom Now" slogan. Early in 1968 King confronted Carmichael, explaining that "the words 'black' and 'power' together give the impression that we are talking about black domination rather than black equality," correctly predicting that this rhetoric would unleash a torrent of white prejudice, which up to that point most whites had been too timid to express openly.[17]

King's words proved prophetic. Before much progress could be made on eradicating racial subordination by integrating schools, workplaces, and neighborhoods, white liberal allies of the civil rights movement were frightened by riot violence they only witnessed on television screens, where they also heard militant Black Power pronouncements. Soon these assertions of muscular nationalism were echoed by Brown, Red, and Yellow Power radicals. These changes laid the political and intellectual foundation for the white conservative counterrevolt. Of course, it had historic roots that reached back to chattel slavery and the Civil War. Since the end of World War II, both the Republican and Democratic parties had endorsed the idea of racial equality, at least in name. But it was only in 1962, when the Kennedy administration assigned federal troops to integrate schools, forcing the admission of James Meredith into the University of Mississippi, that southern opposition to integration and flight from the Democratic Party hastened. In July 1963, 54 percent of whites opined that President Kennedy was "pushing racial integration too fast." Later that same year, a December national opinion poll found that 78 percent of southern whites and 59 percent of northern whites opposed the "actions Negroes have taken to obtain civil rights."[18]

African American civil rights protests in the 1960s were mainly concentrated in the South, staging lunch counter sit-ins starting in

Greensboro, North Carolina, in 1960 and Freedom Rides on interstate buses in 1961; demanding voting rights at Georgia's Albany State College in 1962; protesting against discrimination and police violence, which was best exemplified when Chief Eugene "Bull" Connor gained national attention by using attack dogs and high-pressure water hoses in Birmingham, Alabama, in 1963; and challenging voter disfranchisement at Selma, Alabama, in 1965. There was significant white moral and monetary support from the rest of the country for these civil rights campaigns, but rarely were there significant numbers of white protesters ready to face the consequences of peaceful protest. The probability was high that one would get clubbed, mauled, jailed, and perhaps even killed, as Black activists already had.

When media attention started to shift to the North, with the onset of inner-city riots in 1965 and beyond, white support further fizzled. White northerners had not suffered the pain of Southern Jim Crow laws; their only stake in equality was moral. But when the movement critiqued "institutional racism," whites quickly realized that as beneficiaries of home loan redlining practices, investment portfolios that extracted profits from ghettoes, access to elite educational institutions as legacies, all that was no longer simply aspirational but quite personal. Riots, school busing, Affirmative Action, and the shift from interracialism (represented by King's 1968 Poor People's March on Washington) to Black Power led to the purging and retrenchment of white supporters. What followed by the mid-1970s were various iterations of separatist racial nationalisms. With the 1973 treaty to end the war in Vietnam, one of the principal irritants that previously had accelerated protest—the daily arrival of Black, Puerto Rican, Mexican American, and Native dead soldiers in body bags—was no longer a news item on national television programs. Estimates place the number of American war casualties in Vietnam at 280,000, with Blacks and Mexican Americans accounting for about 40 percent or 112,000 deaths. With the war's end, which also put an end to mandatory military conscription, the peaceful protests that had long been couched as putting an end to colonialism at home and abroad soon fractured and fizzled. With antiwar protesters placated, the civil rights movement lost many of its white allies and its radical transformative potential to end white supremacy and systemic racism. At least for the moment.[19]

If President Johnson waged a war on poverty, Presidents Richard Nixon and later Ronald Reagan waged a war on poor Blacks and Latinos using coded racial rhetoric, birthing the popular white backlash we still live with today. Nixon referred to these whites as a "silent majority." It was for them and his own reelection prospects that he enacted a government of "law and order," waging domestic war against race rebels, on drug use among the poor with punitive mandatory sentences that incarcerated hundreds of thousands of Blacks and Latinos, their prison records limiting their employment options after release.[20]

Social scientists had been moving away from biological notions of race to the idea that what united groups of people from distinct places were their cultural practices and associational patterns. The genocides Europe witnessed during World War II against Jews, Romani, Serbs, and "undesirable others" quickened the emergence of ethnicity as an analytic tool. Harvard sociology professors Nathan Glazer and Daniel Patrick Moynihan, then quite influential in Washington policy circles, led this epistemic shift, trumpeting the utility of ethnicity as a form of national descent that primarily shaped a group's cultural identity. In their book *Beyond the Melting Pot: The Negroes, Puerto Ricans, Jews, Italians, and Irish of New York City*, Glazer and Moynihan explained that many of the differences evident among groups in New York were ethnic not racial, cultural not structural. The low achievement rates of African Americans and Puerto Ricans in the schools were due to the home, family, and community. "It is there that the heritage of two hundred years of slavery and a hundred years of discrimination is concentrated; and it is there that we find the serious obstacles to the ability to make use of a free educational system to advance into higher occupations and to eliminate the massive social problems that afflict colored Americans and the city."[21] They asserted that "[the Negro] has no value and culture to guard and protect"; that Puerto Rican culture "was sadly defective . . . unsure of its cultural traditions, without a powerful faith."[22] In the wake of the Watts riots in Los Angeles in 1965, Moynihan, then as President Johnson's assistant secretary of labor for policy planning and research, authored his much reviled 1965 study *The Negro Family: The Case for National Action*, in which he decried the dysfunction of the Black family, "its present tangle of pathology," which was beyond repair even if presented with legislative aid.[23]

The critiques of domination and subordination, of institutional racism and the need for race-based remedies that had been produced by the radicalization of the civil rights movement, were slowly displaced by a scholarly and public policy shift in an understanding of inequalities as rooted less in race and more in ethnicity. By recuperating and celebrating their ethnic immigrant roots, white Americans who many decades earlier had been reviled as nonwhites began distancing themselves from their white privilege, naturalizing and denying their unmarked racial supremacy, and, most importantly, arguing that they had not participated in colonial conquests, genocide, or slavery. In his 1971 book *The Rise of the Unmeltable Ethnics,* journalist Michael Novak recounted an exchange he had with a Native American who was decrying what Novak's ancestors had done to Indigenous peoples. "I tried gently to remind him that my grandparents never saw an Indian. They came to this country after that. Nor were they responsible for enslaving the blacks (or anyone else). They themselves escaped serfdom barely four generations ago."[24]

A white ethnic revival followed that emphasized America as a "nation of immigrants." In 1972 President Richard Nixon energized the burgeoning white immigrant identity movement by authorizing an Ethnic Heritage Studies Program in public schools. Nixon's goal, as he stated it, was to recognize that "in a multiethnic society a greater understanding of the contributions of one's own heritage and those of one's fellow citizens can contribute to a more harmonious, patriotic, and committed populace . . . All persons in the educational institutions of the Nation should have an opportunity to study the contributions of the cultural heritages made by each ethnic group."[25]

Using the restoration of Ellis Island as the symbolic font for this white ethnic revival, immigrants quickly became this nation's downtrodden, recounting their struggles with adversity and hatred, deeming it comparable to what racial minorities suffered, and, more importantly, inserting themselves into a counternarrative of the American republic in which they could not be held responsible for slavery, colonialism, or its toxic legacies in the form of institutional racism or individual acts of bigotry. White ethnics gained a vocabulary of victimization and perseverance, a self-image as blameless newcomers, while simultaneously preserving their white privileges. In time this generated the language of "reverse discrimination" and proclamations that America was a color-blind society. These ideas gained further legal traction with the Supreme Court's 1978 ruling that Allan Bakke was to be granted admission to the University of California, Davis's medical school. Bakke argued that he had initially been denied admission because of racial quotas reserved for less qualified applicants.[26]

A year after the 1964 Civil Rights Act was signed into law, the 1924 National Quota Act, which over time had forged a unitary white Anglo-Protestant identity through massive immigrant exclusions, was repealed. In the spirit of egalitarianism, immigrants from all of the previously banned countries were allowed entry in the years following 1965. The impact of this change was quickly felt. Before 1980, only 20 percent of the country's population were foreign born; by 1990, 27 percent were; in 2000, 35 percent were. Theorists and students of ethnicity took these staggering statistics of demographic change wrought by immigration as proof-perfect that the United States was no longer a country divided by race; race was a thing of the past. America was now a postracial, color-blind society where previous attempts at compensatory justice for racialized minorities were passé. What few noticed or even mentioned was that by 2000, 35 percent of the foreign born were from Mexico, 26 percent were from Asia, and about 3 percent were from Africa. As these immigrants arrived, they too experienced discrimination as they entered into intense competition with African Americans for jobs earmarked to fulfill Affirmative Action plans and with whites who saw such goals as reverse discrimination. Immigration since 1965 transformed the country economically, culturally, and racially. But lacking now a robust unifying national ideology, immigration heightened ethnic rivalries, notions of zero-sum actions, and nationalist supremacies that have rivaled those of the Civil War.

16 From Pat Buchanan to Donald Trump

THE NATIVIST TURN IN RIGHT-WING POPULISM

Joseph Lowndes

In 2016 Donald Trump staked his presidential campaign first and foremost on a pungent nativism. The virulence of this language was as shocking as his electoral success to many scholars, journalists, and even elites in his own party. He portrayed Mexican immigrants as drug smugglers and rapists, called for mass deportations, promised a wall along the southern border, and proposed a temporary ban on Muslim immigration.[1] Anti-immigrant sentiment had been waxing in Republican Party ranks since the emergence of the Tea Party movement in 2009 and became more acute in Mitt Romney's 2012 campaign, but it had not been the primary driver of GOP politics. Indeed, Trump was nearly alone among his Republican rivals in the 2016 primaries in his focus on immigration. How then did it come to the fore with such ferocity?

Trump's nativism was key to his electoral victory not simply because it played on racist fears of invasion, but because it was embedded in a broader logic of right-wing populism. Nativism and right-wing populism have a symbiotic relationship in U.S. politics because each provides something critical for the other. For nativists, right-wing populism provides the vehicle of class resentment to propagate it. For right-wing populists, nativism provides a clear target—immigrants—to add to its list of threats, alongside African Americans, Jews, and others. In the language of "Middle America" and the "Silent Majority," Trump linked anti-immigrant politics to issues of middle- and working-class economic anxiety, deindustrialization, political powerlessness, and a sense of declining self-worth among white men. Right-wing populist insurgencies have episodically challenged Republican Party orthodoxy over the last half-century. But their origins lay less in nativism than in anti-Black racism. It was not until Pat Buchanan's run in the Republican presidential primaries of 1992 that anti-immigrant sentiment was injected powerfully into GOP politics at the national level. Anti-immigrant politics had, across the 1980s, bubbled up in U.S. politics, but it was Buchanan's campaign that framed it in populist language that would allow it to cross back and forth between the active white supremacist groups like the Ku Klux Klan and the Republican Party. For right-wing populists in the United States, *the people* are threatened by a conspiracy of wealthy elites who are in league with poor people of color and, since the 1990s, nonwhite immigrants as well. In right-wing populist rhetoric, immigrants take jobs, opportunities, and basic social goods away from hardworking native-born white Americans.

To be sure, nativist populism drew on earlier iterations of right-wing populism and depended on what Natalia Molina has called "racial scripts" that transfer the perceived characteristics of one racialized subaltern group to others, but there were new elements as well.[2] One was the idea that immigrants were a direct threat to jobs and wages, allowing racist populists to talk about the rights of American workers. The idea of immigrants stealing jobs reinforced the idea, going back to anti-Chinese campaigns by white labor in the late nineteenth century, that elites used poor immigrants against the white working class. A century later in the 1980s and 1990s, much of the U.S. economic elite had a strong open-borders position, expressed from the campaign speeches of both Reagan and Bush to the editorial page of the *Wall Street Journal*. In the 1990s it became yoked to a critique of "globalism" of proposed free trade agreements such as the North American Free Trade Agreement.

Another new element was the emergent idea that the United States would become a "majority minority" nation by 2050. This became a significant story in the news in the early 1990s, and one that the Right would use to talk about the end of white racial dominance in the United States.

This fear, while widespread in American society, bolstered the Far Right in particular ways because it implicitly endorsed the idea of white racial dominance, demonized people of color, and suggested that resolution to this "problem" would require openly racist state action.

Immigrants were depicted as outside invaders assaulting American culture, language, and institutions. As such, nativism brought the issue of nationalism to the center of right-wing populism in a way that had not been present before. Domestically, it meant that the American nation had to defend itself and its borders from nonwhite others who would destroy it. Internationally, it meant isolationism and an embrace of nationalisms elsewhere.

In some sense, just as nativism gained traction through its embedding in populist discourse, populism would require nativism to impact both the GOP and national politics.

BUCHANAN'S RISE

At the end of the eight years of Reagan's presidency in 1988, the grass-roots conservative movement in the United States had been in some ways supplanted by a much more comfortable conservative establishment. Washington-based lobbies and think tanks on the Right were well anchored and well funded. George H. W. Bush, Reagan's vice president, was the obvious choice for the Republican nominee. But there were misgivings about what would happen to the conservative movement under those conditions. Vice presidents of two-term administrations always struggle to define their own vision, and in the case of Bush he did not have much in the way of his own conservative credentials to begin with.

Both political observers and conservative insiders had begun to discuss another candidate who had *both* establishment qualifications *and* outsider credentials, a staunch movement conservative who was widely known to the American public: Pat Buchanan. Buchanan had been a speechwriter and adviser to Nixon from 1968 to 1973, and had served as communications director at the Reagan White House in the 1980s. In the years in between, Buchanan had been a weekly syndicated columnist. The New Right organizations that grew out of the populist formations of the 1970s also had reasons to draft Buchanan. The New Right no longer fought as outsiders, as they had in the 1970s, and needed new causes to replenish their coffers and ignite support. As former Nixon adviser and columnist Kevin Phillips put it, "I think the New Right has a substantial fund-raising stake in a hot, populist conservative candidate like Pat. He'll get their money moving again."[3] Buchanan was indeed urged by the same New Right entrepreneurs who attempted to find a genuine populist to run in 1976, among them Howard Phillips, Paul Weyrich, and Richard Viguerie—all of whom saw George H. W. Bush as the representative of the "Wall Street wing of the Republican Party."[4] Buchanan ultimately reasoned, however, that he would likely not win if he were to run and might hurt the party in the process. George H. W. Bush ran as the Republican nominee and won the election in 1988.

BUSH, DUKE, AND THE REPUBLICAN PARTY'S IMAGE

Across the next four years, conditions on the ground changed. Among other brewing issues was that of race. Bush may not have been a hard conservative, but the campaign availed itself of white racial animus in the electorate by running the notorious "Willie Horton" political advertisement created by political operative Lee Atwater to make Massachusetts governor Michael Dukakis appear responsible for the crimes of African American convicted rapist William Horton.[5] In the years that followed, Bush had to tack between appearing firm against affirmative action and not looking like the leader of an openly racist party. Bush upheld the Reagan legacy for his party by vetoing a major piece of civil rights legislation, calling it a "quota bill," for which he came under loud and sharp criticism from civil rights organizations with whom he had enjoyed good relations even as vice president. The next year he signed a modified version of the legislation, however, now bringing condemnation from critics on his right.

The president and party's reputation came under greater stress in regard to issues of race when former Ku Klux Klan leader David Duke ran as a Republican for a Louisiana statehouse seat in 1988. Duke represented the boundary line for a party that had depended on white fears and resentments since 1968. Duke's main message throughout was the dispossession of white Christian America through welfare spending, "skyrocketing" Black birth rates, and uncontrolled nonwhite immigration. An inveterate campaigner, Duke had run for various offices since 1975. But his 1988 statehouse run as a Republican caught national attention because he was the anticipated winner in that race.

The moment is telling because of the extraordinary efforts national Republicans put into defeating Duke. George Bush sent a letter to voters in the district calling Duke's Republican opponent John Treen "the clear choice for Jefferson Parish." Even Reagan was summoned to weigh in, recording a radio ad in support of Treen. If the Republican establishment saw Duke as completely at odds with the identity of the GOP, Pat Buchanan had a different understanding of the party's legacy and opportunities. "The way to deal with Duke," said the veteran Nixon strategist, was "the way the GOP dealt with the far more formidable challenge of George Wallace. Take a hard look at Duke's portfolio of winning issues; and expropriate those not in conflict with GOP principles."[6] Buchanan saw populist opportunities in the vulnerabilities of the Bush administration. As the country sank deeper into recession, the president had broken his "Read my lips—no new taxes" campaign pledge, signed a revised version of the "quota bill," launched a war in the Middle East, and continued to speak of a "New World Order." Buchanan's criticisms of Bush reflected an opening schism between two hardening camps—neoconservatives on one side and the mix of libertarians, traditionalists, and populists who came to be called paleoconservatives on the other. This split began during the Reagan years, as populist Right conservatives saw important White House appointments go to neoconservatives in the realm of both domestic and international affairs. Neoconservatives, broadly, had supported the American welfare state of the New Deal, but opposed what they saw as the leftist and Black Power excesses of the 1960s. They tended toward democratic idealism and supported U.S. interventions abroad that would extend American ideals. Paleoconservatives, by contrast, hewed to principles of isolationism, antistatism, and "traditional" values—and, to a greater or lesser degree, open white supremacy.

SAM FRANCIS

One key figure in the paleoconservative movement had decisive impact on Buchanan's political thinking at the time: Sam Francis. Francis was a deputy editorial page editor at the *Washington Times* and became a regular columnist there until his termination in 1995. A gifted writer and polemicist, Francis received the Distinguished Writing Award for Editorial Writing from the American Society of Newspaper Editors in 1989 and again in 1990.[7] For all his beltway credentials on the mainstream Right, Francis was a racist and nativist die-hard who saw the Republican Party as a hopelessly compromised entity that refused to face racial realities. But what made Francis a formidable figure was that he was not merely a racist. He combined beliefs in both biological and cultural racial hierarchy with a broader critique of how state bureaucracies and managerial capitalism disempowered and alienated working- and middle-class Americans. Francis saw what sociologist Donald Warren had called "Middle American Radicals," or MARs for short, as the key to the populist Right's battle against the political and economic elites who presided over America's latter-day decline.

Francis asserted that a managerial "new class" was the late twentieth century's ruling caste, working for both modern capitalism and the bureaucratic state to sell out the interests of a broad working class.[8] Often, Francis elaborated the old populist framework that described a great white middle squeezed between elites above and dependents below. When David Duke came to the offices of the *Washington Times* for an interview in 1990, an unsigned editorial almost surely penned by Francis argued that regardless of Duke's Klan and Nazi past, he ably articulated what many white Americans were feeling.[9] Francis also described Duke's appeal in the right-wing *Chronicles Magazine.* As he put it:

> There was a subtext to what Mr. Duke explicitly and formally said in his speeches and his campaign literature, and the subtext, communicated by the continuous depiction of Mr. Duke in Nazi uniform and Klan hood by his enemies, is that the historic racial and cultural core of American civilization is under attack. Quotas, affirmative action, race norming, civil rights legislation, multiculturalism in schools and universities, welfare, busing, and unrestricted immigration from Third World countries are all symbols of that

attack and of the racial, cultural, and political dispossession they promise to inflict upon the white post-bourgeois middle classes.[10]

If, for Francis, David Duke provided the necessary political spark for a beleaguered white America, it was Buchanan's presidential campaigns that would take up the task of providing political coherence and focus to Middle American radicals, combining more established elements of the Right with emergent forces. "The importance of the Buchanan campaign lies not in its capacity to win the nomination or the national election but in its organization of those forces into a coherent political coalition," he wrote. "That coalition includes the remnants of the 'Old Right,' as well as various single-issue constituencies (pro-lifers, anti-immigration activists, protectionists) to which Buchanan is one of the few voices to speak." For Francis, Buchanan had begun a process that would illuminate "new social forces that only now are forming a common political consciousness ... What is important about these forces is not that a campaign centered on them does not now win major elections (indeed, it would be a fatal error if they succeeded in winning prematurely) but that the Buchanan campaign for the first time in recent history offers them an organized mode of expression that will allow them to develop and mature their consciousness and their power."[11]

THE 1992 ELECTION

Fresh off his gubernatorial race in November 1991, David Duke announced his intention to run in the Republican primaries for president. He began to build a small national organization to achieve ballot status across states, but was strenuously opposed by extant Republican organizations. Within weeks, Buchanan also threw his hat into the ring, seeing an opportunity to successfully challenge a sitting Republican president with very low approval ratings who had been a disappointment to conservatives. Buchanan announced his candidacy on December 10, 1991, ten weeks before primary season. The ongoing recession, Bush's low approval rating among voters, the particular sense of disappointment he generated among conservatives, and his commitment to what he called the "New

World Order" all played a role in Buchanan's decision to run, as did the urging of his intellectual confidants.

Conservatives were torn about Bush's candidacy. Many wanted to see a challenge to Bush from the Right, but much of the conservative establishment—particularly neoconservatives—supported emergent free trade agreements, open immigration, and an expanded global role for the United States in the post–Cold War era. "One has this almost irresistible urge to leap out of your chair and say, 'Pat, this guy deserves to be socked. Do it!'" said David Keene, chairman of the American Conservative Union. "But Pat's mission is not just to sock the President, but to change conservatism in a way I don't like."[12] "His platform in many ways is expected to parallel that of Louisiana state Rep. David Duke, a former Ku Klux Klan wizard," the *Washington Times* noted, but Buchanan had a more elaborate set of ideas and criticisms, even if he was in some ways as potent as Duke in regard to race.[13] Buchanan opposed Bush's signing of the civil rights bill and his turnabout on taxes. To this he would add a distinctly right-wing populist opposition to Bush's support for free trade agreements and intervention in the Middle East, and to the idea of a New World Order generally.

Buchanan's campaign had early success as he wove together rhetoric aimed at "Middle America" and its struggle against foreign competition, capital flight, immigrant labor, high taxes, affirmative action, and welfare. Dubbed "Pitchfork Pat" in the media, he fashioned himself as the people's tribune and challenger to "King George." He referred to the Republican primary contest as "St. Theresa's versus the Redskins," invoking a contrast between white ethnic underdogs and corporate professionals. On the night of a surprising showing in New Hampshire where exit polls showed him getting 40 percent of the Republican primary vote, he told a crowd of supporters in a state that had been particularly hard hit by the recession, "Tonight what began as a little rebellion has emerged into a full-fledged Middle-American revolution. We are going to take our party back from those who have walked away and forgotten about us."

Campaigning in Georgia he stoked the Southern Lost Cause, noting at rallies that two of his great-grandfathers "happened to be troublemakers and rabid secessionists." Bidding for evangelical support in the state, he told an audience in Atlanta, "There's only one candidate in this race who's a conservative and a traditionalist across the board, who believes in lower taxes, in less spending, in traditional values, in standing up for the right to life."[14] He did almost as well there, pulling in 36 percent of the primary vote.

After Georgia, however, the Buchanan campaign had a hard time maintaining momentum. There were no primary victories, and showings above 30 percent became more rare. Moreover, many conservatives had lined up against him by the time the primaries were in full swing. Charles Krauthammer, in a syndicated *Washington Post* column, put it baldly: "The real problem with Buchanan is not that his instincts are antisemitic but that they are, in various and distinct ways, fascistic."[15]

NEW NATIVISM

Over the course of the 1991 Republican primary campaign, Buchanan continued to develop the theme of immigration threat. It had not been an issue on the national agenda since the Immigration Act of 1924 was passed, and most Americans outside the racist Right had not given it a lot of thought. Two days before announcing his candidacy, Buchanan had gone on the ABC News show *This Week with David Brinkley* and said, "I think God made all people good, but if we had to take a million immigrants in, say Zulus, next year, or Englishmen, and put them in Virginia, what group would be easier to assimilate and would cause less problems for the people of Virginia?"[16]

Racist nativism had been a cornerstone of David Duke's message for more than a decade, and it had increasing traction on the Far Right. Organizations (with backing from racist funders including the eugenicist Pioneer Fund) such as John Tanton's Federation of American Immigration Reform had begun to build a national lobby. Sam Francis churned out a steady stream of columns on the subject, hoping to bring it to the attention of a larger public.

Buchanan ratcheted up the nativist language as his 1992 campaign was sputtering out. By May, Bush had more than enough delegate votes to ensure a first-ballot victory at the GOP convention, and Buchanan thus had little to lose in unleashing his most redolent language on the subject. Prior to the California primary, Buchanan gave speeches on immigration, calling for a "border fence" and increased funding for border agents. In the midst of the primary race, South Central Los Angeles erupted in riots following the acquittal of four Los Angeles police officers accused of the beating of Black motorist Rodney King. Buchanan's first response was a kind of tired echo of the campaigns of Alabama segregationist George Wallace: he visited National Guard troops on the street and posed in front of them to take a swipe at Lyndon Johnson's Model Cities program from a quarter-century before, and called for "superior force in dealing with hooligans, criminals, and thugs." This was not enough to distinguish him from Bush, who blamed the riots on "the liberal programs of the '60s and '70s," or even from Democratic candidate Bill Clinton, who said that looters "do not share our values, and their children are growing up in a culture alien from ours" and asserted that government programs should "demand more responsibility from the poor."

Within a few days, however, Daniel Stein, director of the Federation of Immigration Reform, wrote a letter to the California Congressional Delegation blaming illegal immigrants for "helping to deliver America's second-largest city to the furnace of anarchy," which Sam Francis quoted in a *Washington Times* column. Two days later Buchanan followed suit, now adding an anti-immigrant angle to his previous statement. He organized a press conference and photo opportunity at the Mexican border at a hole in the fence, much as Duke had done twelve years previously at a nearby location. White supremacists used the opportunity to stage a more direct message about immigration. White Aryan Resistance leader Tom Metzger showed up, forcing an embarrassing moment from Buchanan's right. Metzger out-Buchananed Buchanan, yelling, "Pat, what are we going to do about all those rich Republicans making millions off the wetbacks in the Imperial Valley?"[17] Buchanan scuttled the photo op and hastened from the scene. Nevertheless, he was back hammering away on nativist themes at rallies across Southern California in the days that followed.

While Buchanan lost the GOP primaries, his run had been forceful enough to warrant a prime-time speaking spot at the Republican Convention. There he delivered what became known as the "Culture War" speech, in which he railed against feminism, lesbians and gays, and affirmative action "quotas." He ended the speech by comparing the Los Angeles riots to a degraded American culture. Describing the 18th Cavalry that had been sent in to quell the unrest, Buchanan said, "Here were 19-year-old boys ready to lay down their lives to stop a mob from molesting old people they did not even know. And as those boys took back the streets of Los Angeles, block by block, my friends, we must take back our cities, and take back our culture, and take back our country."[18]

RUN-UP TO 1996

In 1993 Buchanan founded a group called American Cause as an organizational placeholder for another presidential run, staffed with people from his prior campaign. The focus of its founding conference was "winning the culture war." It included the famous sculptor Frederick Hart, Jewish critic Michael Medved, and African American conservative Ezola Foster, among others. According to paleoconservative philosopher Paul Gottfried, Sam Francis "grumbled all day" at the conference about Buchanan's newfound "inclusiveness." But when his time came to speak, Francis argued that gun rights and cultural symbols such as the Confederate flag were of primary importance, and told Buchanan that he should place immigration side by side with opposition to free trade on the Middle American platform, because they spoke directly to "the racial dispossession of the American people."

Partly as a result of Buchanan's 1992 run, nativism had entered mainstream politics through California's Proposition 187, a 1994 ballot initiative to establish a state-run citizenship screening system and prohibit illegal immigrants from using nonemergency health care, public education, and other services in the state of California. The framing of Prop 187 was strategically populist, taking aim at undocumented residents by portraying them as parasitic on the broadly shared, tax-funded public goods of California. The initiative passed, but was declared unconstitutional in federal district court soon after.

The Far Right moved into a paramilitary, antigovernment phase as evidenced in the emergence of an armed militia movement; an FBI shootout with white supremacists at the Ruby Ridge compound in rural Idaho; the federal government siege of the Branch Davidian compound in Waco, Texas; and, most fatally, in Timothy McVeigh's bombing of a federal building in Oklahoma City in revenge for Ruby Ridge and Waco. Biological racism, meanwhile, went mainstream with the publication of Herrnstein and Murray's popular book *The Bell Curve,* which argued that there was a genetic, racial basis for IQ. Although ultimately discredited by both geneticists and sociologists, the book was enthusiastically reviewed by the *New York Times* and other prominent media. Sam Francis finally stepped over the line and was fired by the *Washington Times* for suggesting at a conference of the "race realist" journal *American Renaissance* that the "genetic endowments" of whites made them the "creating people" of Europe and America. He went on to edit the newsletter of the Council of Conservative Citizens (which was descended from the Citizens Councils of the 1960s but now added racial nativism to neo-Confederate politics) and to write for publications on the Far Right and racist Right linking populism to nativism.

When Buchanan ran again for the Republican nomination in 1996, he shook the GOP establishment in a series of early victories in the Louisiana caucuses and the Alaska primary. After coming in second in the Iowa caucuses behind a tie between Kansas senator Bob Dole and Texas senator Phil Gramm, he won the New Hampshire primary. He worked to keep the Christian Right in his camp through hard antiabortion and antigay rhetoric, and working-class whites through a message of economic nationalism. In southern states he took up the cause of the Confederate flag and, hewing to Sam Francis's advice, kept the issue of illegal immigration from Latin America front and center throughout.

Anti-immigration groups and paleoconservative outlets echoed the new populist spin. One article in the February 1996 issue of *Border Watch,* the organ of the American Immigration Control Foundation (which Francis now headed), asserted that "immigration is enriching the business elites that seek cheap labor" and creating "unpleasant low-paying jobs that do not sustain an American standard of living." The article concluded, "For ordinary middle-class and working-class Americans, immigration has brought alienation, culture-clash, and loss of jobs." *Chronicles,* the magazine of the small paleoconservative Rockford Institute, churned out regular anti-immigrant pieces, attacking Latin American and Southeast Asian immigration on the basis of race, culture, national identity, and populist defense of the white working class.

As in 1992, Buchanan was dogged in the mainstream media for his association with the Far Right. This time, the connections were more tangible. It was discovered that campaign cochair Larry Pratt had appeared with members of the Aryan Nations at a white supremacist Christian Identity meeting in Colorado. Another cochair, Michael Farris, had attended a banquet honoring people convicted of shooting abortion doctors. Two other subnational campaign chairs had organizational ties to David Duke. Republican candidate Bob Dole accused Buchanan of having "extremist views." But other conservatives, concerned to keep Buchananite voters in the party, defended him, including Christian Coalition director Ralph Reed and American Conservative Union head David Keene.

The Buchanan campaign lost steam by Super Tuesday, the day when the largest number of state primaries were held. There would be no prime speaking spot for him at the Republican convention this time. However, his campaign was able, in concert with the Christian Coalition, to capture the Republican platform committee to keep strong antiabortion language and to add an anti-immigrant plank calling for a constitutional change to the Fourteenth Amendment.

Buchanan ran once again for the presidency in 2000, this time as a candidate for the Reform Party on an anti-NAFTA, anti–U.S. intervention, and anti-immigrant platform. As in the last two elections, he talked about immigration in the racial populist terms of crime, wage depression, and culture. In his speech accepting the party nomination, he called for a border wall and linked undocumented immigration to violent crime. Responding to John McCain's speech at the Republican convention, where the Arizona senator said "Walls are for cowards," Buchanan told his audience, "Let me tell the senator a story about a woman who lives in his own home state of Arizona. Her name is Theresa Murray. Senator, she's eighty-two years old. She has arthritis and she lives in Douglas right on that border . . . And around her home is a chain-link fence. And on the top of the chain-link fence are rolls of coiled razor wire as you see on prisons around the country . . . And Mrs. Murray's two pet dogs were killed by thugs who threw meat over the fence with cut glass in it. This lady sleeps with a gun on her bed table at eighty-two because she's been burglarized thirty times."[19]

In another campaign speech that year, Buchanan claimed that "Americans today who do poorly in high school are increasingly condemned to a low-wage existence, and mass immigration is a major reason why," before lamenting the loss of a "common language" and "common culture." Buchanan's Republican candidacies were consequential in providing focus to a nascent Far Right movement, connecting paleoconservative, libertarian, racist, and nativist intellectuals, activists, and writers such as Joe Sobran, Sam Francis, and Charles Murray.

NATIVISM AFTER BUCHANAN

Anti-immigrant politics continued to gain traction in the 1990s, spanning the political spectrum from the Far Right to the Democratic presidency of Bill Clinton. In 1992, Clinton ran as a "New Democrat" and was determined not be pigeonholed as a racial liberal who was soft on crime and welfare. He attempted to win white conservative support in the electorate by demonstrating a willingness to take a tough line on Black crime in his 1992 presidential campaign, and then in the passage of the Violent Crime Control and Law Enforcement Act of 1994. Clinton extended "law and order" politics into immigration politics. In 1996 Clinton signed the Illegal Immigration Reform and Responsibility Act. This act, among other things, barred deportees from entering the United States for three to ten years, called for the hiring of one thousand new Border Patrol agents every five years, authorized the attorney general to construct border barriers, and made the apparatus of the criminal justice system available for mass deportations. Similarly, the right-wing populism Clinton tapped into in his support for welfare reform targeted immigrants as well. The historic Personal Responsibility and Work Opportunity Reconciliation Act severely reduced or eliminated federal eligibility for legal immigrants during their first five years of U.S. residence.[20]

Thus anti-immigrant rhetoric, like other GOP talking points, lost its use value for Republicans by the mid-1990s. As Clinton strategist Mark Penn explained about his candidate's continued success, "We did this by co-opting the Republicans on all their issues—getting tough on welfare, tough on crime, balancing the budget, and cracking down on illegal immigration."[21]

Nativist politics largely lay dormant in the election of 2000. The campaign of George W. Bush courted Latino votes, and the candidate's politics reflected the open-borders position of pro–free trade Republicans. But the

Far Right continued to organize nativist politics ideologically through a network of small paleoconservative journals such as *Chronicles* and the *Unz Review*, more openly racist organizations such as American Renaissance, the hard racist website V-Dare (named for Virginia Dare, purportedly the first English Child born on North American soil) set up by former *National Review* editor Perter Brimelow; organizationally through John Tanton's various organizations such as FAIR and NumbersUSA; politically through right-wing anti-immigrant politicians such as Colorado representative Tom Tancredo, Idaho representative Steve King, and Alabama senator Jeff Sessions. These nativists continued to emphasize crime, welfare, and jobs in a racial populist script. When Bush attempted to pass comprehensive immigration reform, a growing network of grassroots nativists leaned hard on Republicans in Congress, scuttling Bush's ability to do more than enhance the enforcement, border control side of immigration legislation. The Al Qaeda attacks on the Pentagon and World Trade Center on September 11, 2001, allowed nativists to move beyond crime to link immigration to national security. The Bush administration moved swiftly to deport thousands of people on expired visas from North Africa, the Middle East, and Asia and tightened immigration controls through the newly organized Department of Homeland Security, but none of it was authorized in anti-immigrant language as such. Bush was a disappointment to nativists throughout both terms.

Far Right nativists were able to really gain political traction, however, with the election of Barack Obama. Just as earlier nativist victories were built on a populism conceived in anti-Black racism, the election of a Black president who was both the son of an African immigrant and of Muslim descent could link those discourses credibly. Once Obama was elected president, Far Right opponents challenged his legal claim to the office and asserted that he had fabricated a U.S. birth certificate. This rumor, which had circulated during the election season, gained momentum during the first months of Obama's administration. Spokespeople for what came to be called the "birther" movement argued that he held office illegally because of the constitutional requirement that presidents be born on U.S. soil. This movement gained credibility through the tacit and sometimes active consent of major media and political pundits, such as CNN's Lou Dobbs, television and radio talk show host Rush Limbaugh, and GOP figure Liz Cheney. One of the conspiracy theory's major purveyors was real estate magnate and reality television star Donald Trump. Survey data at the time indicated that belief in birtherism correlates strongly with high levels of racial resentment. Even by the middle of his second term, up to a third of U.S. citizens believed that Obama either was born abroad or might have been.[22]

At the same moment, nativist populism was gaining ground in some states, Arizona in particular. There a state bill, SB 1070, would have made it a misdemeanor for noncitizens to be in the state without documentation; made it a crime to shelter, hire, or transport undocumented immigrants; and required police to check the immigration status of anyone suspected of being undocumented. The bill was partially written by Kris Kobach, a longtime legal activist with ties to white nationalist organizations. SB 1070 was largely found to be unconstitutional by the U.S. Supreme Court, not on grounds of civil rights violations, but rather on the basis of federalism.

TEA PARTY NATIVISM

The growing groundswell of nativist politics was taken national and given greater force by another social movement that emerged at the time, the Tea Party. Increasing links to racism between groups and individuals associated with the Tea Party movement led the National Association for the Advancement of Colored People (NAACP) to pass a resolution calling on the Tea Party movement to denounce racist elements in its midst.[23] The NAACP also partnered with the Institute for Research and Education on Human Rights to analyze the presence of racism in the Tea Party movement. The resulting report, *Tea Party Nationalism*, evaluates the presence of racism through the language of Tea Party leaders and participants, of racial symbolism at Tea Party rallies, and of Tea Partiers who are also associated with white supremacist organizations.[24] The report is a thorough investigation of the major Tea Party organizations at both the national and local level. It provides evidence that there are racists in the movement, and that in certain locales, particularly in the South, there is overlap between racist organizations like the Council of Conservative Citizens and

Tea Party groups. Professional Islamophobes such as Pamela Geller have close ties to some Tea Party organizations, and Burghart and Zeskind document hundreds of Tea Party blog posts expressing anti-Muslim sentiment. Nativist activity, particularly in Arizona around Senate Bill 1070, and the campaign to repeal birthright citizenship had Tea Party groups in the vanguard. Klan, neo-Nazi, militia, and border vigilante groups have all tried to make inroads to the Tea Party movement at the local level as well.

This open racist influence on the Tea Party is in the context of a major upsurge in racial nationalism in the United States since 2008. On one end of the spectrum are the birthers and the campaign to repeal the Fourteenth Amendment's birthright citizenship clause, and on the other end, open hate groups. The Southern Poverty Law Center issued a report in February 2011, stating that there are over a thousand Klan and neo-Nazi groups in the United States right now, more than it has ever reported, and over 850 patriot and militia groups in a separate category.[25]

Tea Party organizations continued to make inroads to the GOP through the presidential election of 2012, compelling Republican presidential candidate Mitt Romney to develop a strong stance against undocumented immigrants. He famously stated that his strategy for reducing the number of undocumented residents in the United States was to encourage them to "self-deport." After Romney's loss in 2012, the Republican National Committee underwent a deep self-examination into what had gone wrong, and what the party would need to do to reach a larger electorate. The resulting report, "The Growth and Opportunity Project," laid out a broad plan to recast itself as a party that was less white, male, and socially conservative.[24] As RNC Chair Reince Priebus stated, "We need to campaign among Hispanic, Black, Asian, and gay Americans and demonstrate we care about them, too. We must recruit more candidates who come from minority communities. But it is not just tone that counts. Policy always matters."

TRUMP'S POPULIST NATIVISM

For all the soul-searching that followed Romney's loss, the national leadership of the GOP was unable to steer the party in the direction it proposed in its post-mortem. Indeed, in the 2016 nomination race, the leading candidates took anti-immigrant positions (including Florida Senator Marco Rubio, who helped craft the one major piece of immigration reform legislation since 2012), and the early front-runner Trump called Mexican immigrants "criminals, drug-dealers, and rapists" and called for tracking Muslim Americans and the imposition of a travel ban to the United States on Muslims.[25]

Trump's harsh populist nativism bore the influence of right-wing media personality Ann Coulter, who in 2015 authored a book titled *Adios, America: The Left's Plan to Turn America into a Third-World Hellhole.*[26] Coulter's thinking on Latin American immigration was deeply influenced by Peter Brimelow, founder of a racist anti-immigration website. In the book, Coulter argues that immigrants (not just the undocumented) are undercutting the wages of working-class Americans, burdening public services from welfare to education, and committing violent crimes. As she told one journalist, "Immigration is never going to affect George Soros or Rupert Murdoch or Megyn Kelly or Rachel Maddow—it's not coming to their neighborhoods. They don't know anybody who lost a job because of a bad trade deal. They don't know any steelworkers, coal miners, and they don't particularly care."[27] This populist spin on nativism reflected the language of the Buchanan campaigns of the 1990s and of the right-wing populists who continued to hone in on the paleoconservative and racist Right. As a solution, Coulter called for a border wall, deportation of undocumented immigrants, and a ten-year moratorium on all immigration. Before he announced his candidacy, Trump saw Coulter debate Latino journalist Jorge Ramos and asked for a copy of her book. When Trump announced his candidacy, and as he rolled out his platform on immigration, Coulter's influence was clear.

The 2016 presidential campaign of Donald Trump was also marked by violence in his rhetoric, at his rallies, and among white nationalists more generally. Negative comments about Latino immigrants and Muslims drew people to his rallies, where physical assaults on Black and Latino protesters were common. His rhetoric also inspired attacks, including two men severely beating and urinating on a homeless Latino man in Boston, one of whom said afterward, "Donald Trump was right; all these illegals need to be deported." Far from denouncing the assault, Trump said when asked about it, "I will say that people who are following me are very passionate. They love this country and they want this country to be great again. They are passionate."[28]

Trump was aided in the 2016 election by an assemblage of Far Right ideologues known as the alt-right,[29] a political identity that is distinguished by its overt commitment to both white nationalism and patriarchy. Adept with social media skills, alt-rightists associated with each other across internet platforms such as Reddit and 4chan, and ultimately the right-wing commentary and opinion site Breitbart News. Former Breitbart executive chair Steven Bannon, who left that position to work as chief executive of the Trump campaign, became Trump's chief strategist in January 2017. Bannon is a self-described populist who links his strongly anti-immigrant and anti-Islam stands to an opposition to "globalist" elites who, together with immigrants, have launched an assault on white middle- and working-class Americans. Trump brought other hard-right nativists into his campaign, including Kris Kobach and Stephen Miller, former aide to Alabama senator Jeff Sessions.

In the White House, Trump was able to enact racist nativist policies on a number of fronts. In his very first week in office, Trump announced a travel ban which would have barred entry into the United States to refugees and immigrants from Iran, Iraq, Libya, Somalia, Sudan, Syria, and Yemen—all Muslim-majority countries. A federal court initially blocked the ban, but an amended version of it was later upheld by the U.S. Supreme Court. Later that first month Trump signed an executive order to direct the United States to begin constructing a wall along the U.S.-Mexico border using federal funds. (A year later Trump signed a declaration of National Emergency to divert military funding for more wall construction.) At the U.S.-Mexico border, the Trump administration began to perform public cruelty through a "family separation policy." In line with the administration's "zero tolerance" approach to illegal immigration, federal authorities began separating children from parents or guardians attempting to cross the border, prosecuting the parents and placing the children under the supervision of the Department of Health and Human Services. The Trump administration ramped up both arrests and deportations by the Immigration and Customs Enforcement Agency, and further militarized the U.S. Border Patrol.

Going into the 2020 campaign season, Trump fully embraced the most far-right visions of nativism. Having been impeached in the House of

Representatives and with consistently high disapproval ratings in states he won in 2016—including Ohio, Wisconsin, and Michigan—Trump had to keep his core supporters angry and energized and try to lift Republican support enough to turn states that he narrowly lost, like Minnesota. Trump's intuitive response was, as always, to cry persecution, and then identify his supposed victimization with that of the nation.

Trump's campaign rally in Minneapolis, Minnesota, in October 2019 is a good example of his sharpened public nativist appeals. His speech was notable for its unabashed deployment of "replacement theory"—the long-held colonialist fear, recently repackaged by French white nationalist writer Renaud Camus, that white people are under the grave threat of being supplanted by nonwhite and culturally non-Western immigrants and refugees. Trump's rants ranged from anti-Muslim, red-baiting fabrications about Minnesota congresswoman Ilhan Omar to fear-mongering about Minnesota's refugee Somali community, to a warning that given the chance the Democratic Party would "open the floodgates" to immigrants and refugees, "the likes of which the country has never seen."[30] It was as if Trump had taken this narrative straight from the pages of Steve Bannon's favorite book, *The Camp of the Saints*, Jean Raspail's 1973 racist dystopian novel about the destruction of white countries by migrating hordes from the global South. While Trump's line of attack was notable for its xenophobic brutality, it was not in itself much worse than many of the comments he has made since his first campaign announcement in 2015.

Trump wove together a vivid racialized and gendered conspiracy theory that links immigration, Islam, crime, socialism, and the Democratic Party in one associative chain. This demonization was not new. It fit squarely within what the late political theorist Michael Rogin called the "countersubversive tradition" in the United States—a persecutory fantasy centered on the imagined destructive power of women, immigrants, communists, and people of color that has been used to justify extraordinary violence and repression.[31]

Under current conditions, where the circulation of Far Right conspiracy theories has swollen the ranks of heavily armed paramilitary "patriot" groups and protofascist street-fighting groups, where language of a coming "hot civil war" has animated the former president's Republican Party base as his supporters have sought to defend him from the "Deep State," and where belief in the "great replacement" has driven repeated, episodic mass killings, such language takes on particularly charged and urgent meanings. The Minneapolis event provides us with important insights about this moment. Consider that Republicans who attended Trump's October 2019 rally at the Target Center were escorted to and from their cars by members of the paramilitary Oath Keepers, who bill themselves as "guardians of the republic."[32] Up until that point, the open alliance between the GOP and armed groups had only been employed in the Pacific Northwest, where the Republican Party had already become an increasingly Far Right party of the European variety. The culmination of the Trumpist GOP–Far Right alliance occurred on January 6, 2021, when hundreds of violent protestors stormed the U.S. Capitol to prevent the certification of the presidential election results.[33]

Trump mostly used populist performance in daily White House press briefings and on Twitter to rebuff expert knowledge and epidemiological protocols coming from the World Health Organization (WHO) or the Centers for Disease Control and Prevention (the U.S. agency primarily responsible for pandemic response), to tout untested treatments like the antimalarial drug Hydroxchloroquine, to refuse to wear a mask, to call for the "liberation" of states from lockdown orders, and to ratchet up nationalism and nativism. Trump repeatedly sought to blame China for the spread of the virus. "I think they made a horrible mistake and they didn't want to admit it. We wanted to go in. They didn't want us there," Trump said in one typical statement about the U.S. economic rival. "This virus should not have spread all over the world. They should have put it out."

More consequentially, however, in late April of 2020, Attorney General William Barr told Fox News commentator Laura Ingraham that he had "felt for a long time—as much as people talk about global warming—that the real threat to human beings is microbes and being able to control disease, and that starts with controlling your border. So, I think people will be attuned to more protective measures."[34] Not long after, the Trump administration moved from the threat of foreign microbes to the threat of foreign workers by issuing an executive order suspending the issuance of new green cards. Meanwhile, Education Secretary Betsy DeVos set down policy guidelines to exclude undocumented students from COVID-19 relief aid.[35]

CONCLUSION

In 2016 Pat Buchanan was asked by the *Washington Post* why Donald Trump had succeeded politically where he had failed. Buchanan replied: "What's different today is that the returns are in, the results are known. Everyone sees clearly now the de-industrialization of America, the cost in blood and treasure from decade-long wars in Afghanistan and Iraq, and the pervasive presence of illegal immigrants. What I saw at the San Diego border 25 years ago, everyone sees now on cable TV. And not just a few communities but almost every community is experiencing the social impact."[36] Like any savvy politico, Buchanan made what was a self-conscious political project appear as a self-evident reality.

Nativism has not always depended on populism. At the turn of the twentieth century, anti-immigrant rhetoric was expressed by white Anglo Saxon Protestant elites who saw immigrants as a threat to a rigidly hierarchical class order, not to popular sovereignty. By the same token, right-wing populism has not always depended on nativism. The racial populist Alabama governor and presidential candidate George Wallace, for example, brought eastern and southern European union members on the campaign trail to demonstrate the capaciousness of the coalition he hoped to build. But at this moment in United States political history the coconstitution of nativism and populism, held together by racial demonology, props open a door between Far Right extremists and the mainstream of U.S. politics. The intensification of domestic and global wealth disparity, the growing dysfunction of U.S. political institutions, and the long-term effects of climate catastrophe which will continue to drive refugees across the U.S. border all provide fodder for nativist populism and justification of its brutality.

17 The Alt-Right in Charlottesville

HOW AN ONLINE MOVEMENT BECAME A REAL-WORLD PRESENCE

Nicole Hemmer

There was a frisson of excitement rippling through the white vans carrying marchers to downtown Charlottesville on the morning of August 12, 2017. The night before, they had gathered in the dark and marched under flickering torchlight. But that morning they would assemble in the full light of day, faces clear and bright under the midday sun when the rally kicked off at noon.

It was the alt-right's coming-out rally.

For nearly a decade, the alt-right (a Far Right movement rooted in racist nationalism) had been a largely online phenomenon, a growing network of white supremacists, men's rights activists, antisemites, and others who sought to craft an alternative to American conservatism. Believing the American Right had become too milquetoast and moderate, they wanted to form a Far Right politics centered on white supremacy, patriarchy, and nativism. Though there were publications and public events that attended the rise of the alt-right, its group identity was primarily forged online, a characteristic evident in its meme-based language, trolling-based strategies, and key events like #GamerGate.

The Unite the Right rally in Charlottesville was supposed to be the moment the alt-right crossed over into the real world, demonstrating its physical presence and political strength in the aftermath of President Donald Trump's election. It was meant to show widespread unity on the Right, connecting the most violent fringes of the alt-right with its more respectable avatars.

In that, the alt-right largely failed. But to dismiss the events in Charlottesville as a failure, to see it as a catastrophe that ended the political importance of the alt-right, is a mistake. The events at Charlottesville revealed the intertwined nature of the movement's quest for political acceptance and hunger for political violence, and marked the reorganization, not the dissipation, of the broader movement.

THE EARLY DAYS OF THE ALT-RIGHT

To the extent that it has a definable beginning, the "alternative Right" traces back to 2008, when it was devised by Paul Gottfried, a humanities professor and paleoconservative, and Richard Spencer, a white supremacist. The two worked together at *Taki's Magazine,* a publication that served as a gathering place for members of the Right who felt they no longer fit within the contemporary conservative movement.

Gottfried and Spencer had two different visions for the alternative Right, but they were appropriate coauthors of the term. For Spencer, the phrase was new window dressing for a white supremacist ideology with neo-Nazi roots and ethnic cleansing aims, ideas far, far outside the mainstream. In 2008 he also founded his National Policy Institute, a think tank whose banal name belied its extremist politics.

Gottfried had been tossing around for a word for the movement he had described as "post-paleo." He believed that the original paleoconservative movement, which had emerged in the 1980s and 1990s around noninterventionist nationalism and the traditionalist values of the culture wars, had largely run its course, drained by internecine fights and the graying of its advocates (Pat Buchanan most prominent among them). But he had noticed a new phenomenon emerging in places like the Ron Paul campaigns: a right-wing movement that shared paleoconservatism's noninterventionist and nationalist politics but seemed to have a new energy.[1]

There was one more thing Gottfried believed was wrong with the older paleoconservatives vis-à-vis the post-paleos: they no longer showed any interest in "human cognitive disparities." What could Gottfried have meant by this? He explained that paleoconservatism regrettably showed "little interest in the cognitive, hereditary preconditions for intellectual and cultural achievements" and that some paleos were even drifting into the "liberal immigrationist camp."[2]

In other words, the paleoconservative movement had lost its interest in racist IQ theories, like those found in the pseudoscientific tract *The Bell Curve*, and antiimmigration policy.

Fortunately, he continued, the generation of young professionals who made up the post-paleos had taken readily to those issues and were sharing their work in outlets like *Taki's Magazine* and *VDARE*, a virulently anti-immigration, white nationalist website.[3]

Gottfried distanced himself from Spencer around the time Spencer began giving Nazi salutes in public, but it is not difficult to see how their interests intersected in 2008.[4]

The alt-right's early ties to paleoconservatism, bell-curve racism, and anti-immigrant politics help explain both the origins of the alt-right and the belief by people like Spencer that the movement could eventually find a home in the mainstream Right: after all, all three of those ideas were en vogue on the Right in the 2000s and 2010s, especially as neoconservative policies were undergoing renewed challenge thanks to the Iraq and Afghanistan wars. While in elite Republican circles neoconservatism rarely met sustained challenge, in the conservative base it was far more contested.

Digital outlets like *Taki's Magazine, VDARE, AltRight*, and *Radix Journal* all worked to frame the alt-right as an intellectual project, a challenge to the movement conservatism of magazines like *National Review* and the neoconservatism of magazines like *Weekly Standard*. Alt-right leaders understood the significance of these intellectual homes, and indeed shared lineage with the leading magazine of paleoconservative thought, *The American Conservative*, which was founded in 2002 by Pat Buchanan, Scott McConnell, and Taki Theodoracopulos, the last of whom would found *Taki's Magazine* in 2007.

Without drawing too sharp a line between the early alt-right and paleoconservatism—the networks and ideas overlap significantly—

paleoconservatives emphasized noninterventionist, even isolationist, foreign policy and Christian traditionalism, while the early alt-right focused much more on white supremacy, antifeminism, and anti-immigration ideas. As alt-right leaders integrated more into established networks of white power organizing, some early adherents like Gottfried would distance themselves from the alt-right label, but as an intellectual and organizational project, the post-paleo movement would continue (as seen in the many fractures and rebranding efforts post-Charlottesville).[5]

The intellectualization of the alt-right was only one part of the movement, which flourished online, particularly on discussion and image boards like Reddit, 4chan, and 8chan, as well as in online video game groups and on social-media and video-sharing platforms like Twitter and YouTube. In these digital spaces, the alt-right became a project of radicalization, bringing more and more people, primarily young, college-educated white men, into the movement. While the exact scope of the movement is difficult to determine, given that it operated in amorphous and often anonymous spaces, a fair estimate is that tens of thousands of young, white men of varying class and educational backgrounds from across the United States and Canada identified with the alt-right (though most of the public leaders have college degrees, and the groups recruit on college campuses). The most important shared demographic for the group is that they are almost exclusively white and male.[6]

These digital formats shaped the linguistics of the alt-right, dominated by memes (images that, through widespread sharing and creative modification, serve as symbolic insider referents) and lingo pulled from culture and packed with meaning. Through networks of men's rights activists, white nationalists, gamers, and the like, terms such as *red-pill* and *cuck* became ubiquitous on the alt-right. The first was borrowed from the film *The Matrix* to explain someone who had chosen to see the world as it truly is—that is, to see through the lies of "political correctness" and accept "natural" race and sex hierarchies. The second was borrowed from a porn genre that features Black men having sex with white women as the women's white male partners watch, capturing the emasculation and racial inferiority that the alt-right encourages white men to stand up against.

Other memes had no logical connection to the politics of the alt-right. Pepe the Frog, a cartoon character, had a long history as a popular meme on 4chan and Tumblr before being co-opted by the alt-right. So thoroughly had the alt-right absorbed the Pepe image that it became internet shorthand for the movement, and the frog symbol became a marker in Twitter names and alt-right websites like Gab.ai.

The adoption of a nonsensical character—around which an equally nonsensical mythology sprang up, involving the Egyptian god Kek and the fictional nation of Kekistan, whose flag was modeled off the flag of Nazi Germany's navy—points to one of the most important stylistic innovations of the alt-right, especially in comparison with the white power and neo-Nazi groups that preceded it. Using the tools of irony and jokiness, people aligned with the alt-right were able to disguise their genuine political ideology and slowly introduce newcomers to their ideas, testing people's boundaries by laughing off anything that drew a negative reaction.

This early development of the alt-right occurred mostly out of public view. The first time the movement started to gain media attention was in 2014 because of something called GamerGate. The video game community had long been the province of gamers, who were overwhelmingly young, white, and male. In an effort to expand the sorts of games available and to challenge the overtly masculine and often misogynist nature of gaming, a feminist game designer named Zoe Quinn released a game called Depression Quest in 2013. It is difficult to overstate how innocuous this game was, or to understate the scale of backlash against Quinn and the women journalists who covered her work. Rape threats, death threats, doxing, swatting: the women were subject to the most violent aspects of the gaming community and the misogynist men's rights community.[7]

The attacks on Quinn, Brianna Wu, and Anita Sarkeesian were largely carried out over social media sites like Reddit and 4chan, though at times they crossed into the real world. The main line of grievance in GamerGate was this: video games were now subject to "political correctness" (the dismissive label for concerns about representation), and one more space that had once been the province primarily of white men was being intruded upon by feminists, antiracists, and "social justice warriors," as GamerGaters called them.

GamerGate did not garner much media attention—the concerns of gamers were not considered front-page material—but it did catch the eye of Steve Bannon. Bannon had grown interested in online gaming communities in 2005, when he raised $60 million for Internet Gaming Entertainment, a company that used low-wage Chinese workers to make money playing *World of Warcraft*. He later said that he'd been intrigued by the game's community: "These guys, these rootless white males, had monster power." In 2014 he found that same "monster power" in GamerGate. Where most people saw harassment, Bannon saw potential activists. He believed he could take the energy and anger that fueled GamerGate and bring those gamers, primarily young white men, into a broader politics of populist white nationalism—in other words, into the politics of the alt-right.[8]

Bannon, who was running a right-wing website called Breitbart, had long seen potential in the alt-right. He believed that by focusing on the grievances of white men, it was possible to tap into a broader world of pro-West, antiliberal, anti–civil rights politics that could be harnessed for genuine political change. So he hired a young tech writer named Milo Yiannopoulos, who rose to prominence covering the controversy. Bannon put Milo in charge of the technology section of Breitbart.

Together, Bannon and Milo helped transform Breitbart into a place that could serve as, in Bannon's words to a *Mother Jones* reporter in August 2016, a "platform for the alt-right." Not exactly an alt-right publication, Breitbart was instead a conduit for helping to mainstream the alt-right and gain it legitimacy.

It's important to understand what Breitbart was before GamerGate and the turn to alt-right amplification. The site was founded in 2007 by Andrew Breitbart, a California-based activist who believed conservatives could use the internet in far more effective ways than they had in the early 2000s. So he launched Breitbart, which began as a news aggregator, then increasingly developed an identity as a right-wing populist site, opposed to bigness (its sections were called Big Government, Big Media, Big Hollywood, and the like) and eager to use investigative journalism and exposés to bring down Democrats and the American Left (it was Andrew Breitbart who revealed that Democratic representative Anthony Weiner had been sending sexually suggestive messages to a minor online).

Breitbart, while an online innovator, was not particularly distinguishable from other mainstream conservative media outlets. After Andrew Breitbart died suddenly in 2012, control of the publication fell to Steve Bannon, who had distinctly populist-nationalist politics. Though nationalism wasn't especially en vogue in 2012, populism was. And Bannon, with an eye on the churn in European politics, saw the potential to mobilize a new coalition in the United States, one rooted in disaffected young white men. When he brought Yiannopoulos aboard, he began transforming Breitbart from a conservative site to a right-wing nationalist outlet with increasingly close ties to the European Right and to the online alt-right.

When Donald Trump entered the presidential race in 2015, these forces coalesced. Having worked with Bannon in the past, Trump had learned the language of nationalism. He openly mocked the decision to go to war in Iraq and Afghanistan—catnip to paleoconservatives—and made openly racist anti-immigration rhetoric central to his campaign. These ideas were well outside the consensus of the Republican elite in 2015.[9]

In fact, from the beginning Trump's campaign seemed like one big troll: the announcement speech in his own hotel lobby, the rambling attacks on immigrants and Muslims and other Republicans, the ridiculous nicknames, the self-evident falsehoods, the constant contradictions. Yet he instantly resonated with the GOP base, surging to the top of the polls within a few weeks of his announcement and never losing that top spot.

What read as authenticity and entertainment to many of Trump's supporters looked very different from the perspective of the alt-right. Here was a candidate who put white male grievance at the center of his campaign, who delivered his most outlandish lines with an am-I-serious? smirk, and who seemed to shred the niceties and norms that had once defined American presidential campaigns. When hit, he hit back twice as hard.

These features made the Trump campaign an opportunity for the alt-right. Online, acting primarily under the veil of anonymity, members of the alt-right honed a media strategy that first brought the movement to the attention of mainstream journalists. This was intentional: the alt-right targeted journalists, primarily on Twitter, sending them not just memes but gruesome images from World War II death camps, antisemitic symbols, and photos of lynchings. Suddenly inundated by these images from seemingly hundreds if not thousands of individual accounts, one could scarcely not notice that something was happening.

And still, though journalists had been barraged with swastikas, antisemitic memes, and unprecedented troll attacks that occasionally spilled over into real life in the form of phone calls and letters, the alt-right received no sustained attention prior to Trump's decision in August 2016 to hire Bannon as his campaign chief and Hillary Clinton's decision, a few days later, to deliver a speech on the dangers of the alt-right.

The mainstreaming of the alt-right had begun.

In alt-right circles, the Clinton speech was a moment of celebration. Trump's decision to hire Bannon had made the movement impossible to ignore; Clinton's decision to speak out about the movement had generated national attention. The two events combined raised awareness in a way that many believed could be used as a recruiting tool to expand the movement. After all, they were now associated with the nominee of a major party. Whatever one thought of Donald Trump's chances in late August 2016—and few people believed he was in a position to win—that association nonetheless helped draw the alt-right that much closer to mainstream politics.

COMING OUT

It was in this moment that Richard Spencer became the face of the alt-right. Typical of the coverage he received in the closing days of the campaign (and in the months after) was a piece in the left-wing magazine *Mother Jones*, originally run under the headline "Meet the Dapper White Nationalist Who Wins Even If Trump Loses." The October 27, 2016, piece, which featured Spencer in a tweedy suit eating "slivers of togarashi-crusted ahi from a rectangular plate" at a restaurant in Whitefish, Montana, where he lived, helped shape the image of the alt-right as a movement of handsomely clad, well-educated white men who would happily wolf down fusion cuisine while plotting the future of the white race.[10]

That image benefited the alt-right in a variety of ways, not least by generating unexpectedly flattering, if not fawning, coverage in mainstream media by journalists who mistakenly believed that white nationalists were relics of a long-forgotten past, toothless country bumpkins in tattered Klan robes. That misunderstanding of racism would come with a hefty price tag: in treating Spencer as someone surprisingly respectable, journalists ignored the fact that white nationalist organizers had always adapted to the fashion of their times, only appearing as sepia-toned relics once decades had passed.

In giving Spencer the star treatment, replete with lengthy profiles that detailed his clothes, his diet, his haircut, and, sometimes as almost an afterthought, his virulently racist politics, journalists helped amplify Spencer and added to the air of celebrity that encircled him in late 2016 and into 2017. That amplification had consequences, because Spencer, having found his way into the spotlight, sought a way to stay there.

Donald Trump's surprise victory in November 2016 fed much of the media coverage of Spencer. Suddenly it seemed like the alt-right, like the populist-nationalism Trump and Bannon represented, had been legitimated—far more mainstream than most Americans had thought prior to election night. The DeploraBall, an inauguration event hosted and attended by many of the leading alt-right celebrities, including Spencer, Jack Posobiec, and Gavin McInnes, featured Nazi salutes and a triumphant movement that seemed poised to take over Washington along with the new administration.[11]

But as journalists turned their attention to the new administration and the resistance organizing against it, Spencer set his sights a little further south. At a rally in front of the White House to oppose the bombing of Syria—the alt-right retained its post-paleo commitment to nonintervention, especially when it involved an ally of Russia, to whom the group shared a particular allegiance because of its conservative dictatorial government—he met a young alt-right acolyte named Jason Kessler.

Kessler had been making a name for himself a hundred miles southwest of the capital in his hometown of Charlottesville, Virginia. There, Vice Mayor Wes Bellamy, a newly elected African American member of the city council, had begun advocating for the removal of two massive Confederate statues that stood in public parks in the city's downtown. Activists in town bolstered Bellamy's argument, noting that the Confederate soldiers depicted in the statues, Robert E. Lee and Stonewall Jackson, had never stepped foot in Charlottesville. They also argued that, because 52 percent of the county was enslaved during the Civil War, the Confederate soldiers had been an occupying army and the U.S. soldiers had been liberators, a reality not reflected in the town's statuary.

Because Bellamy was the leading advocate for the statues' removal, Kessler began targeting him, looking for a way to unseat the vice mayor. But he also wanted to use the debate over the statues as a focal point for the alt-right movement. He believed that connecting with Spencer would buy him purchase within the alt-right leadership and that their mutual connection to Charlottesville—Spencer was a University of Virginia alum—could serve as a common bond.

Spencer too was eyeing Charlottesville and the monument battle. Confederate statues had long blurred the line between white nationalism and regional pride, offering plausible deniability for the white supremacists who wanted to use the statues as their new cause du jour. The turn to the statues controversy represented a pivot away from the Trump campaign and toward a battle that would connect them both with a deeper American history and a new audience ripe for radicalization.

On May 13, 2017, Spencer joined Mike Enoch, a neo-Nazi blogger and podcaster, and a hundred or so other self-identified members of the alt-right in Charlottesville. They plowed through the Festival of Cultures, a celebration of the town's diversity featuring booths from different countries. The celebration was being held in Lee Park in the shadow of the statue of Robert E. Lee, one of the statues whose removal was under debate. The white supremacists crowded around the Germany booth in a tribute to Adolf Hitler, then made their way to Jackson Park and the statue of Stonewall Jackson, where they made their speeches.[12]

These speeches, full-throated declarations of white supremacy, did not try to hide or temper their politics. The fight was not just about the statues, Spencer declared, it was about white heroes and white history and the effort to stamp out white culture. He put in bald terms what defenders of the Confederacy seldom stated or even acknowledged: the deeply racist history behind the statues and their subjects.[13]

If the daytime event was about white supremacy—a catalogue of the superiority of the white race and white history—the nighttime event was about white power—a demonstration of the physical intimidation and violence that the alt-right was willing to use to enforce that claim of supremacy. A hundred members of the alt-right returned to Lee Park with torches. They circled the statue of Lee and chanted "Blood and soil" and "You will not replace us."

Two weeks later, Jason Kessler filed for a permit for a rally in Lee Park, scheduled for August 12, 2017.

UNITE THE RIGHT

The Unite the Right rally was billed as a free speech event with two over-arching goals: to forge a broad right-wing coalition that included the alt-right and to frame the group's organizing as a testament to the Left's intolerance for the First Amendment.

It would end up shattering the alt-right coalition and associating it irredeemably with terroristic violence.

The strain on the alt-right coalition was a function of efforts to broaden it. The lineup for the day included Spencer, Kessler, Enoch, Ku Klux Klan organizer David Duke, neo-Nazi Anthime Gionet (a.k.a. Baked Alaska), libertarian candidate and Far Right activist Austin Gillespie (a.k.a. Augustus Sol Invictus), white supremacist and men's rights activist Christopher Cantwell, neo-Nazi organizer Matt Heimbach of the Traditionalist Worker Party, white supremacist and conspiracist John Ramondetta (a.k.a. Johnny Monoxide), former chief technology officer of *Business Insider* and alt-right troll Pax Dickinson, and neo-Confederate Michael Hill.[14]

That lineup, plus the May statue rally and torch-burning, had put white supremacy at the center of the Charlottesville activism. While groups like the Proud Boys (of which Jason Kessler was a member) were present in Charlottesville throughout the summer of 2017 and during the events of August 11 and 12, their leaders had tried to put distance between the "alt-light" or "civil nationalists" and the alt-right as early as the DeploraBall in January of that year.

The Proud Boys were organized in 2016 by *Vice* magazine founder Gavin McInnes as a men's-only neofascist organization dedicated to political violence. The group, which the Southern Poverty Law Center estimated had around six thousand members in 2017, was closely associated with the alt-right and the men's rights movement, but McInnes worked to separate the group, to an extent, from the more openly white supremacist organizations and leaders within the alt-right. This offshoot rebranded itself the "alt-light," hinting at its leaders' efforts to moderate their image. McInnes and other members of the so-called alt-light, like Mike Cernovich, Jack Posobiec, and Milo Yiannopoulos, had worked alongside Richard

Spencer and associated with the alt-right into 2016; after Trump's election, when political power and influence seemed more attainable, they distanced themselves from Spencer and his allies.[15]

No moment better captured these shifts than competing rallies in Washington, DC, in late June 2017, seven weeks before the Unite the Right rally. The organizer of the "Rally for Free Speech," Colton Merwin, made a last-minute change to the speakers' list, adding Spencer. As soon as he did, activists Laura Loomer and Jack Posobiec pulled out of the event, and Posobiec organized a counterrally, the "Rally against Political Violence." The competing rallies, both operating under appealing but inaccurate names, were physical representations of how split the movement had become.[16]

The Unite the Right rally crystallized those tensions, as McInnes denounced the planned gathering and warned Proud Boys not to attend (though many did). The objections to the Unite the Right rally flowed from several sources: rejection of Spencer's leadership, part of the internecine fights within the alt-right; concern over the open neo-Nazi identity of some of the speakers; and even worry that the gathering would be infiltrated by law enforcement.

But whatever the motivation, it was clear by mid-2017 that a portion of the alt-right wanted to return to its "post-paleo" roots, to a time when the movement, while still defined by white male chauvinism, was not so publicly aligned with white power organizing.

Yet the divisions at the leadership level were not so cleanly reflected in the movement more broadly, and the ostensible aims of the Unite the Right rally—building a coalition, defending free speech, protecting Confederate statues—continued to shape the planned activities for the day, as well as the rules surrounding it. Participants were urged not to give Nazi salutes, and, having worked closely with law enforcement in preparation for the day, the organizers anticipated a scene of stark contrasts, with the speakers orating from the park while counterprotesters clashed with police.

That planned symbolism was important, because for months the alt-right had been honing a set of arguments meant to help mainstream the movement: wanting only their God-given right to speak freely, the alt-right had revealed the intolerance, violence, and un-Americanness of a Left that refused to let them speak. It was a smart tactic, because by framing the political stakes not as white supremacy versus antiracism but as free speech versus censorship, the alt-right could effectively flip the tolerance-intolerance framework around white supremacy (something that, in other circumstances, they have done quite effectively).[17]

Such a plan could have succeeded, perhaps, but it was dramatically undercut by the decision to hold an unannounced torchlight march on August 11, the evening before the Unite the Right rally. That march began as an act of political intimidation and ended as an act of political violence, as hundreds of white men (and a handful of white women) marched onto the University of Virginia's campus without prior notice or authorization, shouting slogans like "Jews will not replace us." When they arrived at their intended rallying point, the statue of Thomas Jefferson outside the university's famed Rotunda (an attempt to claim Jefferson as part of the lineage of white heroes), they found a small group of antiracist students and activists circling the statue. The marchers surrounded the protesters and then began to beat them as police looked on nearby.

The torchlight march unmade the argument, defended in court just hours earlier, that the Unite the Right rally was about political speech rather than political violence. At 8 p.m., U.S. District Court judge Glen Conrad had sided with the American Civil Liberties Union, on free speech and free assembly grounds, to allow the rally to be held in downtown Charlottesville rather than moved to a more isolated, and more defensible, spot a mile away. Less than two hours later, the torchlight march showed that the judge had erred, that the core issue was in fact public safety, because the alt-right activists were planning to engage in political violence.

But no new order was issued, and the rally was allowed to proceed as planned.

By the next morning, none of the stated premises of the Unite the Right rally were intact. Rather than uniting a broad right-wing coalition around the issue of Confederate nostalgia and white rights, the organizers had exposed the sharp limits of a political movement that openly displayed Nazi symbols and chanted antisemitic slurs. The violence at the Rotunda had exposed the inauthenticity of the free speech claims and made it impossible to pin the violence of the day on antiracist and antifascist counterprotesters. Even had the rest of the day gone as planned, had the white supremacists and neo-Confederates and neo-Nazis given their speeches and marched in and out of the park under police protection, the rally was already a failure on its declared terms (though, as I'll discuss in the next section, the stated goals and the actual goals of the rally should not be assumed to be the same).

As it happened, the rally did not go as planned. As the speakers huddled in the rear of the park, alt-right supporters and white supremacist activists, many of them armed, gleefully clashed with counterprotesters, unimpeded by the massive police presence that encircled the downtown area. When the park was cleared well in advance of the planned start time, white supremacists rolled through the city's narrow streets. One group savagely beat counterprotester DeAndre Harris in a parking garage next to the police station in what was, at the time, the bloodiest violence of the day.

A little over ninety minutes later, at 1:41 p.m., twenty-year-old James Alex Fields Jr., who earlier in the day had been seen carrying a shield with the emblem of Vanguard America, a neo-Nazi organization, sped his gray Dodge Charger into a crowd of counterprotesters, killing an activist named Heather Heyer and injuring dozens of others in an act of terroristic violence.

In December 2018, a Virginia jury found Fields guilty of first-degree murder, malicious wounding, and leaving the scene of a fatal crash. His sentence: life plus 419 years and $480,000 in fines. Six months later, Fields pleaded guilty to twenty-nine federal hate-crime charges, and received twenty-nine life sentences.[18]

THE AFTERMATH

The shocking images from Charlottesville roiled the nation for the next week, though the ultimate cost to the alt-right was not immediately clear. That's in part because, in the days following the violent march and terror attack, President Trump equivocated in his response. His infamous statement that there were "very fine people" on both sides was understood by alt-right activists as an endorsement of their cause.

Yet in the weeks and months that followed, fallout mounted. A few high-profile activists were arrested, including one of the scheduled speakers, Christopher Cantwell. The Traditionalist Worker Party, a neo-Nazi organization founded by scheduled speaker Matthew Heimbach with about five hundred members, dissolved. Participants in the torchlit march were doxed (that is, had their personal information, including their identities, released online by antiracist and antifascist activists) and several lost their jobs as a result. Identity Evropa, the neo-Nazi group with about one thousand members that coined the chant "You will not replace us," saw its membership rapidly decline and was forced to rebrand as the American Identity Movement.

An independent review conducted by Tim Heaphy, a former U.S. attorney, found that the police had been ill-prepared and had failed to properly coordinate across local, state, and national units. The commonwealth's attorney told police, incorrectly, that they could not restrict weapons, when they could—and should—have prohibited nonfirearm weapons. Commanders told their units not to intervene except in the most severe cases of violence, and the style of intervention—closing down the park and pushing the alt-right ralliers into the counterprotesters—served to ramp up, rather than deescalate, the violence.[19]

In national politics, Charlottesville made some people and moments temporarily toxic. Steve Bannon left the White House five days after the violence in Charlottesville, and soon after took his nationalist project abroad, helping organize nationalist movements in Europe. And while Donald Trump continued to defend his post-Charlottesville comments— in 2019, he insisted he had "answered perfectly"—there was a coordinated campaign on the Right to deny that Trump even made the comments, calling it "the Charlottesville lie."[20]

New legal techniques developed by counterterrorism expert Mary McCord disarmed and depressed scheduled rallies in Tennessee, and the tiny turnout for a rally in Boston suggested that whatever the alt-right had hoped to achieve in Charlottesville, the events of August 11 and 12 had sealed the movement's fate, discrediting white supremacy, shattering the alt-right, and exposing the emptiness of the movement's First Amendment claims.[21]

That, anyway, is the conventional wisdom surrounding Charlottesville. But it paints far too rosy a picture.

First, the terrorism in Charlottesville must be understood as part of an unbroken, and indeed increasing, line of Far Right white supremacist terror attacks. Though future historians may be able to fill in the gaps of our current knowledge, from our perspective, we can see a rise in terroristic white power violence as early as 2011, when white supremacists David Pederson and Holly Grigsby went on a multistate killing spree. A year later, Wade Michael Page, who had neo-Nazi and white supremacist ties, killed six people at a Sikh temple in Wisconsin. A white supremacist killed three people in two shootings at Jewish centers in Kansas City, and the next year Dylann Roof murdered nine Black worshippers in Charleston, South Carolina.[22]

Nor did the attacks end with Charlottesville: the 2018 shooting at a Pittsburgh synagogue was the deadliest antisemitic attack in U.S. history.

This timeline narrowly focuses on white power violence in the United States, but a broader lens brings in major terror attacks in Norway and New Zealand as well as "incel" massacres in the United States and Canada. Charlottesville did not disrupt this violence; it only added to it.

Second, the decline of particular figures within the alt-right should not be mistaken for a decline in the ideology of the alt-right. As the earlier fissures in the movement show, the "post-paleo" energy had already started to reorganize in ways more acceptable to mainstream politics. Repackaged as "Western civilization" and "civic nationalism," many of the same ideas that fueled the alt-right have been retooled in ways that create plausible deniability about alt-right ties while still advancing the core political values.

Through this lens, Charlottesville must still be understood as a major recruitment event, even as the rally drew condemnation from most parts of mainstream culture and politics. The ideas, images, and rhetoric of the alt-right were made much more visible because of the coverage of those events, and whatever the short- and medium-term damage to the movement and the alt-right brand, as a tool for recruitment and radicalization it was likely a success.

How much of a success is difficult to trace in the present. The large-scale deplatforming of Far Right websites and personalities has made the networks more difficult to map, as more and more participants are moving onto secure channels like Discord and semiprivate platforms like Gab. The post-Charlottesville deplatforming was limited in time and scope—Richard Spencer is back on Twitter, the openly racist and antisemitic website The Daily Stormer is back on the regular web, and activists have found a number of workarounds for fundraising to sidestep their ejection from major sites like PayPal and Patreon. Following the Capitol attack in January 2021, another large-scale deplatforming pushed many Far Right activists off Facebook and Twitter, temporarily shut down the alternative social media site Parler, and introduced a new wave of activists to encrypted apps like Telegram and Discord. As such, some of these networks remain difficult to trace and, at this point, impossible to view through a historical lens.

Finally, despite the push for new domestic terrorism laws and the FBI's recognition of white power terrorism as a serious and growing problem, law enforcement and media still tend to treat white power terrorism with a lone-wolf framework. The United States lacks a domestic terrorism law, for important civil-liberties reasons, but federal law enforcement has also been reluctant to use conspiracy laws for these sorts of cases. At the same time, a combination of disinformation campaigns, partisan motivation to reject political framing, and reporting that focuses on mental illness and individual histories makes it difficult for the analysis of organized white supremacist violence to break through.

The assault on the Capitol in January 2021 adds an important coda to this story. Looked at from the perspective of the events in Charlottesville, it is a chilling sign of how much success the Far Right has had in integrating itself and its ideas into pro-Trump politics. If events at Charlottesville ultimately failed to "unite the Right," the mix of Proud Boys, Oath Keepers, and other Far Right groups at the Capitol, incorporated with a much larger right-wing crowd acting under the banner of Trump flags rather than Nazi flags, signifies that the white power and violent Right has indeed integrated itself into the broader pro-Trump Right.

That Right does not look like the alt-right of 2017. Charlottesville did indeed mark the end of the alt-right as it was once understood—a coming-out party that failed spectacularly. But the events of 2017 advanced the movement's underlying objectives in ways we are still working to understand. The organizing around Charlottesville, rather than a static moment that marked a beginning or an end, should be understood as one moment in a contested process of political negotiation and radicalization.

18 The Whiteness of Blue Lives

RACE IN AMERICAN POLICING

Joseph Darda

When Colin Kaepernick took a knee against police killings of Black people, Congress took a stand for blue lives.

In 2018, a coalition of conservative and liberal legislators, including most members of the House Freedom Caucus and the Congressional Black Caucus, backed a bill that would make it a hate crime to "knowingly assault a law enforcement officer."[1] The bill's authors argued, without evidence, that attacks on officers had escalated and demanded coverage under civil rights law as crimes stemming from a kind of antiblue racism. The Protect and Serve Act of 2018, better known as the Blue Lives Matter bill, sailed through the House in a vote of 382 to 35. Orrin Hatch, the long-serving conservative from Utah, introduced it in the Senate to counter what he described as "heinous, cowardly assaults" on police.[2] Democrats signed on, vowing to "make sure that all of our officers know we have their back."[3] In the fifth year of the Black Lives Matter movement, with officer deaths nearing an all-time low, conservatives and liberals came together to declare that blue lives mattered more.

The Protect and Serve Act borrowed language from a wave of legislation at the state level. In 2016, John Bel Edwards, the Democratic governor of Louisiana, signed the first Blue Lives Matter bill into law. More than twenty other states introduced their own, including South Carolina, which, as more than a few critics observed, lacked a hate-crime statute to which it could add officers. The bills answered demands from the Blue Lives Matter countermovement, which had formed after the murder of two NYPD officers in late 2014, and received the endorsement of the Fraternal Order of Police, the nation's largest law enforcement association. When Edwards signed the Louisiana bill, adding officers and firefighters to the state's hate-crime statutes, Chuck Canterbury, the president of the FOP, described it as a long-overdue recognition of antiblue bias. "Since 1999, we've been saying that police officers that are ambushed merely for the color of their uniform are being subjected to hate crimes," he said in an interview with NPR.[4] The order's executive board then consisted of seven white men, including Canterbury, who often made allusions to the civil rights movement ("merely for the color of their uniform") in advocating for himself and other officers.

Although the Fraternal Order of Police leans conservative and Blue Lives Matter bills had more success in red states, the legislation did not belong to the Right but, at least until the summer of 2020, formed a broad consensus among conservatives and liberals. President Barack Obama signed the Blue Alert Act into law in 2015, creating a national communications network, modeled after amber alerts, for collecting and sharing information regarding threats to officers' lives. Nancy Pelosi, the longtime House Democratic leader, voted for the Protect and Serve Act, along with 161 of her Democratic colleagues.

In the wake of the 2015 Charleston church shooting, in which twenty-one-year-old Dylann Roof, seeking to foment a race war, murdered nine Black churchgoers, liberal news media committed more resources to investigating the networks, online and off, that had attracted Roof's generation to neo-Confederate, neo-Nazi, and neo-Rhodesian ideologies (Roof subscribed to them all).[5] And they should. But stories about self-declared race warriors can also distract us from the more mundane forms that white racial dominance takes in the United States. Reading about someone like Roof makes white people feel secure because they know they would never say or do what he did. Most white people don't make declarations about their racial identities—they don't issue manifestos or sew Rhodesian flags onto their clothes—but rather find other outlets through which to advance their racial interests. Most frame their racial demands as either skating below (individual) or rising above (universal) identitarian concerns, balancing an assertion of radical individualism with a racial claim to the nation, feigning color blindness while dressing white skin in NYPD blue or USMC green, binding whiteness to the badge and the flag. White men who have never worn a uniform often benefit the most from calls for police officers' and veterans' rights because the whiteness of the officer and the vet in the national imagination allows them to claim their grievances and entitlements when it serves them and set them aside when it doesn't. Not all officers are white, of course. But all blue lives are because white people invented them to undercut Black demands.

Civil rights organizations condemned the Blue Lives Matter bills for distorting civil rights law. "Hate crimes are about an identity-based bias, an immutable characteristic that a person cannot change," a Louisiana organizer told the *New York Times* in 2016, after her state enacted the first Blue Lives Matter law. "Adding a professional category changes and confuses the meaning of that."[6] The bills confused identities with uniforms, awarding redundant legal armor to police. (Most state legal codes, including Louisiana's, mandated increased sentences for assaults on officers without the addition of hate-crime safeguards.) But the civil rights organizer's observation also gestured to how white men had held on to their racial and gender status after civil rights and feminism: through mutable identities constructed in the image of the officer and the vet that allowed them to bridge conservative color blindness and liberal multiculturalism. Conservatives could celebrate white officers and vets as deracinated embodiments of the nation. Liberals could treat them as minoritized heroes whose voices must be heard. The Blue Lives Matter countermovement wielded an old trick, hailing white men as universal and marginal, deracinated (identified with state-issued uniforms) and minoritized (deserving hate-crime safeguards). White men who claim blue lives assert their national belonging as agents of the law while bemoaning that the law doesn't serve them as blue minorities. What did they do to be so white and blue?

In 1993, Cheryl Harris, then teaching at the Chicago-Kent College of Law after a stint in the city attorney's office, contributed a field-defining article to the *Harvard Law Review*, tracing the legal construction of, as her title announced, "Whiteness as Property." In the 1930s, Harris's grandmother, a light-skinned Black woman, moved from the South to Chicago, where, struggling to raise her two daughters, she sought a job at a segregated retail store in the central business district. She got the job, and the job got her and her daughters through some lean times. No one at the store ever knew that she lived on the South Side, a Black woman working in a white store. Harris's grandmother could see that whiteness had a cash value. It constituted a kind of asset. When she walked into that store as a white woman, she crossed a material line, not, her granddaughter wrote, "merely passing, but *tres*passing."[7]

From the founding of the nation, whiteness has, through an ever-shifting racial calculus, cohered as a material belonging, a status that entitled men to land and to the value of their own labor. The law designated it as a condition for the theft of Indigenous lands and Black lives. A man, with few exceptions, needed to own whiteness before he could own land and other people. Laws changed over time, but, as Harris's grandmother knew, whiteness remained and remains a treasured asset in the United States, where it can be the difference between surviving hard times and not making it at all. Harris's characterization of her grandmother's racial transgression as a crime—not merely passing, but trespassing—suggests how that material whiteness has endured for so long. The legal construction of whiteness coincided with the establishment of some of the first modern police departments, which served to secure the holdings of white elites from the assumed threat of Indigenous and Black people without legal claim to their own assets, neither land nor often their own bodies. White landowners demanded the whiteness of blue lives. Blue lives fortified that white wealth.[8]

White claims to blue lives have often surfaced at times of Black gains, from Reconstruction to the civil rights era to the election of the first Black president, allowing white men to act out their racial interests without acknowledging them as racial. In his 1935 classic *Black Reconstruction in America*, W. E. B. Du Bois traced the end of Reconstruction to the decision of white laborers to align themselves with white landowners rather than Black laborers, to form a cross-class racial coalition rather than a cross-racial class coalition. White owners encouraged white laborers to invest in their racial interest, to invest in their whiteness as "a sort of public or psychological wage." White workers received that racial wage in the form of enfranchisement, education, racial deference, and—in an often overlooked dimension of Du Bois's famous claim—inclusion in police departments and the army. "The police were drawn from their ranks, and the courts, dependent upon their votes, treated them with such leniency as to encourage lawlessness," he wrote.[9] White owners would not share their wealth with white laborers, but they would let them wear blue and green, safeguarding their wealth at home and securing their fortunes abroad. Du Bois described the white racial wage as a feeling of national belonging conferred on white men through an identification with uniforms that authorized violence.

In the years after World War II, blue lives turned red, white, and blue. Thousands of white men returned from combat, where they had served in segregated units, and brought their training as soldiers and marines to their local sheriff's office. For them, a war on crime felt like a natural continuation of their service. William Parker, the chief of the LAPD from 1950 until his death in 1966, led the militarization of law enforcement, which earned him the condemnation of civil rights leaders and admiration in *Life* as the nation's "second most respected" law enforcement officer after J. Edgar Hoover.[10] Parker had served in the world war, overseeing General Dwight Eisenhower's "police and prisons plan for the European invasion," and returned to California with a war-mindedness he never lost.[11] In a 1952 address to the National Automatic Merchandising Association (a trade association for vending machine businesses) in Chicago with the ominous title "Invasion from Within," he described police as, borrowing and amending the nickname for the British army, a "thin blue line" standing between the "law abiding elements of society and the criminals that prey upon them." Parker's "professionalization"—a term he used to mean militarization—of the LAPD had transformed Los Angeles into, he told the Chicago audience, "the nation's 'white spot' in the black picture" of rising crime.[12]

Parker believed that the nation faced an invasion from within, an invasion that originated from LA's Black and Latinx neighborhoods and necessitated a blue army to combat it. (He broadcast that belief through his office but also as a consultant on the radio and TV drama *Dragnet* and the genre it all but invented.) When the Civil Rights Commission asked him in

1960 about accusations of anti-Black racism against him and the LAPD, he answered, "I think the greatest dislocated minority in America today are the police."[13] Parker could see—before the civil rights legislation of the mid-1960s, before the Johnson, Nixon, and Reagan administrations' wars on crime, before the Blue Lives Matter bills of the 2010s—the value of blue lives to white interests. He turned his white officers into embodiments of the nation (soldiers in a war on crime) while maintaining that no one lived more marginal lives in antiblue America.

In 2014, with police killings of unarmed Black people in the headlines, Andrew Jacob, a white University of Michigan student, sat down in his dorm room and designed a flag for officers: a black and white American flag with a horizontal blue line below the stars. He named it, with an unknowing nod to Parker, the thin blue line flag. Jacob ordered a thousand flags from an overseas manufacturer and created an Amazon store. The flags sold out. He ordered more, and they sold out again. He and his friend Pete Forhan, a white UM classmate, founded Thin Blue Line USA and, over the coming months, sold tens of thousands of flags and added more merchandise, including sweatshirts, window decals, bracelets, beer coolers, dog and cat accessories, and onesies for infants. Jacob and Forhan first met on their high school swim team in West Bloomfield, Michigan, an affluent Detroit suburb. Neither came from a police family, but they felt that officers did not receive the veneration they deserved and wanted to honor their service. "The black above represents citizens, and the black below represents criminals," Jacob told the *Detroit News* in 2017, describing his design. "So the thin blue line separates the two and maintains order."[14] The flag signifies a nation facing, as Parker might have said, a war from within, with a blue army standing between besieged citizens and invading criminals.

Thin Blue Line USA later added a line of shirts and hats that combined Jacob's flag design with the logo of the Punisher, the Marvel antihero who first arrived in Spider-Man comics in 1974 as an Italian American Vietnam veteran waging a vigilante war on street crime (a minoritized ethnic American and "veteran American" turned blue American). Introducing a new black, white, and blue Punisher hat, Thin Blue Line's "law enforcement liaison" said, "At the end of the day, whether on this earth or somewhere else, the criminal always gets punished."[15]

Although Klansmen and neo-Nazis carried the thin blue line flag next to the Confederate southern cross and the Nazi swastika at the 2017 Unite the Right march in Charlottesville, Virginia, Jacob and Forhan maintained their distance from, without denouncing, their torch-burning customers. The two white men, who built a business out of a movement countering the assertion that Black lives matter, insisted that they sold their flag to take a stand not against Black people but for police officers. That message worked, attracting conservative and liberal officials who either believed that officers needed the refuge of hate-crime laws or knew that to say otherwise would be to risk their offices and careers. The whiteness of blue lives allowed white men, including men who had never worn a uniform, to imagine themselves at the center and margin of national life, universal Americans in blue and minoritized "blue Americans." Although the large-scale Black Lives Matter demonstrations of 2020 threatened to reveal the white racial interests embedded in the government's recurring wars on crime and terrorism, white officers and veterans continue to form a rare site of consensus in the new culture wars. No one wins in a culture war, except, for now, white men dressed in police blue and army green.

No one needed to tell the forty-fifth president of the United States, who wielded blue lives against Black lives and veterans against kneeling Black athletes. Two weeks after taking office, Donald Trump signed an executive order directing Attorney General Jeff Sessions to review legal strategies for enhancing the rights and resources of law enforcement. Sessions lifted restrictions on access to grenade launchers, armored vehicles, and other castoff gear from the Pentagon. When the *Times* asked administration officials why local police departments needed the 1,623 bayonets that they claimed a 2015 Obama executive order had denied them, the officials, caught off guard, suggested that they could be used to cut seatbelts.[16]

"We must confront and condemn dangerous anti-police prejudice," President Trump declared in 2018 at the National Law Enforcement Officers Memorial in Washington, where Canterbury, the FOP president, introduced him as the headliner of a Peace Officers Memorial Day event. "Can you believe there's prejudice with respect to our police?" he asked the audience of uniformed officers and their families, who nodded.[17] The people who benefit most from the assertion that blue lives matter don't often walk the beat themselves. Some sell flags and sweatshirts. Some run for office. Some do nothing. Trump dragged some of the ugliest white supremacist substructures of the nation out from under a thin veil, but he never forgot that blue still sells better than white. That night, he ordered that the White House be lit with blue lights to honor fallen officers. The lights, amid a storm, crossed with lightening, blazed through the night, leaving visitors with a haunting image of whiteness after civil rights: a big white house that could almost, if you didn't look too close, be blue.

19 There Are No Lone Wolves

THE WHITE POWER MOVEMENT AT WAR

Kathleen Belew

On April 19, 2020, in the grip of social distancing and fear about the novel coronavirus that inexorably changed our world, the United States quietly passed the twenty-fifth anniversary of the Oklahoma City bombing. With its death toll of 168 people—including 19 young children—and the injury of hundreds more, the bombing was the largest deliberate mass casualty on American soil between Pearl Harbor and 9/11. It was a cataclysm, a shock, a horror in the heartland of America. Yet despite its historical significance, people remember the bombing as the work of a lone wolf or a few bad apples. People who visit the memorial in Oklahoma City, view documentaries on Netflix, or read more casually about the 1990s might easily come away with no story of the white power movement: a generations-long groundswell with a complex ideology that continues to propel mass violence in the present.

Our eyes are turned on other horrors. Our news is full of hate crimes, exclusions legal and illegal, cruelty and violence in speech and in action. But the historical context can illuminate the whirlwind of the present.

The problem of understanding the Oklahoma City bombing and other acts of political violence as "lone wolf" attacks derives partly from the movement itself, which has successfully disguised its degree of coherence and organization. But it also results from failures that we can repair by telling better stories. The lone wolf myth rests on journalistic accounts that fail to capture social connections between and ideology of white power actors; activist accounts that fail to take seriously the violent and organizational capacity of white power groups; policymakers and law enforcement officers who use piecemeal, rather than systemic, response mechanisms for a broad and transnational problem; and a general public that has no frame of reference to understand these acts of violence. Indeed, the most common story seems to be one about individual communities that would break us from one another.

The Oklahoma City bombing, in other words, was not the act of a "lone wolf." This phrase is misleading and damaging, directing our attention away from long histories and complex relationships, away from systemic inequality and organized ideology in order to focus on individual perpetrators. Instead, the bombing was a culminating action of the white power movement. It was carried out by a broad and organized social movement supported by decades of networking, deep belief, and a shared sense of the coming end of the world.

What would it mean to know that story, to teach it in our history textbooks, to recognize its repercussions in the present? My hope is that the history of organized hate could have a utility in confronting the present and imagining a different future.

Our moment, indeed, gives us opportunities to think deeply about what it means to study and write the history of the present. In one sense, this is simply about the urgent project of contributing to public discourse. In another, it follows the Foucauldian mandate of understanding a genealogy of the present such that we might decode the moment in which we find ourselves.

But I find the most useful model in Lisa Lowe's *The Intimacies of Four Continents,* in which she situates her pursuit as a way of troubling and revealing what she calls "the politics of knowledge that give us the received history of our present,"[1] and thereby revealing different possibilities of response and action. In other words, the project of "history of the present" isn't just decoding or explaining, but is fundamentally about creating space for new courses of action. It's about expanding the realm of the possible, about broadening our shared imaginary. History of the present might not only decode and explain, but also lay bare the assumptions of "received knowledge" and perhaps reveal a different path.

Because let me be perfectly clear: without a different response, today's wave of white extremist violence will certainly crush beneath it the lives of more victims, their families, and their communities, and may indeed seep further into governance.

My first book, *Bring the War Home,* presents a history of the white power movement from its formation after the Vietnam War to the 1995 Oklahoma City bombing.[2] It reveals a broad-based social movement united through narratives, symbols, and repertoires of war. This movement connected neo-Nazis, Klansmen, and skinheads; people in every region of the country; people in suburbs and in cities and on mountaintops. It joined men, women, and children; felons and religious leaders; high school dropouts and aerospace engineers; civilians and veterans and active-duty troops. It was a social movement that included a variety of strategies—but its most significant legacies have evolved from its 1983 revolutionary turn to declare war against the federal government and other enemies. The strategies that stem from that pivotal turn include, first, the use of computer-based social network activism, beginning in 1984, that has only amplified in the present, and second, "leaderless resistance." That strategy, perhaps most easily explained as cell-style terror, was implemented in large part to foil the many government informants who infiltrated Klan groups in the 1960s and to stymie court prosecution. But it has had a much more durable and catastrophic effect in its clouding of public understanding. It has allowed the movement to disappear, leaving behind a fiction of supposed "lone wolf" terrorists, bad apples, and errant madmen.

The 1983–95 period featured many episodes of white power coordination, social networking, and spectacular violence, but at no point in this period was there a meaningful stop to this movement's organizing. Even in the wake of the Oklahoma City bombing, there was no durable shift in public understanding, no major prosecution that hobbled the movement. There was no meaningful and permanent response to white power activism in surveillance organization and resources, juror education, prosecutorial strategy, or military policy. The piecemeal responses in each of these areas utterly failed to contain white power as a growing and broad-based social movement. Not even lawsuits, which were in many ways the most effective measure attempted, delivered a full stop to white power organizing and violence.

In the two years since the release of *Bring the War Home*, it has become more urgent than ever to think carefully about the terminology that shapes and delimits understanding of this movement. My use of the term *white power* here is meant precisely to do the work of recognizing both the revolutionary ideology put forward by this movement and the links between groups and belief systems too often understood as disparate.

White power should not be confused with *white supremacy*. Although this certainly *was* a white supremacist movement, the activists we consider here today are one very small and violent component of that broad and complex category. White power should not be called *white nationalist*, which carries with it a distortion that threatens to contribute to public misunderstanding. People hear this term and think of overzealous patriotism. But the nation in white nationalism since 1983 was not the United States, but rather a transnational "Aryan nation" that connected white people around the world. The interests of white nationalism were and are fundamentally opposed to those of the United States, at least insofar as the United States is imagined as an inclusive constitutional democracy.

Nor should we confuse white power with the alt-right, a specific and recent subset of organizing with large overlaps into the white power movement. The alt-right is new; white power is decades, even generations old.

White power—which was also the most common phrase used by these activists in self-description—most accurately conveys this movement. *White supremacist extremism*, which has come into more frequent use in the aftermath of Charlottesville—especially among scholars who study this groundswell outside of the United States—also conveys both its seriousness and its specificity, but was not used by white power activists or their opponents in the earlier period.

This linguistic clarification is necessary because academics, journalists, and activists alike are late to the study and understanding of white power ideology and activism. We have failed to listen to the deadly intent of these actors. This is part of a broad misunderstanding of this violence that emerges from the urge to categorize and contain belief systems that people find fringe, shocking, or oppositional. Thus we see stories about the

Tree of Life synagogue attack as antisemitic violence, the Christchurch shooting as Islamophobic violence, the El Paso shooting as anti-immigrant violence, the attempted assassinations by a Coast Guard officer as political violence, and the militias on our border and parading armed through our capital cities as "neutral." They are, of course, acts of antisemitic, Islamophobic, anti-immigrant, and political violence. But they are also actions motivated by a common white power ideology. Understood through a focus on perpetrators, they are part of the same story. Seeing them together, instead of as lone wolf actions, we can begin to see a trend, a wave, a rising tide.

We have also failed to understand perpetrators on their own terms. For example, a large part of the scholarly work on the white power movement, already divorced from that on other kinds of perpetrators, has attempted to categorize and quantify the various branches of the movement—attempting to establish how many Klansmen, how many neo-Nazis, how many Skinheads, etc. In fact, this question is often irrelevant to the way that white power activists understood their own participation in the movement. The historical archive reveals that people regularly circulated between groups and belief systems, that they often held concurrent memberships, and that they used a wide variety of flexible and interchangeable symbols and ideologies.

Indeed, the white power movement is distinct from earlier mobilizations of the Klan and earlier neo-Nazi movements because of its ideological, generational, and religious diversity. Leaders wrote about the imperative of accepting members that people found shockingly different (like Christian Identity rural survivalists banding together with urban skinheads).

The white power groundswell was certainly a fringe movement, but it was comparable with better-known mobilizations such as the anticommunist John Birch Society. Membership numbers are a poor measure of white power activity, with records often distorted or destroyed. Nonetheless, scholars and watchdog groups who seek an aggregate count of the movement's varied branches—one that includes, for instance, both Klansmen and neo-Nazis rather than only one of these often overlapping self-designations—estimate that in the 1980s the movement included around 25,000 "hard-core members;" an additional 150,000–175,000 people who bought white power literature, sent contributions to groups, or attended rallies or other movement events; and another 450,000 who did not themselves purchase materials or participate, but who read the literature.[3] The John Birch Society, in contrast, reached 100,000 members at its 1965 peak and, while much less violent, has garnered much more public awareness and scholarly attention.[4]

So: why don't we have a story of Oklahoma City? Why didn't people understand white power, when Birch still comes up so regularly? In fact, we knew about white power activism as it happened. The episodes I cover in *Bring the War Home* appeared in major newspapers, on public access television, on talk shows and morning shows, and on the radio. But nevertheless, white power activism was misunderstood by many Americans, and unconfronted and unresolved such that the movement could resurface in our present moment. I argue that this comes down to three things.

The first is a change in movement organizing strategy. Beginning in 1983, a new strategy, "leaderless resistance," depended upon the action of independent cells without direct contact with movement leadership. The strategy, which had the specific aim of preventing prosecution, was distributed through movement literature and adopted widely throughout the underground. Leaderless resistance changed recruitment goals, emphasizing the importance of a small number of fully committed activists rather than large memberships of less-committed followers.[5] Because of this change, membership numbers could not forecast activity or the movement's capacity for violence.

The second was a number of failed trials. The Department of Justice attempted a large-scale trial of thirteen white power activists and leaders in 1987–88 in Fort Smith, Arkansas, on federal charges including seditious conspiracy. This involved the fruits of several smaller stings by FBI and ATF agents that had resulted in plea bargains, and several people testified against their fellow activists in order to shorten their own sentences, keep their families together, or assure their protection. Their descriptions of the race war were vivid: thirty gallons of cyanide seized just before it could be used to poison the water of a major city; assassinations of a talk radio personality, fellow group members, and state troopers; a reign of paramilitary training, parading, and harassment of various enemies; and two huge laundry hampers of military-grade weapons pushed through the courtroom. Seditious conspiracy was wholly evident, declared outright in the writings and speeches of the movement, and out-fitted with semi- and fully automatic rifles, machine guns, rocket launch-ers, antitank M72s, and grenades. Witnesses described how white power separatist compounds manufactured their own Claymore-style land mines and trained in urban warfare.

However, the Fort Smith trial failed; all thirteen activists walked free. A historical analysis of the trial raises several questions about its efficacy. Two jurors had romantic pen-pal relationships with two defendants, and one of these couples married after the trial, casting doubt upon the impar-tiality of the jury. Defendants, representing themselves, gave lengthy char-acter testimony about their tours in Vietnam, arguing that those who had served their country in wartime could not possibly be seditious conspira-tors against it (the historical record does not support this argument). Large swaths of evidence were excluded, as were jurors familiar with white power activity in the area (which had been widely reported in local news sources). One juror later spoke of a white supremacist view, though common to the region, that the Bible prohibited race-mixing. And white power women did enormous performative work in the courtroom to attempt to establish the good character of the defendants. Their actions led to sympathetic journalistic and scholarly accounts that clouded the movement's violent record and allowed it to appeal to the mainstream.

Finally, the third and last element was the large-scale and durable for-getting of everything we knew about white power activism. The sedition trial represented such an embarrassment that—along with the tragedies that were also public relations disasters at Ruby Ridge and Waco in the early 1990s—it would impact the investigative strategies used in Oklahoma City. The acquittals at Fort Smith caused the Department of Justice and some agents in the FBI reluctance in attempting an investiga-tive and prosecutorial strategy that would attempt to portray the Oklahoma City bombing as the work of a movement. Indeed, the bureau had institutionalized a policy to pursue only individual actors in white power violence, with "no attempts to tie individual crimes to a broader movement."[6] This strategy not only worked to obscure the bombing as part of a social movement but, in the years following bomber Timothy McVeigh's conviction and execution, effectively erased the movement itself from public understanding.

The evidence of McVeigh's involvement in the white power movement is too extensive to document at length here, but a few highlights include his choice of a building that had been a movement target since the early 1980s, the use and distribution of a movement novel titled *The Turner Diaries* in formulating his plan for the bombing, McVeigh's presence as high-level security for movement leadership in the Michigan Militia, his membership in a Klan chapter, his contacts and attempted contacts with the white power groups Arizona Patriots, National Alliance, and the separatist compound at Elohim City, and the date of the bombing on the anniversary not only of the Waco siege but the execution date of a prominent white power activist who had once targeted, yes, the federal building in Oklahoma City. Additional evidence abounds, and not at the level of conspiracy theory: a simple social geography of McVeigh's life prior to the bombing places him decisively in the white power movement as a follower of the strategy of "leaderless resistance."

All this is to say that white power activity in the United States is not new, nor has it been as shadowy as we may have imagined. It was known, and then forgotten, and it is this process of forgetting that directs our attention to the parameters of public debate and public memory, and to what might be different in our current moment that might open the way for confronting racist formations in our society.

A history focused on perpetrators reveals that many of the purportedly inexplicable acts of violence in the present are motivated by a coherent and deliberate ideology. The March 2019 attack on two mosques in Christchurch, New Zealand, that left forty-nine people dead and scores more injured was not a lone wolf attack or the work of a few isolated radicals. It was, again, part of the white power movement, a broad groundswell that has joined people together in common purpose, social relationships, and political ideology. This movement formed in the United States after the Vietnam War, using narratives of violence and the symbols and weapons of that conflict to bring together Klansmen, neo-Nazis, skinheads, and other white radicals.

The materials left behind by the alleged Christchurch attacker—not just the manifesto, but also the social media posts and the white messages scrawled on the weapon and magazines used in the attack—definitively locate his ideology in this movement. He references the Fourteen Words, a slogan written by the U.S. white power activist David Lane, who was incarcerated in the late 1980s after his participation in a white power terror cell called the Order. That group stole millions of dollars from armored cars and department stores to distribute to white power cells around the country, assassinated enemies, and attacked infrastructure targets in an attempt to foment race war.

The Fourteen Words refer to the central mission of the white power movement, which is to ensure a white future and the birth of white children. The Christchurch gunman also refers to a "future for our people," expressing the apocalyptic fear of racial annihilation that has animated white power activism for decades. The manifesto ends with highly stylized, idyllic images of white mothers and children. This focus on women is also a mainstay of the white power movement and its intense emphasis on white reproduction, worries about the hyperfertility of people of color, and the fear of racial extinction.

These ideas about genocide and population replacement aren't new, nor do they constitute a conspiracy theory responding only to growing populations of Muslim immigrants. White power activists share views with other conservatives on many social issues, but they understand these issues as deeply related to racial extinction. They have written about this in precisely this way for decades. They opposed interracial marriage, abortion, and gay and lesbian movements, they said, because these would decrease the white birthrate; they opposed immigration because they feared they would be overrun. They framed these issues with ideas about the purity of white women—who, they said, would have to bear three children each in order to avoid racial extinction—and with hateful invective about hyperfertile racial others.

The white power movement was profoundly transnational, motivated by ideas that have long roots in the United States and elsewhere but are not bounded by nation. As with many transnational movements, white power was both shaped by inflows from other places—like skinhead culture from Great Britain—and exported as a specific white power ideology, shaped by U.S. paramilitarism, abroad. Groups like Aryan Nations sent their materials around the world in the 1980s and 1990s, and activists in Australia and New Zealand could read white power newspapers from the United States and send for materials. White power groups like Wotansvolk and the World Church of the Creator even set up chapters and memberships in other countries. Wotansvolk had representation in forty-one countries by 2000, and World Church of the Creator had chapters in a multitude of places including New Zealand, Canada, Norway, and South Africa. The language and strategy of white power also spread through books like *The Turner Diaries,* a novel-turned-manual-turned-lodestar that appeared in places like Apartheid South Africa and sold more than fifty thousand copies in the few decades after it was released. The places white power activists chose to pollinate map onto an idea of whiteness that transcends national boundaries.[7]

Understanding these acts of violence as politically motivated, connected, and purposeful would fundamentally change the way we understand, speak, and write about such attacks—a crucial first step toward a different response.

The future envisioned by the white power movement is also profoundly radical, and not just the overzealous patriotism that many people think of when they hear the word *nationalism.* Indeed, the mass casualties wrought by this movement are not, in themselves, the movement's goal. They are means to an end, a way to awaken a broader white public to what white power activists see as obvious: the threats posed to the white race by immigration and racial others. The violence is meant to mobilize white people around the world to wage race war.

The Christchurch manifesto talks about just this strategy. In a section about the use of guns, the attacker writes about how he hopes to spur a seizure of guns that would then enrage the Right in the United States and provoke further conflict. This strategy is directly out of *The Turner Diaries.*[8]

Indeed, that novel is the crucial text in understanding the way futurity works in the white power movement. It sets out to answer the question that undergirds the entire project: how could a tiny fringe movement hope to overthrow the most powerful, militarized superstate in the history of the world?

In *The Turner Diaries,* the narrator describes the problem as "a gnat trying to assassinate an elephant." The novel then lays out a plan in which white power cells and undercover operatives carry out assassinations, attacks on infrastructure targets, and sabotage to awaken a broader white public to their cause. Through guerilla warfare and cell-style terror, they are able to seize an air force base with nuclear weapons, provoke a nuclear exchange between the United States and the Soviet Union (and Israel), and take over first the nation and then the world in its aftermath. The details are worth understanding, and I have explored them elsewhere. Here I want to focus first on the inherent apocalypticism braided through these beliefs, and on the role of the white bystander / broader white public in the future imagined by the movement.

In the period of my study, apocalypticism was enormously important not only to the white power movement but in broader political culture. In the rising evangelical congregations of the 1980s and 1990s, the ones that read Tim LaHaye's *Left Behind* novels and planned for the rapture, the fears of the Cold War became intertwined with faith belief. After the fall of the Berlin Wall in 1989, I argue, there was a fundamental crisis of narrative—people with these ingrained fears of the end of the world still held them, but now operated without a clear narrative enemy or agent of the end.

This worked in an even stronger and more direct way in the white power movement, where activists connected ideas of a radical political future with their belief in imminent apocalypse. Christian Identity, one of the movement's two most prominent theologies, foretold the imminent end of the world. But whereas evangelical belief offered the promise of the rapture—in which the faithful would be peacefully transported to heaven before the bloodshed of the tribulations—Christian Identity called its adherents to arms. The faithful either would have to outlast the tribulations to see the return of Christ, becoming survivalists, or would have to take up arms to clear the world of nonbelievers in the End Times. Nonbelievers, in Christian Identity, included all nonwhite people. In other words, Christian Identity transfigured race war into holy war.[9]

These views of the world—encroaching threats on the white population, the idea of demographic transformation as racial extinction, and the looming fear of the coming end of the world—have come to impact mainstream political formations in all sorts of new and imbricated ways in the 2000s, and not just in the aftermath of the 2016 election.

Historical context could pave the way to better reporting, more sound activism, and better public understanding. There are no lone wolves.

There are, from time to time, people who carry out acts of violence that are not motivated by political ideology, as in the case of the 1999 attack on Columbine High School. It would not be correct to attribute the Columbine attack to the white power movement. But in the attacks on the Tree of Life Synagogue, the Anders Breivik attack in Norway, the El Paso shooting, and Dylann Roof's attack on AME worshippers in Charleston, we need look no further than the manifestoes to see that even those people who have never met another activist in real life can find themselves radicalized by a social network, imbricated in an ideology, and motivated by decades of history.

The grain of hope is that connecting these stories together could make possible a new coalition politics between the many communities impacted by exclusion, hate, and violence—that in our moment we might see a knitting together of people that could create different possibilities of response and action.

Conclusion

A HISTORY OF THE PRESENT

Ramón A. Gutiérrez and Kathleen Belew

As we conclude this *Field Guide to White Supremacy*, humans across the globe face the spread of the COVID-19 virus, which is rapidly choking the breath and vital organs of young and old, poor and rich, women, men, and nonbinary persons of every creed and color. No end to the pandemic appears on the immediate horizon, with the United States currently facing the highest proportion of deaths in the world. Already 33 million people have been infected in the United States, with 600,000 deaths, a number rapidly increasing daily. National and local quarantines, travel bans, business closures, and the mandatory use of masks in some states have slowed the contagion's spread, but in turn these measures have provoked a deep economic recession both in the United States and across the globe, with layoffs, job losses, bankruptcies, unemployment, and food insecurities arguably as great as those experienced during the Great Depression of the 1930s.

The COVID-19 pandemic has affected the republic's racialized populations differentially, particularly those who historically have borne the brutal brunt of settler colonialism and racial capitalism. They are now the country's poorest and its sickest. Take, for example, the impact of the virus on just one Indigenous group in the United States. During the eighteenth-century,

Thousands of people take the oath of allegiance to the United States and become citizens, July 5, 1976, Miami Beach, Florida. (AP Photo/BH)

the Spanish soldiers who colonized the Kingdom of New Mexico and Arizona waged what they rationalized as "just wars" against the nomadic Navajos (*Dines* in their native language), killing resisters and marketing their captive children, women, and men as slaves throughout Mexico, Central America, and Cuba. In the nineteenth century the Dinés suffered a similar fate at the hands of the U.S. Army. Starting in 1863, in the midst of the Civil War, American Union soldiers conducted scorched-earth campaigns against the Diné and the Mescalero Apache, forcefully removing them from their ancestral lands, much as had been done to the Cherokee, Muscogee (Creek), Seminole, Chickasaw, and Choctaw between 1831 and 1842. The trauma of this removal, which led to several hundred deaths from starvation and disease during this 250-mile march, is still vividly remembered by these Indigenous nations as the "Long Walk." The "severe poverty, addiction, suicide and crime on reservations all have their roots in the Long Walk," notes Diné historian Jennifer Denetdale.[1] The Navajo Nation currently has the highest per capita coronavirus infection rates in the United

States, largely because its members live in poverty in multigenerational homes, where a single person has often infected an entire household and then members of extended families. Forty percent of Diné homes have no indoor plumbing or running water, both crucial necessities to stem the virus's spread. The Navajo live in a food desert. To purchase food, people must densely congregate at the small number of stores that sell groceries. This, in conjunction with the lack of good health care, explains the origin of the virus and its rapid spread; when this book went to press, it tallied 30,914 infections and 1,334 deaths in the Navajo Nation.[2]

If we turn our gaze to populations historically disadvantaged by their origins as African slaves and conquered subjects of American imperial expansion, we discover that Blacks and Latinas/os are three times more likely to be infected than their white neighbors. Data from the Centers for Disease Control and Prevention conclude that these two groups are "nearly twice as likely to die from the virus as white people," and four times as likely to die in Wisconsin, Michigan, Missouri, and Kansas. Latinos and Hispanics in thirty states are twice as likely as whites to get infected, and four times higher in eight states. Though Latinos represent only 10 percent of Virginia's population, they account for almost 50 percent of all known COVID infections.[3] What explains these rates? Many Blacks and Latinos have frontline, poorly paid jobs that prevent them from sheltering in place or working from home. They commute to jobs on crowded public buses and trains, work side by side with others, live in tightly packed apartments in multigenerational families, and suffer from a range of comorbidities, such as obesity and diabetes, without access to healthy food or quality health care over the course of their lives.[4] For those few who had managed to gather a down payment and purchase a home, the Great Recession of 2008 liquidated the dominant form of capital accumulation racialized minorities typically had: their home equity vanished at the hands of predatory lenders.

The COVID-19 pandemic has exposed the economic, social, and racial fault lines wrought by forty years of neoliberal governance in the United States, which has transferred through taxation the earnings of the majority of the population to the top 10 percent, eliminated safety nets for the poorest and most vulnerable, and ensured low or nonexistent taxation of the rich and global corporations.

The racial tensions stoked by hopelessness, poverty, and the precarity of life during a pandemic have heightened the police and state violence that minorities face. We all watched in horror as George Floyd found himself face down, pinned to the ground by four members of the Minneapolis Police Department on May 25, 2020, suspected of passing a counterfeit twenty-dollar bill at a nearby convenience store. Gasping for air, with the knee of officer Derek Chauvin dug into his neck, Floyd cried out more than twenty times, "I can't breathe." He called to his dead mother for help, gasping, "They'll kill me. They'll kill me." They did. As his body went limp and unresponsive, Officer Chauvin shouted at Floyd, "Stop yelling, it takes a hell of a lot of oxygen to talk." He did, but only because he was already comatose and soon pronounced dead.[5]

Was this pure happenstance, an unfortunate accident, or systemic racism? The way in which the police murdered Floyd resembled the illegal chokehold that took Eric Garner's life in 2014, as he too uttered similar words at the precipice of death. What police records show is that over the last ten years at least seventy persons in police custody have died while gasping, whispering "I can't breathe." The majority were Black Americans apprehended for suspicious behavior (being Black while walking across the tracks, Black while jogging in a white neighborhood) and minor, non-violent infractions. Yet, they were placed in chokeholds, tased many times, hogtied, placed face down on the ground, or had their heads covered with hoods, purportedly to protect arresting officers from spit and bites.[6]

The American criminal justice system is the largest in the world. As the year 2016 began, some 6.7 million persons were under correctional control, 2.2 million of them incarcerated. As the Sentencing Project informed the United Nations in 2018, Black Americans "are more likely than white Americans to be arrested; once arrested, they are more likely to be convicted; and once convicted, and they are more likely to experience lengthy prison sentences. African American adults are 5.9 times as likely to be incarcerated than whites and Hispanics are 3.1 times as likely. As of 2001, one of every three black boys born in that year could expect to go to prison in his lifetime, as could one of every six Latinos—compared to one of every seventeen white boys." The incarceration statistics for women by race and ethnicity are less stark but equally revealing of race and class divides.[7]

In our heterosexist culture, being lesbian, gay, trans, or a nonbinary person also places people in disproportionate danger. "Latin Gay Night" at the Pulse nightclub in Orlando, Florida, started out as usual on Saturday, June 12, 2016, a merry night of drinking, dancing, seductions, and romance. But as the night turned into day, the Pulse became the scene of the most violent massacre of Latinas/os in American history. At approximately 2:00 a.m. Omar Mateen, a twenty-nine-year-old security guard, entered the nightclub armed with two semiautomatic weapons—a pistol and rifle—methodically shooting at random targets, leaving forty-nine dead and fifty-three wounded, the second most deadly attack up to that date since 9/11. Why? Allegedly it was retaliatory for the U.S. airstrikes that killed Abu Waheeb, a leader in the Islamic State in Iraq and the Levant, in May of 2016. Why was Matten's rage targeted on the club's Latina/o LGBTQ clientele? Why didn't he choose a military target, a federal installation, or some other much more symbolic objective? We will never know. He left no manifesto explaining his act of terror.

Three years later, on August 3, 2019, a Walmart store in El Paso, Texas, was the scene of an equally hateful attack on Mexicans, most of them Americans. This time twenty-two died and twenty-five were badly wounded. The killer, Patrick Crusius, a twenty-one-year-old white power activist from Allen, Texas, did post a manifesto. "This attack is a response to the Hispanic invasion of Texas. They are the instigators, not me. I am simply defending my country from cultural and ethnic replacement brought on by an invasion." In the screed Crusius posted on the Internet before he drove to El Paso, he railed about the worldwide conspiracy to subordinate the "white race" by non-Europeans and nonwhites, what is often described by white power activists as "The Great Replacement." It is a conspiracy theory first articulated by Renaud Camus in his 2011 book similarly titled, warning his French compatriots of the impact immigrants and their birthrates were having on their European culture. Crusius also expressed admiration for the Christchurch shooter, who on March 15, 2019, had attacked Muslims gathered at mosques in New Zealand, murdering fifty-one and injuring forty-nine. Both attacks, as well as the idea of replacement, share an unbroken historical genealogy with the earlier white power movement that used similar strategies and mass attacks.[8]

Most of these examples illustrate what scholars describe as systemic racism with vivid force. But its most subtle and insidious forms go unrecognized. Some years ago, a trans friend named Alex was asked about the pain she suffered during her gender-conforming surgery. "Did it hurt when they cut off your testicles?" "No," Alex replied, "not really." "Did it hurt when they split open your penis to fashion a vagina?" Again, she replied, "No. All of that was done under general anesthesia. There was some pain after surgery. But what really hurt was when they cut my paycheck in half." What Alex and most women understand is that, in the patriarchal society in which we live, women are routinely paid much less than what a man earns for the same task.[9] *Woman* signifies inferiority and subordination, though with no biological or psychological basis. In American society we constantly emphasize gender differences, which are minor and account mostly for the timing of human developmental processes. Factually, there are more gender similarities.[10] Why the emphasis on difference? Rebecca Solnit herein suggests that it authorizes patriarchy, misogyny, and a rape culture that wounds and kills thousands of women yearly. The statistics Croix Saffin cites show that the majority of violent acts against transpersons are also against transwomen of color.

What continues unabated in this moment of existential crisis are the forms of hatred documented and described in this guide—racism, xenophobia, misogyny, homophobia, antisemitism, and transphobia. These have been made all the more lethal by the coronavirus and by populist politicians who have seized on the pandemic to exacerbate the polity's historic divides by race, national origins, religion, gender, and affectional preferences, enhancing their own power by scapegoating others, breeding divisions, and conjuring outlandish conspiracy theories to leave the populace mired and twisted in their understanding of words. We must fear the "Kung flu," we our told by the executive who was once deemed the leader of the "free world." Black Lives [really don't] Matter! All lives matter is the retort President Trump openly endorses. His July 4, 2020, "Salute to America" speech lampooned those peaceful protesters demanding that police departments be defunded, labeling them antidemocratic Antifa groups composed of anarchists, fascist thugs, and looters, who he promised would "be dominated by force," a promise made good in Portland, Oregon, in subsequent days.

Given our country's past, where systemic racism and xenophobia have been met by protesting, will this latest wave of massive mobilization have lasting effects? Will the life of George Floyd and the many other unarmed Black, Brown, and Asian women and men executed by the police in the name of law and order, and by white power activists, fundamentally change how policing is done?

Protests demanding racial justice that stirred the moral conscience of the republic have radically changed since the 1960s. Then peaceful protest was concentrated in the American South. When the mostly peaceful protest spread across the country, some seven hundred events demanding racial justice took place, with fifteen thousand persons arrested. Much larger rebellions that turned violent with arson and looting occurred in Los Angeles (August 11, 1965), Newark (July 12–17, 1967), Detroit (July 23, 1967), and across more than one hundred cities after the assassination of Rev. Dr. Martin Luther King Jr. on April 4, 1968. In all of these cases, violence was met in kind by local police and federal troops. And it was at this point that white allies fled the civil rights movement.

Today, the United States is a much more racially, ethnically, and religiously diverse country. Fifty-nine percent of the population is white, 19 percent Hispanic, 13 percent Black, 6 percent Asian, and .74 percent Native American and Alaskan; proportions are rapidly changing. If one simply surveys where Black Lives Matter demonstrations recently occurred after the murder of George Floyd, they are no longer regionally concentrated in the North or South. They were national in scope, in all fifty states, be they red or blue. Even in small, predominantly white towns in the Midwest, protests demanding an end to police violence and "systemic" and "institutional" racism have occurred. According to historian Peniel Joseph, there were seven thousand antiracist demonstrations in twenty-four hundred locations with over twenty million participants. These were mostly peaceful, mobilized by grassroots organizations, churches, labor unions, college and university students, global corporations, even by the membership of the National Basketball Association. Video recordings showed the participants as being 61 percent white, 12 percent Black, 12 percent Asian, 9 percent Hispanic, and 5 percent multiracial/other. What violence occurred was sparked by local police forces and federal troops mobilized by the president to restore "law and order" after acts of arson and looting, intensified by armed right-wing militias.[11]

Indeed, in the lead-up to the presidential elections of 2020, the nation experienced spasms of militant Right activity by white power activists, militiamen, and others on the fringe—sometimes directly called into being and directed by the president. These groups included both ideological fanatics and casual participants moved to anarchic violence by a set of social frustrations including the pandemic, masking requirements, economic uncertainty, racial justice protests, and political divisiveness. This volatile formula moved many people to radical action, and only some unknown percentage of these acted with the long-awaited white power race war in mind. Nevertheless, they raised paramilitary forces, organized, trained, and armed themselves, and will not easily disband in the years to come.

Indeed, as the January 6, 2021, storming of the Capitol reveals, the white power movement had already mobilized among the Trump base and among QAnon supporters, widening its reach and capacity at precisely the most dangerous moment for opportunistic action. The insurrection was meant not as a mass casualty attack, but as a show of force, to prove that a band of white self-proclaimed "patriots" could strike at the heart of democracy. As we untangle the relationships between groups and activists, between lawmakers and police who aided and abetted their cause, and between competing narratives of the event, our only hope of confronting this threat to the idea of America is in better understanding our history.

And there may be reason to hope. Sociologist Douglas McAdam, a long-time analyst of social movements in the United States, recently concluded that "these protests are achieving what very few do; setting in motion a period of significant, sustained, and widespread social and political change," which eluded the 1960s civil rights movement, Occupy Wall Street protesters, and those who organized against mass shootings at churches, synagogues, schools, movie theatres, and shopping malls.[12] And communities impacted by white power and white supremacist violence— communities of color all over the country, but also in places like Charlottesville and Charleston, Pittsburgh, and El Paso—now share their targeting with all of us. White Power has now attacked us all, and we all hold this in common.

Perhaps this is the moment when systemic forms of racism, xenophobia, misogyny, homophobia, antisemitism, and transphobia will finally be, if not eviscerated, then profoundly tempered, radically shrinking the space between the egalitarian ideas of the American Creed and the realities of racial inequality.

Notes

INTRODUCTION

1. Nicholas Fandos, "Senate Leader Says President 'Provoked' Mob," *New York Times*, January 20, 2021, 1, 23.

2. See, for instance: Peter Silver, *Our Savage Neighbors: How Indian War Transformed Early America* (New York: W. W. Norton, 2008); Alexandra Minna Stern, *Eugenic Nation: Faults and Frontiers of Better Breeding in Modern America* (Berkeley: University of California Press, 2005); Matthew Frye Jacobson, *Whiteness of a Different Color: European Immigrants and the Alchemy of Race* (Cambridge, MA: Harvard University Press, 1998); Peggy Pascoe, *What Comes Naturally: Miscegenation Law and the Making of Race in America* (Oxford: Oxford University Press, 2009).

SECTION I BUILDING, PROTECTING, AND PROFITING FROM WHITENESS

1. On settler colonialism, see: Lorenzo Veracini, *Settler Colonialism: A Theoretical Overview* (New York: Palgrave, 2010); Gerald Horne, *The Apocalypse of Settler Colonialism: The Roots of Slavery, White Supremacy, and Capitalism in 17th Century North America* (New York: Monthly Review Press, 2017); Natchee Blu Barnd, *Native Space: Geographic Strategies to Unsettle Settler Colonialism*

(Corvallis: Oregon State University Press, 2017); Edward Cavanagh, *The Routledge Handbook of the History of Settler Colonialism* (New York Routledge, 2017); Adam Dahl, *Empire of the People: Settler Colonialism and the Foundations of Modern Democratic Thought* (Lawrence: University Press of Kansas, 2018); Mahmood Mamdani, *Neither Settler nor Native: The Making and Unmaking of Permanent Minorities* (Cambridge, MA: Harvard University Press, 2020); Natsu Taylor Saito, *Settler Colonialism, Race, and the Law: Why Structural Racism Persists* (New York: NYU Press, 2020).

2. James Madison Papers, vol. 75: February 4, 1826, Library of Congress, as quoted in Nicholas De Genova, *Racial Transformations: Latinos and Asians in the Remaking of the United States* (Durham, NC: Duke University Press, 2006), 1.

3. Senator John C. Calhoun, "Speech on Mexico's Annexation," *The Congressional Globe*, January 4, 1848, 96–100.

4. For the classic works on racial capitalism, see: C. L. R. James, *The Black Jacobins: Toussaint L'Ouverture and the San Domingo Revolution* (London: Secker and Warburg, 1938); Eric Williams, *Capitalism & Slavery* (New York: Russell & Russell, 1944); Cedric J. Robinson, *Black Marxism: The Making of the Black Radical Tradition* (London: Zed, 1983); Robin D. G. Kelley, *Race Rebels: Culture, Politics, and the Black Working Class* (New York: Free Press, 1996); Walter Johnson, *River of Dark Dreams: Slavery and Empire in the Cotton Kingdom* (Cambridge, MA: Harvard University Press, 2013); Edward Baptist, *The Half Has Never Been Told: Slavery and the Making of American Capitalism* (New York: Basic Books, 2014); Sven Beckert, *Empire of Cotton: A Global History* (New York: Alfred A. Knopf, 2014); Caitlin Rosenthal, *Accounting for Slavery: Masters and Management* (Cambridge, MA: Harvard University Press, 2018).

5. Nancy Leong, "Racial Capitalism," *Harvard Law Review* 126, no. 8 (June 2013): 2151–2226.

6. Cybelle Fox, *Three Worlds of Relief: Race, Immigration, and the American Welfare State from the Progressive Era to the New Deal* (Princeton, NJ: Princeton University Press, 2012).

7. Ira Katznelson, *When Affirmative Action Was White: An Untold History of Racial Inequality in Twentieth-Century America* (New York: W. W. Norton & Company, 2005), 113–41.

CHAPTER 1. NATION V. MUNICIPALITY

1. According to the U.S. Census Bureau's 2018 population estimates, the total population of Hobart is 9,496, with 78.3 percent of the population identifying as white (non-Hispanic or Latino) and 10.6 percent of the population identifying as American Indian / Alaska Native. See www.census.gov/quickfacts/fact/table /hobartvillagewisconsin,US/INC110217.

2. Hugh Danforth, letter to the editor, *Kalihwisaks,* October 31, 2002, 7A.

3. Hugh Danforth, letter to the editor, *Kalihwisaks,* April 4, 2002, 10A.

4. Dawes Severalty Act, February 8, 1887, 24 Stat. 388. For an overview of Oneida history during the allotment period, see L. Gordon McLester III and Laurence M. Hauptman, *The Oneida Indians in the Age of Allotment, 1860–1920* (Norman: University of Oklahoma Press, 2008).

5. "Petition of the Oneidas for Admission to Brown County," *Daily State Gazette* (Green Bay, WI), February 13, 1890, 3.

6. "Oneida Reservation, Proposed to Invest the Indians with Local Town Governments," *Oshkosh Northwestern,* April 24, 1903, 4.

7. "Ready for Legislature, Bill to Create Townships for Reservation Is Drafted," *Appleton Post,* April 23, 1903, 3; "Would Annex Part of the Reservation," *Post-Crescent* (Appleton, WI), February 1, 1908, 8.

8. "Five New Members in County Board," *Green Bay Semi-Weekly Gazette,* April 11, 1908, 1; "Oneida Organized into a Township," *Post-Crescent,* April 7, 1910, 1.

9. Hugh Danforth, letter to the editor, *Kalihwisaks,* November 29, 2002, 6A.

10. Rebecca M. Webster, "Service Agreements: Exploring Payment Formulas for Tribal Trust Lands on the Oneida Reservation," *American Indian Quarterly* 39, no. 4 (2015): 347–63.

11. John Greendeer, "State of the Tribes Address," Wisconsin State Assembly, March 13, 2012, https://wiseye.org/2012/03/13/assembly-floor-session-with-state-of-the-tribes-address-part-1-of-4/.

12. Paul Egelhoff, letter to the editor, *Kalihwisaks,* February 6, 2003, 7A; see also James M. Murray, *Local Economic Impacts of Oneida Gaming* (Green Bay: University of Wisconsin–Green Bay, 1992), UW–Green Bay Archives, call no. HV6721.W5 L6 1992x.

13. Katherine J. Kramer, *The Politics of Resentment: Rural Consciousness in Wisconsin and the Rise of Scott Walker* (Chicago: University of Chicago Press, 2016); Dan Kaufman, *The Fall of Wisconsin: The Conservative Conquest of a Progressive Bastion and the Future of American Politics* (New York: W. W. Norton, 2018).

14. On the broader significance of the local in U.S. political history, see Thomas J. Sugrue, "All Politics Is Local: The Persistence of Localism in Twentieth-Century America," in *The Democratic Experiment: New Directions in American Political History,* ed. Meg Jacobs, William J. Novak, and Julian E. Zelizer (Princeton, NJ: Princeton University Press, 2003), 301–26.

15. Thomas Biolsi, *Deadliest Enemies: Law and Race Relations on and off Rosebud Reservation,* 2nd ed. (Minneapolis: University of Minnesota Press, 2007).

16. For an overview of allotment, see Frederick E. Hoxie, *A Final Promise: The Campaign to Assimilate the Indians, 1880–1920,* 2nd ed. (Lincoln: University of Nebraska Press, 2001); Indian Reorganization Act, June 18, 1934, 48 Stat. 984.

17. California v. Cabazon Band of Mission Indians, 480 U.S. 202 (1987); Indian Gaming Regulatory Act, October 17, 1988, 102 Stat. 2467. See also Steven Andrew Light and Kathryn R. L. Rand, *Indian Gaming and Tribal Sovereignty: The Casino Compromise* (Lawrence: University Press of Kansas, 2005).

18. Oneida Tribe of Indians of Wisconsin, "20–20 Vision Acquisition Plan," General Tribal Council Resolution 10–26–98A.

19. In regard to casino gaming transforming relationships between Native nations and the United States and the resulting dilemmas of Indigenous governance, see Jessica Cattelino, "The Double Bind of American Indian Need-Based Sovereignty," *Cultural Anthropology* 25, no. 2 (2010): 235–62.

20. For related histories, see Meghan Y. McCune, "It's a Question of Fairness: Fee-to-Trust and Opposition to Haudenosaunee Land Rights and Economic Development," in *Gambling on Authenticity: Gaming, the Noble Savage, and the Not-So-New Indian*, ed. Becca Gercken and Julie Pelletier (East Lansing: Michigan State University Press, 2018), 111–34.

21. "Exhibit J: Service Agreement between the Oneida Nation in Wisconsin and the Village of Hobart," affidavit of Rebecca Webster, Oneida Tribe of Indians of Wisconsin v. Village of Hobart, Wisconsin (Civil File No. 06-C-1302), 1. The Oneida Indian Nation of New York also wrestled with municipal tax authority. The nation reacquired fee land within its traditional territory and the city of Sherrill taxed it. In *City of Sherrill v. Oneida Indian Nation of New York*, 544 U.S. 197 (2005), the U.S. Supreme Court ruled the Oneida Indian Nation of New York could not challenge the imposition of local property taxes on this fee land, because the land had passed out of the Oneidas' control nearly two hundred years earlier and was only recently reacquired by the Oneidas. The *Sherrill* decision was based upon the unique factual circumstances in New York and does not speak to reservations allotted under the General Allotment Act.

22. Affidavit of Rebecca Webster, *Oneida Tribe of Indians*, para. 33.

23. "Exhibit J: Service Agreement," 1.

24. "Exhibit N," affidavit of Rebecca Webster, *Oneida Tribe of Indians*, 2.

25. "Welcome to the Centennial Centre at Hobart!," Village of Hobart, Wisconsin, www.hobartwi.govoffice3.com/index.asp?Type=B_BASIC&SEC = {00C876AE-F179–4FE3–8820-E6A9CFAC6B03}.

26. "A Developer and Land Buyer's Dream: Step into Centennial Centre at Hobart," Village of Hobart, Wisconsin, www.hobart-wi.org/vertical/sites/% 7B354A483F-042E-454E-A570–720BFEDE46D9%7D/uploads/%7BC5432 DAF -85FF-4703–9984-DD2F5CD6BC34%7D.PDF.

27. "Downtown Hobart: Centennial Centre Is the Village's Effort to Create the Heart of the Community," *Marketplace Magazine* 21, no. 4 (2010): 12.

28. Willman, "A Less Than Neighborly Neighbor," 1.

29. Oneida Tribe of Indians of Wisconsin v. Village of Hobart, Wisconsin, 542F. Supp. 2d 908 (2008).

30. "Exhibit P: Village of Hobart News," affidavit of Rebecca Webster, *Oneida Tribe of Indians*, 4.

31. Affidavit of Rebecca Webster, *Oneida Tribe of Indians*, para. 39.

32. Ryan Lenz, "Seeing Red," *Intelligence Report*, February 17, 2016, www .splcenter.org/fighting-hate/intelligence-report/2016/seeing-red.

33. Oneida Tribe of Indians of Wisconsin, "Resolution Regarding Government-to-Government Relations with the Village of Hobart (Business Committee Resolution #2–20–08-C)," 3.

34. Willman claims that there are over one thousand incorporated municipalities located within Indian reservations throughout the United States.

35. Willman, interview; Carcieri v. Salazar (No. 07–526), 497 F.3d 15. Regarding *Carcieri v. Salazar*, the federal government has considered the Wisconsin Oneidas to be among the tribes that were under federal jurisdiction as of June 18, 1934, when the Indian Reorganization Act became law. The Village of Hobart, however, has stated: "It is the Village's position that there was no 'Tribe now under federal jurisdiction' as defined by § 479 of the IRA as interpreted by the *Carcieri* court" ("Village of Hobart's Opening Brief," Village of Hobart v. Midwest Regional Director, Bureau of Indian Affairs, Docket No. IBIA 11–058).

36. Willman, interview.

37. Affidavit of Carol Cornelius, *Oneida Tribe of Indians*, para. 19.

38. "Oneida Organized into a Township."

39. Affidavit of Carol Cornelius, *Oneida Tribe of Indians*, para. 24.

40. Kevin Bruyneel, *The Third Space of Sovereignty: The Postcolonial Politics of U.S.-Indigenous Relations* (Minneapolis: University of Minnesota Press, 2010), 171.

41. Elaine Willman, "Hobart—The Not-So-Hidden Spirit of the Community," *Press*, June 24, 2011, 17.

42. Along these lines, see Bruyneel, *Third Space*, 171–216; Alyosha Goldstein, "Where the Nation Takes Place: Proprietary Regimes, Antistatism, and U.S. Settler Colonialism," *South Atlantic Quarterly* 107, no. 4 (2008): 833–61.

43. Heidel, "Response."

44. Willman, interview.

45. See Osawa, *Lighting the Seventh Fire;* and Nesper, *The Walleye War.*

46. Bruyneel, *Third Space*, 197–98.

47. Willman, interview.

48. Ezra Klein, "Romney's Theory of the 'Taker Class,' and Why It Matters," *New York Times*, September 17, 2012, www.washingtonpost.com/blogs/wonkblog /wp/2012/09/17/romneys-theory-of-the-taker-class-and-why-it-matters/.

49. Willman, interview.

50. Works that characterize the U.S. West as historically dependent upon federal support include Patricia Nelson Limerick, *The Legacy of Conquest: The Unbroken Past of the American West* (New York: W. W. Norton, 1987); and

Richard White, *"It's Your Misfortune and None of My Own": A New History of the American West* (Norman: University of Oklahoma Press, 1991).

51. Oneida Tribe of Indians of Wisconsin v. Village of Hobart, 732 F.3d 837 (2013).

52. Elaine Willman, "The Spreading Epidemic of Tribalism in America," NewsWithViews.Com, January 11, 2016, www.newswithviews.com/Willman /elaine100.htm.

53. Anne-Marie d'Hauteserre, "Explaining Antagonism to the Owners of Fox-woods Casino Resort," *American Indian Culture and Research Journal* 34, no. 3 (2010): 121.

54. For a discussion of these themes at greater length, see Alexandra Harmon, *Rich Indians: Native People and the Problem of Wealth in American History* (Chapel Hill: University of North Carolina Press, 2010).

55. For an examination of these issues in a Pequot context, see d'Hauteserre, "Explaining Antagonism," 107–27.

56. Katherine A. Spilde, "Rich Indian Racism: The Uses of Indian Imagery in the Political Process," paper presented at 11th International Conference on Gambling and Risk Taking, Las Vegas, NV, June 20, 2000, www.indian gaming .org/library/articles/rich-indian-racism.shtml.

57. Cattelino, "The Double Bind."

58. Jeff Bollier, "Hot in Hobart: Residential Boom Continues, County VV Plans Take Shape," *Green Bay Press-Gazette*, June 12, 2019, 1A.

59. Ben Rodgers, "Teaming Up on 29, Governments Coming Together for Grant," *Press Times*, June 26, 2018, https://gopresstimes.com/2018/06/26 /teaming-up-on-29-governments-coming-together-for-grant/.

60. Kevin Boneske, "Equalized Property Value Nearing $1 Billion," *Press Times*, August 16, 2019, 1.

61. U.S. Census Bureau QuickFacts, www.census.gov/quickfacts/fact/table /hobartvillagewisconsin,US/INC110217.

62. Oneida Nation v. Village of Hobart, Wisconsin, U.S. District Court for the Eastern District of Wisconsin, Green Bay Division, Case No. 16-CV-1217.

63. Oneida Nation v. Village of Hobart, Wisconsin, Seventh Circuit, No. 19–1981 (2020); Paul Srubas, "Government Sides with Oneida Tribe in Dispute with Hobart," *Green Bay Press-Gazette*, October 3, 2019, 1A.

64. Oneida Tribe of Indians of Wisconsin, "2033 Land Acquisition Plan," GTC Resolution 09–18–10-A.

65. Dawn Walschinski, "Hobart Groundwater Claim Washed Down the Drain," *Kalihwisaks*, October 31, 2013, 4A; Fred R. Shapiro, "The Most-Cited Legal Scholars," *Journal of Legal Studies* 29, no. S1 (January 2000): 409–26. For a legal forum on the Oneida-Hobart jurisdictional disputes, see Rebecca M. Webster, "Tribal and Local Governments: Jurisdictional Challenges within

Shared Spaces," State Bar of Wisconsin, January 1, 2016, www.wisbar.org /NewsPublications/Pages/General-Article.aspx?ArticleID=2455.

CHAPTER 2. A CULTURE OF RACISM

1. Epigraph quotations: Lyndon B. Johnson, speech delivered at Howard University, June 4, 1965, www.lbjlib.utexas.edu/johnson/archives.hom/speeches .hom/650604.asp; Barack Obama, speech delivered at Morehouse College, May 19, 2013, www.ajc.com/news/news/local/prepared-text-for-president-obamas -speech-at-moreh/nXwk2/.

2. John Eligon, "A Teenager Grappling with Promise and Problems," *New York Times,* August 25, 2014, A1, A11.

3. "Goldie Taylor Lectures Nicholas Kristof for Suggesting Protesters Focus Less on Michael Brown," *Twitchy,* January 23, 2015, http://twitchy.com /2015/01/23/goldie-taylor-lectures-nicholas-kristof-for-suggesting-protesters- focus-less-on-michael-brown/.

4. Thomas Jefferson, *Notes on the State of Virginia,* chapter 14 (Paris, 1785), http://xroads.virginia.edu/~hyper/JEFFERSON/ch14.html.

5. Barbara J. Fields, "Slavery, Race and Ideology in the United States of America," *New Left Review* 181, no. 1 (1990): 95–118.

6. Karen Fields and Barbara J. Fields, *Racecraft: The Soul of Inequality in American Life* (London: Verso, 2012), 134.

7. US Congress et al., *The ISIS Threat: The Rise of the Islamic State and Their Dangerous Potential* (Providence, RI: Providence Research, 2014).

8. Frank Main, "Treasure Trove of Memos Shows Emanuel's Politics in White House," *Chicago Sun-Times,* June 20, 2014, http://chicago.suntimes.com /chicago-politics/7/71/163978/treasure-trove-of-memos-shows-emanuels-politics -in-white-house.

9. Rahm Emanuel, interviewed by Scott Pelley, "Emanuel: Chicago's Escalating Crime about 'Values,'" CBS News, July 10, 2012, www.cbsnews.com/news /emanuel-chicagos-escalating-crime-about-values/.

10. ABC7 Chicago, "Obama Addresses Chicago Violence in Message to Students," August 14, 2012, http://abc7chicago.com/archive/8773637/.

11. Hal Dardick and Kristen Mack, "Emanuel Admits He Erred on Details of Protest Rule Changes," *Chicago Tribune,* October 4, 2012, http://articles .chicagotribune.com/2012-10-4/news/ct-met-emanuel-protesters-20120104_1 _mayor-rahm-emanuel-protest-leader-nato.

12. Terry Blounte, "Foote: Lynch Sending Wrong Message to Kids," ESPN.com, February 3, 2015, http://espn.go.com/nfl/story/_/id/12272608/arizona -cardinals-linebacker-larry-foote-says-marshawn-lynch-seattle-seahawks-sending -wrong-message-kids.

13. Jonathan Chait, "Barack Obama vs. the Culture of Poverty," *Daily Intelligencer*, March 28, 2014, http://nymag.com/daily/intelligencer/2014/03/barack-obama-vs-the-culture-of-poverty.html.

14. Institute on Assets and Social Policy, "The Roots of the Widening Racial Wealth Gap," report, quoted in Jamelle Bouie, "The Crisis in Black Homeownership," *Slate*, July 24, 2014, www.slate.com/articles/news_and_politics/politics/2014/07/black_homeownership_how_the_recession_turned_owners_into_renters_and_obliterated.html.

15. Patricia Cohen, "For Recent Black College Graduates, a Tougher Road to Employment," *New York Times*, December 24, 2014.

16. Ta-Nehisi Coates, "Black Pathology and the Closing of the Progressive Mind," *The Atlantic*, March 21, 2014, www.theatlantic.com/politics/archive/2014/03/black-pathology-and-the-closing-of-the-progressive-mind/284523/.

17. Quoted in Ronald Reagan, "We Will Be a City upon a Hill," speech delivered to the first Conservative Political Action Conference, January 25, 1974, http://reagan2020.us/speeches/City_Upon_A_Hill.asp.

18. Quoted in Greg Jaffe, "Obama's New Patriotism," June 3, 2015, *Washington Post*, www.washingtonpost.com/sf/national/2015/06/03/obama-and-american-exceptionalism/.

19. Michael Dobbs and John M. Goshko, "Albright's Personal Odyssey Shaped Foreign Policy Beliefs," *Washington Post*, December 6, 1996, www.washingtonpost.com/wp-srv/politics/govt/admin/stories/albright120696.htm.

20. Reagan, "We Will Be a City upon a Hill."

21. Ta-Nehisi Coates, "Other People's Pathologies," *The Atlantic*, March 30, 2014, www.theatlantic.com/politics/archive/2014/03/other-peoples-pathologies/359841/.

22. Quoted in Jim Cullen, *The American Dream: A Short History of an Idea That Shaped a Nation* (Oxford: Oxford University Press, 2004).

23. Hal Draper, "Who's Going to Be the Lesser-Evil in 1968?" *Independent Socialist*, January–February 1967, Marxists Internet Archive, www.marxists.org/archive/draper/1967/01/lesser.htm.

24. Franklin D. Roosevelt, speech delivered in Chicago, October 14, 1936, www.presidency.ucsb.edu/ws/?pid = 15185.

25. David M. P. Freund, *Colored Property: State Policy and White Racial Politics in Suburban America* (Chicago: University of Chicago Press, 2007).

26. David Harvey, *Rebel Cities: From the Right to the City to the Urban Revolution* (London: Verso, 2012).

27. Freund, *Colored Property*; Arnold R. Hirsch, *Making the Second Ghetto: Race and Housing in Chicago 1940–1960* (Chicago: University of Chicago Press, 1998); Beryl Satter, *Family Properties: Race, Real Estate, and the Exploitation of Black Urban America* (New York: St. Martin's Press, 2009); Kenneth T. Jackson, *Crabgrass Frontier: The Suburbanization of America* (New York: Oxford

University Press, 1985); Kenneth L. Kusmer and Joe William Trotter, *African American Urban History since World War II* (Chicago: University of Chicago Press, 2009); Gregory Squires, ed., *Unequal Partnerships: The Political Economy of Urban Redevelopment in Postwar America* (New Brunswick, NJ: Rutgers University Press, 1989).

28. Arnold R. Hirsch and Raymond A. Mohl, *Urban Policy in Twentieth-Century America* (New Brunswick, NJ: Rutgers University Press, 1993); Squires, *Unequal Partnerships;* Gregory D. Squires, *Capital and Communities in Black and White: The Intersections of Race, Class, and Uneven Development* (Albany: State University of New York Press, 1994).

29. N. D. B. Connolly, *A World More Concrete: Real Estate and the Remaking of Jim Crow South Florida* (Chicago: University of Chicago Press, 2014).

30. Penny M. von Eschen, *Race against Empire: Black Americans and Anticolonialism, 1937–1957* (Ithaca, NY: Cornell University Press, 1997); Mary L. Dudziak, *Cold War Civil Rights: Race and the Image of American Democracy* (Princeton, NJ: Princeton University Press, 2000).

31. Quoted in Leon F. Litwack, *How Free Is Free? The Long Death of Jim Crow* (Cambridge, MA: Harvard University Press, 2009), 82.

32. Litwack, 83.

33. Hirsch, *Making the Second Ghetto*, 65.

34. Lyndon B. Johnson, remarks to the US Chamber of Commerce, April 27, 1964, www.presidency.ucsb.edu/ws/?pid = 26193#axzz2h 3amO72U.

35. Alexander von Hoffman, "The Lost History of Urban Renewal," *Journal of Urbanism* 1, no. 3 (2008): 281–301.

36. Landon R. Y. Storrs, *The Second Red Scare and the Unmaking of the New Deal Left* (Princeton, NJ: Princeton University Press, 2013), 2.

37. Storrs, 3–4.

38. Manning Marable, *Race, Reform, and Rebellion: The Second Reconstruction in Black America, 1945–1990* (Jackson: University Press of Mississippi, 1991), 28.

39. Marable, 31; Von Eschen, *Race against Empire;* Nikhil Pal Singh, *Black Is a Country: Race and the Unfinished Struggle for Democracy* (Cambridge, MA: Harvard University Press, 2004).

40. Karen Ferguson, *Top Down: The Ford Foundation, Black Power, and the Reinvention of Racial Liberalism* (Philadelphia: University of Pennsylvania Press, 2013).

41. Quoted in Alice O'Connor, *Poverty Knowledge: Social Science, Social Policy, and the Poor in Twentieth-Century U.S. History* (Princeton, NJ: Princeton University Press, 2009), 117.

42. O'Connor, 117.

43. O'Connor, 117–18.

44. O'Connor, 122.

45. Martin Luther King Jr., "I Have a Dream," speech delivered at the March on Washington, DC, August 28, 1963, www.ushistory.org/documents/i-have-a-dream .htm.

46. Martha Biondi, *To Stand and Fight: The Struggle for Civil Rights in Postwar New York City* (Cambridge, MA: Harvard University Press, 2003), 1.

47. Malcolm X and Alex Haley, *The Autobiography of Malcolm X* (New York: Grove Press, 1965), online edition, 67, www.epubsbook.com/2015/4318_67 .html.

48. Malcolm X, speech at the founding rally of the Organization of Afro-American Unity, New York, June 28, 1964, www.blackpast.org/1964-malcolm -x-s-speech-founding-rally-organization-afro-american-unity.

49. Jack M. Bloom, *Class, Race, and the Civil Rights Movement* (Bloomington: Indiana University Press, 1987), 204.

50. Gerald Horne, *The Fire This Time: The Watts Uprising and the 1960s* (Boston: Da Capo Press, 1997).

51. Johnson, remarks to Chamber of Commerce.

52. Daniel Patrick Moynihan, *The Negro Family: The Case for National Action* (Washington, DC: US Department of Labor, Office of Policy Planning and Research, 1965), www.blackpast.org/primary/moynihan-report–1965.

53. Kenneth Bancroft Clark, *Dark Ghetto: Dilemmas of Social Power* (New York: Harper & Row, 1965), 15.

54. Felicia Ann Kornbluh, *The Battle for Welfare Rights: Politics and Poverty in Modern America* (Philadelphia: University of Pennsylvania Press, 2007), 17–18.

55. William J. Novak, "The Myth of the 'Weak' American Stat," *American Historical Review* 113, no. 3 (2008): 752.

56. Kornbluh, Battle for Welfare Rights, 41.

57. "President Lyndon B. Johnson's Commencement Address at Howard University: 'To Fulfill These Rights,' June 4, 1965," www.lbjlib.utexas.edu/johnson / archives.hom/speeches.hom/650604.asp (accessed June 9, 2015).

58. "Negroes, Whites Agree on Riot Victims," *Boston Globe*, August 15, 1967.

59. Martin Luther King Jr., *The Essential Martin Luther King, Jr.: "I Have a Dream" and Other Great Writings* (Boston: Beacon Press, 2013).

60. Philip Sheldon Foner, ed., *The Black Panthers Speak* (Chicago: Haymarket, 2014), 51.

61. Colette Gaiter, "Visualizing a Revolution: Emory Douglas and the Black Panther Newspaper," AIGA website, June 8, 2005, www.aiga.org/visualizing -a-revolution-emory-douglas-and-the-black-panther-new/.

62. *New York Times* editorial, "The Race Problem: Why the Riots, What to Do?" August 6, 1967.

63. "Negroes, Whites Agree"; Louis Harris, "Races Agree on Ghetto Abolition and Need for WPA-Type Projects," *Washington Post*, August 14, 1967.

64. Kerner Commission and Tom Wicker, *Report of the National Advisory Commission on Civil Disorders* (New York: Bantam Books, 1968).

65. Stan Karp, "Challenging Corporate Ed Reform," *Rethinking Schools* (Spring 2012), www.rethinkingschools.org//cmshandler.asp?archive/26_03 /26_03_karp.shtml.

66. Nia-Malika Henderson, "What President Obama Gets Wrong about Acting White,'" *Washington Post*, July 24, 2014, www.washingtonpost.com/blogs /she-the-people/wp/2014/07/24/what-president-obama-gets-wrong-about-acting -white/.

67. Barack Obama, "Remarks by the President on 'My Brother's Keeper' Initiative," Whitehouse.gov, February 27, 2014, www.whitehouse.gov/the-press -office/2014/02/27/remarks-president-my-brothers-keeper-initiative.

68. U.S. Department of Justice, Civil Rights Division, *Investigation of the Ferguson Police Department* (Washington, DC: Government Printing Office, 2015), 77, http://purl.fdlp.gov/GPO/gpo55760.

CHAPTER 3. POLICING THE BOUNDARIES OF THE
WHITE REPUBLIC

1. Epigraph quotations: David T. Wellman, *Portraits of White Racism*, 2nd ed. (Cambridge: Cambridge University Press, 1993), 55; Carlyle McKinley, *An Appeal to Pharaoh: The Negro Problem and Its Radical Solution* (New York: Fords, Howard & Hulbert, 1889), 202, quoted in George M. Frederickson, *The Black Image in the White Mind: The Debate on Afro-American Character and Destiny, 1817–1914* (Middletown, CT: Wesleyan University Press, 1971), 265.

2. White supremacy has been defined as "a particular kind of oppressive social system [in which] . . . whiteness and nonwhiteness are recognized racial identities; whites have and exert differential power in creating and controlling the evolution of the social system in question, and/or in blocking changes to it that would substantially reduce their domination, whose end is originally the systemic, significant, and illicit differential advantaging of all or most whites as a group with respect to nonwhites as a group in various important social spheres." Charles W. Mills, "White Supremacy," in *The Routledge Companion to Philosophy of Race*, ed. Paul C. Taylor, Linda Martin Alcoff, and Luvell Anderson (New York: Routledge, 2018), 475.

3. Markus Dirk Dubber, "'The Power to Govern Men and Things': Patriarchal Origins of the Police Power in American Law," *Buffalo Law Review* 52, no. 4 (Fall 2004): 1277–78, quoting Slaughter-House Cases, 83 U.S. 36, 49–50 (1873).

4. Jonathan A. Bush, "Free to Enslave: The Foundations of Colonial American Slave Law," *Yale Journal of Law & the Humanities* 5, no. 2 (Summer 1993): 417, 421, 425–26, 434; see also Markus Dirk Dubber, *The Police Power: Patriarchy*

and the Foundations of American Government (New York: Columbia University Press, 2005), 61.

5. An Act for Preventing, Suppressing and Punishing the Conspiracy and Insurrection of Negroes and Other Slaves (passed December 10, 1712), in *The Colonial Laws of New York from the Year 1664 to the Revolution*, vol. 1 (Albany, NY: James B. Lyon, 1894), 761-67; A. Leon Higgenbotham Jr., *In the Matter of Color* (New York: Oxford University Press, 1978), 119; Thelma Wills Foote, *Black and White Manhattan: The History of Racial Formation in Colonial New York City* (New York: Oxford University Press, 2004), 132-33. Although the huge majority of slaves were Black, a significant number of slaves were Natives.

6. An Additional Act to an Act Entitled "An Act for the Better Ordering and Governing Negroes and All Other Slaves," sec. 9 (passed December 18, 1714), in *Statutes at Large of South Carolina*, vol. 7, ed. David J. McCord (Columbia, SC: Printed by A. S. Johnstone, 1840), 367.

7. An Act for Preventing, Suppressing and Punishing the Conspiracy and Insurrection of Negroes and Other Slaves.

8. Kunal M. Parker, *Making Foreigners: Immigration and Citizenship Law in America, 1600-2000* (Cambridge: Cambridge University Press, 2015), 40.

9. Lorenzo J. Greene, *The Negro in Colonial New England, 1620-1776* (1942; repr., Eastford, CT: Martino Fine Books, 2016), 312-13, 121.

10. Parker, *Making Foreigners*, 40.

11. An Act for the Better Regulation and Government of Free Negroes and Persons of Color; and for Other Purposes, sec. 1 (passed December 21, 1822), in *Statutes at Large of South Carolina*, vol. 7, ed. David J. McCord (Columbia, SC: Printed by A. S. Johnstone, 1840), 461.

12. An Act for the Better Regulation and Government of Free Negroes and Persons of Color; and for Other Purposes, sec. 3, 461.

13. Illinois Constitution of 1848, art. 14.

14. Indiana Constitution of 1851, art. 13.

15. Oregon Constitution of 1857, art. 1, sec. 35.

16. Frederickson, *Black Image*, 266.

17. Alden T. Vaughan, *Roots of American Racism: Essays on the Colonial Experience* (New York: Oxford University Press, 1995), 18.

18. Johnson v. M'Intosh, 21 U.S. (8 Wheat.) 543 (1823).

19. *Johnson*, 21 U.S. (8 Wheat.) at 543.

20. Cherokee Nation v. Georgia, 30 U.S. (5 Pet.) 1 (1831).

21. *Cherokee Nation*, 30 U.S. (5 Pet.) at 1.

22. Stuart Banner, *How the Indians Lost Their Land: Law and Power on the Frontier* (Cambridge, MA: Harvard University Press, 2005), 191-92.

23. Theda Perdue and Michael D. Green, *The Cherokee Nation and the Trail of Tears* (New York: Viking, 2007), 123.

24. Gary Clayton Anderson, *Ethnic Cleansing and the Indian: The Crime That Should Haunt America* (Norman: University of Oklahoma Press, 2014), 162–63.

25. Crandall v. Nevada, 73 U.S. 35 (1867).

26. In re Ah Fong, 1 F.Cas. 213, 216–17 (C.C.D. Cal. 1874).

27. People v. Compagnie Generale Transatlantique, 107 U.S. 59 (1883).

28. Parker, *Making Foreigners*, 119.

29. Kelly Lytle Hernandez, "America's Mass Deportation Is Rooted in Racism," *The Conversation*, February 26, 2017, https://theconversation.com/americas-mass-deportation-system-is-rooted-in-racism-73426.

30. Elmer Clarence Sandmeyer, *The Anti-Chinese Movement in California* (Urbana: University of Illinois Press, 1991), 65.

31. Chinese Exclusion Case (Chae Chan Ping v. United States), 130 U.S. 581, 609 (1889).

32. Fong Yue Ting v. United States, 149 U.S. 698, 707, 730 (1893).

33. Parker, *Making Foreigners*, 126.

34. The Cherokee Tobacco, 78 U.S. 616 (1870).

35. United States v. Kagama, 118 U.S. 375, 380 (1886).

36. *Kagama*, 118 U.S. at 384–85.

37. Sarah H. Cleveland, "Powers Inherent in Sovereignty: Indians, Aliens, Territories, and the Nineteenth Century Origins of Plenary Power Over Foreign Affairs," *Texas Law Review* 81, no. 1 (Nov. 2002): 62.

38. Lone Wolf v. Hitchcock, 187 U.S. 553, 565 (1903).

39. Parker, *Making Foreigners*, 135.

40. See José A. Cabranes, *Citizenship and the American Empire: Notes on the Legislative History of the United States Citizenship of Puerto Ricans* (New Haven, CT: Yale University Press, 1979), 20. According to Article IX of the Treaty of Paris, "The civil rights and political status of the native inhabitants of the territories hereby ceded to the United States *shall be determined by the Congress*" (emphasis added).

41. Downes v. Bidwell, 182 U.S. 244, 268 (1901).

42. *Downes*, 182 U.S. at 286–87.

43. 182 U.S. at 287–344.

44. Mae Ngai, *Impossible Subjects: Illegal Aliens and the Making of Modern America* (Princeton, NJ: Princeton University Press, 2004), 22.

45. Cong. Globe, 30th Cong., 1st Sess. 98 (1848).

46. Michael A. Olivas, "The Chronicles, My Grandfather's Stories, and Immigration Law: The Slave Traders Chronicle as Racial History," *Saint Louis University Law Journal* 34, no. 3 (Spring 1990): 436–38.

47. Bob Franco Carpinteria, "Trip Down Racism Lane," CoastalView.com, August 8, 2018, www.coastalview.com/opinion/trip-down-racism-lane/article_2d2df0b6-9b55-11e8-b024-ab26e178c20e.html.

48. Ngai, *Impossible Subjects,*155–56.

49. Kelly Lytle Hernandez, *Migra!: A History of the U.S. Border Patrol* (Berkeley: University of California Press, 2010), 156 n28.

50. Trump v. Hawaii, 585 U.S. ___, 138 S. Ct. 2392 (2018).

51. The numbers of deportations here and following are my calculations, based on the U.S. Department of Homeland Security, *2018 Yearbook of Immigration Statistics,* table 39.

52. Sarah Pierce, Jessica Bolter, and Andrew Selee, *U.S. Immigration Policy under Trump: Deep Changes and Lasting Impacts* (Transatlantic Council on Migration, Migration Policy Institute, July 2018), 1–2.

53. John Gramlich, "How Border Apprehensions, ICE Arrests and Deportations Have Changed under Trump," Pew Research Center, March 2, 2020, www.pewresearch.org/fact-tank/2020/03/02/how-border-apprehensions-ice-arrests-and-deportations-have-changed-under-trump/.

54. William J. Clinton, "Address before a Joint Session of the Congress on the State of the Union," January 24, 1995, American Presidency Project, www.presidency.ucsb.edu/node/221902.

55. Barack Obama, "Address before a Joint Session of the Congress on the State of the Union," January 28, 2014, American Presidency Project, www.presidency.ucsb.edu/node/305034.

56. Yolanda Vázquez, "Enforcing the Politics of Race and Identity in Migration and Crime Control Policies," in *Race, Criminal Justice, and Migration Control,* ed. Mary Bosworth, Alpa Parmar, and Yolanda Vázquez (New York: Oxford University Press, 2017), loc. 4093–4101, 4146–54 of 7550.

57. Michael Shear and Julie Hirschfeld Davis, "Shoot Migrants' Legs, Build Alligator Moat: Behind Trump's Ideas for the Border," *New York Times,* October 1, 2019, www.nytimes.com/2019/10/01/us/politics/trump-border-wars.html.

58. Marc R. Rosenblum and Ariel G. Ruiz Soto, *An Analysis of Unauthorized Immigrants in the United States by Country and Region of Birth,* Migration Policy Institute, August 2015, www.migrationpolicy.org/research/analysis-unauthorized-immigrants-united-states-country-and-region-birth.

59. Vázquez, "Enforcing the Politics of Race and Identity in Migration and Crime Control Policies," loc. 4064 of 7550.

60. Vázquez, loc. 4108.

61. Leo R. Chavez, *Covering Immigration: Popular Images and the Politics of Nation* (Berkeley: University of California Press, 2001).

62. Vázquez, "Enforcing the Politics," loc. 4130.

63. Jens Manuel Krogstad, Jeffrey S. Passel, and D'Vera Cohn, "5 Facts about Illegal Immigration in the U.S.," Fact Tank, Pew Research Center, June 12, 2019, www.pewresearch.org/fact-tank/2019/06/12/5-facts-about-illegal-immigration-in-the-u-s/.

64. Vázquez, "Enforcing the Politics," loc. 4130; Krogstad, Passel, and Cohn, "5 Facts."

65. As stated by Douglas S. Massey, "It is not just a border but *the* border." Douglas S. Massey, "The Mexico-U.S. Border in the American Imagination," *Proceedings of the American Philosophical Society* 160, no. 2 (June 2016): 160.

66. Samuel P. Huntington, *Who Are We?: The Challenges to America's National Identity* (New York: Simon & Schuster, 2004), 312; Maria del Far Marina, *White Nativism, Ethnic Identity and U.S. Immigration Policy Reforms* (New York: Routledge, 2018), 25.

67. Peter Brimelow, *Alien Nation: Common Sense about America's Immigration Disaster* (New York: Random House, 1995), xvii, 10.

68. John Tanton, WITAN IV Paper, 2, 4 (1986), quoted in Antonio J. Califa, "Declaring English the Official Language: Prejudice Spoken Here," *Harvard Civil Rights–Civil Liberties Law Review* 24, no. 2 (Spring 1989), 326–27, 326n217, 327n218, 327n222.

69. Leo Chavez, "Fear of White Replacement: Latina Fertility, White Demographic Decline, and Immigration Reform," this volume, quoting Barbara Ehrenreich (2015).

70. Chavez, this volume.

71. Chavez, this volume; "Laura Ingraham: Demographic Changes 'National Emergency,'" BBC News, August 10, 2018, www.bbc.com/news/world-us -canada-45146811.

72. For the term "Latino threat," consult Leo R. Chavez, *The Latino Threat: Constructing Immigrants, Citizens, and the Nation* (Stanford, CA: Stanford University Press, 2008). I use the term *Latino* here and after to refer to persons of Mexican and Central American ancestry, who constitute the huge majority of persons being deported and excluded. I use this term for reasons of economy and to lessen repetition of the terms "Mexican and Central American."

73. Kevin R. Johnson, "Race, the Immigration Laws, and Domestic Race Relations: A 'Magic Mirror' into the Heart of Darkness," *Indiana Law Journal* 73, no. 4 (1998): 1152–53.

74. Jennifer M. Chacón and Susan Bibler Coutin, "Racialization through Enforcement," in *Race, Criminal Justice, and Migration Control,* ed. Mary Bosworth, Alpa Parmar, and Yolanda Vázquez (New York: Oxford University Press, 2017), loc. 4609–17 of 7550.

75. Cody Wofsy and Caitlin Borgmann, "U.S. Border Patrol Detained U.S. Citizens for Speaking Spanish in Montana," ACLU, February 14, 2019, www.aclu .org/blog/immigrants-rights/ice-and-border-patrol-abuses/us-border-patrol -detained-us-citizens-speaking.

76. Rick Rojas et al., "Families of El Paso Victims Waited in Anguish after Shooting," *New York Times,* August 5, 2019, www.nytimes.com/2019/08/05/us /el-paso-victims.html.

77. Douglas S. Massey, "The Real Purpose of the Border Wall," in Robert Schenkkan, *Building the Wall: The Play & Commentary* (New York: Arcade, 2017), 109.

78. Frederickson, *Black Image,* 266.

CHAPTER 4. THE ARC OF AMERICAN ISLAMOPHOBIA

1. Jenna Johnson, "Trump Calls for 'Total and Complete Shutdown of Muslims Entering the United States,'" *Washington Post,* December 7, 2015. Epigraph quotation: In re Ahmed Hassan, 48 F. Supp. (Eastern District of Michigan Court, 1942), 843, 845.

2. Jeremy Diamond, "Trump on Latest Iteration of Muslim Ban: 'You Could Say It's an Expansion,'" CNN, July 24, 2016.

3. For a chronological log of President Trump's anti-Muslim pronouncements, see Jenna Johnson and Abigail Hauslohner, "'I Think Islam Hates Us': A Timeline of Trump's Comments about Islam and Muslims," *Washington Post,* May 20, 2017, www.washingtonpost.com/news/post-politics/wp/2017/05/20/i-think -islam-hates-us- a-timeline-of-trumps-comments-about-islam-and-muslims/. Although the Supreme Court ruled otherwise, critics of the travel ban executive order cite these statements as indicative of his intent to discriminate against Muslims. Trump v. Hawaii, 138 S. Ct. 2392, 2408 (2018), holding that "the President lawfully exercised that discretion based on his finding . . . that entry of the covered aliens would be detrimental to the national interest.".

4. The six additional states are Nigeria, Myanmar, Eritrea, Kyrgyzstan, Sudan, and Tanzania.

5. See Vince Warren, "Anti-Muslim Hate Is a Continuation, Not an Aberration," *Huffington Post,* December 11, 2015.

6. See Khaled A. Beydoun, "Between Muslim and White: The Legal Construction of Arab American Identity," *NYU Annual Survey of American Law* 69 (2013): 29, 34.

7. Khaled A. Beydoun, "Islamophobia: Toward A Legal Definition and Framework," *Columbia Law Review* 116 (2016): 108.

8. Edward Said, *Orientalism* (New York: Vintage, 1979).

9. Leti Volpp, "The Citizen and the Terrorist," *UCLA Law Review* 49 (2002): 1586.

10. Volpp, 1586n40.

11. Wajahat Ali et al., *Fear, Inc.: The Roots of the Islamophobia Network in America* (Washington, DC: Center for American Progress, 2011), 9–10.

12. Beydoun, "Islamophobia," 112–14n____.

13. For a comprehensive history of the era, see Ian Haney López, *White by Law: The Legal Construction of Race* (New York: NYU Press, 1996).

14. Naturalization Act of 1790, Act of March 26, 1790, Chapter 3, Statute 103. The law was reformed in 1798 to "establish a uniform rule of naturalization" and extended the qualifying residency. Naturalization Act of 1795, Act of January 29, 1795, Chapter 20, Statute 414.

15. Hiroshi Motomura, *Americans in Waiting: The Lost Story of Immigration and Citizenship in the United States* (New York: Oxford University Press, 2006), 115-16.

16. Motomura, 115-16.

17. John Tehranian, *Whitewashed: America's Invisible Middle Eastern Minority* (New York: NYU Press, 2009), 15.

18. Beydoun, *Between Muslim and White*, 33n____.

19. This case came before the creation of Lebanon and Syrian as modern nation-states.

20. Ex Parte Shahid (Eastern District of South Carolina, 2013), 812.

21. *Shahid,* at 813n____.

22. *Shahid* at 816.

23. Khaled A. Beydoun, "America Banned Muslims Long Before Donald Trump," *Washington Post,* August 18, 2016.

24. Khaled A. Beydoun, "Islamophobia Has a Long History in the US," BBC News, September 29, 2015.

25. Sahar Aziz, "Sticks and Stones, The Words That Hurt: Entrenched Stereotypes Eight Years After 9/11," *CUNY Law Review* 13 (2009): 33-36.

26. Volpp, "Citizen and the Terrorist," 1595.

27. Volpp, 1595.

28. Linda Bosniak, *The Citizen and the Alien: Dilemmas of Contemporary Membership* (Princeton, NJ: Princeton University Press, 2008), 30.

29. Bosniak, 30.

30. Khaled A. Beydoun, "Acting Muslim," *Harvard Civil Rights–Civil Liberties Law Review* 53 (2018): 1.

SECTION II ITERATIONS OF WHITE SUPREMACY

1. William D. Carrigan and Clive Webb, *Forgotten Dead: Mob Violence against Mexicans in the United States, 1848-1928* (Oxford: Oxford University Press, 2013). On lynching, see for instance Christopher Waldrep, *The Many Faces of Judge Lynch: Punishment and Extralegal Violence in America* (New York: Palgrave Macmillan, 2002), 10, 21; Richard Maxwell Brown, *Strain of Violence: Historical Studies of American Violence and Vigilantism* (New York: Oxford University Press, 1975), vii, 5; W. Fitzhugh Brundage, *Lynching in the New South: Georgia and Virginia, 1880-1930* (Urbana: University of Illinois Press, 1993), 3; Stewart Tolnay and E. M. Beck, *A Festival of Violence: An Analysis of*

Southern Lynchings, 1882-1930 (Urbana: University of Illinois Press, 1995) 246, quoting Edward L. Ayers, *Vengeance and Justice: Crime and Punishment in the 19th-Century American South* (Oxford: Oxford University Press, 1984), 238; and Michael J. Pfeifer, *Rough Justice: Lynching and American Society: 1874-1947* (Urbana: University of Illinois Press, 2004) 3, 10, 149–50.

2. Jacqueline Dowd Hall, "'The Mind That Burns in Each Body': Women, Rape and Racial Violence," in *Powers of Desire: The Politics of Sexuality*, ed. Ann Snitow, Christine Stansell, and Sharon Thompson (New York: Monthly Review Press, 1983), 328–49.

3. On women as slave owners, see Stephanie E. Jones Rogers, *They Were Her Property: Women as Slave Owners in the American South* (New Haven: Yale University Press, 2019). On women and Jim Crow lynching, see Timothy B. Tyson, *The Blood of Emmett Till* (New York: Simon & Schuster, 2017). On the participation of women in vigilante violence, see also Benjamin H. Irvin, "Tar, Feathers, and the Enemies of American Liberties, 1768–1776," *New England Quarterly* 76, no. 2. (June 2003): 197–238; Christopher Waldrep, *Lynching in America: A History in Documents* (New York: NYU Press, 2006); and Linda Gordon, *The Great Arizona Orphan Abduction* (Cambridge, MA: Harvard University Press, 2001). On the defense of white female bodies as justification for racial violence, see also Peggy Pascoe, *What Comes Naturally: Miscegenation Law and the Making of Race in America* (Oxford: Oxford University Press, 2009).

CHAPTER 7. ANTI-ASIAN VIOLENCE AND U.S. IMPERIALISM

1. Press statement, "New Data Examines Political Anti-Chinese Rhetoric and Anti-AAPI Hate," June 18, 2020, http://asianpacificpolicyandplanningcouncil.org.

2. Beth Lew-Williams, *The Chinese Must Go! Violence, Exclusion, and the Making of the Alien in America* (Princeton, NJ: Princeton University Press, 2018).

3. Alexander Saxton, *The Indispensable Enemy: Labor and the Anti-Chinese Movement in California* (Berkeley: University of California Press, 1971); Manu Karuka, *Empire's Tracks: Indigenous Nations, Chinese Workers, and the Transcontinental Railroad* (Berkeley: University of California Press, 2019).

4. Cedric Robinson, *Black Marxism: The Making of the Black Radical Tradition* (Chapel Hill: University of North Carolina Press, 2000); Kelly Lytle Hernández, *City of Inmates: Conquest, Rebellion, and the Rise of Human Caging in Los Angeles, 1771-1965* (Chapel Hill: University of North Carolina Press, 2017).

5. Lucie Cheng and Edna Bonacich, eds., *Labor Immigration under Capitalism: Asian Workers in the United States before World War II* (Berkeley: University of California Press, 1984).

6. Cheryl L. Harris, "Whiteness as Property," *Harvard Law Review* 106, no. 8 (June 1993): 1707–91.

7. Monica Muñoz Martinez, *The Injustice Never Leaves You: Anti-Mexican Violence in Texas* (Cambridge, MA: Harvard University Press, 2018); Jessie Kindig, "Looking beyond the Frame: Snapshot Photography, Imperial Archives, and the U.S. Military's Violent Embrace of East Asia," *Radical History Review* 126 (2016): 147–58.

8. John Johnson Jr., "How Los Angeles Covered Up the Massacre of 17 Chinese," *LA Weekly*, March 10, 2011.

9. Matt Reimann, "At Rock Springs Massacre, 28 People Were Killed Because White Miners Feared Chinese Immigrants," *Timeline*, February 2, 2017.

10. Erika Lee, *The Making of Asian America: A History* (New York: Simon & Schuster, 2015), 94.

11. Paul A. Kramer, *The Blood of Government: Race, Empire, the United States, and the Philippines* (Chapel Hill: University of North Carolina Press, 2006).

12. Dean Saranillio, *Unsustainable Empire: Alternative Histories of Hawai'i Statehood* (Durham, NC: Duke University Press, 2018).

13. Kelly Lytle Hernández, *Migra! A History of the U.S. Border Patrol* (Berkeley: University of California Press, 2010).

14. Jasbir K. Puar, *The Right to Maim: Debility, Capacity, Disability* (Durham, NC: Duke University Press, 2017), xiii; Monica Kim, *The Interrogation Rooms of the Korean War* (Princeton, NJ: Princeton University Press, 2019).

15. Quoted in Nick Turse, *Kill Anything That Moves: The Real American War in Vietnam* (New York: Picador, 2013).

16. Kathleen Belew, *Bring the War Home: The White Power Movement and Paramilitary America* (Cambridge, MA: Harvard University Press, 2018), 40.

17. Helen Zia, *Asian American Dreams: The Emergence of an American People* (New York: Farrar, Straus, and Giroux, 2001), 55–81; *Who Killed Vincent Chin?*, dir. Christine Choy and Renee Tajima-Peña (1987), film.

18. Statement by Coalition to Stop Violence against Asians in America, August 21, 1986, box 1, folder: CAAAV, Asian Labor Resource Center Records, Tamiment Library, NYU.

19. Wong/Woo Support Committee Update, Coalition against Anti-Asian Violence, April 10, 1987, box 1, folder: CAAAV, Asian Labor Resource Center Records, Tamiment Library.

20. *The CAAAV Voice: Newsletter of the Committee against Anti-Asian Violence* 1, no. 3 (Fall 1989): 2.

21. Chinese Progressive Association Housing Committee Pamphlet, box 1, folder: Chinese Community, Karl Akiya Papers, Tamiment Library.

22. Circular, Concerned Committee for the Chung Park Project, April 9, 1985, box 1, folder: LDC Correspondence and Mailing List, Rocky Chin Papers, Tamiment Library.

23. Asia/Pacific Statement on Apartheid, n.d., box 5, folder: South Africa, Rocky Chin Papers, Tamiment Library.

24. CriticalResistance.org.

25. Ruth Wilson Gilmore, "COVID-19, Decarceration, and Abolition," Online Teach-In sponsored by Haymarket Books, April 16, 2020.

26. The organization's website is at https://caaav.org.

27. Nudutdol, "Coronavirus Statement," https://nodutdol.org/coronavirus / (accessed January 16, 2021).

28. Nudutdol, "In Support of Black Liberation," https://nodutdol.org/in-support -of-black-liberation/ (accessed January 16, 2021).

CHAPTER 8. HOMOPHOBIA AND
AMERICAN NATIONALISM

1. Lizette Alvarez and Richard Pérez-Peña, "Orlando Gunman Attacks Gay Nightclub, Leaving 50 Dead," *New York Times,* June 12, 2016.

2. Rebecca Solnit, "The Longest War," chap. 5 of this volume.

3. Jack Halberstam, "Who Are 'We' after Orlando?," Bully Bloggers (blog), June 22, 2016, https://bullybloggers.wordpress.com/2016/06/22/who-are-we-after -orlando-by-jack-halberstam/.

4. Justin Torres, "In Praise of Latin Night at the Queer Club," *Washington Post,* June 13, 2016.

5. G. D. H. Cole, *A History of Socialist Thought,* vol. 5: *Socialism and Fascism, 1931-1939* (London: Macmillan, 1960), 6.

CHAPTER 9. WOUNDS OF WHITE SUPREMACY

1. National Coalition of Anti-Violence Programs, "Lesbian, Gay, Bisexual, Transgender Queer and HIV-Affected Hate and Intimate Partner Violence in 2017," http://avp.org/wp-content/uploads/2019/01/NCAVP-HV-IPV-2017-report.pdf.

2. Madeleine Roberts, "Marking the Deadliest Year on Record, HRC Releases Report on Violence against Transgender and Gender Non-Conforming People," Human Rights Campaign, www.hrc.org/press-releases/marking-the-deadliest -year-on-record-hrc-releases-report-on-violence-against-transgender-and-gender -non-conforming-people.

3. The FBI is required to track statistics based on gender and gender identity, but police agencies are not required to report hate crimes to the FBI.

4. Dan Avery, "Anti-Transgender Hate Crimes Soared 20 Percent in 2019," NBC News, November 17, 2020, www.nbcnews.com/feature/nbc-out/anti -transgender-hate-crimes-soared-20-percent-2019-n1248011.

5. National Center for Transgender Equality, "Failing to Protect and Serve: Police Department Policies towards Transgender People," https://transequality .org/issues/resources/failing-to-protect-and-serve-police-department-policies-to wards-transgender-people.

6. Alex Paterson, "News Outlets Misidentified Nearly Two Out of Three Victims of Anti-Trans Violence in 2020," *Media Matters for America,* November 19, 2020, www.mediamatters.org/justice-civil-liberties/news-outlets-misidentified -nearly-two-out-three-victims-anti-trans-violence.

7. Paterson. Of the remaining 121 articles, despite updates made to reflect the status of the investigation, the misgendering language or deadnaming was never corrected. Among those victims who were misgendered are: Yampi Méndez Arocho, Monika Diamond, Johanna Metzger, Penélope Díaz Ramírez, Nina Pop, Helle Jae O'Regan, Jayne Thompson, Dominique "Rem'mie" Fells, Riah Milton, Brayla Stone, Merci Mack, Shaki Peters, Bree Black, Marilyn "Monroe" Cazares, Dior H Ova, Queasha D Hardy, Summer Taylor, Lea Rayshon Daye, Kee Sam, Aerrion Burnett, Mia Green, Felycya Harris, and Sara Blackwood.

8. Madeleine Roberts, "Marking the Deadliest Year on Record, HRC Releases Report on Violence against Transgender and Gender Non-Conforming People," Human Rights Campaign, www.hrc.org/press-releases/marking-the-deadliest -year-on-record-hrc-releases-report-on-violence-against-transgender-and-gender -non-conforming-people.

9. White supremacy is a racist ideology that is based on the belief that white people are superior to people of other races and that therefore white people are and should be dominant. This is embedded in individuals, institutions, and cultural norms/values. White supremacy is describing social, political, and economic systems of domination based on racial categories that benefit those defined and perceived as white. White supremacy is a system of structural power that privileges, centralizes, and elevates white people as a group (not just some white people). White supremacy is not just neo-Nazis/KKK members, white nationalists, or "conservative white rednecks." Like polluted air, white supremacy is the systemic toxic messages that our culture constructs around race whereby whites are the norm or standard for being human. Racism, in its most simplistic form, is prejudice/discrimination plus power. Racism is a system of advantage/privilege, prejudice/discrimination, and oppression based on race. And this privilege, advantage, and oppression is reinforced individually, institutionally, and culturally. There is only one racist system in the United States, and that is white supremacy. Racism can only come from the group that dominates, has power and privilege, because this results in the oppression of other groups. Racism, then, is not a two-way street. When whites experience hatred by people of color or are stereotyped, or discriminated against through the actions of people of color, as awful as that is and feels, that does not create a Black supremacy or Asian supremacy or Latinx privilege or Indigenous privileges or result in

white oppression. There is no system that supports that reversal. Whites still have white privilege, and those privileges are still reinforced in institutions by white supremacy. See Crystal M. Fleming. *How to Be Less Stupid About Race* (Boston: Beacon Press, 2018).

10. See the Transgender Law Center's "Trans Agenda for Liberation" for donating, volunteering, or supporting BIPOC trans–led work, https:// transgenderlawcenter.org/trans-agenda-for-liberation.

11. "HRC Mourns Sasha Garden and Calls for Review of Police Conduct During Investigation," Human Rights Campaign, July 20, 2018, www.hrc.org /news/hrc-mourns-sasha-garden-and-calls-for-review-of-police-conduct-during -inves.

12. Sasha Garden, "Sasha Garden: 5 Fast Facts You Need to Know," *Heavy,* https://heavy.com/news/2018/07/sasha-garden/.

13. Colin Wolf and Monivette Cordeiro, "A Transgender Women Died Today, and How It Was Reported Was Awful," *Orlando Weekly,* July 19, 2018, www .orlandoweekly.com/Blogs/ archives/2018/07/19/a-transgender-woman-died-in-orlando-today-and-how-it- was-reported-was-awful.

14. Wolf and Cordeiro.

15. Wolf and Cordeiro.

16. Wolf and Cordeiro.

17. Wolf and Cordeiro.

18. Wolf and Cordeiro.

19. Wolf and Cordeiro.

20. Cissexism is the systemic/institutional rewarding and privileging of cis- ness and cisgender.

21. BIPOC (Black, Indigenous, people of color) is a phrase used to centralize the unique experiences of racism that Black and Indigenous communities face.

22. Cristi Hegranes, "Badlands Confidential," *SF Weekly,* June 29, 2005, www.sfweekly.com/2005-06-29/news/badlands-confidential/.

23. Alex Abad-Santos, "Philadelphia's New, Inclusive Gay Pride Flag Is Making Gay White Men Angry," *Vox,* June 20, 2017, www.vox.com/culture/2017/6/20 /15821858/gay-pride-flag-philadelphia-fight-explained.

24. George Johnson, "White Gay Privilege Exists All Year, but It Is Particu- larly Hurtful During Pride," *Think: NBC News,* June 30, 2019, www.nbcnews .com/think/opinion/white-gay-privilege-exists-all-year-it-particularly-hurtful -during-ncna1024961.

25. Manisha Krishnan, "So Many Gay Dudes Are Depressingly Racist on Dat- ing Apps," *Vice,* January 21, 2016, www.vice.com/en/article/bnpavv/so-many-gay -dudes-are-depressingly-racist-on-dating-apps. In July, 2020 Grindr stated that it would remove the ethnicity filter from its next version.

26. Charmaine Lang, "To the White LGBTQ Community: Your (Racist) Slip Is Showing," *Colorlines*, June 29, 2020, www.colorlines.com/articles/white-lgbtq-community-your-racist-slip-showing-op-ed.

27. See Robin DiAngelo's *What Does It Mean to Be White: Developing White Racial Literacy* (New York: Peter Lang Publishing, 2016); and *White Fragility: Why It's So Hard for White People to Talk about Racism* (Boston: Beacon Press, 2018) for more discussion of this.

28. Johnson, "White Gay Privilege."

29. Tehama Lopez Bunyasi and Candis Watts Smith. "Do All Black Lives Matter Equally to Black People? Respectability Politics and the Limitations of Linked Fate," *Journal of Race, Ethnicity, and Politics* 4, no. 1 (March 2019): 180–215, www.cambridge.org/core/journals/journal-of-race-ethnicity-and-politics/article/do-all-black-lives-matter-equally-to-black-people-respectability-politics-and-the-limitations-of-linked-fate/CBC842CABC6F8FAA6C892B08327B09DA.

30. Kimberly F. Balsam, Yamile Molina, Blair Beadnell, Jane Simoni, and Karina Walters, "Measuring Multiple Minority Stress: The LGBT People of Color Microaggressions Scale," *Cultural Diversity and Ethnic Minority Psychology* 17, no. 2 (2011): 163–74, www.ncbi.nlm.nih.gov/pmc/articles/PMC4059824/.

31. In 2016, the median white family had 41 times more wealth than the median Black family and 22 times more wealth than the median Latino family, and an estimated 28 percent of Black households and 26 percent of Latinx households had zero or negative wealth in 2019, twice the level of whites. See "Facts: Racial and Economic Inequality," Inequality.org, https://inequality.org/facts/racial-inequality/. There is also over a 30-percentage-point gap in home ownership between white and Black families. In 1960, when racial segregation was legal, there was a 27-percentage-point gap in home ownership, meaning that there is a greater gap today than there was during Jim Crow segregation. See Courtney Connley, "Why the Homeownership Gap Between White and Black Americans Is Larger Today Than It Was Over 50 Years Ago," CNBC, August 21, 2020, www.cnbc.com/2020/08/21/why-the-homeownership-gap-between-white-and-black-americans-is-larger-today-than-it-was-over-50-years-ago.html. Additionally, data from the Small Business Administration indicates that just over 19 million businesses, or 70.9 percent of all U.S. businesses, are white owned. Blacks own about 2.6 million businesses, or 9.5 percent of all U.S. businesses, and Latinos own 3.3 million businesses, or 12.2 percent of all American businesses. But the 19 million white-owned businesses have 88 percent of the overall sales and control 86.5 percent of U.S. employment, while black businesses have a mere 1.3 percent of total American sales and 1.7 percent of the nation's employees. Latino businesses have 4 percent of U.S. sales and 4.2 percent of U.S. employment. See Brian Marshall, "Are We There Yet? The State of Black Business and the Path to Wealth," *BLNDED Media*, February 13, 2019, http://blndedmedia.com/are-we-there-yet/.

32. PovertyUSA.org, "The Population of Poverty USA," 2018, www.povertyusa.org/facts.

33. National LGBTQ Task Force, "New Analysis Shows Startling Levels of Discrimination Against Black Transgender People," www.thetaskforce.org/new-analysis-shows-startling-levels-of-discrimination-against-black-transgender-people/.

34. National LGBTQ Task Force.

35. National Center for Transgender Equality, "The Report of the 2015 U.S. Transgender Survey," December 2016, www.transequality.org/sites/default/files/docs/usts/USTS%20Full%20Report%20-%20FINAL%201.6.17.pdf.

36. Evan Urquhart, The Joy of Having a Job," Slate, June 16, 2020, https://slate.com/human-interest/2020/06/trans-job-discrimination-scotus-bostock-decision.html.

37. "Federal Government Eliminates Health Care Protections for Transgender Americans," June 19, 2020, The Commonwealth Fund, www.commonwealthfund.org/blog/2018/federal-protections-health-care-risk-transgender-americans.

38. "Federal Government Eliminates Health Care Protections."

39. "Federal Government Eliminates Health Care Protections."

40. Erika Stallings, "This Is How the American Healthcare System is Failing Black Women," O Magazine, October 2018, www.oprahmag.com/life/health/a23100351/racial-bias-in-healthcare-black-women/.

41. Katie Keith, "HHS Strips Gender Identity, Sex Stereotyping, Language Access Protections from ACA Anti-Discrimination Rule," Health Affairs, June 13, 2020, www.healthaffairs.org/do/10.1377/hblog20200613.671888/full/.

42. Theo Santos, Lindsay Mahowald, and Sharita Gruberg, "The Trump Administration's Latest Attack on Transgender People Facing Homelessness," Center for American Progress, September 3, 2020, www.americanprogress.org/issues/lgbtq-rights/reports/2020/09/03/490004/trump-administrations-latest-attack-transgender-people-facing-homelessness/.

43. "Federal Government Eliminates Health Care Protections."

44. In February 2021, the Biden Administration issued an executive order directing all federal agencies to uphold the June 2020 Supreme Court ruling that prohibits discrimination based on sexual orientation and gender identity. See Tracy Jan, "HUD Expands Fair Housing Protections for Transgender People," Washington Post, February 11, 2021, www.washingtonpost.com/business/2021/02/11/hud-expand-fair-housing-protections-transgender-people/.

45. "Addressing Anti-Transgender Violence," Human Rights Campaign, May 2019, http://assets2.hrc.org/files/assets/resources/HRC-AntiTransgenderViolence-0519.pdf.

46. Rebecca L. Stotzer, "Violence against Transgender People: A Review of United States Data," Aggression and Violent Behavior 14, no. 3 (May 2009): 170–79; Laramie R. Smith, Jennifer Yore, Daniel P. Triplett, Lianne Urda, Tootu

Nemoto, and Anita Raj, "Impact of Sexual Violence across the Lifespan on HIV Risk Behaviors among Transgender Women and Cisgender People Living with HIV," *JAIDS: Journal of Acquired Immune Deficiency Syndromes* 75, no. 4 (August 2017): 408–16.

47. Sara Matsuzaka and David E. Koch, "Trans Feminine Sexual Violence Experiences: The Intersection of Transphobia and Misogyny," *Affilia: Journal of Women and Social Work* 34, no. 1 (2019): 28–47, https://journals.sagepub.com /doi/pdf/10.1177/0886109918790929.

48. Julie Compton, "Is Transmisogyny Killing Transgender Women?" NBC News, August 24, 2015, www.nbcnews.com/feature/nbc-out/transmisogyny -killing-transgender-women-n415286.

49. Compton.

50. Tuck Woodstock, "Who Is Committing Violence against Trans Women?" *Portland Monthly,* October 2, 2020, www.pdxmonthly.com/news-and-city -life/2020/10/who-is-committing-violence-against-trans-women.

51. This is often called the trans panic defense. See Alexandra Holden, "The Gay/Trans Panic Defense: What It Is and How to End It," American Bar Association, Summer 2019, www.americanbar.org/groups/crsj/publications/member -features/gay-trans-panic-defense/

52. Meredith Talusan, "Unerased: Counting Transgender Lives," *Mic,* December 8, 2016, https://unerased.mic.com/.

53. Talusan.

54. Talusan.

55. Talusan.

56. Alex Berg, "Analysis: How 'Toxic Masculinity' Fuels Transgender Victimization," *Think: NBC News,* August 4, 2017, www.nbcnews.com/think/nbc-out /analysis-how-toxic-masculinity-fuels-transgender-victimization-ncna789621.

57. Zariah Taylor, "VOX 5: Reasons Why 'Black-on-Black Crime' Is Not a Valid Argument against the Black Lives Matter Movement," *Afterschool Snack,* September 8, 2020, www.afterschoolalliance.org/afterschoolsnack/VOX-5 -Reasons-why-Black-on-Black-crime-is-not-a-valid_09–08–2020.cfm.

58. Jeffrey Kluger, "Domestic Violence Is a Pandemic Within the Covid-19 Pandemic," *Time,* February 3, 2021, https://time.com/5928539/domestic -violence-covid-19/.

59. Gina Martinez and Tara Law, "Two Recent Murders of Black Trans Women in Texas Reveal a Nationwide Crisis, Advocates Say," *Time,* June 12, 2019, https://time.com/5601227/two-black-trans-women-murders-in-dallas -anti-trans-violence/.

60. Anna North, "The Movement to Decriminalize Sex Work, Explained," *Vox,* August 2, 2019, www.vox.com/2019/8/2/20692327/sex-work-decriminalization -prostitution-new-york-dc.

61. North.

62. Molly Smith and Juno Mac, *Revolting Prostitutes: The Fight for Sex Workers' Rights* (New York: Verso Publishing, 2018).

63. "Why Sex Work Should Be Decriminalized," Human Rights Watch, August 7, 2019, www.hrw.org/news/2019/08/07/why-sex-work-should-be-decriminalized.

64. North, "Movement to Decriminalize Sex Work."

65. Liz Tung, "FOSTA-SESTA Was Supposed to Thwart Sex Trafficking. Instead, It's Sparked a Movement," *WHYY*, July 10, 2020, whyy.org/segments/fosta-sesta-was-supposed-to-thwart-sex-trafficking-instead-its-sparked-a-movement/.

66. Tung.

67. Natasha Riddle, "Sex Workers Struggle to Find Housing in DC. A Bill to Decriminalize Their Job Can Help," *Greater Greater Washington,* July 17, 2019, https://ggwash.org/view/72972/decriminalize-sex-work-housing-access-for-black-and-brown-trans-women-dc

68. Riddle.

69. Jenavieve Hatch, "First Congress Took Sex Worker' Websites. Now It's Coming for Their Bank Accounts," *Huffington Post,* May 29, 2018, www.huffpost.com/entry/human-trafficking-banking-bill-sex-workers_n_5b045577e4b0740c25e5efd1.

70. Taia Handlin, "Financial Services Are Shutting Out Sex Workers," *BTRtoday,* June 7, 2018, www.btrtoday.com/read/featured/financial-services-are-shutting-out-sex-workers/.

71. North, "Movement to Decriminalize Sex Work."

72. Jasmine Sankofa, "From Margin to Center: Sex Work Decriminalization Is a Racial Justice Issue," *Amnesty International,* December 12, 2016, www.amnestyusa.org/from-margin-to-center-sex-work-decriminalization-is-a-racial-justice-issue/.

73. Molly Crabapple, "New York Cops Will Arrest You for Carrying Condoms," *Vice,* March 5, 2013, www.vice.com/en/article/3b5mx9/new-york-cops-will-arrest-you-for-carrying-condoms.

74. Those 2.3 million people include 1,833 in state prisons, 110 in federal prisons, 1,772 in juvenile correctional facilities, 3,134 in local jails, 218 in immigration detention facilities, and 80 in Indian Country jails as well as in military prisons, civil commitment centers, state psychiatric hospitals, and prisons in the U.S. territories. See Wendy Sawyer and Peter Wagner, "Mass Incarceration: The Whole Pie 2020," *Prison Policy Initiative,* March 24, 2020, www.prisonpolicy.org/reports/pie2020.html. See "Highest to Lowest Prison Population Rate," World Prison Brief, www.prisonstudies.org/highest-to-lowest/prison_population_rate?field_region_taxonomy_tid = All.

75. Sawyer and Wagner, "Mass Incarceration."

76. Sawyer and Wagner.

77. Lea Hunter, "What You Need to Know about Ending Cash Bail," *Center for American Progress*, March 16, 2020, www.americanprogress.org/issues/criminal -justice/reports/2020/03/16/481543/ending-cash-bail/.

78. Hunter.

79. Alexa Van Brunt, "Poor People Rely on Public Defenders Who Are Too Overworked to Defend Them," *The Guardian*, June 17, 2015, www .theguardian.com/commentisfree/2015/jun/17/poor-rely-public-defenders-too -overworked.

80. Naomi Murakawa, foreword to *We Do This 'Til We Free Us: Abolitionist Organizing and Transforming Justice* by Mariame Kaba (Chicago: Haymarket Books, 2021), xvii.

81. National Center for Transgender Equality, "Prison and Detention Reform," 2012, www.transequality.org/sites/default/files/docs/resources/NCTE_ Blueprint_for_Equality2012_Prison_Reform.pdf.

82. Heath Fogg Davis, "The Sex Markers We Carry," *Beyond Trans: Does Gender Matter?* (New York: NYU Press, 2017).

83. Mariame Kaba, "Black Women Punished for Self Defense Must Be Freed from Their Cages," in *We Do This 'Til We Free Us: Abolitionist Organizing and Transforming Justice* (Chicago: Haymarket Books, 2021), 49–53.

84. Perfect victims tend to be defined as middle-upper-class white cis women who have no history of drug use, are employed, educated, and have had no prior contact with the criminal justice system. See also Mariame Kaba, "Part II," in *We Do This 'Til We Free Us: Abolitionist Organizing and Transforming Justice* (Chicago: Haymarket Books, 2021), 29–52.

85. National Center for Transgender Equality, "Prison and Detention Reform."

86. National Center for Transgender Equality.

87. National Coalition of Anti-Violence Programs, "Hate Violence Against Transgender Communities," 2013, https://avp.org/wp-content/uploads/2017/04 /ncavp_transhvfactsheet.pdf; National Center for Transgender Equality, "Reducing Incarceration and Ending Abuse in Prisons," 2015, https://transequality.org /sites/default/files/docs/resources/NCTE_Blueprint_2015_Prisons.pdf

88. National Center for Transgender Equality, "Reducing Incarceration."

89. National Center for Transgender Equality.

90. Woodstock, "Who Is Committing Violence?"

91. Battered Women's Support Services, "Transmisogyny 101: What It Is and What We Can Do About It," August 14, 2018, www.bwss.org/transmisogyny-101 -what-it-is-and-what-can-we-do-about-it/.

92. Joshua Manson, "Transgender Women of Color Face Crushing Rates of Incarceration, Solitary Confinement, and Abuse," *Solitary Watch*, July 22, 2019, https://solitarywatch.org/2019/07/22/transgender-women-of-color-face-crushing -rates-of-incarceration-solitary-confinement-and-abuse/.

93. "Solitary Confinement Should Be Banned in Most Cases, Says Expert," *UN News,* October 18, 2011, https://news.un.org/en/story/2011/10/392012 -solitary-confinement-should-be-banned-most-cases-un-expert-says.

94. Joshua Manson, "Transgender Women of Color Face Crushing Rates of Incarceration, Solitary Confinement, and Abuse," *Solitary Watch,* July 22, 2019, https://solitarywatch.org/2019/07/22/transgender-women-of-color-face-crushing -rates-of-incarceration-solitary-confinement-and-abuse/.

95. "The Equality Act," Human Rights Campaign, March 13, 2021, www.hrc .org/resources/the-equality-act?utm_source = GS&utm_medium = AD&utm_ campaign = BPI-HRC-Grant&utm_content = 451187702350&utm_term = discrimination%20acts&gclid = CjwKCAjwu5CDBhB9EiwA0w6sLXDAxBm5 g0PgbAD3E-6M1zU9mBUrYKlKmL_8KB-US2kF-WV864HwEhoC4n0QAvD_ BwE.

96. "Statement by President Joseph R. Biden, Jr. on the Introduction of the Equality Ace in Congress," The White House, February 19, 2021, www .whitehouse.gov/briefing-room/statements-releases/2021/02/19/statement-by-president-joseph-r-biden-jr-on-the-introduction-of-the-equality-act-in-congress/.

97. The House of Representatives passed this bill in February of 2021. When this volume went to press, it was unclear if it would pass the Senate and make it to President Biden to sign into law. See Danielle Kurtzleben, "House Passes the Equality Act: Here's What It Would Do," NPR, February 24, 2021, www.npr .org/2021/02/24/969591569/house-to-vote-on-equality-act-heres-what-the-law -would-do.

SECTION III ANTI-IMMIGRANT NATION

1. Michael C. LeMay and Elliott Robert Barkan, eds., *Immigration and Naturalization Laws and Issues: Primary Documents in American History and Contemporary Issues* (Westport, CT: Greenwood Press, 1999), 6–9.

2. A number of states did grant citizenship to free Blacks.

3. There are a number of studies that chronicle how European immigrants once racialized as Black and nonwhite became white over time. Noel Ignatiev, *How the Irish Became White* (New York: Routledge, 1995); Karen Brodkin, *How Jews Became White Folk and What that Says about Race in America* (New Brunswick, NJ: Rutgers University Press, 1998); Matthew Frye Jacobson, *Whiteness of a Different Color: European Immigrants and the Alchemy of Race* (Cambridge, MA: Harvard University Press, 1999); Thomas Guglielmo, *White on Arrival: Italians, Race, Color and Power in Chicago, 1890-1945* (New York: Oxford University Press, 2003); Jennifer Guglielmo and Salvatore Salerno, eds., *Are Italians White?: How Race Is Made in America* (New York: Routledge, 2003).

4. John Higham, *Strangers in the Land: Patterns of American Nativism, 1860–1925* (New Brunswick, NJ: Rutgers University Press, 1955); Erika Lee, *America for Americans: A History of Xenophobia in the United States* (New York: Basic Books, 2019), 113–45.

5. Mae M. Ngai, *Impossible Subjects: Illegal Aliens and the Making of Modern America* (Princeton, NJ: Princeton University Press, 2004).

6. President Johnson quoted in Ngai, 259.

7. Douglas S. Massey, Jorge Durand, and Nolan J. Malone, *Beyond Smoke and Mirrors: Mexican Immigration in an Era of Economic Integration* (New York: Russell Sage Foundation, 2002), 40.

8. Kitty Calavita, *Inside the State: The Bracero Program, Immigration, and the I.N.S.* (New York: Routledge, 1992); Deborah Cohen, *Braceros: Migrant Citizens and Transnational Subjects in the Postwar United States and Mexico* (Chapel Hill: University of North Carolina Press, 2011); Ana Elizabeth Rosas, *Abrazando el Espíritu: Bracero Families Confront the US-Mexico Border* (Berkeley: University of California Press, 2014); Mireya Loza, *Defiant Braceros: How Migrant Workers Fought for Racial, Sexual, and Political Freedom* (Chapel Hill: University of North Carolina Press, 2016).

CHAPTER 11. FEAR OF WHITE REPLACEMENT

1. The U.S. Census uses the terms Hispanic and Latino interchangeably, as will I herein. A Latino is generally understood as a person from Latin America, while Hispanic usually includes persons from Spain.

CHAPTER 12. UNMAKING THE NATION OF IMMIGRANTS

1. Gallup, "Topic: Immigration," https://news.gallup.com/poll/1660/immigration.aspx.

2. Center for Immigration Studies, "A Pen and a Phone: 79 Immigration Actions the Next President Can Take," CIS website, April 6, 2016, https://cis.org/Report/Pen-and-Phone.

3. President Lyndon B. Johnson's Remarks at the Signing of the Immigration Bill, Liberty Island, New York, October 3, 1965, www.lbjlibrary.org/lyndon-baines-johnson/timeline/lbj-on-immigration.

4. Mae Ngai, *Impossible Subjects: Illegal Aliens and the Making of Modern America* (Princeton, NJ: Princeton University Press, 2004).

5. Ward Sinclair, "U.S. and Mexico Embroiled in Dispute Over 'Tortilla Curtain,'" *Washington Post*, December 24, 1978, www.washingtonpost.com

/archive/politics/1978/12/24/us-and-mexico-embroiled-in-dispute-over-tortilla
-curtain/0f9b055a-5989–4600–8ecb-a642b8a14777/.

6. Quoted in Otis L. Graham Jr., *Immigration Reform and America's Unchosen Future* (Bloomington, IN: AuthorHouse, 2008), 32.

7. AP, "Ku Klux Klan Plans Border Patrol to Help Fight Illegal Alien Problem,"
New York Times, October 18, 1977, www.nytimes.com/1977/10/18/archives
/ku-klux-klan-plans-border-patrol-to-help-fight-illegal-alien.html.

8. Harris N. Miller, "'The Right Thing to Do': A History of Simpson-Mazzoli,"
in *Clamor at the Gates: The New American Immigration*, ed. Nathan Glazer (San
Francisco: Institute for Contemporary Studies, 1985), 49.

9. Works that highlight the role played by Tanton and FAIR include Raymond
Tatalovich, "Official English as Nativist Backlash," in *Immigrants Out!: The New
Nativism and the Anti-Immigrant Impulse in the United States*, ed. Juan F. Perea
(New York: NYU Press, 1997), 78–102; Jean Stefancic, "Funding the Nativist
Agenda," in Perea, ed., *Immigrants Out!*, 119–35; Daniel J. Tichenor, *Dividing
Lines: The Politics of Immigration Control in America* (Princeton, NJ: Princeton
University Press, 2002); Elena R. Gutiérrez, *Fertile Matters: The Politics of Mex-
ican-Origin Women's Reproduction* (Austin: University of Texas Press, 2008);
and Daniel Martinez HoSang, *Racial Propositions: Ballot Initiatives and the
Making of Postwar California* (Berkeley: University of California Press, 2010).

10. John Tanton, "Say Goodbye to the North Country," *The Torch (East Grand
Traverse Bay)*, January 29, 1972, box 1, "Memoir file 1960s–1983," John Tanton
Papers, Bentley Historical Library, University of Michigan (hereafter Tanton
Papers).

11. Paul Schulman, "Can Lady Liberty Ever Say No?," *Sunday Record* (Hack-
ensack, NJ), October 6, 1974, box 1, "Memoir file 1960s–1983," Tanton Papers.

12. File on Sierra Club Population Committee, 1968–70, box 6, Tanton Papers.

13. Memo from ZPG, Inc. to Trustees of Equilibrium Fund, Re: Proposed
Immigration Program, April 25, 1974, box 2, folder: ZPG Immigration Project,
Tanton Papers.

14. "A Funding Proposal for a Program of Applied Research, Public Education
and Policy Development on United States Immigration Policy Submitted by Zero
Population Growth Foundation Inc," June 20, 1977, box 2, folder: ZPG Immigration Project, Tanton Papers.

15. Letter from John Tanton to Richard Brannick, president, National Border
Patrol Council, December 30, 1975, box 3, folder: National Border Patrol INS
Council, Tanton Papers.

16. "A Proposal for the Federation for American Immigration Reform Submitted to the ZPGF Board of Directors," by Roger L. Conner, executive director, and
John Tanton, chairman of the board, January 9, 1979, box 2, folder: ZPG Immigration Project, Tanton Papers.

17. "Proposal for the Federation."

18. In May 1982, for example, a Merit survey found that 84 percent of the public expressed concern about the number of "illegal aliens" in the country. Between October 1977 and October 1983, the percent of the public who believed that penalties should be imposed on employers that hire "illegal aliens" jumped from 72 to 79 percent. Polls cited in Edwin Harwood, "American Public Opinion and U.S. Immigration Policy," *Annals of the American Academy of Political and Social Science* 487, issue on Immigration and American Public Policy (September 1986): 201–12, www.jstor.org/stable/1046063. As he writes, "The portrait that emerges is one of considerable ambivalence and inconsistency in public attitudes toward both legal and illegal immigrants" (207). Scholars have noted that immigration is a policy issue where public opinion is strongly shaped by elite discourse and views. Lina Newton, *Illegal, Alien, or Immigrant: The Politics of Immigration Reform* (New York: NYU Press, 2008). Additionally, the framing of these polls is suspect; in their oral histories, Roger Conner and Garrett Hardin each discuss organizational ties to the Roper polling shop through the environmental/population movement, and how they pushed Bud Roper to poll on immigration and population. Soon other polls followed, adding immigration questions. Garrett Hardin oral history, July 13, 1983, www.garretthardinsociety.org /gh/gh_oral_history_tape11.html; Roger Conner, Tenth Anniversary Oral History Project for the Federation for American Immigration Reform, interviewed by Otis Graham Jr., January 27, 1989, 50, box 23, folder 4 (hereafter Conner oral history), Federation for American Immigration Reform Records, Special Collections MS2195, George Washington University (hereafter FAIR Records).

19. Conner oral history, 50.

20. John Tanton, "A Skirmish in a Wider War," Oral History Project for the Federation for American Immigration Reform, interviewed by Otis Graham, Jr. April 20–21, 1980, 41, box 1 (hereafter Tanton oral history), Tanton Papers. Epigraph quotation: Early FAIR pamphlet, "The FAIR Way," box 1, "Personal Folder," Tanton Papers.

21. Conner oral history, 32.

22. Conner oral history, 32.

23. Reminiscences, Sidney A. Swensrud, 1990, interviewed by David H. Fowler for the Columbia University Oral History Archives, recorded December 19–20, 1988, January 27–30, 1989, and October 17, 1989, 168–69, box 22, folder 9, FAIR Records.

24. John Tanton, "The Great Escape," early 1970s, 5, box 1, "Memoir file 1960s–1983," Tanton Papers.

25. "FAIR Advertisement," *The North Woods Call,* February 6, 1980, 9, box 1, "Memoir File 1960s–1983," Tanton Papers.

26. "A Chronology of Immigration Reform," box 2, folder 1, Otis Graham Jr. Papers, Special Collections MS2195, George Washington University (hereafter Graham Papers).

27. FAIR published a number of pamphlets: "Illegal Immigration and the New Reform Movement" (1980), "Illegal Immigration: The Problem, the Solutions" (1982), "Breaking Down the Barriers: The Changing Relationship between Illegal Immigration and Welfare" (1982), and hosted a conference on "Illegal Immigration: The Solvable Problem" (May 1980). "A Chronology of Immigration Reform," box 2, folder 1, Graham Papers.

28. "FAIR Advertisement."

29. Robert Reinhold, "Catholic Church Rejects Request to Assure Aliens on 1980 Census," *New York Times,* December 6, 1979, www.nytimes.com /1979/12/06/archives/catholic-church-rejects-request-to-assure-aliens-on-1980 -census.html; Robert Reinhold, "Dispute over Aliens Snarls Census Plans," *New York Times,* December 21, 1979, www.nytimes.com/1979/12/21/archives /dispute-over-aliens-snarls-census-plans-lawsuit-challenges-the.html.

30. Conner oral history, 51.

31. Conner oral history, 52.

32. Conner oral history, 54.

33. Conner oral history, 56.

34. *Immigration Reform and Control Act of 1982: Joint Hearings Before the Subcommittee on Immigration, Refugees, and International Law of the Committee on the Judiciary, House of Representatives and Subcommittee on Immigration and Refugee Policy of the Committee on the Judiciary, United States Senate, Ninety-seventh Congress, Second Session, on H.R. 5872, S. 2222* (Washington, DC: Government Printing Office, 1982), April 1, 1982, 179.

35. Letter from Alan Simpson to the President, April 12, 1982, box 351, folder 2, Alan K. Simpson Papers, Collection 10449, American Heritage Center, University of Wyoming.

36. Conner oral history, 89.

37. Jack Rosenthal, "Immigration and the Missing Nail," *New York Times,* March 1, 1981, www.pulitzer.org/winners/jack-rosenthal.

38. "A Chronology of Immigration Reform," box 2, folder 1, Graham Papers; GAO Report, "Illegal Aliens: Information on Selected Countries' Employment Prohibition Laws," for the Chairman, Subcommittee on Immigration, Refugees, and International Law, Committee on the Judiciary, House of Representatives, October 1985.

39. Jack Rosenthal, "A Flood outside Our Door," *New York Times,* January 5, 1986, www.nytimes.com/1986/01/05/books/a-flood-outside-our-door.html.

40. Tanton oral history, 44.

41. Dan Stein, Oral History Project for the Federation for American Immigration Reform, interviewed by John Tanton, August 5, 1994, 35, box 23, folder 5, FAIR Records (hereafter Stein oral history).

42. In 1994, a FAIR press release claimed 55,000 members nationwide. In 1995, it claimed 75,000. Press releases, box 1, folders 8 and 9, FAIR Records. In

a 2006 article, Chris Hayes reported that FAIR said it had 198,000 members. Chris Hayes, "Keeping America Empty," April 24, 2006, https://chrishayes.org /articles/keeping-america-empty/.

43. Tanton oral history, 48.

44. Conner oral history, 56.

45. Conner oral history, 103.

46. Tanton oral history, 57. Also: "I remember large arguments going on between Patrick Burns and K.C. about direct mail contents and whether those kinds of issues were permissible. I didn't get too directly involved at the time, but ultimately, the organization seems to have crafted a public image of being a little bit liberal in the eyes of conservatives, and a little bit conservative in the eyes of liberals." Stein oral history, 29.

47. Conner oral history, 81.

48. Brendan O'Connor, "The Eugenicist Doctor and the Vast Fortune behind Trump's Immigration Regime," *Splinter News*, July 5, 2018, https://splinternews .com/the-eugenicist-doctor-and-the-vast-fortune-behind-trump-1827322435; Solana Larsen, "The Anti-Immigration Movement: From Shovels to Suits," *NACLA Report on the Americas* 40, no. 3 (May/June 2007): 14–18.

49. Stein oral history, 47.

50. Stein oral history, 31.

51. Stein oral history, 37.

52. Stein oral history, 38.

53. Maria Cristina Garcia, "National (In)security and the 1996 Immigration Act," *Modern American History* 1, no. 2 (July 2018): 233–36.

54. Stein oral history, 54.

55. Sarah Jones, "The Notorious Book That Ties the Right to the Far Right," *New Republic*, February 2, 2018, https://newrepublic.com/article/146925/notorious -book-ties-right-far-right; Michael Malice, "Alt-Right Bible 'Camp of the Saints' Proves Everyone's Still Insane," *The Observer*, May 2, 2018, https://observer .com/2018/05/the-insanity-of-alt-right-bannon-approved-the-camp-of-the-saints/.

56. Otis L. Graham, Jr. *Immigration Reform and America's Unchosen Future* (Bloomington, IN: AuthorHouse, 2008), 292.

57. John Tanton WITAN memo, October 26–27, 1986, box 121, folder 10, FAIR Records.

58. Tanton oral history, 72.

59. Memo from John Tanton to FAIR Board, May 4, 1988, box 2, folder 1, Graham Papers.

60. Letter from John Tanton to Cordelia Scaife May, October 6, 1997, www.documentcloud.org/documents/4523828-20070911144638OCR.html.

61. Letter from John Tanton to Robert K. Graham, August 7, 1995, www.documentcloud.org/documents/4523842-1995-08-07-LETTER-Robert-K -Graham-Meeting-With.html.

62. Stein oral history, 60.

63. Tanton once linked to Spencer's American Patrol from his website, though he took the link down. https://web.archive.org/web/20080924075339/https://www.johntanton.org/info/links.html.

64. Max Blumenthal, "Vigilante Injustice," *Salon.com*, May 23, 2003, www.salon.com/2003/05/22/vigilante_3/.

65. Information on Park at Colorado Alliance for Immigration Reform (CAIRCO), https://web.archive.org/web/20130126192709/https://www.cairco.org/book/export/html/287. See also Robert Park, "Mass Immigration and the Invasion Clause," *Social Contract Press*, https://web.archive.org/web/20181012230018/https://www.thesocialcontract.com/booklets/common-sense-mass-immigration/invasion-article-4-section-4.html;; Park's website "Immivasion," https://web.archive.org/web/20180811003640/http://immivasion.us/.

66. John Tanton, "End of the Migration Epoch?" *Social Contract Press* 4, no. 3 (Spring 1994), https://web.archive.org/web/20190922133103/https://www.thesocialcontract.com/artman2/publish/tsc0403/article_329.shtml.

67. John F. Rohe, *Mary Lou & John Tanton: A Journey into American Conservation* (Washington, DC: FAIR Horizon Press, 2002), 115.

68. John Tanton, "The Color Line," *Social Contract Press* 8, no. 4 (Summer 1998), https://web.archive.org/web/20191017023116/https://www.thesocialcontract.com/artman2/publish/tsc0804/article_756.shtml.

69. Samuel Francis, "Whose Future?," *Social Contract Press* 8, no. 4 (Summer 1998), https://web.archive.org/web/20191017022940/https://www.thesocialcontract.com/artman2/publish/tsc0804/article_761.shtml.

CHAPTER 13. THE EXPULSION OF IMMIGRANTS

1. On the long, bipartisan history of the deportation machine and authorities' reliance on voluntary departure and self-deportation, see Adam Goodman, *The Deportation Machine: America's Long History of Expelling Immigrants* (Princeton, NJ: Princeton University Press, 2020).

2. On the persistence of xenophobia throughout U.S. history, see Erika Lee, *America for Americans: A History of Xenophobia in the United States* (New York: Basic Books, 2019).

3. Gregory Krieg, "14 of Trump's Most Outrageous 'Birther' Claims—Half from after 2011," CNN, September 16, 2016, www.cnn.com/2016/09/09/politics/donald-trump-birther/index.html; "Full Text: Donald Trump Announces a Presidential Bid," *Washington Post*, June 16, 2015, www.washingtonpost.com/news/post-politics/wp/2015/06/16/full-text-donald-trump-announces-a-presidential-bid.

4. Donald J. Trump, "Executive Order: Enhancing Public Safety in the Interior of the United States," January 25, 2017; Donald J. Trump, "Executive Order: Border Security and Immigration Enforcement Improvements," January 25, 2017; Donald J. Trump, "Executive Order: Protecting the Nation from Foreign Terrorist Entry into the United States," January 27, 2017.

5. "Press Briefing by Press Secretary Sean Spicer," February 21, 2017, www.whitehouse.gov/briefings-statements/press-briefing-press-secretary-sean-spicer-022117/.

6. Franklin Foer, "How ICE Went Rogue," *The Atlantic*, September 2018.

7. Goodman, *Deportation Machine*, 303n6.

8. Jonathan Blitzer, "Trump's Public-Charge Rule Is a One-Two Punch against Immigrants and Public Assistance," *New Yorker*, September 28, 2018, www.newyorker.com/news/dispatch/trumps-public-charge-rule-is-a-one-two-punch-against-immigrants-and-public-assistance; DHS, "DHS Implements Inadmissibility on Public Charge Grounds Final Rule," February 24, 2020, www.dhs.gov/news/2020/02/24/dhs-implements-inadmissibility-public-charge-grounds-final-rule.

9. Brent D. Griffiths, "Trump: 'We cannot allow all of these people to invade our country,'" *Politico*, June 24, 2018, www.politico.com/story/2018/06/24/trump-invade-country-immigrants-667191; Department of Justice, Office of Public Affairs, "EOIR Announces Largest Ever Immigration Judge Investiture," September 28, 2018, www.justice.gov/opa/pr/eoir-announces-largest-ever-immigration-judge-investiture; Transactional Records Access Clearinghouse, "Immigration Court's Active Backlog Surpasses One Million," https://trac.syr.edu/immigration/reports/574/ (accessed September 18, 2019).

10. Goodman, *Deportation Machine*, 304n8; Zolan Kanno-Youngs and Kirk Semple, "Citing Virus to Justify a Crackdown the President Has Long Sought," *New York Times*, March 21, 2020, A7; Emily Kassie and Barbara Marcolini, "'It Was Like a Time Bomb': How ICE Helped Spread the Coronavirus," *New York Times*, July 10, 2020, www.nytimes.com/2020/07/10/us/ice-coronavirus-deportation.html.

11. Department of Justice, Office of Public Affairs, "Attorney General Announces Zero-Tolerance Policy for Criminal Illegal Entry," April 6, 2018; Julia Preston, "Zero Tolerance Lives On," The Marshall Project, September 14, 2018, www.themarshallproject.org/2018/09/14/zero-tolerance-lives-on; Comment from Border Patrol on zero tolerance, June 18, 2018, https://assets.documentcloud.org/documents/4519977/June-18-2018-Comment-From-Border-Patrol.pdf.

12. Caitlin Dickerson and Ron Nixon, "White House Weighs Separating Families to Deter Migrants," *New York Times*, December 21, 2017, A15; Laura Briggs, *Taking Children: A History of American Terror* (Oakland: University of California Press, 2020), 132–57; Amnesty International, "USA: 'You Don't Have Any

Rights Here': Illegal Pushbacks, Arbitrary Detention & Ill-Treatment of Asylum-Seekers in the United States," 2018, 1–72. On earlier prevention through deterrence measures, see Goodman, *Deportation Machine*, 73–106, 174–75.

13. Devin Miller, "AAP a Leading Voice against Separating Children, Parents at Border," *AAP News*, June 14, 2018, www.aappublications.org/news/2018/06/14/washington061418; Ron Nixon, "Official Likens Shelters to Summer Camp," *New York Times*, July 31, 2018, A13; Ginger Thompson, "Listen to Children Who've Just Been Separated from Their Parents at the Border," ProPublica, June 18, 2018, www.propublica.org/article/children-separated-from-parents-border-patrol-cbp-trump-immigration-policy; Dan Barry, Miriam Jordan, Annie Correal, and Manny Fernandez, "Scrubbing Toilets and No Hugging: A Migrant Child's Days in Detention," *New York Times*, July 14, 2018, A1; Goodman, *Deportation Machine*, 305n11.

14. Jeremy Raff, "ICE Is Pressuring Separated Parents to Choose Deportation," *The Atlantic*, July 6, 2018, www.theatlantic.com/politics/archive/2018/07/how-ice-pressures-separated-parents-to-choose-deportation/564461/; Sarah Stillman, "Migrants Say They Are Still Being Threatened with Child Separation," *New Yorker*, June 26, 2018, www.newyorker.com/news/dispatch/migrants-say-they-are-still-being-threatened-with-child-separation; Adam Isacson, "Southwest Border Data Shows 'Zero Tolerance' Didn't Deter Migrants after All," WOLA, July 5, 2018, www.wola.org/analysis/southwest-border-data-shows-zero-tolerance-didnt-deter-migrants/.

15. Interview transcript, "Bob Woodward and Bob Costa with Donald Trump," March 31, 2016, www.washingtonpost.com/wp-stat/graphics/politics/trump-archive/docs/donald-trump-interview-with-bob-woodward-and-robert-costa.pdf.

16. Julia Carrie Wong, "'Psychological Warfare': Immigrants in America Held Hostage by Fear of Raids," *The Guardian*, February 18, 2017, www.theguardian.com/us-news/2017/feb/18/us-immigration-raids-fear-trump-mexico.

17. Testimony of Thomas D. Homan, acting director of ICE, "Immigration and Customs Enforcement & Customs and Border Protection FY18 Budget Request," before House Committee on Appropriations, June 13, 2017.

18. Noelle Phillips, "Jeanette Vizguerra Leaves Sanctuary after 86 Days Avoiding Immigration Authorities," *Denver Post*, May 12, 2017; Laurie Goodstein, "Immigrant Father Shielded from Deportation by a Philadelphia Church Walks Free," *New York Times*, October 11, 2017, A17.

19. Alexandra Hall, "America's Dairyland and Trump in the Rearview Mirror as Workers Return to Mexico," Wisconsin Public Radio and the Wisconsin Center for Investigative Journalism, June 18, 2017, www.wisconsinwatch.org/2017/06/americas-dairyland-and-trump-in-the-rearview-mirror-as-workers-return-to-mexico/.

20. Claire Galofaro and Juliet Linderman, "Immigrants Wait in Fear after Raids; Trump Takes Credit," Associated Press, February 12, 2017; Emily Baum-

gaertner, "Immigrants Abandon Public Nutrition Services," *New York Times,* March 6, 2018, A17; Katherine Hernandez, "Fearing Deportation, Food Vendors Are Leaving New York City's Streets," NPR, January 12, 2018, www.npr.org /sections/thesalt/2018/01/12/577462634/fearing-deportation-food-vendors-are -leaving-new-york-city-s-streets; Cora Engelbrecht, "Fewer Hispanics Report Domestic Abuse. Police Fault Deportations," *New York Times,* June 3, 2018, A12.

21. Sarah Elizabeth Richards, "How Fear of Deportation Puts Stress on Families," *The Atlantic,* March 22, 2017, www.theatlantic.com/family/archive/2017/03 /deportation-stress/520008/; Goodman, *Deportation Machine,* 308n21.

22. Glenn Thrush and Maggie Haberman, "Giving White Nationalists an Unequivocal Boost," *New York Times,* August 15, 2017, A1; Ryan Devereaux, "US Citizenship and Immigration Services Will Remove 'Nation of Immigrants' from Mission Statement," *The Intercept,* February 22, 2018, https://theintercept .com/2018/02/22/u-s-citizenship-and-immigration-services-will-remove-nation -of-immigrants-from-mission-statement/.

CHAPTER 14. THE DETENTION AND DEPORTATION
REGIME AS A CONDUIT OF DEATH

1. "United States Immigration Detention: Quick Facts," Global Detention Project, 2017, www.globaldetentionproject.org/countries/americas/united -states. For the location of the Service Processing Centers, see "INS Detention and Deportation Program," U.S. Citizenship and Immigration Services Historical Library, Washington, DC.

2. The concept of an immigration industrial complex is used in the following scholarship: Deepa Fernandes, *Targeted: Homeland Security and the Business of Immigration* (New York: Seven Stories Press, 2011); Robert Koulish, *Immigration and American Democracy: Subverting the Rule of Law* (New York: Routledge, 2010); Tom K. Wong, *Rights, Deportation, and Detention in the Age of Immigration Control* (Stanford, CA: Stanford University Press, 2015).

3. Jessica Ordaz, "Protesting Conditions inside El Corralón: Immigration Detention, State Repression, and Transnational Migrant Politics in El Centro, California," *Journal of American Ethnic History* 38, no. 2 (2019): 65–93; Jessica Ordaz, *The Shadow of El Centro: A History of Migrant Incarceration and Solidarity* (Chapel Hill: University of North Carolina Press, 2021).

4. "Deadly Force and Human Rights Violations against Undocumented Workers in CA," American Friends Service Committee—United States—Mexico Border Program Records, MSS 0644, box 1, folder 3, June–December 1985, University of California–San Diego.

5. Yen Le Espiritu, *Body Counts: The Vietnam War and Militarized Refuge(es)* (Berkeley: University of California Press, 2014), 177.

6. "Deadly Force and Human Rights Violations."

7. Philip Martin, "Trade and Migration: NAFTA's Migration Hump," in *NAFTA and the Future of the U.S.-Mexico Relationship*, ed. Melissa Floca (San Diego: University of California, Center for U.S.-Mexico Studies, 2017), 39.

8. Patricia Fernández-Kelly and Douglas S. Massey, "Borders for Whom? The Role of NAFTA in Mexico-U.S. Migration," *Annals of the American Academy of Political and Social Science* 610 (2007): 99; Bill Ong Hing, *Ethical Borders: NAFTA, Globalization, and Mexican Migration* (Philadelphia: Temple University Press, 2010), 5.

9. Peter Andreas, *Border Games: Policing the U.S.-Mexico Divide* (Ithaca, NY: Cornell University Press, 2000), x.

10. Joseph Nevins, *Dying to Live: A Story of U.S. Immigration in an Age of Global Apartheid* (San Francisco: City Lights Books, 2008), 116.

11. Supplemental Materials to the Intervention before the 55th Session of the United Nations Commission on Human Rights, Submitted on Behalf of Human Rights Advocates by American Civil Liberties Union of San Diego and Imperial Counties and California Rural Legal Assistance Foundation, Claudia E. Smith private collection, 15.

12. Letter from Claudia E. Smith, Law Offices of California Rural Legal Assistance, to Fernando Trulin, March 5, 1996, Claudia E. Smith private collection, 1; Bill Ong Hing, "The Racism and Immorality of the Operation Gatekeeper Death Trap," *Border Criminologies* (blog), April 13, 2015, www.law.ox.ac.uk /research-subject-groups/centre-criminology/centreborder-criminologies/blog /2015/04/racism-and.

13. Wendy A. Vogt, *Lives in Transit: Violence and Intimacy on the Migrant Journey* (Berkeley: University of California Press, 2018), 3.

14. Letter from Claudia E. Smith and Roberto L. Martinez, director of the American Friends Service Committee U.S.-Mexico Border Program, to Doris Meissner, INS commissioner, October 24, 1994, Claudia E. Smith private collection, 3; Letter from Claudia E. Smith to John P. Chase, director, Internal Audit, INS, March 6, 1995, Claudia E. Smith private collection, 4.

15. Smith and Martinez to Meissner, October 24, 1994, 4.

16. Vogt, *Lives in Transit*, 112.

17. Bianca Quilantana, "Remembering the Forgotten," *Southwestern College Sun*, April 10, 2017.

18. Letter to Marion Standish, California Endowment Public Officer, from Claudia E. Smith, August 8, 1997, Claudia E. Smith private collection, 1.

19. Nevins, *Dying to Live*, 66.

20. Morgan Baskin, "Field Notes from a Cemetery for the Nameless," *Pacific Standard*, March 31, 2017.

21. Petitioners' Supplemental Memo to the Inter-American Commission on Human Rights of the Organization of American States on Behalf of Petitioners

American Civil Liberties Union of San Diego and Imperial Counties and California Rural Legal Assistance Foundation v. The United States of America, Claudia E. Smith private collection, 3–4.

22. Tatiana Sanchez, "Remains of Hundreds of Unidentified Immigrants Are Buried in Imperial County Cemetery," *Los Angeles Times*, June 18, 2016.

23. Judith Butler, *Precarious Life: The Powers of Mourning and Violence* (London: Verso, 2004), 34.

24. Baskin, "Field Notes."

25. Sophia Lee, "Remembering the Lost Dead: Graves without Names on the U.S. Southern Border," *Sophia's World*, March 4, 2019. Burial costs are approximately $1,200 per person, and cremation costs $645 per person.

26. Quilantana, "Remembering the Forgotten."

27. Sanchez, "Remains of Hundreds"; Baskin, "Field Notes." Monica Muñoz Martinez also writes about remembrance, anti-Mexican violence, and tombstones; see Martinez, *The Injustice Never Leaves You: Anti-Mexican Violence in Texas* (Cambridge, MA: Harvard University Press, 2018).

28. Vogt, *Lives in Transit*, 109.

29. Esther Morales, "Tireless Warrior I," *Humanizando la Deportacion*, no. 11a (2017), http://humanizandoladeportacion.ucdavis.edu/; Martha Escobar, *Captivity beyond Prisons: Criminalization Experiences of Latina (Im)migrants* (Austin: University of Texas Press, 2016), 79.

30. Esther Morales, "Tireless Warrior II," *Humanizando la Deportacion*, no. 11b (2017), http://humanizandoladeportacion.ucdavis.edu/.

31. Escobar, *Captivity beyond Prisons*, 93.

32. Letter from Claudia E. Smith and Roberto L. Martinez to Doris Meissner, October 24, 1994, Claudia E. Smith private collection, 4.

33. Smith and Martinez to Meissner, 5.

34. Smith to Chase, March 6, 1995, 4.

35. Smith to Chase, 4.

36. Smith and Martinez to Meissner, October 24, 1994, 6. Some of the short-term detention cells inside Border Patrol centers are located in El Centro, Calexico, Indio, Imperial Beach, Campo, San Clemente, El Cajon, and Chula Vista, California, and Nogales, Ajo, Tucson, Douglas, Blythe, and Yuma, Arizona.

37. U.S. Department of Justice, INS, *Service Processing Center Design Guide*, JV6414.DE9F21d, 20, U.S. Citizenship and Immigration Services Historical Library, Washington, DC; Mark Dow, *American Gulag: Inside U.S. Immigration Prisons* (Berkeley: University of California Press, 2004), 200.

38. Ordaz, "Protesting Conditions."

39. Dow, *American Gulag*, 200.

40. Dow, 201.

41. Dow, 201.

42. A. R. Mackey, *INS Annual Report*, June 30, 1951, U.S. Immigration and Customs Enforcement Historical Library, Washington, DC, 56.

43. Florida Immigrant Advocacy Center, "Dying for Decent Care: Bad Medicine in Immigration Custody," February 2009, 11 & 21-23.

44. Florida Immigrant Advocacy Center, 21.

45. Florida Immigrant Advocacy Center, 11, 23.

46. Elsa Guadalupe-Gonzales, Department of Homeland Security, ICE Report of Investigation, Report no. 4 003, U.S. Immigration and Customs Enforcement, Freedom of Information Library, www.ice.gov/foia/library, 1.

47. Guadalupe-Gonzales, 3.

48. Guadalupe-Gonzales, 6.

49. Guadalupe-Gonzales, 8.

50. Guadalupe-Gonzales, 9.

51. Guadalupe-Gonzales, 14.

52. Guadalupe-Gonzales, 22.

53. Smith and Martinez to Meissner, October 24, 1994, 2; Letter from Claudia E. Smith to John P. Chase, March 13, 1995, Claudia E. Smith private collection, 1.

54. Smith and Martinez to Meissner, October 24, 1994, 1; Letter from Claudia E. Smith to John P. Chase, February 9, 1995, Claudia E. Smith private collection, 2.

55. Smith to Chase, March 6, 1995, 3. Antonio Gomez is a pseudonym.

56. Memo to Western District Directors and Chief Patrol Agents from the Office of the Western Regional Director, Re: Regional Transportation System Plan, March 28, 1995, Claudia E. Smith private collection, 2.

57. Memo to Western District Directors and Chief Patrol Agents, 6, 13.

58. Memo to Western District Directors and Chief Patrol Agents, 8-10.

59. Letter from Claudia E. Smith to Doris Meissner, September 11, 1995, Claudia E. Smith private collection, 2.

60. Smith to Meissner, 2.

61. Letter from Claudia E. Smith to Doris Meissner, July 7, 1997, Claudia E. Smith private collection, 3.

62. Letter from a Concerned Taxpayer and Patrol Agent to Claudia E. Smith, October 5, 1995, Claudia E. Smith private collection, 1.

63. Letter from Concerned Taxpayer, 3.

64. Lisa M. Cacho, *Social Death: Racialized Rightlessness and the Criminalization of the Unprotected* (New York: NYU Press, 2012), 37.

65. Tom K. Wong, *The Politics of Immigration: Partnership, Demographic Change, and American National Identity* (New York: Oxford University Press, 2017), 82; Patrisia Macias-Rojas, *From Deportation to Prison: The Politics of Immigration Enforcement in Post-Civil Rights America* (New York: NYU Press, 2016), 9.

66. Michael Welch, *Detained: Immigration Laws and the Expanding INS Jail Complex* (Philadelphia: Temple University Press, 2002), 3.

67. Wong, *Politics of Immigration*, 83.

68. Daniel Jauregui Mariz, "First They Americanize You, Then They Throw You Out," *Humanizando la Deportacion*, no. 6 (2017), http://humanizandolade portacion.ucdavis.edu/.

69. Emma Sanchez de Paulsen, "The Wall Separates Families, but Never Feelings," *Humanizando la Deportacion*, no. 4 (2017), http://humanizandolade portacion.ucdavis.edu/.

70. Jessica Nalbach, "Deportation the Effects on the Soul, Part I: Dwelling in the Past," *Humanizando la Deportacion*, #66a (2018), http://humanizandolade portacion.ucdavis.edu/.

71. Gerardo Sanchez Perez, "Cruel Deportations," *Humanizando la Deporta-cion*, no. 1 (2017), http://humanizandoladeportacion.ucdavis.edu/.

CHAPTER 15. A RECENT HISTORY OF
WHITE SUPREMACY

1. Gunnar Myrdal, *An American Dilemma: The Negro Problem and Modern Democracy* (New York: Harper & Row, 1962, 20th Century Edition), lxxi, lxxv, 75.

2. Ira Katznelson, *When Affirmative Action Was White: An Untold History of Racial Inequality in Twentieth-Century America* (New York: W. W. Norton, 2005), 113–41; Brian Gifford, "The Camouflaged Safety Net: The U.S. Armed Forces as a Welfare State Institution," *Social Politics* 13 (Fall 2006): 372–99.

3. Michael J. Bennett, *When Dreams Came True: The GI Bill and the Making of Modern America* (McLean, VA: Brassey's Publications, 1996), 26.

4. Margot Canaday, *The Straight State: Sexuality and Citizenship in Twenti-eth-Century America* (Princeton, NJ: Princeton University Press, 2009).

5. Kathleen Hill Frydl, "The GI Bill" (PhD diss., University of Chicago, 2000), 309–10; Angélica Aguilar Rodriguez, Julian Vasquez Heilig, and Allison Proch-now, "Higher Education, the GI Bill, and the Postwar Lives of Latino Veterans and Their Families," in *Latina/os and World War II: Mobility, Agency, and Ide-ology,* ed. Maggie Rivas-Rodriguez and B. V. Olguín (Austin: University of Texas Press, 2014), 59–74, Davis quote on 59, Rivas quote on 61.

6. Steven Rosales, "Fighting for Peace at Home: Mexican American Veterans and the 1944 GI Bill of Rights," *Pacific Historical Review* 8, no. 4 (November 2011): 597–627, Medina quote on 597.

7. Rosales, 604.

8. Suzanne Mettler, *Soldiers to Citizens: The G.I. Bill and the Making of the Greatest Generation* (New York: Oxford University Press, 2005), 7.

9. Harley Browning, Sally Lopraeto, and Dudly Poston Jr., "Income and Veteran Status: Variations among Mexican Americans, Blacks and Anglos," *American Sociological Review* 38, no. 1 (February 1973): 74–85.

10. Matthew D. Lassiter, *The Silent Majority: Suburban Politics in the Sunbelt South* (Princeton, NJ: Princeton University Press 2006); Margot Canaday, *The Straight State: Sexuality and Citizenship in Twentieth-Century America* (Princeton, NJ: Princeton University Press, 2009), 137–49.

11. "The NAACP Was Established February 12, 1909," *The Crisis*, www.thecrisismagazine.com/single-post/2019/02/12/The-NAACP-Was-Established-Febuary-12-1909 (accessed October 20, 2020).

12. League of United Latin American Citizens: Mission, https://lulac.org/about/mission/ (accessed September 15, 2020).

13. Rosales, "Fighting for Peace," 614–15.

14. Mae M. Ngai, *Impossible Subjects: Illegal Aliens and the Making of Modern America* (Princeton, NJ: Princeton University Press, 2004), 235.

15. National Advisory Commission on Civil Disorders, *Report of the National Advisory Commission on Civil Disorders* (Washington, DC: Government Printing Office, 1968), 1–2.

16. Stokely Carmichael and Charles Hamilton, *Black Power: The Politics of Liberation in America* (New York: Random House, 1967); Ramón A. Gutiérrez, "Internal Colonialism: The History of a Theory," *Du Bois Review: Social Science Research on Race* 1 (Summer 2004): 281–96.

17. Martin Luther King Jr., *Where Do We Go From Here: Chaos or Community?* (Boston: Beacon Press, 1968), 31.

18. Paul B. Sheatsley, "White Attitudes toward the Negro," *Daedalus* 95 (Winter 1996): 321; Hazel Erskine, "The Polls: The Speed of Racial Integration," *Public Opinion Quarterly* 32 (Fall 1968): 514.

19. Douglas McAdam, "We've Never Seen Protests like These Before," *Jacobin*, June 20, 2020, www.jacobinmag.com/2020/06/george-floyd-protests-black-lives-matter-riots-demonstrations.

20. Elizabeth Kai Hinton, *From the War on Poverty to the War on Crime: The Making of Mass Incarceration* (Cambridge, MA: Harvard University Press, 2016).

21. Nathan Glazer and Daniel Patrick Moynihan, *Beyond the Melting Pot: The Negroes, Puerto Ricans, Jews, Italians, and Irish of New York City* (Cambridge, MA: MIT Press, 1963), 49–50.

22. Ian F. Haney López, "'A Nation of Minorities': Race, Ethnicity, and Reactionary Colorblindness," *Stanford Law Review* 985 (2007): 1009.

23. Daniel P. Moynihan, *The Negro Family: The Case for National Action* (Washington, DC: Government Printing Office, 1965).

24. Michael Novak, *The Rise of the Unmeltable Ethnics: Politics and Culture in the Seventies* (New York: Macmillan, 1971), xx.

25. Matthew Frye Jacobson, *Roots Too: White Ethnic Revival in Post-Civil Rights America* (Cambridge, MA: Harvard University Press, 2006), 50–64.

26. Howard Ball, *The Bakke Case: Race, Education, and Affirmative Action* (Lawrence: University Press of Kansas, 2000).

CHAPTER 16. FROM PAT BUCHANAN TO DONALD TRUMP

1. Alexander Burns, "Donald Trump, Pushing Someone Rich, Offers Himself," *New York Times*, June 16, 2015.

2. Natalia Molina, *How Race Is Made in America: Immigration, Citizenship and the Historical Power of Racial Scripts* (Berkeley: University of California Press, 2014).

3. Steven V. Roberts, "Washington Talk: Politics; To Be or Not to Be a Protest Candidate," *New York Times*, January 19, 1987.

4. Gerald M. Boyd, "Bush Says He Has Earned Support of Right Wing," *New York Times*, June 2, 1988; Anne Devroy, "Bush Vetoes Civil Rights Bill," *New York Times*, October 23, 1990.

5. See Tali Mendelberg, *The Race Card: Campaign Strategy, Implicit Messages, and the Norm of Equality* (Princeton, NJ: Princeton University Press, 2001).

6. Timothy Stanley, *The Crusader: The Life and Tumultuous Times of Pat Buchanan* (New York: St. Martin's Press, 2012), 134.

7. "Sam Francis, Columnist, 57, Dies," *Washington Times*, February 16, 2005.

8. Samuel Francis, *Beautiful Losers: Essays on the Failure of American Conservatism* (Columbia: University of Missouri Press, 1994), 230.

9. John Ganz, "The Year the Clock Broke," *The Baffler*, November 18, 2018.

10. Samuel Francis, "The Education of David Duke," *Chronicles Magazine*, January 1, 1992.

11. Samuel Francis, "From Household to Nation: The Middle American Populism of Pat Buchanan," *Chronicles Magazine*, February 1, 1996.

12. Steven Holmes, "The 1992 Campaign: Republicans; Buchanan's Run Shows Fissures in the Right," *New York Times*, February 4, 1992.

13. Ralph Z. Hallow, "On the Right, a New Challenge," *Washington Times*, November 14, 1991.

14. Robin Toner, "The 1992 Campaign: Republicans; Marching through Georgia," *New York Times*, February 26, 1992.

15. Charles Krauthammer, "Buchanan Explained." *Washington Post*, March 1, 1992.

16. Krauthammer.

17. Remarks made on ABC News, *This Week with David Brinkley*, December 8, 1991.

18. Patrick J. Buchanan, "Cultural War," speech at the Republican National Convention, August 17, 1992, www.c-span.org/video/?31255–1/pat-buchanan -1992-republican-convention-address.

19. Patrick J. Buchanan, Reform Party Nomination Acceptance Speech, August 12, 2000, www.americanrhetoric.com/speeches/patbuchananreform partyacceptance.htm.

20. Audrey Singer, "Welfare Reform and Immigrants," Brookings Institution, May 2004, www.brookings.edu/research/welfare-reform-and-immigrants/.

21. Daniel Denvir, *All-American Nativism: How the Bipartisan War on Immigrants Explains Politics as We Know It* (New York: Verso Books, 2020), 103.

22. Philip A. Klinkner, Nicholas Anastasi, Jack Cartwright, Matthew Creeden, Will Rusche, Jesse Stinebring, and Hashem Zikry, *The 2012 Election and the Sources of Partisan Polarization: A Survey of American Political Attitudes* (Clinton, NY: Arthur Levitt Public Affairs Center, Hamilton College, 2013).

23. Ashley Southall, "NAACP Challenges Tea Party on Racism," *The Caucus* (blog), *New York Times*, July 13, 2010, http://thecaucus.blogs.nytimes .com/2010/07/13/n-a-a-c-p-challenges-tea-party-on-racism/?scp = 1&sq = %20 jealous%20naacp%20resolution%20on%20tea%20party%20%20&st = cse.

24. Devin Burghart and Leonard Zeskind, *Tea Party Nationalism* (Kansas City, MO: Institute for Research and Education on Human Rights, 2010).

25. "SPLC Hate Group Count Tops 1,000 as Radical Right Expansion Continues," *Hatewatch* (blog), Southern Poverty Law Center, February 23, 2011, www .splcenter.org/blog/2011/02/23/new-report-splc-hate-group-count-tops-1000 -as-radical-right-expansion-continues/.

26. Ann H. Coulter, *Adios, America: The Left's Plan to Turn Our Country into a Third World Hellhole* (Washington, DC: Regnery, 2015).

27. Mitchell Sunderland, "How Anne Coulter Created Donald Trump," *Vice. com*, September 8, 2016, www.vice.com/en_us/article/kwkba3/how-ann-coulter -created-donald-trump. See also Tom Platak, Anne Coulter Interview, part 1, *Chronicles Magazine*, June 8, 2016.

28. Justin Wm. Moyer, "Trump Says Fans Are 'Very Passionate' after Hearing One of Them Allegedly Assaulted Hispanic Man," *Washington Post*, August 21, 2015.

29. George Hawley, *Making Sense of the Alt-Right* (New York: Columbia University Press, 2019).

30. Joseph Lowndes, "Trump and the Shifting Landscape of Political Conflict: What Minneapolis Can Teach Us," *Public Seminar*, October 16, 2019, https://publicseminar.org/essays/trump-and-the-shifting-landscape-of-political -conflict/.

31. Michael Rogin, *Ronald Reagan the Movie: And Other Episodes in Political Demonology* (Berkeley: University of California Press, 1988).

32. "Oath Keepers: Guardians of the Republic," web archive at Library of Congress, Washington, DC, www.loc.gov/item/lcwaN0003728/ (available only on site).

33. Stella Cooper, Ben Decker, Anjali Singhvi, and Christiaan Triebert, "Tracking the Oath Keepers Who Attacked the Capitol," *New York Times,* January 29, 2021, www.nytimes.com/interactive/2021/01/29/us/oath-keepers-capitol-riot.html.

34. James Hohmann, "The Daily 202: Barr Memo Threatening Lawsuits against Coronavirus Restrictions Is a Warning Shot," *Washington Post,* April 28, 2020.

35. Morgan Chalfant and Niv Elis. "Trump Steps Up Effort to Blame China for Coronavirus," *The Hill.com,* May 4, 2020, https://thehill.com/homenews/administration/496047-trump-steps-up-effort-to-blame-china-for-coronavirus.

36. Chris Cillizza, "Pat Buchanan Says Trump Is the Future of the Republican Party," *Washington Post,* January 12, 2016.

CHAPTER 17. THE ALT-RIGHT IN CHARLOTTESVILLE

1. Paul Gottfried, "The Decline and Rise of the Alternative Right," *Taki's Magazine,* December 1, 2008, www.takimag.com/article/the_decline_and_rise_of_the_alternative_right/.

2. Gottfried.

3. VDARE's founder Peter Brimelow has worked to distance the magazine from labels like "white nationalist" in order to buy it more purchase in mainstream politics, but its content, name (short for Virginia Dare, the first "white" person recorded born in what would become the United States), and Brimelow's own work fit the descriptor.

4. Paul Gottfried, "Don't Call Me the 'Godfather' of Those Alt-Right Neo-Nazis. I'm Jewish," *National Post,* April 17, 2018, https://nationalpost.com/opinion/paul-gottfried-dont-call-me-the-godfather-of-those-alt-right-neo-nazis-im-jewish.

5. On the alt-right intellectual origins, see George Hawley, *Making Sense of the Alt-Right* (New York: Columbia University Press, 2017). Two worthwhile overviews of the movement are David Niewert, *Alt-America: The Rise of the Radical Right in the Age of Trump* (London: Verso, 2017); and Thomas J. Main, *The Rise of the Alt-Right* (Washington, DC: Brookings Institution, 2018).

6. For an overview of the online culture of the alt-right, see Angie Nagle, *Kill All the Normies: The Online Culture Wars from Tumblr and 4chan to the Alt-Right and Trump* (Winchester, UK: Zero Books, 2017), and Heather Suzanne

Woods and Leslie A. Hahner, *Make America Meme Again: The Rhetoric of the Alt-Right* (New York: Peter Lang, 2019).

7. On GamerGate, see Bailey Poland, *Haters: Harassment, Abuse, and Violence Online* (Lincoln, NE: Potomac Books, 2016), esp. chap. 5; and Zoe Quinn, *Crash Override: How Gamergate (Nearly) Destroyed My Life, and How We Can Win the Fight against Online Hate* (New York: PublicAffairs, 2017).

8. Joshua Green, *Devil's Bargain: Steve Bannon, Donald Trump, and the Nationalist Uprising* (New York: Penguin, 2017), 80–83, 145.

9. Green, 5–6, 44–47.

10. John Harkinson, "Meet the White Nationalist Trying To Ride the Trump Train to Lasting Power," *Mother Jones*, October 27, 2016, www.motherjones.com /politics/2016/10/richard-spencer-trump-alt-right-white-nationalist/; Nicole Hemmer, "Tweedy Racists and 'Ironic' Anti-Semites," *Vox*, December 2, 2016, www.vox.com/the-big-idea/2016/12/2/13814728/alt-right-spencer-irony-racism -punks-skinheads

11. Katie Glueck, "Alt-Right Celebrates Trump's Election at D.C. Meeting," *Politico*, November 19, 2016, www.politico.com/story/2016/11/alt-right-washington-dc-meeting-231671; Joseph Goldstein, "Alt-Right Gathering Exults in Trump Election With Nazi-Era Salute," *New York Times*, November 21, 2016, www .nytimes.com/2016/11/21/us/alt-right-salutes-donald-trump.html?_r = 0.

12. Andrew Marantz, "Birth of a White Supremacist," *New Yorker*, October 9, 2017, www.newyorker.com/magazine/2017/10/16/birth-of-a-white-supremacist.

13. Video of the May rally, www.youtube.com/watch?v = B-syXRg6TRE.

14. Timothy J. Heaphy, "Independent Review of the 2017 Protest Events in Charlottesville, Virginia," November 24, 2017.

15. Alan Feuer, "Proud Boys Founder: How He Went from Brooklyn Hipster to Far-Right Provocateur," *New York Times*, October 16, 2018, www.nytimes .com/2018/10/16/nyregion/proud-boys-gavin-mcinnes.html.

16. Andrew Marantz, "The Alt-Right Branding War Has Torn the Movement in Two," *New Yorker*, July 6, 2017. www.newyorker.com/news/news-desk/the-alt -right-branding-war-has-torn-the-movement-in-two.

17. Author interviews with Risa Goluboff and Dahlia Lithwick, April 2018.

18. Paul Duggan, "James A. Fields Jr. Sentenced to Life in Prison in Charlottesville Car Attack," *Washington Post*, December 11, 2018; Joe Heim and Paul Duggan, "James A. Fields Jr., Avowed Neo-Nazi in Charlottesville Car Attack, Sentenced to Life in Prison," *Washington Post*, June 29, 2019.

19. Heaphy, "Independent Review," 2017.

20. Jake Bittle, "Remember Trump's Charlottesville Comments? Conservatives Don't," *New Republic*, September 10, 2019, https://newrepublic.com /article/154960/trump-charlottesville-comments-conservative-campaign-erase -from-memory.

21. Author interview with Mary McCord, May 2018.

22. Peter Bergen, Albert Ford, Alyssa Sims, and David Sterman, "Terrorism in America after 9/11," *New America Foundation.* www.newamerica.org/in-depth/terrorism-in-america/what-threat-united-states-today/.

CHAPTER 18. THE WHITENESS OF BLUE LIVES

1. Protect and Serve Act of 2018, H.R. 5698, 115th Cong. (2018).

2. Orrin Hatch, "Hatch, Heitkamp Protect Police with New Legislation to Address Ambushes and Violence against Officers," news release, May 7, 2018, www.hatch.senate.gov/public/index.cfm/2018/5/hatch-heitkamp-protect-police-with-new-legislation-to-address-ambushes-and-violence-against-officers.

3. Quoted in Hatch.

4. Chuck Canterbury, "Fraternal Order of Police President Calls Targeting of Officers a Hate Crime," interview by Ari Shapiro, *All Things Considered*, July 8, 2016, www.npr.org/2016/07/08/485281280/fraternal-order-of-police-president-calls-targeting-of-officers-a-hate-crime.

5. See, for example, ex-skinhead Christian Picciolini's 2017 memoir *White American Youth*, which earned him a slot on *Fresh Air* and a TED talk, and Eli Saslow's *Rising Out of Hatred*, his 2018 book about former white supremacist youth leader Derek Black.

6. Quoted in Richard Pérez-Peña, "Louisiana Enacts Hate Crimes Law to Protect a New Group: Police," *New York Times*, May 26, 2016.

7. Cheryl I. Harris, "Whiteness as Property," *Harvard Law Review* 106, no. 8 (1993): 1711.

8. The critical race theorist Nikhil Singh shows how the state used and created racial divisions in distinguishing war from law enforcement. In refusing to acknowledge colonial wars as wars, he writes, "colonialism supported a foundational differentiation between the conduct of war between equal sovereigns, as an extension of specific and limited political and state aims, and the means by which imperial sovereigns asserted jurisdiction, seized territory, and exercised a more or less open-ended police power over ungoverned, unproductive, unsettled spaces and the 'unfit peoples' who inhabited them." That differentiation forged what Singh elsewhere terms the "whiteness of police," from which arose the whiteness of blue lives. Singh, *Race and America's Long War* (Berkeley: University of California Press, 2017), 54–55; Singh "The Whiteness of Police," in "Whiteness Redux or Redefined?," ed. Cynthia A. Young and Min Hyoung Song, forum, *American Quarterly* 66, no. 4 (2014): 1092. For more on the relation between war, law enforcement, and race making, see Lesley Gill, *The School of the Americas: Military Training and Political Violence in the Americas* (Durham, NC: Duke University Press, 2004); Kimberley L. Phillips, *War! What Is It Good For? Black Freedom Struggles and the U.S. Military from World War II to*

Iraq (Chapel Hill: University of North Carolina Press, 2012), 12–13, 280–82; Stuart Schrader, *Badges without Borders: How Global Counterinsurgency Transformed American Policing* (Berkeley: University of California Press, 2019); and Micol Seigel, *Violence Work: State Power and the Limits of Police* (Durham, NC: Duke University Press, 2018).

9. W. E. B. Du Bois, *Black Reconstruction in America: An Essay toward a History of the Part Black Folk Played in the Attempt to Reconstruct Democracy in America, 1860–1880* (New York: Russell and Russell, 1935), 700.

10. Quoted in Spencer Crump, *Black Riot in Los Angeles: The Story of the Watts Tragedy* (Los Angeles: Trans-Anglo, 1966), 27.

11. O. W. Wilson, introduction to *Parker on Police*, by William H. Parker, ed. Wilson (Springfield, IL: Charles C. Thomas, 1957), 60.

12. William H. Parker, "Invasion from Within," in *Parker on Police*, ed. O. W. Wilson (Springfield, IL: Charles C. Thomas, 1957), 60.

13. *Hearings before the United States Commission on Civil Rights* (Washington, DC: Government Printing Office, 1960), 327.

14. Stephanie Steinberg, "Thin Blue Line USA Honors Fallen Officers with Bracelets, Shirts," *Detroit News*, May 31, 2017.

15. Quoted in Steinberg.

16. Adam Goldman, "Trump Reverses Restrictions on Military Hardware for Police," *New York Times*, August 28, 2017.

17. Donald Trump, "Remarks by President Trump at the 37th Annual National Peace Officers' Memorial," WhiteHouse.gov, May 15, 2018, www.whitehouse .gov/briefings-statements/remarks-president-trump-37th-annual-national-peace -officers-memorial/.

CHAPTER 19. THERE ARE NO LONE WOLVES

1. Lisa Lowe, *The Intimacies of Four Continents* (Durham, NC: Duke University Press, 2015), 173.

2. Kathleen Belew, *Bring the War Home: The White Power Movement and Paramilitary America* (Cambridge, MA: Harvard University Press, 2018).

3. These numbers, drawn from Southern Poverty Law Center and Center for Democratic Renewal estimates, appear in Betty A. Dobratz and Stephanie L. Shanks-Meile, *The White Separatist Movement in the United States: "White Power, White Pride!"* (New York: Twayne Publishers, 1997); Raphael S. Ezekiel, *The Racist Mind: Portraits of American Neo-Nazis and Klansmen* (New York: Penguin, 1995); Abby L. Ferber and Michael Kimmel, "Reading Right: The Western Tradition in White Supremacist Discourse," *Sociological Focus* 33, no. 2 (May 2000): 193–213.

4. D. J. Mulloy, *The World of the John Birch Society: Conspiracy, Conservatism, and the Cold War* (Nashville, TN: Vanderbilt University Press, 2014), 2–3, 15–41.

5. On "leaderless resistance" changing movement attitudes towards recruitment as a measure of success, see Dobratz and Shanks-Meile, *White Separatist Movement,* 25. On membership numbers as secondary to a movement's structure of struggle, see Sidney Tarrow, *Power in Movement: Social Movement, Collective Action and Politics* (Cambridge: Cambridge University Press, 1994), 15.

6. Quoted from FBI internal documents in Andrew Gumbel and Roger G. Charles, *Oklahoma City: What the Investigation Missed—and Why It Still Matters* (New York: William Morrow, 2012), 262; Edward T. Linenthal, *The Unfinished Bombing: Oklahoma City in American Memory* (Oxford: Oxford University Press, 2001).

7. On transnational activity, see Robert W. Balch, "The Rise and Fall of Aryan Nations: A Resource Mobilization Perspective," *Journal of Political and Military Sociology* 34, no. 1 (Summer 2006): 81–113; Mattias Gardell, *Gods of the Blood: The Pagan Revival and White Separatism* (Durham, NC: Duke University Press, 2003); Abby L. Ferber, *White Man Falling: Race, Gender, and White Supremacy* (Lanham, MD: Rowman and Littlefield, 1998).

8. *The Turner Diaries* was first printed in serial in National Alliance, *Attack!,* 1974–76, box 31, folder 9, Stimely Collection, University of Oregon, Eugene, and then published as Andrew Macdonald, *The Turner Diaries* (Hillsboro, WV: National Vanguard Books, 1978).

9. Ideas about outlasting the Tribulations also appeared in mainstream evangelical accounts such as Tim LaHaye's popular *Left Behind* novels, the first of which appeared in 1995.

CONCLUSION

1. Jennifer Nez Denetdale, *The Long Walk: The Forced Navajo Exile* (New York: Chelsea House, 2008).

2. Jeffrey Ostler, "Disease Has Never Been Just Disease for Native Americans," *The Atlantic,* April 29, 2020; COVID Statistics, October 8, 2020; Alexandra Sternlicht, "Navajo Nation Has Most Coronavirus Infections Per Capita in the U.S. Beating New York, New Jersey," *Forbes Magazine,* May 20, 2020; Hollie Silverman, Konstaintin Toropin, Sara Sidner, and Leslie Perrot, "Navajo Nation Surpasses New York State for the Highest Covid-19 Infection Rate in the US," CNN, May 18, 2020.

3. María Godoy and Daniel Wood, "What Do Coronavirus Racial Disparities Look Like by State?," NPR podcast, May 30, 2020.

4. Richard A. Oppel Jr., Robert Gebeloff, K. K. Rebecca Lai, Will Wright, and Mitch Smith, "Racial Disparity in Cases Stretches All Across the Board," *New York Times,* July 6, 2020, A1, A6–7.

5. Richard A. Oppel Jr. and Kim Baker, "'They'll Kill Me,' Floyd Pleaded, Records Reveal," *New York Times,* July 9, 2020, A1, A18.

6. Mike Baker, Jennifer Valentino-DeVries, Manny Fernandez, and Michael LaForgia, "In 70 Deaths in Police Custody, the Same Three Gasped Words," *New York Times,* June 30, 2020, A1, A14–15.

7. The Sentencing Project, "Report to the United Nations on Racial Disparities in the U.S. Criminal Justice System," April 19, 2018, 1.

8. Lauren Villagran, "Walmart Shooter Allegedly Penned White Supremacist Rant in 'Bible of Evil,'" *El Paso Times,* August 4, 2019; Charlotte Graham-McLay, "Death Toll in New Zealand Mosque Shootings Rises to 51," *New York Times,* May 2, 2019.

9. Ramón A. Gutiérrez, "Decolonizing the Body: Kinship and the Nation," *American Archivist* 57, no. 1 (Winter 1994): 86–99.

10. Janet Shibley Hyde, "Gender Similarities and Differences," *Annual Review of Psychology* 65 (2014): 373–98.

11. Peniel Joseph, Interview, PBS News Hour, October 28, 2020.

12. Douglas McAdam, "We've Never Seen Protests like These Before," www.jacobinmag.com/2020/06/george-floyd-protests-black-lives-matter-riots-demonstrations (accessed July 15, 2020).

Acknowledgments

For their hard work and good spirits, the editors wish to thank Niels Hooper, Enrique Davila, Cleo Nevakivi-Callanan, Rachel Sass, Alyssa Smith, Maureen McCord, Mia Bay, Natalia Molina, Monica Muñoz Martinez, Elizabeth McRae, Nick DeGenova, and Michele White. Special thanks are also due to the staff at the University of California Press, Summer Farah and Francisco Reinking, as well as Ben Alexander and Andrew Christenson, who worked on the copyediting and indexing of this book. This volume was made possible by the generous support of the Center for the Study of Race, Politics and Culture, the Franke Institute for the Humanities, the International House, the Global Studies Mobility Project, the Department of History, the Social Sciences Division at the University of Chicago, and the Chauncey and Marion Deering McCormick Foundation.

Contributors

KATHLEEN BELEW is an assistant professor of history at the University of Chicago, where she specializes in the recent history of the United States. Her first book, *Bring the War Home: The White Power Movement and Paramilitary America* (Harvard University Press, 2018), documented the white power movement from the late 1970s to the Oklahoma City bombing in 1995. Belew's research has been featured on "Fresh Air," "Weekend Edition," and CBS News, and her book has provided the backbone of major reporting projects in the *New York Times,* PBS "Frontline," and more. She has testified before Congress, to intelligence agencies, and to tech companies about the threat of white power violence.

KHALED A. BEYDOUN is a critical race theorist, an associate professor of law at Wayne State University School of Law, and a senior faculty affiliate of the Islamophobia Research and Documentation project at the University of California, Berkeley. He is one of this country's leading scholars on Islamophobia, national security and anti-terrorism law, and civil liberties. Author of *American Islamophobia: Understanding the Roots and Rise of Fear* (University of California Press, 2018), his opinions are frequently featured in the *Washington Post,* the *New York Times,* the *San Francisco Chronicle, Time, Salon,* and television and radio broadcasts of CNN, the BBC, Fox, NBC, and ABC News.

JAMELLE BOUIE is an American journalist, a columnist for the *New York Times,* and a political analyst for CBS News known for his incisive reporting on stories relating to race, from the Ferguson uprising sparked by the police murder of

Michael Brown in 2014 to Black Lives Matter. He was formerly chief political correspondent for *Slate* magazine and a staff writer for *The Daily Beast.* Bouie attended the University of Virginia, where he graduated with a degree in political science and government.

JUDITH BUTLER is the Maxine Elliot Professor in the Departments of Rhetoric and Comparative Literature at the University of California, Berkeley. She is the author of *The Psychic Life of Power, Excitable Speech, Bodies that Matter, Gender Trouble, Frames of War,* and with Slavoj Zizek and Ernesto Laclau, *Contingency, Hegemony, Universality.* Her latest book, *The Force of Nonviolence* (Verso, 2020), argues for a new political imaginary.

LEO R. CHAVEZ is a professor of anthropology at the University of California, Irvine, a nationally recognized expert on Latina/o immigrants, and the author of *Anchor Babies and the Challenge of Birthright Citizenship* (Stanford University Press, 2017), *The Latino Threat: Constructing Immigrants, Citizens, and the Nation* (Stanford University Press, 2008, 2013), *Covering Immigration: Popular Images and the Politics of the Nation* (University of California Press, 2001), and *Shadowed Lives: Undocumented Immigrants in American Society* (Wadsworth Press, 1998, 2013).

JOSEPH DARDA is an associate professor of English at Texas Christian University. He is the author of *How White Men Won the Culture Wars: A History of Veteran America* (University of California Press, 2021) and *Empire of Defense: Race and the Cultural Politics of Permanent War* (University of Chicago Press, 2019).

RODERICK FERGUSON is a sociologist by training, a past president of the American Studies Association, and currently professor and chair of the Department of Women's, Gender, and Sexuality Studies at Yale University. He is a prolific author on African American cultural, gender, and queer topics, including *One-Dimensional Queer* (Polity Press, 2019), *We Demand: The University and Student Protests* (University of California Press, 2017), *The Reorder of Things: The University and Its Pedagogies of Minority Difference* (University of Minnesota Press, 2012), and *Aberrations in Black: Toward a Queer of Color Critique* (University of Minnesota Press, 2004).

ADAM GOODMAN teaches in the Department of History and the Latin American and Latino Studies Program at the University of Illinois Chicago. His award-winning book *The Deportation Machine: America's Long History of Expelling Immigrants* (Princeton University Press, 2020) was a finalist for the Los Angeles Times Book Prize in History. Goodman is co-organizer of the #ImmigrationSyllabus project and the Newberry Library's Borderlands and Latino/a Studies Seminar.

CARLY GOODMAN is a historian of immigration, writer, and visiting assistant professor at La Salle University, where she teaches courses on global history and migration history. She is a coeditor of the *Washington Post*'s "Made by History," where she edits commentary and analysis from the nation's leading historians. She received her history PhD from Temple University in 2016, where her dissertation, "Global Game of Chance: The U.S. Diversity Visa Lottery, Transnational Migration, and Cultural Diplomacy in Africa, 1990–2016," won an Honorable Mention from the Oxford University Press USA Dissertation Prize in International History.

EMILY GORCENSKI is a data scientist and social justice activist. A survivor of the 2017 neo-Nazi violence in her home city of Charlottesville, Virginia, Emily uses her tech skills and firsthand experience to shine a light on white supremacist violence nationwide. Her project tracking Far Right crimes in America, First Vigil, led her to be named one of *Bitch* magazine's most influential feminists of the year in 2018.

RAMÓN A. GUTIÉRREZ, who counts a MacArthur Fellowship among his many recognitions, is the Preston & Sterling Morton Distinguished Service Professor of U.S. History and the College at the University of Chicago. He is author of field-defining works including the multiple-prizewinning *When Jesus Came, the Corn Mothers Went Away: Marriage, Sexuality, and Power in New Mexico, 1500-1846* (Stanford: Stanford University Press, 1991). He has edited editions of several of the field's most prominent journals and has published several coauthored works, most recently *Relational Formations of Race: Theory, Method, and Practice* (University of California Press, 2019) with Natalia Molina and Daniel HoSang. Gutiérrez is a preeminent scholar in Latina/o, borderlands, and Western history, who has taught U.S. immigration history for more than thirty years.

NICOLE HEMMER is an associate research scholar with the Obama Presidency Oral History Project at Columbia University, cohost of the podcasts *Past Present* and *This Day in Esoteric Political History,* and the author of *Messengers of the Right: Conservative Media and the Transformation of American Politics* (University of Pennsylvania Press, 2016). She wrote and produced the podcast *A12*, which told the story of the 2017 Charlottesville protests.

DOUG KIEL is assistant professor of history at Northwestern University. He is a citizen of the Oneida Nation and studies Native American history, with particular interests in the Great Lakes region and twentieth-century Indigenous nation rebuilding. He is working on a book manuscript titled *Unsettling Territory: Oneida Indian Resurgence and Anti-Sovereignty Backlash.* Beyond the university, Kiel has worked in several museums, testified as an expert witness in regards to Indigenous land rights, and in 2008 was as an Indigenous Fellow at the United Nations Office of the High Commissioner for Human Rights (OHCHR) in Geneva, Switzerland. He currently serves on the advisory committee for the renovation of the Field Museum's exhibition on Native North America.

JOSEPH E. LOWNDES is an associate professor of political science at the University of Oregon, where his teaching, research, and publications focus on right-wing politics, race, populism, and U.S. political development. He is the author of *From the New Deal to the New Right: Race and the Southern Origins of Modern Conservatism* (Yale University Press, 2008), and coauthor with Daniel Martínez HoSang of *Producers, Parasites, Patriots: Race and the New Right-Wing Politics of Precarity* (University of Minnesota Press, 2019).

SIMEON MAN is a historian of race and empire in the twentieth-century United States and an interdisciplinary scholar of American studies, Asian American studies, and comparative ethnic studies. He is associate professor of history at University of California–San Diego. His first book, *Soldiering through Empire: Race and the Making of the Decolonizing Pacific* (University of California Press, 2018), received an Honorable Mention for the Theodore Saloutos Memorial Book Prize from the Immigration and Ethnic History Society.

CASSIE MILLER is a senior research analyst at the Southern Poverty Law Center's Intelligence Project, where her research focuses on far-right extremism and political violence. She came to the SPLC as a Mellon Foundation/American Council for Learned Societies Public Fellow after receiving her PhD in history from Carnegie Mellon University. She is frequently called upon to speak to government officials and policymakers about the far right, and has appeared as an expert on *BBC Panorama*, NPR's *On Point, Democracy Now!,* and elsewhere.

CYNTHIA MILLER-IDRISS is an award winning author and scholar of Far Right extremism and higher education. She is professor of education and sociology and runs the Polarization and Extremism Research & Innovation Lab (PERIL) in the Center for University Excellence (CUE) at the American University in Washington, DC. She is also director of strategy and partnerships at the U.K.-based Centre for Analysis of the Radical Right and serves on the international advisory board of the Center for Research on Extremism (C-REX) in Oslo, Norway. Dr. Miller-Idriss has testified before the U.S. Congress and frequently serves as a keynote speaker and expert panelist on trends in white supremacist extremism to global academic and policy communities as well as staff and representatives in U.S. and international government agencies and embassies.

JESSICA ORDAZ is an assistant professor of Ethnic Studies at the University of Colorado Boulder. She received her doctorate in American History from the University of California, Davis. During the 2017-2018 academic year, Ordaz was the Andrew W. Mellon Sawyer Seminar postdoctoral fellow at the University of Washington, which focused on comparative racial capitalism. Her first book, *The Shadow of El Centro: A History of Migrant Incarceration and Solidarity*, was released in March 2021. Her second project will explore the multifaceted history of veganism and plant-based diets throughout the Americas, focusing on colonization, food politics, and social justice.

JUAN F. PEREA is the Curt and Linda Rodin Professor of Law and Social Justice and associate dean for research and faculty at the Loyola School of Law in Chicago, with expertise in constitutional and employment law. He is the editor of *Immigrants Out!: The New Nativism and the Anti-Immigrant Impulse in the United States* (NYU Press, 1997) and coauthor of several legal casebooks.

CROIX A. SAFFIN is a trans, feminist educator who teaches sociology and cultural and ethnic Studies at Bellevue College. They have a passion for teaching and a general love of empowering students to act toward social change. Croix is involved in a variety of social justice initiatives and is currently active in facilitating conversations around whiteness (especially in the wake of George Floyd's murder and the role whiteness is playing in protests across the country) and discussing the complexities and erasure of transmasculine identities.

REBECCA SOLNIT is a writer, historian, and political activist; a columnist at *The Guardian* and a regular contributor to Literary Hub. She has authored more than twenty widely acclaimed books on feminism, North American and indigenous history, popular power, social change and insurrection, wandering and walking, and hope and disaster. *Whose Story Is This?*, *Call Them by Their True Names* won the 2018 Kirkus Prize for Nonfiction, and *River of Shadows: Eadweard Muybridge and the Technological Wild West* won the National Book Critics Circle Award in criticism and the Lannan Literary Award. Her memoir, *Recollections of My Nonexistence*, appeared in March 2020.

KEEANGA-YAMAHTTA TAYLOR writes and speaks on Black politics, social movements, and racial inequality in the United States. She is author *Race for Profit: How Banks and the Real Estate Industry Undermined Black Homeownership*, published in 2019 by University of North Carolina Press. *Race for Profit* was a semifinalist for the 2019 National Book Award and a finalist for the Pulitzer Prize in History in 2020. She is assistant professor of African-American history at Princeton University and a contributing writer at *The New Yorker*.

Index

Founded in 1893,
UNIVERSITY OF CALIFORNIA PRESS
publishes bold, progressive books and journals
on topics in the arts, humanities, social sciences,
and natural sciences—with a focus on social
justice issues—that inspire thought and action
among readers worldwide.

The UC PRESS FOUNDATION
raises funds to uphold the press's vital role
as an independent, nonprofit publisher, and
receives philanthropic support from a wide
range of individuals and institutions—and from
committed readers like you. To learn more, visit
ucpress.edu/supportus.

Made in the USA
Monee, IL
07 September 2022